The Jack Benny Times
1984-1989

The newsletter of the
International Jack Benny Fan Club

© Copyright 2001, Laura Leff

PREFACE

From "The Official History of the International Jack Benny Fan Club", February, 1987:

> The International Jack Benny Fan Club officially started on January 1, 1980. Laura Lee, aged ten years, was the sole founder and President. The first newsletters were individually typed and included copies of articles on Jack Benny and his colleagues. Four honorary members were soon added: George Burns, Irving Fein, Fred deCordova, and Itzhak Perlman. Membership grew slightly in the first years, but the club was still in obscurity. Because of constraints on Laura's time, the newsletters eventually fell out of publication and the club became dormant.
>
> In mid-1983, Laura discovered an article about a Jack Benny fan in Connecticut: Jay Hickerson. Laura contacted him about the small club and her desire for more members. Jay himself became a member and mentioned the club in his publication, Hello Again, named after Jack's immortal opening line. Laura received many letters of inquiry, and the small club began to expand. Seeing the renewed interest, in June of 1984 the newsletter was reinstated under the name The Jack Benny Times. In September of 1984, it became a bimonthly publication containing news and articles about Jack Benny, and information about gaining material on him such as tapes, books, and magazines. The fan club was then publicized in many other publications, as well as in radio interviews with Laura.
>
> In 1984, the word spread overseas about the club--with members in Europe, the club became international. In 1986, the Times was enlarged to encompass more articles...

And the years went by. When I restarted the Times in 1984, I was 15 years old. My enthusiasm was boundless, and I was determined to put whatever I could into the newsletter (and often did). The Times ran through the most eventful 11 consecutive years of my life: graduating high school; moving from my hometown of Grand Rapids, Michigan, to Fort Wayne, Indiana; getting my Bachelor's and Master's degrees; moving to California; starting a career; losing my mother; and getting married. I always had a difficult task of getting them out on time--which I usually didn't--but looking back, it's almost a miracle that they came out at all. I frequently commented, "It may not come out on time, but it *will* come out!"

It truly was the members that made it happen. People generously submitted stories, questions, xeroxes, and magazines, many of which are still waiting to be used. So often I would get busy, distracted, or discouraged; then a note would arrive saying, "I really enjoy the newsletter," making it all worthwhile. Even in 1994 when the entire year was one issue because of major personal changes, it was answered by an outpouring of support. And there were those who never said anything, but faithfully sent their checks for $6.39 every year.

There are some fantastic memories behind these articles: driving three hours to meet Phil Harris, pleading with a <u>Sugar Babies</u> stagehand for five minutes with Mickey Rooney, talking with Tony Butala at 3AM by a hotel swimming pool, cutting a Statistics class to interview Dennis Day, attending Jack's induction into the Television Academy Hall of Fame, and many others. I hope that the warmth and excitement of these occasions can come through the words, making you feel like you were there, experiencing it along with me.

I took a break in 1996, and the Vice President temporarily assumed day-to-day responsibilities. I returned in 2000, with the next issue of the <u>Times</u> coming out late that year. A few years from now, I look forward to the second volume of bound <u>Times</u>, with more information, interviews, and memories.

To Jack, for being Jack Benny.
To Jack's friends, for sharing their memories.
To Dan, for understanding.
To Joe, for his advice and support.
And to the members, for always being there.

Enjoy,

Laura Leff

Laura Leff
President, IJBFC

The Jack Benny Times

Vol. 4, No. 1   NATIONWIDE DISTRIBUTION   June, 1984

By popular demand, The Jack Benny Times has been reinstated. The files are bulging with requests for memberships and info from all over the nation. To our new members, we welcome you. To the continuing members, thank you for sticking with us during the "lull."

*** A FEW OF OUR NEW MEMBERS ***

****JAY HICKERSON--Jay is involved in many of the national radio clubs and is the publisher of his own newsletter, Hello Again, named after Jack's famous opening line. He is reputed to have one of the largest JB collections in America. It is thanks to him that we have many of our newest members. In my opinion, any of our members who do not already subscribe to his newsletter should definitely look into it. For info, write him at: Box C, Orange, CT 06477.
****BOB BURNHAM--Bob is an active OTR recording dealer. His collection is also quite extensive and contains several of the master recordings of the JB show. His company also does equalizing and mastering along with general recordings. I know that several of you have complainesd about the quality of your various tapes; here's the man for you. Write him at: BRC Productions, P.O. Box 39522, Redford, MI 48239.
****LORA PALMER--Lora is our most enthusiastic new member. OTR is just one of her many hobbies such as tutoring and working at her local Braille workshop.
****ROBERT PIEKARSKI--Robert is a member of MARE, (Milwaukee Area Radio Enthusiasts), and, according to Lora Palmer, he also has quite a large JB collection.

* ATTENTION * ATTENTION * ATTENTION *

The "Jack Benny Logs" are out!!! Our own Jack Hickerson has published one which can be purchased for $6.00. This log spans 1932-1955. Although the log is missing a few shows from 1932-4, it is nearly complete from 1935 on.
Mr. Ron Barnett also has published a similar log. Because he is not a member, I have very little information on it. However, you can write him about it at: Box 9593, Alexandria, VA 22304.

§ SUGGESTED READING §

The Big Radio Comedy Program, edited by Ross Firestone. Hardbound, $15. This book contains several script copies from twenty different radio programs. There are thirty pages on Jack alone, plus chapters on Fred Allen, Burns and Allen, and many others. This is almost as much fun as actually listening to the shows.

CAN'T FIND A BOOK? Try Renaissance Book Shop, the second largest used book shop in America. 834 North Plankton, Milwaukee, Wisc. 53203. (414) 271-6850.

Copyright 1989, Laura Lee

* LEST WE FORGET *

June 30--One year ago today, Mary Benny, wife of Jack, passed away. For her funeral, two flower arrangements were sent in the name of the Jack Benny Fan Club. One of our own members, Fred deCordova, did the eulogy.

§ NARA §

Lora Palmer has made some information about the North American Radio Archives available to us. As the pamphlet reads:

"The North American Radio Archives, commonly known as the NARA, is a non-profit, educational organization incorporated under the laws of California[.] Membership allows the individual access to NARA's vast collections and lending libraries of radio broadcasts, books, magazines, scripts, slides and other paraphenalia associated with the history of radio."

For further information, write: Jackie Thompson, 3601 Lakewood Dr., Cincinnati, OH 45248.

One last note...
Publisher's Central Bureau has a division called the "Nostalgia book Club." Each month, members are sent a mailing with one featured book and a list of several other selections. This would interest any nostalgia buff on anything from radio to music to movies. For further info write: Publisher's Central Bureau, 1 Champion Ave./Dept. 270, Avenel, NJ 07131.

If you have any information, announcements, or comments please drop me a line.

Laura Lee, Jack Benny Fan Club Offices, 1620 Old Town Dr. SE, Grand Rapids, Mich. 49508.

Volume 4, No. 2   NATIONWIDE DISTRIBUTION   July, 1984

** NEW FRIENDS **

****GARY McBEE---Gary has been a fan of Jack Benny since childhood and is a teacher at City High School in Grand Rapids.
****PETER, ROBIN, and MELANIE PTERNEAS--This is one of our family memberships. Melanie, our youngest member, was introduced to Jack Benny when she heard a tape of one of Jack's shows which her parents had borrowed from the library. I'm sure that this should made many of our members happy to know that the next generation still has the ability to appreciate Jack's brand of humor.
****JOHN YOUNG--Another long-time fan of Jack Benny, John is an English teacher at East Kentwood High School.

§ ATTENTION § ATTENTION § ATTENTION §

In this month's issue of The Jack Benny Times there are two inserts of particular importance. The first one is from Jay Hickerson which concerns the ninth convention of the Friends of Old-Time Radio. You will note that Frank Nelson, the famous character actor who was closely associated with Jack Benny is attending this convention.

The other one is from Bob Burnham concerning his upcoming TECHNICAL GUIDE TO COLLECTING OLD TIME RADIO book. Bob has been extremely generous in offerring free trader ads to the members of the Jack Benny Fan Club. Please note that the deadline is ***JULY 28, 1984.***

¥ HONORARY MEMBERS ¥

Some of you have been asking for a list of our honorary members. Well, here it is.

> George Burns
> Fred deCordova
> Irving Fein
> Itzhak Perlman
> Ronald Reagan

Itzhak quite appreciated his honorary membership to the club, and wrote a very nice note thanking us. He also invited me backstage at his October 1983 concert here in Grand Rapids. I took along my mini tape-recorder and caught some of the conversation. Next month I will try to transcript some of Itzhak's

comments about Jack and his relationship with him.

Copyright 1989, Laura Lee

LEST WE FORGET

(not the well-known announcer from early television.)

July 28--Alex Brier passed away of a heart attack on July 28, 1981. He is sorely missed by many of us.

ß PASS ALONG THE WORD ß

From <u>Hello Again</u>, "Received newspaper clipping about Old-Time Radio, Box 27301, Denver (left in Jan. 1983) run by Richard Abel who apparently moved to Florida. He was investigated for mail fraud."

£ SUGGESTED READING £

George Burns, <u>Living It Up, Or, They Still Love Me In Altoona</u>. Published in hardcover and paperback. Paperback priced at $2.50 In this book, there is a chapter entitled "The Quiet Riot," George's nickname for Jack. It is packed full of humorous stories about George and Jack, many of their laughs, and many of the "rotten" tricks that he played on Jack. This provides for very enjoyable reading for anybody. The rest of the book is great, too.

That's about it for this month. As always, if you have any announcements, anecdotes, or vice versa write me.

Laura Lee, The Jack Benny Fan Club Offices, 1620 Old Town Dr. SE, Grand Rapids, Michigan, 49508

See you next month!!!

FREE TRADER ADS TO MEMBERS OF JACK BENNY CLUB!

DEADLINE 7/28/84

BRC Productions
Old time radio recordings, services and supplies
P.O. Box 39522 — Redford, Michigan 48239-0522

OLD TIME RADIO'S NEWEST AND MOST EXCITING PUBLICATION EVER IS NEARING COMPLETION. IT'S A ONE TIME ONLY BOOK, WHICH WILL BE MARKETED AND SOLD FOR YEARS TO OLD TIME RADIO ENTHUSIASTS ACROSS THE U.S. AND CANADA.

A TECHNICAL GUIDE TO COLLECTING OLD TIME RADIO

PROGRAMS is destined to become the "bible" of collectors everywhere... The most comprehensive and complete "handbook" ever published on this most unique hobby... It's a technical reference book loaded with tips and techniques on how to get the best sounding recordings of old time radio possible, but it's much much more!!

"A Technical Guide" probes the many questions collectors are always faced with--cassette versus reel, double speeding and double tracking, four track or two track, equipment, setting levels, equalizing, a detailed sound quality analysis of a typical radio show... Connections between tape recorders are also covered, equipment recommendations, recording tape -- "used" Ampex 641, monitoring systems, tape editing, disk dubbing... ALL THESE TECHNICAL QUESTIONS ARE COVERED, PLUS MANY MORE.

But "A Technical Guide" is a lot more than a technical guide--Other exclusive sections include tips on getting your collection organized and preparing your catalog, FIVE methods are listed for building your collection and getting the best-sounding copies, plus a chapter covering a variety of ways of getting more enjoyment out of the hobby other than listening. A complete listing of OTR clubs and publications is also provided along with sources for equipment and blank tape.
Well over 40 pages of useful information are offered in the book, plus a special section on the history of old time radio collecting--a guest appearance by collector/dealer Joe Webb are included.
It's all inclusive--a thorough how-to book on the hobby for both beginners and veterans--written and researched by Bob Burnham, a collector/dealer for over 10 years, and former broadcaster, engineer and production director in the Detroit area.
We've included ALL THIS MATERIAL, but would like to add two additional sections with your help... We feel the dealers involved in selling radio programs and supplies to radio program collectors play a major part in the growth and development of the hobby. In addition, the collectors themselves are of course, the backbone of old time radio.
For these reasons, we are pleased to announce effective immediately, BRC PRODUCTIONS is accepting both commercial and non-commercial advertisements in this one-time-only book. Non-commercial ads will be featured in a section amounting to a "Collector's Directory." The "Dealers" section will include both a classified section as well as display ads -- full page, half page and quarter page ads available at reasonable rates. All advertisers may purchase a copy of the book at discount rates.

"YOUR PROFESSIONAL OLD TIME RADIO SOURCE"

A TECHNICAL GUIDE TO COLLECTING OLD TIME RADIO PROGRAMS
A BRC Publication

Commercial Advertising Rates
Applies to all individuals or companies offering a service or product of interest to old time radio collectors --

DISPLAY ADS -- All copy should be camera ready --

Full Page -- $18.00 / Page size is 5-1/2 X 8-1/2" /Your original should be proportional
Half Page -- $10.00   to this size. No charge for reduction.
Quarter Page 6.00

CLASSIFIED - COMMERCIAL

30¢ per word including name and address. No minimum.

All commercial advertisers receive a $1.00 discount off purchase price of the book.

Non-Commercial Advertising Rates
Trader Directory Listing

~~$3.00~~ per insertion -- COMPLETE THE FORM AT RIGHT ~~AND ENCLOSE PAYMENT~~.

A TECHNICAL GUIDE TO COLLECTING
OLD TIME RADIO PROGRAMS---A BRC Publication
Non-commercial Advertising Form
Old Time Radio Trader Directory Application

Provide the below information ~~and payment~~ for inclusion in our publication.

NAME_____

ADDRESS_____

CITY/STATE_____ZIP_____

PHONE (   )_____COLLECTING MODE_cass ree

SIZE OF COLLECTION_____Years Collecting____

Optional: OCCUPATION_____AGE____

Types of shows interested in [mystery/comedy, etc.]____

Specific shows collected_____

Other OTR related activities_____

All collectors listed in the "Technical Guide" directory rec a $1.00 discount off purchase price of the book.

DEADLINE FOR TRADER DIRECTORY INSERTION- 7/28/
Mail to - BRC PRODUCTIONS, BOX 39522, REDFORD, MI.
****All Advertisements must be paid for in advance****

A TECHNICAL GUIDE TO COLLECTING
OLD TIME RADIO PROGRAMS---A BRC Publication
Commercial Advertising Form -- Dealer Section

NAME/COMPANY_____

ADDRESS_____

CITY/STATE_____ZIP_____

PHONE (   )_____

TYPE OF AD(S) REQUIRED   CHECK ON
[ ] Full Page -- Number of Pages____   Copy Enclosed
[ ] Half Page   Copy Under Separate Cover-
[ ] Quarter Page
[ ] Classified   Number of Words____

$_____AMOUNT ENCLOSED -- AD PROOFS? [ ]Yes [
Advertising Proofs are available after publication. Add $1 if you wish to receive proofs. No cancellations after deadline date.

CLASSIFIED AD COPY_____

DEADLINE FOR DEALER SECTION INSERTION - 7/28/84 -
All advertisers receive a $1.00 discount off price of the book.
PLEASE WRITE OR TYPE YOUR AD CLEARLY. WE ARE NOT RESPONSIBLE FOR ERRORS DUE TO ILLEGIBLE WRITING.

THE JACK BENNY TIMES
Volume 4, No.3   NATIONWIDE DISTRIBUTION   July addition

§ ATTENTION § ATTENTION § ATTENTION §

On July 14, 1984, Mr. Kenny Delmar passed away. Mr. Delmar played the character of Senator Beauregard Claghorn on The Fred Allen Show. Of the "residents" of Allen's Alley, one is still alive and well. The person that I am referring to is Mr. Parker Fenelly who played Titus Moody. Parker was not only a close friend of Kenny Delmar, but also a friend of the Jack Benny Fan Club. He has provided our records with much information about both Jack and Fred. Even though some of you have expressed that "(you) will hate Fred Allen to (your) grave," I see it only fitting and proper to make a request of all of the members of the Jack Benny Fan Club. My request is that you send a small note or sympathy card to Parker expressing the fact that there are people in this world that still remember Allen's Alley. His address is: 597 Croton Ave., Peekskill, New York 10566. Thank you.

...also!

Just this evening I received some news that has big potentials. There is a chance that I might be able to serve an internship at a local radio station. This internship would give me the chance to have my own weekly radio show. They are considering me because they wish to have a program based on old radio comedy. I would produce, direct, edit, and script the show myself. They also have told me that I would be able to advertise the Jack Benny Fan Club over the airwaves. Although this hasn't materialized yet, there is always that chance. I will report pro or con on this issue in next month's issue.

Laura Lee, The Jack Benny Fan Club offices, 1620 Old Town Dr. SE, Grand Rapids, Michigan 49508.

Copyright 1989, Laura Lee

THE JACK BENNY TIMES

Volume 4, No. 4   NATIONWIDE DISTRIBUTION   August, 1984

** IN CASE YOU HAVEN'T ALREADY HEARD... **

The radio show has come through and is a success!!! My first show was the last week in July, and it was dedicated to Jack Benny (of course). My most recent program was that of the 24th, and it centered around Fibber McGee and Molly. The program is called Laughs From the Past, and for you Grand Rapids area members it is on Fridays from 8 to 9 a.m. on WEHB 89.9 f.m. I hope you will tune in! In the future I will have many more shows on Jack Benny because most of my collection is made up of his shows. Itzhak Perlman has already offered to do an interview when he can find the time, and Chris Costello, daughter of Lou Costello, has also offered to give an interview whenever I can find the time!!! My next program will be September 7 or 14 because our station is moving, and we are not sure when we will be back on the air.

§ A FEW MORE THANKS §

I wish to thank all of the members who were kind enough to send Parker Fennelly a sympathy card in lieu of Kenny Delmar's passing. It is very much appreciated. Also, I thank those of you whose letters I have received during the past month and have not yet been able to answer. With the radio show coming in, my spare time has just about been cut in half, and my correspondence has taken the proverbial "back seat." Hopefully, I will be able to get around to it by 1985!

££ READING ££

In this month's Reader's Digest there is a fairly good article on Jack. It is entitled "Unforgettable Jack Benny" by Maurice Zolotow. It is five pages long, and it has some interesting information. Although there are several incorrect dates listed, the article itself is well-structured and well-written. Mr. Zolotow had interviewed Jack several times, so he does have sufficient grounds for writing the article.

** A FEW WORDS FROM ITZHAK PERLMAN *

Last month, I promised that I would transcribe some of my conversation with Mr. Perlman. Here is the transcription.
> "...He thought I was the funniest guy in the world, and for me that was the best compliment... [In reference to Jack's violin playing] He really practiced...We once had lunch on a Sunday, and he [said] ,'Come to my office and we'll have lunch,'...and I came to the office, and there he was, seriously practicing! He was very serious about his music... a great showman.

Copyright 1989, Laura Lee

> "...He was a great performer...Somebody said he was the greatest straight man in show business because, in a sense, when you think about what he did he was a great reactor. He reacted to people around him...When somebody said something to him ...just the look in his eyes... he was a great artist...Not only that, but to think that he was so successful on radio and then he moved successfully to television which a lot of people didn't do. Once they were radio stars and then moved into television, they were finished; he kept with the times."

By the way, if Itzhak ever comes to your city, you must go see him. He's absolutely fabulous.

¥ MEMBERS' ACTIVITIES ¥

Enclosed is a copy of the information on how to obtain Bob Burnham's new book. I hope you all order it.

Once again, if you wish to subscribe to Jay Hickerson's newsletter, (which I highly recommend,) write him at: Box C, Orange, Conn. 06477.

Also, we extend a BIG "thank you" to Lora Palmer for contributing postage stamps for the fan club mailings.

ONE LAST NOTE...

Mr. Tom Mastel in San Jose wrote and called a certain line in Hello Again to my attention. I thought that you'd be interested. "Brad Ashton, 7 Abbotshall Ave., Southgate, London, N14 7JU, England. Brad has available 3000 hours-mostly comedy- including all available J. Benny."

If you have any announcements, news, notes, etc., please write me at:

The Jack Benny Fan Club Offices, 1620 Old Town Dr. SE, Grand Rapids, Michigan, 49508

The next issue will be in October.

Sorry it's a bit late. There was a problem with the printer.

TM - BRC Prod.

IT'S HERE!

OLD TIME RADIO'S MOST COMPLETE & COMPREHENSIVE HANDBOOK

<u>18 CHAPTERS -- OVER 50 PAGES</u> -- COVERING...
  The history of old time radio collecting and trading...
   Recording techniques and equipment...
    Improving and organizing your collection...
     Recording tape, tape editing, disk dubbing...
      Logs -- an essential tool for serious collectors...
  <u>DIRECTORIES</u> of all known OTR clubs and publications...
   <u>Sources</u> for equipment and prices for most commonly used OTR tape decks...
   Blank tape and other special interest supplies of interest to collectors...
    <u>DEALER ads</u> from across the U.S. for old time radio tapes and supplies...
PLUS THE TECHNICAL GUIDE'S OWN DIRECTORY OF OLD TIME RADIO COLLECTORS, FROM COAST TO COAST, PLUS CANADA.

AVAILABLE NOW!

$7.50

POST PAID

ADVERTISERS DEDUCT $1.00

BRC Productions

Old time radio recordings, services and supplies

P.O. Box 39522 — Redford, Michigan 48239-0522

BRC Productions
Old time radio recordings, services and supplies
P.O. Box 39522 — Redford, Michigan 48239-0522

BRC PRODUCTIONS PRESENTS...
Mysteries, Adventures, and more!

OLD TIME RADIO ON REEL & CASSETTE TAPES
$10.00 per reel number - Ampex 641 (used in new box) [4 TRACK]*
5 reels - $45.00 --- 10 reels - $90.00
$15.00 per reel number - SCOTCH 177 (new tape in new box - factory packaged and wound on heavy duty 3M reel)
5 reels - $68.00 --- 10 reels - $135.00

CASSETTE [Music grade -- custom wound blanks in Norelco box]
Custom recorded from our reel masters with fully compatible noise reduction.
$7.00 per hour [1 - 9 tapes] Order 5 cassettes, pick one free.
$6.50 per hour [10 - 24 tapes] Pick 2 free cassettes for every 10 ordered.
$6.00 per hour [25 or more tapes] Pick 2 free cassettes with every 10 ordered.
$5.50 per hour [entire reel master recorded on cassette]

SHIPPING & HANDLING   ADD:
ORDERS UNDER $10.00 $1.50   BRC PRODUCTIONS pays shipping
ORDERS FROM $10 - 49.99 $2.50   on all orders totalling $100
ORDERS FROM $50 - 79.99 $3.00   or more!
ORDERS FROM $80 - 99.99 $4.00
*half track prices for reel tapes are double given rates. Other formats available

REEL 4400 THE SHADOW
The Plot Murder 2/27/38
Hounds in the Hills 2/20/38
The Silent Avenger 3/13/38
The White Legion 3/20/38
Hypnotic Death 2/12/39
Friend of Darkness 2/19/39
Horror in Wax 2/26/39
Sabotage by Air 3/5/39
Murder, Incorporated 12/17/39
The Stockings Were Hung 12/24/39
The Cat that Killed 12/31/39
Murder in the Death House 1/7/40

REEL 6125 THE WHISTLER
Evening Stroll 1/1/50
Return to Riondo 1/8/50
Escape to Skull Island 1/15/50
The Go Between 1/22/50
Burden of Guilt 1/29/50
Desert Reckoning 2/21/50
Five Cent Call 2/19/50
Appointment for Murder 2/26/50
Chinese Elephant Puzzle 3/5/50
Strange Meeting 3/12/50
The Oriana Affair 3/19/50
Lady in the Snow 3/26/50

REEL 4074 BULLDOG DRUMMOND
Hi-Jackers (audition & first show)
George Coulouris as Drummond 9/28/41
Blind Man's Bluff 1943 [Hortons]
Axis Submarines 1943
Help Wanted 8/13/45
Claim Check Murders 1/17/47
#11 Death at the Races
#12 Death Loops the Loop
#25 Death Uses Disappearing Ink
The Bookstore
The Fatal Right [Tums]

REEL 6304 BULLDOG & CADETS
BULLDOG DRUMMOND---
#29 The Circus
#30 The Deadly Stand In
TOM CORBETT, SPACE CADET
#1 1/28/52
#2 1/28/52
#5 2/12/52
#6 2/12/52
#7 2/19/52
#8 2/19/52
#9 2/26/52
#10 2/26/52

REEL 6305 THAT HAMMER GUY
Mickey Spillane's Mike Hammer (sound quality varies)
Zelda's Brother
Man in Wheelchair Fools All
Fayne Durando
Laura Fenton [Dog Collar]
Hank Busby Story
Wakefield Dame
Murdered Dame in Park
Mark Judson
Jim Gordon
Sgt. William McTusick
Pete Morrison

****
UNLESS NOTED OTHERWISE,
Each program listed runs approximately 1/2 hour. Each reel contains approximately 6 hours of programming [4 track].
****

REEL 6301 MARK TRAIL
#1 Lumber King of Timber Mt. 1/30/50
#2 Polluted Waters 2/1/50
#3 Satan & Devil's Herd 2/3/50
#4 Chief Lightfoot&Buffalo 2/6/50
#8 Whisperfoot 2/15/50
#15 Wildlife Acres 3/3/50
#16 Vampires from the Deep 3/6/50
#17 Killer that Strikes from the Sky 3/8/50
#21 Rapids of No Return 3/17/50
#22 The Rabid Foxes 3/20/50
#23 The Eyeglass Monster 3/22/50
#24 The Deluge 3/24/50

REEL 6302 MARK TRAIL
Capturing Big Horn Sheep 3/27/50
Coyotes from the Sky 4/3/50
Miracle Man of Junction Valley 4/19/50
The Thumping Beaver 4/24/50
Fishing Contest 4/26/50
Missing Deer 5/10/50
The Snake Hill Survey 5/15/50
Claws of the Killer Bear 5/17/50
The White Camel 9/22/50
The Purse Strings of Danger 9/25/50
Highway of Terror 10/6/50
Monster of the Gulf 10/9/50

REEL 6303 MARK TRAIL
The Forty-year Freeze 10/11/50
The Witch of Lost Forest 10/13/50
Strange Invitation of Death 10/16/50
Wings of the vampire 10/18/50
Killers of Lost Forest 10/20/50
The Sticks of Fear 10/23/50
The Silver Sky 10/25/50
The Avenging Arrow 10/27/50
ROCKY JORDAN [CBS]
Consignment for Naples 4/4/49
Word of Bishop 6/4/50
Money of a Bishop 7/30/50
Holiday Weekend 4/9/50

REEL 4515 GUNSMOKE
#193 Scared Kid 12/18/55
#194 Twelfth Night 12/25/55
#195 Pucket's New Year 1/1/56
#196 Doc's Revenge 1/8/56
#197 How to Cure a Friend 1/15/56
#198 Romeo 1/22/56
#199 Bureaucrat 1/29/56
#200 Legal Revenge 2/5/56
#201 Kitty's Outlaw 2/12/56
#202 New Hotel [reh] 2/19/56
#203 New Hotel [b. cast] 2/19/56
#204 Who Lives by the Sword 2/26/56

REEL 4516 GUNSMOKE
#205 The Hunter 3/4/56
#206 Bringing Down Father 3/11/56
#207 The Man who would be Marshall 3/18/56
#208 Hanging Man 3/25/56
#209 How to Sell a Ranch 4/1/56
#210 Widow's Mite 4/8/56
#211 The Executioner 4/15/56
#212 Indian Crazy 4/22/56
#213 Doc's Reward 4/29/56
#214 The Photographer 5/6/56
#215 Cows and Cribs 5/13/56
#216 Buffalo Man 5/20/56

REEL 4517 GUNSMOKE
#217 Man Hunter 5/27/56
#218 The Pacifist 6/3/56
#219 Daddy-O 6/10/56
#220 Cheap Labor 6/17/56
#221 Sunday Supplement 6/24/56
#222 Gun for Chester 7/1/56
#223 Passive Resistance 7/8/56
#224 Letter of the Law 7/15/56
#225 Lynching Man 7/22/56
#226 Lost Rifle 7/29/56
#227 Sweet and Sour 8/5/56
#228 Snake Bite 8/12/56

REEL 4518 GUNSMOKE
#229 Annie Oakley 8/19/56
#230 No Sale 8/26/56
#231 Old Pal 9/2/56
#232 Belle's Back 9/9/56
#233 Thick 'n Thin 9/16/56
#234 Box of Rocks 9/23/56
#235 The Brothers 9/30/56
#236 The Gamblers 10/7/56
#237 Gunshot Wound 10/14/56
#238 Till Death Do Us 10/21/56
#239 Dirty Bill's Girl 10/28/56
#240 Crowbait Bob 11/4/56

REEL 4519 GUNSMOKE
#241 Pretty Mama 11/11/56
#242 Brother Whelp 11/18/56
#243 Tail to the Wind 11/25/56
#244 Speak to Me Fair 12/2/56
#245 Braggart's Boy 12/9/56
#246 Cherry Red 12/16/56
#247 Beeker's Barn 12/23/56
#248 Hound Dog 12/30/56
#249 Devil's Hindmost 1/6/57
#250 Ozymandias 1/13/57
#251 Categorical Imperative 1/20/57
#252 1/27/57 (missing)

REEL 4520 GUNSMOKE
#253 Cold Fire 2/3/57
#254 Hellbent Harriet 2/10/57
#255 Doubtful Zone 2/17/57
#256 Impact 2/24/57
#257 Colleen so Green 3/3/57
#258 Grebb Hassle 3/10/57
#259 Spring Freshet 3/17/57 (missing)
#260 Saddle Sore Sal 3/24/57
#261 Chicken Smith 3/31/57
#262 Rock Bottom 4/7/57 (missing)
#263 Saludos 4/14/57
#264 Bear Trap 4/21/57

****
Gunsmoke programs star William Conrad as Matt Dillon.

REEL 4521 GUNSMOKE
#265 4/28/57 (missing)
#266 5/5/57 (missing)
#267 Sheep Dog 5/12/57
#268 One Night Stand 5/19/57
#269 Pal 5/26/57
#270 Ben Tolliver's Stud 6/2/57
#271 Dodge Podge 6/9/57
#272 Summer Night 6/16/57
In 1957, listeners voted the next five Gunsmoke shows as the best of the series.
#273 Home Sugery 6/23/57
#274 The Buffalo Hunter 6/30/57
#275 Word of Honor 7/7/57
#276 Bloody Hands 7/14/57

REEL 4522 GUNSMOKE
#277 Kitty Caught 7/21/57
#278 Cow Doctor 7/28/57
#279 Big Hands 8/4/57
#280 Jay Hawkers 8/11/57
#281 The Peace Officer 8/18/57
#282 Grass 8/25/57
#283 Jobe's Son 9/1/57
#284 Loony McCluny 9/8/57
#285 Child Labor 9/15/57
#286 Custer 9/22/57
#287 Another Man's Poison 9/29/57
#288 The Rooks 10/6/57

REEL 4523 GUNSMOKE
#289 The Margin 10/13/57
#290 Professor Lute Bone 10/20/57
#291 Man and Boy 10/27/57
#292 Bull 11/3/57
#293 Gunshy 11/10/57
#294 The Queue 11/17/57
#295 Odd Man Out 11/24/57
#296 Jud's Woman 12/1/57
#297 Long as I Live 12/8/57
#298 Ugly 12/15/57
#299 Twelfth Night 12/28/57
#300 Where'd they Go 12/29/57

REEL 4524 GUNSMOKE
#301 Pucket's New Year 1/5/58
#302 Second Son 1/12/58
#303 Moo Moo Raid 1/19/58
#304 One for Lee 1/26/58
#305 Kitty's Killing 2/2/58
#306 Joke's on Us 2/9/58
#307 Brugers Folly 2/16/58
#308 The Surgery 2/23/58
#309 The Guitar 3/2/58
#310 Laughing Gas 3/9/58
#311 Real Sent Johnny 3/16/58
#312 Indian 3/23/58

The first 17 reels of Gunsmoke are also available. Also ask for our free 1983 and 1984 supplement. Our catalogs are available in 2 volumes--$3.00 for both, or $2.00 each.

The Jack Benny Times

Volume 4, No. 5　　NATIONWIDE DISTRIBUTION　　Sept.-Oct. 1984

§§ PRESIDENT'S MESSAGE §§

Hello to all the new and potenially new members, and "Hello again" to all the continuing members! This issue begins the bi-monthly cycle of the Times. From now until May the Jack Benny Times will come out every other month by reason of homework on my part. However, I hope that the bi-monthly will be twice as good as the monthly installments.

£ A FEW NEW MEMBERS £

****REX RIFFLE--Rex has been collecting Jack's shows on cassette for almost ten years. Perhaps some of you would be interested in contacting him in trading or buying. Write him at: 24 Central Ave., Buckhannon, West Virginia, 26201.

****JOE ANNE PETERSON--Joe Anne is an English teacher at City High, my patron institution. She is trying for first place in our most enthusiastic members; she just might have it, too! If anyone needs spiritual inspiration, write her! c/o City High School, 226 Bostwick NE, Grand Rapids, Mich. 49503.

****TOM MASTEL--Tom decided to become a member.(ha!) He owns his own realty company in California. If anyone wants to buy a house out there, contact him at: 1547 Arbutus Dr., San Jose, California 95118.

****PHILP R. EVANS--Phil is searching for someone with a VHS who can record the TV shows Jack did. He already has about 20 shows. I myself have over 65 on Beta. If any of you know a way to put shows from Beta on to VHS or has a VHS, please contact him. 701 Knotts St., Apt. G, Bakersfield, Calif., 93305.

****JOHN T. SCHLAMP--John hasn't said much in his letters, but he has stated that he is also a collector of Jack's shows on tape. Perhaps we could help him increase that collection. 320 South Drive, Paramus, N.J., 07652.

¥¥ FAMILY ALBUM ¥¥

We are assembling a Jack Benny Fan Club Family Album. We would very much appreciate it if you could send information about yourself that you would like included in the album and, if convenient, a recent photo. Please also send the date of certification on your membership certificate. There is no particular deadline, so take your time. Thank you.

µµ LEST WE FORGET µµ

October 1, 1944-- On this date, Jack broadcast his first show sponsored by Lucky Strike.

October 14, 1934--On this date, Jack Benny started the Jell-O Program. He served this same sponsor for ten years. (See previous page)

October 28--This is the birthday of one of our honorary members, Fred deCordova.

** THANKS!!! **

I wish to thank all those members who sent in donations. The money is going toward the printing costs of the <u>Times</u>. Just last month we lost a Xerox machine for copies, and we are forced to go to a formal printer which is more costly. Thank you again.

ßß TV LIST ßß

Next month we hope to have a listing of all the Jack Benny television shows now in syndication. Please send another copy, Phil!! The other one was inadvertently marked!

£ LATE MEMBER £

****ROB COHEN--Rob is a collector from Ohio. He is looking to you dealers out there for information about your tapes of Jack's radio shows. Phil, this gentleman records the T.V. shows--might want to get in touch with him!! 655 Brice Road, Reynoldsburg, OH 43068.

I'm going to cut this short because I realize that this issue is going to be late. History and English do take priority!! I will definitely make it up next month. Remember, if you have any requests, information or announcements, write me!

Laura Lee, The Jack Benny Fan Club Offices, 1620 Old Town Dr. SE, Grand Rapids, Mich. 49508

Copyright 1989, Laura Lee

The Jack Benny Times

Vol.4, No.6　　　NATIONWIDE DISTRIBUTION　　　Nov.-Dec. 1984

** PRESIDENT'S MESSAGE **

Merry Christmas!!!
Happy Channukah!!!

Now let's get down to the business.

** JACK BENNY TV SHOW LOG **

Philip Evans, one of our newer members, has most graciously sent us another copy of the Jack Benny TV show log. This listing includes all the Jack Benny television shows now in circulation. Unfortunately, many of the programs Jack did were live and never captured on tape. However, any of you that have cable television or satellite dishes can tune Jack in on CBN at 10:00 pm e.s.t.

§§ OTRWEAR!!! §§

Enclosed is Bob Burnham's flyer on his new "otrwear." They are t-shirts with "I love old time radio" printed on the front. Also, he is still selling copies of his Technical Guide to Collecting Old Time Radio Programs for $7.50. I highly recommend this booklet for references for tape dealers, clubs and above all, information on making better recordings of old radio shows. For further information, refer to the enclosed sheet.

¥¥ RJR ENTERPRISES ¥¥

Rusty Wolfe of RJR Enterprises wrote me in November requesting information on the fan club. He is not a member as of yet, but perhaps he will decide to become one. In the meantime, he gave me a bit of information that I thought you might be interested in; a Jack Benny mug. Apparently, a place called the Memory Mug Company has one. It has a drawing of Jack Benny on it and says "Coffee isn't cheap." I have just gotten around to writing them myself, so I cannot supply any more information than that. When I do get a response from them, I will follow up on this article. For those of you who would like to write yourselves, the address is: Memory Mugs Company, 1030 Boyer Street, Dubuque, Iowa 52001.

Rusty himself has quite a few Jack Benny shows on casette. For more information, you can write him at: RJR Enterprises, 1626 North Gunbarrel Road, P.O. Box 21428, Chattanooga, Tennessee 37421.

Copyright 1989, Laura Lee

** FRIENDS OF OLD-TIME RADIO **

YOu might remember that in a pest issue, I mentioned that Frank Nelson was going to be at the Friends of Old-Time Radio convention. Well, the convention has come and gone, but the sound lives on!!! (I know I ended the sentence with a preposition. It rhymed!!) Audio tapes can be obtained by sending 6 reels or $12.00 to Joseph Webb, Box 268, Glen Cove, NY 11542. The tape used is Ampex 641 in a new box sent 4th class special handling.

To receive video tapes from Ken Piletic, 705 South Oltendorf Rd., Streamwood, Ill. 60103: 1) VHS only, 2) SLP speed, 3) send SASE to Ken for details.

µ LEST WE FORGET µ

December 26, 1974 between 11:30 and 11:57 pm-- On this date at this time, Jack Benny passed away. However, no one is ever dead until they are forgotten.

¥¥ JACK BENNY LIVES !!! ¥¥

Bill "Rocky" Lane of Brigham City, Ut. sent us an article that he found in the Grit Newspaper on Jack Benny. He estimates that he has about 138 Jack Benny shows in his collection. However, his favorite is Lum and Abner. He will buy or trade. Write him at: 236 W. 6th South, Brigham City, Ut. 84302.

$$ THANKS A MILLION $$

I wish convey my sincerest gratitude to all the members who made donations to the fan club. (It's tax deductible, you know.) The money once again is going toward the printing costs of this installment of the Times.

Thanks a million!!!

ßß DEALERS' GUIDE ßß

For all of you besides Bob Burnham and Rusty Wolfe who deal in old-time radio show recordings, we need your name. I have lost track of who deals in recordings, who trades and who just collects. I would like to put together a listing of radio show dealers for a future Times issue. I am sure of the above two people, but I'm not sure of anyone else. Please just drop me a note and I'll include you.

££ TUNE IN!!! ££

On December 28, I am broadcasting the famous 1945 Jack Benny New Year's Program. All GR members should tune in! 89.9 fm, If you have any other notes, comments or announcements write me!! Jack Benny Fan Club Offices, 1620 Old Town Dr. SE, Grand Rapids, Mich. 49508

THE JACK BENNY SHOW

On the air 10/28/50, off 9/10/65. CBS, NBC. 30 min. B&W Film. 104 episodes. Although 343 episodes were made, only 104 are syndicated as most of the shows were done live. Only the episodes from the 1960s are rerun. Broadcast: Oct 1950-Jan 1959 CBS Sun 7:30-8; Oct 1959-Jan 1960 CBS Sun 10-10:30; Oct 1960-Jun 1962 CBS Sun 9:30-10; Sept 1962-Jun 1963 CBS Tue 9:30-10; Sept 1963-Sept 1964 CBS Tue 9:30-10; Sept 1964-Sept 1965 NBC Fri 9:30-10. Producer: Fred De Cordova (filmed episodes only). Prod Co/Synd: Universal TV.

CAST: Cast members portrayed themselves: Jack Benny, Eddie "Rochester" Anderson, Don Wilson, Dennis Day, Mary Livingstone (Mrs. Jack Benny), Frank Nelson, and Mel Blanc as Prof. LeBlanc.

Jack Benny plays himself in this situation comedy focusing on his home and working life. Episodes revolve around Jack, his faithful servant Rochester, and Mary Livingstone, who played his girlfriend but in real life was his wife. *The Jack Benny Show* is frequently seen on late-night television and is considered one of television's classic comedies.

How Jack Found Mary
Rochester and Roy dry dishes. The knives have "Hilton" written on them. Jack tells how he first met Mary.

Bedroom Burglar Show
Burglars enter Jack's bedroom, he calls the police and finds out the Beverly Hills police have an unlisted number.

Carnival Story
Jack goes to a carnival and gets into a lion's cage, thinking it is really Mr. Kitzel in a lion's suit.

6 O'Clock in the Morning Show
A disc jockey wakes Jack up with a silly question.

ium and then Jack asks Mary to go along.

Mary Has May Company Reunion
Mary invites Jack to a reunion she is giving for the May Company girls who used to work with her.

Don Invites Gang to Dinner
Don thanks everyone for some anniversary presents and invites the gang over for dinner.

Isaac Stern Show
GS: Isaac Stern. Jack threatens to jump out of the window because he is not a good violinist, so Isaac Stern plays for him.

Jack in Paris
GS: Maurice Chevalier. In Paris, Mary and Jack go up to the top of the Eiffel Tower, and Jack finds Maurice Chevalier in a local shop.

Jack Locked in Tower of London
Jack takes a lesson in English money

their Jack Benny Fan Club meeting In Pasadena.

Jack Arrested for Disturbing the Peace
Jack goes to bed, can't fall asleep, gets up to play the violin and gets arrested for disturbing the peace.

Jack Goes to Doctor
GS: Oscar Levant. Jack is irritable and unreasonable at rehearsal, so Oscar Levant persuades him to go to his doctor.

Jack Goes to Nightclub
GS: Danny Thomas. Jack takes his sponsor and wife to a nightclub, one with no comedians, but the regular entertainer is sick so Danny Thomas takes over.

Rochester Falls Asleep, Misses Program
Roy invites Rochester up to his cabin for the weekend. He turns on Jack's show, falls asleep and misses it.

Jack Dives into Empty Swimming Pool in Palm Springs
In Palm Springs, Jack jumps into an empty swimming pool and has to stay in bed for a whole week.

Massage and Date with Gertrude
Jack gets massage with chicken fat and then takes Gertrude to a restaurant.

Jack Hunts for Uranium
Don talks Jack into hunting for uran-

and then goes on a sightseeing tour of Trafalgar Square and the Tower of London.

Jack Falls into Canal in Venice
Waiting for a gondola, Jack falls into a canal, twice.

Jack Hires an Opera Singer in Rome
A crowd at the Rome airport wants an opera singer's autograph.

Ginger Rogers Show
GS: Ginger Rogers. A producer tells Jack they have to find a new script for the next show, so he asks Ginger Rogers and Fred Astaire for their help.

Hillbilly Act
Jack says he hasn't changed since he was young so he takes off his shirt and acts like a hillbilly.

Jack Goes to the Races
Dennis gives a long routine on how to pick horses. Meanwhile, Jack bets on the sponsor's horse and wins.

Jack's Life Story
GS: Van Johnson. Jack's ego has gone to his head when he hears they are going to film his life story.

Jack Takes Beavers to Dentist
The mother of one of Jack's Beavers asks Jack to take the boy to the dentist, who then pulls Jack's tooth by mistake.

Railroad Station Program
At the railway station the ticket Jack was supposed to get went to a fat girl, and it turns out the girl is Jack's daughter.

The Bergen Show
GS: Edgar Bergen. Jack tells jokes about ventriloquists and then goes over to see Edgar Bergen at his house, and finds Charlie McCarthy and Mortimer Snerd are real children.

Pasadena Fan Club
Two old ladies ask Jack to come to

Jack Goes to Vault
Two men from the Treasury visit Jack to see all the devices he has worked up over the years to protect his money.

Don's Anniversary
It's Don's anniversary and Jack tells the story of how he found Don.

Jack Goes to Concert
GS: Jimmy Stewart. Jack and Barbara Nichols go to the same concert as Mr. and Mrs. Stewart. Jack mistakenly goes to their house after the concert because of fog.

Death Row Sketch
GS: Mamie Van Doren. Jack's wife is playing around with the boarder, so Jack ends up in jail condemned for murder.

Jimmy Stewart Show
GS: Jimmy Stewart. Barbara Nichols and Jack join the Stewarts at a nightclub to celebrate the Stewarts' wedding anniversary.

Musicale
A look into Jack's past reveals: Sunday musicales at his house.

Jack at Supermarket
Rochester beats Jack at cards so Jack has to do the housework, including the dreaded chore of going supermarket shopping.

Jack Casting for TV Special
Jack wrote his life story and is casting it for TV. He casts a child agent to play him as a boy and the child is as cheap as he.

Lunch Counter Murder
Jack is running a lunch counter when two tough guys come in to rob him, so Jack shoots them both.

Hong Kong Suit
Jack goes to the barber shop but no one will cut his hair because he is wearing a suit he got in Hong Kong for $12.00.

Jack Gets a Passport
Jack is planning a trip to Australia and is having trouble getting a passport.

Tennessee Ernie Ford Show
Jack visits Tennessee Ernie Ford on his farm in Northern California.

Modern Prison Sketch
GS: Mickey Rooney. Mickey explores what might happen to prisons if they continue to be easier and easier on prisoners.

Jack Goes to Cafeteria
Jack has difficulties taking Jane Morgan to lunch as everything is too expensive.

Dennis's Surprise Party
Jack decides to give Dennis a surprise party for his birthday.

Jack on Trial for Murder
GS: Raymond Burr. Jack is being sued for having a chicken which disturbs the peace, and dreams Raymond Burr is his lawyer and he loses.

Jack Followed Home
Jack is followed home after having Bobby Rydell on his show. It turns out to be Dennis who is out to kill him for having Bobby on the show.

Golf Show
Jack goes out to play golf and no one will play against him.

Jack Writes Song
Jack finds a song he wrote years ago and he tries to get Dimitri Tiomkin to write an arrangement of it.

Jack Does Opera
Jack sings an excerpt from an opera with Roberta Peters and Don Wilson.

Ghost Town Western Sketch
GS: Gisele MacKenzie. Jack imagines he is a western hero with a gun that shoots backwards.

Jack Going Back into Pictures
Billy Wilder wants Jack for a part in a

Blanc shows up as Mr. Fingue, whose specialty is imitating dogs and horses, and then he impersonates an organ.

The Story of Jack Refereeing Wrestling Match
Jack is insulted when he has not been asked to appear at a charity fair, then he gets his chance when one of the guests cancels out.

Bob Hope Show
Bob and Jack reminisce over their old days at the office of the Weber Theatrical Agency.

Jack Plays Tarzan
GS: Carol Burnett. In a Tarzan sketch, Jack drives three gorillas crazy with his violin playing, while Jane decides to leave home.

Jack Fires Don
Jack is about to replace Don when they have a dispute over a famous naval saying and neither would back down.

The Peter Lorre-Joanie Sommers Show
Jack goes to a doctor to treat his cold, but the doctor is a plastic surgeon. Meanwhile, an escaped criminal causes havoc in the studio.

Jack Becomes a Surgeon
Jack applies to medical school. In a sketch, Jack is a crazy doctor operating on a patient.

Jack Goes to Las Vegas
Jack hires only two Mills Brothers and tricks the other into joining them to sing.

Variety Show
George Burns comes on to introduce Ann Margret, his latest discovery.

Main Street Shelter
Rochester gives Jack's jacket to a mission, unaware that there is $200 in the lining. Jack goes down to get it back and is mistaken for a bum.

English Sketch
Jack is in love with Diana Dors, Peter Lawford's wife. However, Jack trades Diana for a stamp collection in order to get his picture in the papers.

How Jack Found Rochester
Jack is on the train coming East, Rochester is the porter on the train. Jack gets Rochester fired, so he hires him as his butler.

picture, but it is a very small part.

Alexander Hamilton Story
Jack dreams that he is Alexander Hamilton, first Secretary of the Treasury o the U.S.

Julie London Show
Jack sings songs with Julie London.

Jack Is Violin Teacher
Jack takes a look at what would happen if he had been a violin teacher.

Jack and the Cab Driver
After a plane is airborne, Jack discovers an emotional cab driver unable tc say goodbye has come along on thi trip.

The Story of My Gang Comedy
Members of "Our Gang" pay a visi and Jack, Rochester, Spanky McFarland and Darla Hood perform a sketch

Air Force Sketch
Jack tries to teach Raymond Burr hov to become a comedian. Then Raymond asks Jack to turn a WWII battl scene into a comedy.

The Phil Silvers Show
While Phil Silvers borrows Jack's pant for his appearance, Jack borrow Don's pants. Later, Don arrives wearing the pants Phil returned.

Jack Meets Japanese Agent
Jack introduces guest Romi Yamada who does a song. Jack wants him tc appear again on the show so he deal with his Japanese agent.

The Lawrence Welk Show
Jack has written a torch song anc wants Lawrence Welk to perform it; he does, as a polka.

Jack Meets Max Bygraves
Jack tells the story of how he met Max Bygraves, one of England's top performers.

The Story of the New Talent Show
It is the new talent show and Me

Jack Answers Request Letters
Jack answers request letters from his fans.

Riverboat Sketch
Carol Burnett plays a Southern belle along with Jack's riverboat gambler routine.

Jack Takes Boat to Hawaii
Jack goes to Hawaii when he meets Jayne Mansfield and Schlepperman.

Johnny Carson Guests
Johnny Carson sings, dances, plays the drums and converses with Jack.

The Tall Cowboy Sketch
Guest Clint Walker makes his singing debut and leads Jack into the world of the western star.

The Robert Goulet Show
Robert and Jack both vie for affection from the same girl.

The Ed Sullivan Show
Ed and Jack play opposing attorneys in the trial of a beautiful Parisienne accused of slaying her husband.

How Jack Found Dennis
Jack takes a look back in time at how he discovered Dennis Day. Jack tells how his quest for a singer for his old radio show led him to many faces.

Jack Takes a Violin Lesson
Professor LeBlanc gives Jack music lessons.

Peter, Paul and Mary
Peter, Paul and Mary show Jack how folklore can be adapted to songs. Jack then succeeds in getting the three to record a song he wrote.

How Jack Met George Burns
George and Jack demonstrate what and who killed vaudeville.

Bobby Darin Guests
Jack thinks Bobby would be the perfect man to play him in a movie based on his life.

Nat King Cole Guests
A musical show has Nat singing and playing piano in a musical group that has Jack on the violin.

Jack Goes to Allergy Doctor
Jack goes to two doctors to determine why his arm itches, and doesn't like either method of dealing with his problem.

The Lettermen Guest
Jack plays an enterprising college dormitory student rooming with the Lettermen.

Hillbilly Sketch
Jack and guest Connie Francis play hillbillies concerned over their 28-year-old son who they think doesn't know the facts of life.

Andy Williams Guests
Andy accompanies Jack to a big opening, which turns out to be the opening of a meat market.

Jack Makes Comedy Record
Jack urges guest Bob Hope to join forces with him in recording a comedy record.

The Kingston Trio Guests
Jack is arrested and thrown into the Tijuana jail for being double parked, while the Kingston Trio sing "Tijuana Jail."

The Smothers Brothers Show
The Smothers Brothers relive a London bombing raid when Jack entertained servicemen at the Palladium.

The Income Tax Show
Jack has his income tax return investigated for a $3.90 dinner deduction, an amount the IRS can't believe is so small.

The Lucille Ball Show
Jack and Lucille give their version of the story behind Paul Revere's famous midnight ride.

Jack Adopts a Son
GS: Milton Berle. Jack plays a man who has everything in life except a son, so he tries to adopt a lad named Marvin.

Wayne Newton Show
Jack, Wayne, and Louis Nye donate their talents to help underprivileged Beverly Hills children jet to camp on the French Riviera.

Jack Jones Show
Jack and Jack Jones spoof ways of coping with problems that confront the teaching profession.

Jack Goes to Gym
It is Rochester's day off and he won't lift a finger, so Jack takes up body building to impress his girl.

We're one year old!

Old Time Radio is alive and well in the pages of the DIGEST!

The hobby needs a voice and the DIGEST would like to be that voice.

Our recipe is to have a nice mix of current articles by collectors with material from old radio publications of the past.

One year $12.50 for 6 issues.

Royal Promotions
4114 Montgomery Rd.
Cincinnati, Ohio 45212

Jack Does the USO Show
Jack answers letters and tells his listeners about the USO show. At the end of the show, two Japanese soldiers arrive claiming they'll surrender if Jack will stop playing his violin.

The Spanish Sketch
Jack introduces Rita Moreno who acts out a movie scene with Jack in a Spanish cafe.

The Frankie Avalon Show
Frankie discusses how he became a guest star on Jack's show.

The Connie Francis Show
Jack introduces Connie Francis who does a sketch about Stephen Foster.

Don Breaks Leg
An ecdysiast performs her specialty to Jack's chagrin. Don Wilson takes a broken leg, and his son Harlow takes over Don's job.

Jack Directs Film
Jack crashes the set where Jimmy Stewart is making a film and gives his advice on how movies should be made.

Amateur Show
GS: George Jessel. Jack holds his annual amateur show which ends in pandemonium when all the contestants feel they have won.

Harlow Gets a Date
Jack does all he can to please a sponsor, including getting his daughter an escort for sightseeing, only Don's son Harlow has no interest in girls.

Jack Benny's Style Makes People Laugh

Fred Allen once said Jack Benny couldn't ad-lib a belch after a Hungarian dinner. Allen may have been right in implying that Benny couldn't write his own material. But Benny knew what was funny and he knew how to deliver jokes. His comedic timing was flawless.

Benny once speculated that he might have become a symphony violinist had there been no vaudeville. However, when he was a young man in the Navy, his violin playing was not enthusiastically received so he began interspersing the fiddling with jokes and found he could make people laugh. From then on he used the violin as a prop. When he actually played, it was most often a deliberately off-key rendition of "Love in Bloom."

After a few years in vaudeville, he decided radio was where his future lay. His radio show premiered in 1932 and was an immediate hit.

Part of his success came because he surrounded himself with interesting characters and often allowed himself to become the butt of their jokes. Rochester (Eddie Anderson) served as his gravel-voiced chauffeur. Announcer Don Wilson pompously extolled the virtues of Jell-O in six delicious flavors. Benny's real-life wife, Mary Livingston, read imaginary letters from her "mother" over the air. Andy Devine always greeted Benny with "hiya Buck" before launching into some amusing banter with Benny. And Mel Blanc's talent for voices provided several other amusing characters.

There was a succession of tenors with little-boy voices for Benny to heckle — Kenny Baker, Frank Parker and Dennis Day — and the Sportsmen Quartet that Benny kept firing.

When Benny made the transition to television in 1952, he pretty much kept the same cast of characters and he developed a springy walk and folded-arms stance for the benefit of the audience who could now see as well as hear him. When beset by life's vicissitudes he had only to put his hand to his cheek and deliver a disgusted "Wellllll!" and the audience howled.

Within the framework of the show, Benny assumed traits we'd probably dislike in others. For instance, he was touchy and bristled at derogatory references to his receding hairline and violin playing.

He was vain and never admitted to being over 39. Once he was heard to remark, "I just celebrated my 39th birthday — for the 12th time."

And he was stingy. He put only one gallon of gas at a time in his ancient Maxwell car.

There were lots of running gags on the show — the balky Maxwell, Rochester's sarcasm, the clanging doors of the underground vault where Benny supposedly kept his money.

For a while there was also a "feud" with Fred Allen that went on for weeks and finally climaxed with a mock fist fight on Benny's program.

In real life Benny was a kind man who over-tipped in restaurants and raised millions of dollars for charity.

He died in 1974 and almost to the very end, he was doing what he loved most. He was making people laugh.

Just published — "The Zany World of Joy Duane," a 96-page paperback book containing more than 75 humorous stories. Send $4.95, plus 90 cents for postage and handling, to Grit Publishing Co., P.O. Box 245, Williamsport, Pa. 17701.

NOW - Exclusively from BRC Productions..."OTRWEAR."

I LOVE OLD TIME RADIO!

$8.50 POST PAID

T-SHIRTS
High quality 50% cotton - 50% polyester with blue trim and blue printing. Your choice of medium, large or ex-large.

BRC Productions
P.O. Box 39522, Redford, Michigan 48239
Old time radio recordings, services and supplies

IT'S HERE
OLD TIME RADIO'S MOST COMPLETE & COMPREHENSIVE HANDBOOK

$7.50 POST PAID
ADVERTISERS DEDUCT $1

BY BOB BURNHAM

18 CHAPTERS, OVER 50 PAGES COVERING
The history of old time radio collecting and trading
Recording techniques and equipment
Improving and organizing your collection
Recording tape editing, data dubbing
Logs — and covers of focal log sources, collectors
DIRECTORIES of all known OTR clubs and publications
SOURCES for equipment and prices for most commonly used OTR tape decks
Blank tape and other special supplies of interest to collectors
DEALER ads from across the U.S. for old time radio tapes and supplies
PLUS THE TECHNICAL GUIDE'S OWN DIRECTORY OF OLD TIME RADIO COLLECTORS, FROM COAST TO COAST, PLUS CANADA.

BRC Productions P.O. Box 39522, Redford, Michigan 48239
Old Time Radio Recordings, Services and Supplies

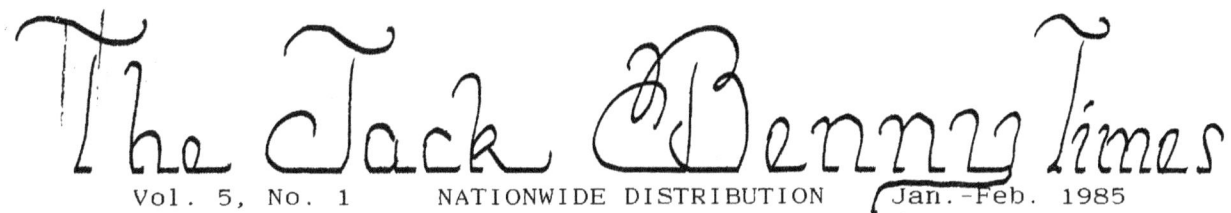

Vol. 5, No. 1   NATIONWIDE DISTRIBUTION   Jan.-Feb. 1985

** PRESIDENT'S MESSAGE **

WELL...On January 1 of this year, the Jack Benny Fan Club celebrated its fifth anniversary!!! We've come a long way from a four-member club!!! I'm happy to say that the fan club is now recognized by several national otr publications and considered a legitimate club. I thank each and every one of you for being not only great co-members, but good friends as well.

§§ A FEW NEW MEMBERS §§

****ROB COHEN--Rob is looking to enlarge his collection of Jack's radio shows, television programs and movies. He says that he is willing to trade programs with other members. Write him at: 2680 Cannon Pt., Apt. 3D, Columbus, Ohio, 43209.
****DONNIE PITCHFORD--Let's see...who the heck is this guy? Oh, yeah. He's the guy who hates Lum and Abner so much that he's head of their fan club. He also has his own printing shop called D.S.Co. If anyone is interested in either of these, just drop him a note!!! 202 Alta, Longview, Texas, 75604.
****DAVID MILLER--David is a friend of Donnie Pitchford and a member of the Lum and Abner Society. David, please write a letter and tell me about yourself!
****PHIL "HARRIS" BAIRD--Phil is another die-hard Jack Benny fan. About all I know about him is that he was Donnie Pitchford's college room-mate for two semesters and they used to end the day watching Jack's show on TV. Does it really put you to sleep?!
****RUSTY WOLFE--Rusty is a part of RJR enterprises (Refer to last issue). He has quite a variety of radio shows along with several of Jack's programs for sale. Write him at: RJR Enterprises, 1626 North Gunbarrel Rd., P.O. Box 21428, Chattanooga, Tennessee, 37421.
*****BOB HOPE--Need I say more?
*****ISAAC STERN--For those of you who don't know, Isaac Stern is a world-famous violinist and a close friend of Jack's. During the time Jack was giving benefit concerts, Isaac served as his "agent."

¥URGENT¥URGENT¥URGENT¥

If any of you haven't heard, the Citizen's Stamp Advisory Committee is considering issuing a commemorative stamp in honor of Jack Benny. We ask that if you have some free time in the near future, please jot a note supporting the idea. Send your cards and letters to: Jack Benny Commemorative Stamp Committee, P.O. Box 48559, Los Angeles, California, 90048. Also, please tell them to stop addressing me as "Mr. L. Lee".

Copyright 1989, Laura Lee

μ FAMILY ALBUM μ

Just a reminder to old members and information for new...
I thank those of you who have sent in photos and write-ups for the Jack Benny Fan Club Family Album. It's bound in red leather with gold trim. The pages are parchment and have guilded edges. It's quite handsome. For your own entry in the album, you need only enclose whatever information you'd like included and a photo. Send them to the address at the end of the newsletter. Thank you.

ßß JACK BENNY LIVES!!! ßß

Enclosed with this issue is a copy of a portion of an article on communications from the November/December 1984 issue of <u>The Digest of Chiropractic Economics</u>. Please don't tell anyone--I don't want to go to jail. Anyhow, it has been given to the club by Ms. Kati Patsakos of Grand Rapids. We give our sincere thanks to her.

If you have any news, anecdotes or announcements, write me!!! Laura Lee, Jack Benny Fan Club Offices, 1620 Old Town Dr. SE, Grand Rapids, Mich. 49508.

LEST WE FORGET LIKE I DID...

February 14--On this date in 1894, Jack Benny was born and immediately became 37.

No, that's not a mistake. The first time he was asked his age on radio, he said it was 37. About 10 years later he turned 39.

January 14--On this date in 1927, Jack and Mary were wed.

January 20--On this date in ____, one of our honorary members, George Burns was born.

February 13--On this day in 1870, Emma Kubelsky, Jack's mother, was born.

February 28--On this day in 1977, Eddie "Rochester" Anderson passed away.

and just for good measure...

January 7--On this date in 1926, George Burns and Gracie Allen were married.

One of Jack Benny's most memorable one liners, which usually broke up the audience with hysterical laughter, illustrates this point. In a skit, he was held up by an armed robber demanding "Your money or your life." Benny's reply consisted of just two words, but to appreciate his answer you have to keep in mind that he carefully nourished the reputation of being a Scrooge.

As the armed bandit points a gun and asks him for his money, Benny is going through body and nonverbal expressions as a man debating with himself whether he should give it to him or not. Keep in mind he had himself depicted as so tight with money that his wallet would almost squeak when he opened it. (And then to those of us who are old enough, who can never forget Benny's old Maxwell jalopy and its familiar clackety clack. Of course we all knew he was simply too tight with his money to part with any of it for a new car. He'd always find a good excuse or two why his old jalopy was still a perfectly good car). Again the armed bandit repeated, "All right, which is it going to be, your money or your life?" and with perfect timing and intonation Benny responded with, "I'm thinking."

Unless you're a fan of Jack Benny and remember his style of comedy it is even difficult to appreciate the humorous impact of his answer. The answer by itself isn't even funny, but if you could watch him bring his hand up to his chin, watch his very subtle facial reactions, the way he uses his eyes for expression and then at the precise moment with perfect timing throw his hand out in frustration as he answers, "I'm thinking," you could appreciate his communicative genius. He was a master of his trade of just how and when to say what he said. He supported this with all the appropriate nonverbal, vocal and visual language of communication and did it in perfect timing.

That one liner, just two words, became a classic in Benny's long and distinguished career. It's like that old saying "It's not what you say, but the way you say it." And we could improve on that expression with "It's not entirely what you say, but **also** the way that you say it."

Jack Benny Times

Vol. 5, No. 2 INTERNATIONAL DISTRIBUTION March-April 1985

A FEW NEW MEMBERS

****BRAD ASHTON--Brad is a writer for television and radio in Europe. At one time he wrote for Groucho Marx, who he quoted as saying, "Jack Benny is my best friend and I hate him. He makes ten times as much money as I do with only half my talent." He is interested in trading old radio shows. He is helping me get in touch with Larry Adler, a concert harmonica player who appeared several times with Jack, and Ernest Maxin who produced all Jack's shows made in England. Hopefully I will be able to transcribe interviews with them for upcoming issues. In the meantime if you would like to write Brad, his address is: 288 St. Paul's Road, Islington, London N1 2LR, England.

****DAVID SPANGLER--David played a big part in the Jack Benny Train, celebrating Jack's birthday. There is a clipping with more information on it which will be published in a later Times. He is the proud owner of the class ribbons of the Jack Benny Junior High School Class of 1978. If you'd like to find out how that came about, write to him at: 3550 N. Lake Shore Drive, Apt. 616, Chicago, Illinois, 60657.

****SAREE HALEVY--Having not heard from her since I sent her her certificate, I can't say anything except that she's a friend of David Spangler! Please send information!!!

****BILLIE LEE BREHM--At long last...a member!!! The article by Tom Hennessy is being brought to you by Billie; we thank you. They have a catalog of old radio programs for sale, so if you would be interested, the address is: 13402 Leibacher Ave., Norwald, California 90650.

*****NORM CROSBY--As if you didn't know, Norm is the chairman of the Jack Benny Commemorative Stamp Committee. Just after the release of the Jan.-Feb. issue of the Times, I received a not from him saying that all indications seem to say that it will go. We hope so!!!

*****GEORGE BUSH--George has been a hearty supporter of the Jack Benny stamp. His side job is being Vice-President of the United States.

*****MICKEY ROONEY--Needs no introduction. (See later article.)

AUCTION§AUCTION§AUCTION

Here it is, the announcement you've all been waiting for; at last!!! I have found two very interesting magazines which I am now putting up for auction, the proceeds going to the Jack Benny Fan Club treasury.

The Procedure: If you would like to bid on either or both of the items, send me a letter specifying which item and your bid. SEND NO MONEY NOW. Both winners will be notified by mail. ALL BIDS MUST BE RECEIVED BY JUNE 30.

The Items: LOOK Magazine, May 15, 1945. This has a <u>very</u> nice picture of Jack on the cover. He is wearing a tux and playing the violin. It has a 7-page article with lots of pictures. The magazine itself is complete and in nearly mint condition. Many other interesting articles and ads.

LOOK Magazine, November 1, 1955. This, too, has a nice picture of Jack on the cover. He is resting his chin on his hands and holding his violin. It really shows off his blue eyes!!! There's a 5-page article with lots to read. The magazine is complete and in good condition. It also has other timely articles and ads.

Current high bids will be printed in the next <u>Times</u>.

£ MEMBERS CLOSE-UP £

In mid-April I personally presented Mickey Rooney with a membership certificate. He most generously granted me an interview; here is a small portion of it:

> It's so wonderful to know that you keep his (Jack's) memory alive. There aren't many people who keep celebrities' (memories)...You're to be commended...It's wonderful that you keep this great love for him because he was a wonderful man, and he was a lovely person. Where is the George Burns Fan Club?...But I can understand your wanting to keep the torch lit for Jack, because it's certainly a worthy endeavor...All I can say...is don't ever stop loving this great, great man, and don't ever forget his greatness, and I wish you all the luck and happiness with your fan club and may it be forever and ever.

During the interview he questioned why there were no fan clubs for Judy Garland, Clark Gable, Jimmy Cagney, Bob Hope, Abbott and Costello and many others. If any of you know of any, please drop me a line as soon as possible. Maybe you could start one!!! Anyhow we thank Mickey Rooney for the interview and send him our best wishes.

Also I received a letter from Isaac Stern thanking us for his membership. Here is what he had to say about Jack:

> He was an old and devoted friend and we shared a deep mutual affection. Jack

> always loved music and the violin, and
> the thing that I admired most about him
> was that he never made fun of artists,
> only of himself in relation to violin
> playing. He was one of the greatest
> gentlemen I had ever met and a warm and
> generous spirit.

What more is there to say? Thank you Isaac Stern.

¥CORRECTIONRS AND UPDATES¥

Answering the demand of 20,000,000 members, we are here today to tell you that DONNIE PITCHFORD DOES NOT OWN HIS OWN PRINTING SHOP!!! HE IS NOT THE NEXT HITLER, AND HE DOES NOT BOW DOWN TO SATAN!!! HE HAS NOT VICIOUSLY MURDERED SEVENTY PEOPLE, AND HE IS NOT (as far as we know) HAVING AN AFFAIR WITH HIS SECRETARY. He does, however, have some Lum and Abner Movie Poster Cards for sale. Write him at 202 Alta, Longview, Texas 75604.

Phil "Harris" Baird also sent me a letter with some info on himself. He is 25, has been married since December, 1982 and has a baby boy. He is called Phil Harris because he almost constantly has a can of Mountain Dew in his hand. He was first introduced to OTR in Stephen F. Austin University where the radio station played OTR shows.

John Schlamp also sent me a letter telling a litle more about himself. Although he has been collecting for 18 years, he is still interested in buying shows. The two obits included with this issue were sent by him, and we give our sincere thanks for them.

µLEST WE FORGETµ

March 14, 1947--The Benny-Allen Feud officially ended on this day.
March 17, 1956--Fred Allen passed away, a victim of a heart attack.
MARCH 23   --JACK BENNY DAY
March 29, 1932--On this day Jack made his radio debue on Ed Sullivan's show.
April 26, 1982--Don Wilson passed away at 82 years of age.

A FINAL NOTE

Dear Members,
    I am going to be moving this summer to Ft. Wayne; because of this, the July and August issues will be combined into one. By the way, for those of you who haven't heard the good news, I am graduating this June, and I have been accepted into Purdue. All I can say is THANK GOODNESS!!!
    If you do have any articles, announcements or would just like to chat about life in general, contemplate the ex-

istance of God or plot the overthrow of the universe with potential expansion to the entire galaxy, write me!!!

Laura "Benny" Lee, Jack Benny Fan Club Offices, 1620 Old Town Dr. SE, Grand Rapids, Michigan 49508.

Sorry about the delay!

- Comics B6
- Entertainment B7

Tom Hennessy

'Cheapskate' Jack Benny left us richer

This column was to have been written last month. Illness intervened.

•

The funniest person in my memory slipped away 10 years ago. He was born in 1894 and died Dec. 26, 1974. At the time of his death, he was 39.

His name would have remained Benny Kubelsky if he had stayed in Waukegan, Ill., maybe as a bookkeeper, which was once a possibility. But God must have known the world needed a laugh more than it needed another bookkeeper.

So He gave us Jack Benny.

When Benny was 16, he fancied himself a violinist, having just landed a job with a local orchestra. Mayer Kubelsky thought otherwise, and one day told his son, "Benny, to you, you're a violinist. To me, maybe you're a violinist. But to Jascha Heifetz, you're a bum."

In vaudeville, Benny tried using the violin for laughs, but soon found he got more by using his wit. The rest, as they say, is show biz history.

Millions of us grew up — or old — laughing at Jack Benny and the gags of his that became national fixtures, such as his perpetual claim that he was 39 or the endless jokes about his being cheap. (In truth, he was very generous.)

In depression and war, we still managed to laugh at miser Benny's subterranean vault. And the wheezing sound of his antique Maxwell automobile. And those railroad station announcements: "Train leaving on Track Five for Anaheim, Azusa, and Cuc — *long pause* — amonga." (It was the first time much of America had even heard of

One had Jack in the shower. Needing to tip a delivery boy, Rochester, Benny's butler, extracts a quarter from his boss' trousers hanging on the bathroom door. Jack emerges from the shower, takes the trousers in both hands, pauses and calls out, "Rochester, who took a quarter from my pocket?"

Another show featured this exchange:
Holdup man: "Your money or your life."

Very long pause.
Holdup man: "Quit stalling. I said your money or your life."
Benny: "I'm thinking it over."

He made a 1945 movie called *The Horn Blows at Midnight*. When it bombed, he took it in stride, even working the disaster into his scripts. For example, Jack drives up to a studio gate, only to be fired on by the guard.

"Don't you recognize me?" he asks. "I'm Jack Benny. I made a movie here at Warner Brothers — *The Horn Blows at Midnight*. Didn't you see it?"

The guard says, "See it? I directed it."

Benny needed no script to be funny. He was opening in Earl Carroll's *Vanities* one night and was doing a skit that had him romancing a farmer's daughter as she milked a live cow. Suddenly, the cow began delivering something other than milk. And delivering and delivering.

By the time the cow finished, the audience was in hysterics. Holding up a hand, Benny at last quieted them and said, "Folks, you'll have to forgive the cow. This is opening night and she's just as nervous as we are."

The Benny formula included a lot of jokes about his violin playing, said to be terrible. Like gags about his thrift, they had no basis in fact. He was actually accomplished enough to play with numerous symphonies. But the myth persisted.

After doing a concert in Washington, D.C., one evening, Benny, complete with violin case, went to a party being given by President Lyndon Johnson. At the White House he was stopped by a Secret Service man demanding to know what was in the case.

Thinking the fellow had not recognized him, Benny facetiously said, "A machine gun." And the agent answered, "Thank God, I thought it was your violin."

It took 8½ hours of sorting through Benny material to write this column. For all that, I don't care for it. It says nothing about the characters that appeared on his shows or about his radio "feud" with Fred Allen or his warm, zany relationship with George Burns. Nor does it come close to telling how truly funny the man was or how kind and sensitive.

There is talk these days about putting

Readers are anti-abortion, pro-Benny

Although I ... disagree with most of your (abortion) column, I join with you in condemning the bombing of abortion clinics. And so do President Reagan and the Rev. Jerry Falwell.

(Also) loved your tribute to my all-time favorite, Jack Benny. You were wrong about one thing the "post-Benny" people (those born after his heyday). My nephews were 6 and 5 at the time of Jack's passing.... Yet, from hearing my old time radio tapes, Jack and his wonderful cast are just as real and alive to the boys as they are to us.

— Frank G. Williams
Paramount

Your nephews have good taste — in comedians and uncles.

As an ardent admirer of Jack Benny, your column returned some memories. We were all poor in those days and Jack's musings hit home to us. Our poor family had two Maxwell cars (one at a time, fortunately). They were automotive disasters. If you were dressed up for a date, you had to get out and lift the hood and suck on the vacuum tank until it would work again.... What a sorry place the world has become; so few real comics left.

— Al Browning
Lakewood

Hey, Al, remember the TV show when Benny's doing his monologue and out come 10 penguins, each on roller skates? Audience goes crazy. So the following week, he's doing his monologue again and out comes one penguin on roller skates. Benny turns to him and says, "If I told you once, I told you a hundred times. The check is in the mail."

You liberals are all alike. I got so mad about your column about the subway commando that I went out and bought three more guns. However, your column on obesity endeared yourself to me.... The girls at your office tell me that when you sit on a small chair you have a hangover. Your wife told me you've gotten so fat under the Reagan administration that she had to let your bedsheets out. Have a Goodyear, blimp.

— Frank J. Sullivan
Los Alamitos

Nice to hear from you, Frank, but this is the last time I print your audition for vaudeville.

'... and all the gang'

When Jack Benny died last week, his obituary was the lead story in The Record. For young readers—younger than, say, 30—it might have seemed a little strange that a newspaper would devote to the death of an old comedian as much attention as to the demise of a head of state.

But it wasn't strange at all. Jack Benny was more than a comedian. For years he was an integral part of the ordinary life of the nation. That is, he was, for many Americans, part of the family. Every Sunday evening, millions of radios would be switched on at 7 o'clock for the Benny show.

The show was often quite funny, for Mr. Benny's stable of writers was the best that money could buy, and his sense of timing was without peer. Jack Benny didn't even try to compete with the likes of Fred Allen, the wit who could tell a dozen jokes a minute.

Mr. Benny's talent was subtler than that. What he did was to create an obviously fictitious but wholly endearing collection of serial audio biographies. He was at the center of each episode, of course, portraying a miserly, penny-pinching fellow who played the violin atrociously and with inexplicable persistence, who could not resist an opportunity to attack the character or ability of Mr. Allen, and who professed an intimate friendship with the British actor Ronald Colman, a friendship that Mr. Colman would regularly repudiate with frosty hauteur.

But the character that Mr. Benny created for himself was only half the show. Just as important were the audio personalities that Mr. Benny would chat with, Sunday after Sunday. There was the butler, Rochester, with a voice like gravel sloshing in a cement mixer; the dumb, boyish tenor, Dennis Day; the fat announcer, Don Wilson; the tipsy bandleader, Phil Harris, and a whole stable of train announcers, unctuous department store floorwalkers, and racing touts.

The plot line typically would be about the process of preparing the show itself; an episode would begin at home, with Mr. Benny and his wife, Mary Livingston, getting ready to leave in their ancient Maxwell automobile for the studio, and encountering one little mishap after another. Unlike the television comedy shows of today, which are anchored to one or two stage sets, in a radio drama the characters could go anywhere, courtesy of a sound effect or two. We have particularly fond memories of Mr. Benny's occasional visits to the money vault in the basement of his own house. These would be attended by a cornucopia of audio effects: steel doors opening and clanging shut, burglar alarms sounding, rusty screeching noises, and finally the wistful voice of the vault attendant, who had been immured in these gloomy depths so long that he had lost all track of time.

Jack Benny and friend, 1959

The Benny show would begin with some trivial bit of business and weave into the story one after another of these tried-and-true elements. Rarely did anything surprising happen. It was predictable, from first to last. It was, in McLuhanese, a cool medium. That is, it was low-key, not flashy and aggressive.

Thinking back to those shows, which ran for years through the tail end of the Depression and through the tumult of World War II—attended by huge ratings Sunday in and Sunday out—we suspect that what people sought and obtained from Jack Benny was a sense of family, of continuity and human values. Listeners knew exactly how each character would react in any circumstance, knew the foibles of these characters and forgave them.

Take, for instance, what became the best-known joke of the Benny series: A hold-up man accosts the star in the street and says, "Your money or your life." There is no answer. Seconds tick by, and more seconds. The hold-up man, impatient, says "Hey, mister, I said, 'Your money or your life'!" To which Mr. Benny responds, "I'm thinking! I'm thinking!" Reading that now, in the cold Aquarian light of 1974, the line does not seem terribly funny. In the early 1940s it was convulsive. And the reason it was is that Jack Benny had spent so many Sunday nights establishing his miserly character — a character that was nevertheless gentle and human — that listeners knew before he could say anything that the choice in the robbery was for him as harrowing as it was hilarious to the audience.

Well, the days of that sort of comedy seem gone forever. Mr. Benny tried with indifferent success to transplant his format first to motion pictures and then to television. It never worked as well in these visual media as it did on the radio. Perhaps that's because the characters he created were so ephemeral that they required more imaginative involvement by the audience than is possible when the actors in a drama can be seen. Don Wilson could never be as fatuous in the flesh as one could imagine him being, listening to his voice. In television today, the Mary Tyler Moore show comes closest to the Benny format, but the difference in media does make a difference in perception.

Jack Benny, in sum, made a significant albeit characteristically self-deprecating contribution to American humor. It is a contribution that will endure as long as there are people around to remember "Jack and Mary and all the gang."

Vol. 5, No. 3   INTERNATIONAL DISTRIBUTION   May-June 1985

§ PRESIDENT'S MESSAGE §

Sorry this is a bit late--I've been very busy lately working on the house and all, getting it ready to put on the market. By the way, I'm not sure exactly when I'll be moving, but I know that I have to be in Ft. Wayne on August 22; that's the day I start college!!! In the meantime we'll be staying here until the house is sold. If we move at a time significantly earlier than August 22, I'll send out some cards. Anyhow, my future address is:

>   15430 Lost Valley Drive
>   Ft. Wayne, Indiana 46825

This issue of the Times will be abbreviated because of lack of time and material. I'll try to make up for it when things are more settled in my life!!!

*AUCTION*AUCTION*AUCTION*

Ladies and gentlemen, there are NO BIDS currently on the magazines that are up for auction!!! These are two of the best magazines pertaining to Jack that I've ever found--and I've been searching for a long time. If you are reluctant to bid without seeing the merchandise, I have a photo of both magazines which I will "loan" to anyone who would be interested. Do you realize that someone could practically steal these beauties for a low bid just because no one else tried? It would keep Jack awake all night knowing just how little he would have had to bid to get them. (But please be reasonable--don't bid 50¢.)

μμ FAMILY ALBUM μμ

The Jack Benny Fan Club Family Album is coming together beautifully. For each member, the left page is the photo and name inscribed in German calligraphy. The right page is a short biography, usually written by the member. If you do not wish to take the time to write anything down or submit a photo at this time, just drop me a line and I'll write up something myself and leave room for a photo if you would like to submit one at a later date. Addresses are not published with the bio. The album has impressed several new members that I have met personally, and one who shall remain nameless, said that it was really encouraging to see such a warm, personal fan club. Of course...only the classiest enjoy Jack Benny!!!

£RADIO RECORDINGS£

Heritage Radio Classics sent me a catalog of theirs listing many radio programs that they have available on cassette. One of them is called "Jack Benny's Life Story," a two-hour special with many clips and interviews of members of the cast. It sound quite in-

Copyright 1989, Laura Lee

teresting. If you would like to write to them, their address is: P.O. Box 16, Chestnut Hill, Massachusetts, 02157.

ß STATUES ß

Are any of you really deprived? Are any of you lacking that something in life that would make your existence really feel complete? Do you wake up sometimes and feel like there is a gap in your world? You can solve that problem now by writing the Tinder Box, Water Tower Shopping Center, Chicago, Illinois or Judy's Pastime, Ft. Wayne, Indiana (more specific address in next issue) for information on how to order your own personal statue of Jack Benny.

¥ MORE RECORDINGS ¥

Some of you have expressed an interest in getting some of Jack's movies on video tape. I personally have <u>TheHorn Blows at Midnight</u>, <u>George Washington Slept Here</u>, <u>Buck Benny Rides Again</u>, and a clip from <u>Transatlantic Merry-Go-Round</u>. I also have <u>It's In the Bag</u> starring Fred Allen--a movie in which Jack had second star billing and a somewhat cameo appearance. I may be able to get all of <u>Transatlantic</u> at a later date. Anyhow, if anyone is interested in copies of these, please send me a note and I'll see if I can arrange something. I also have a set of two tapes from KCRW in California of a collection of clips and interviews called <u>The Jack Benny Story</u>. (Totally different from Radiola version.) By the way, they were a gift from a very dedicated member, Pat Mechling. I don't think these tapes are available anywhere else, so if anyone is interested and will supply the tape, I'll copy it free.

ENCLOSURES

Our first article was sent by David Spangler. It's from the Chicago Tribune about the new mayor of Waukegan. I'll try to get some more news about Waukegan in future issues. Thanks, David!!!

The other two I dug out of my files. One was an article about a lottery winner a few years ago. I marked it up a bit, but you can still read it. The other is one from a 1961 Reader's Digest. I couldn't get the full article, so I settled for the digest. I hope you enjoy them.

I haven't heard from many of you in quite a while, so please send me a letter to bring me up to date. My mailbox is getting dusty!!!

Laura Lee, Jack Benny Fan Club Offices, 1620 Old Town Dr. SE, Grand Rapids, Michigan, 49508.

CHI TRIB
5/7/85

Section 2 ★

Inside

Tribune photo by John Irvine

Sabonjian's back as boss

Robert Sabonjian now seems as much of a town fixture as Waukegan native Jack Benny. Sabonjian, "the Mayor Daley of Waukegan," was sworn-in Monday for his sixth term. Story, Page 3.

New mayor old face in Waukegan

By Robert Enstad

One of Bill Morris' last acts as mayor of Waukegan on Monday was to hang a framed picture of himself on the wall facing the desk of the incoming mayor, Robert Sabonjian. On the picture Morris wrote: "Good luck and Godspeed. Bill."

Next to that picture is a portrait Sabonjian left of himself 8 years ago when his 20-year reign as Waukegan mayor was derailed by Morris. On his portrait Sabonjian had written, "Good luck, you Irish S.O.B. Bob."

As Morris and Sabonjian once again prepared to trade places in the mayor's office Monday, their years of bitterness and distrust of each other remained. Sabonjian said he hoped that upon his swearing-in Monday night for a sixth term, "the old mayor gets the hell out [of City Hall]. There is no love lost."

He didn't need to worry. Morris planned to be home, "probably in bed," when City Clerk William Durkin administered the oath to Sabonjian.

The return of Robert "The Rock" Sabonjian, 69, was significant because from 1957 to 1977 he was a Waukegan institution. Ruling the city with an iron hand, he was often called "the Mayor Daley of Waukegan," and he often was the subject of ridicule, praise and government investigation into alleged corruption.

Charges by Morris in the recent campaign that Sabonjian consorted with unsavory characters has led Sabonjian to threaten a libel suit.

"It is not going to be a frivolous suit," Sabonjian said Monday.

Morris said he isn't scared, because the best defense of libel is the truth. A libel suit, Morris said, might bring out some things about his opponent that he should leave buried.

Morris said the threat of a libel suit is typical of Sabonjian's character, adding: "He has a solid reputation that he doesn't just beat you, he tries to drive you out of town."

Morris said he will stay in Waukegan but probably won't run for public office again.

For Sabonjian it was a day of

Robert Sabonjian

saying goodbye to colleagues at an insurance agency, where he has worked for eight years. He will have a quiet family dinner at home before re-entering City Hall for the first time in eight years.

"I don't mean to act blasé about the whole thing," Sabonjian said, "but this is the sixth time."

In his first three terms as mayor, he was elected as a Democrat. The next two terms he was elected as a Republican. He won as a Republican this year.

Sabonjian said he will start his 21st year as mayor by appointing new police and fire chiefs and other top administrators and by attacking what he calls "government waste in city government."

And, Sabonjian said, "I want to bring the people together again."

Morris spent Monday cleaning out his office, playing racketball, hanging his portrait and preparing for a Wisconsin canoe trip. He believes he is leaving behind a good legacy.

"We have a new police station, new fire station, newly remodeled City Hall, and we have a new 800-slip boat harbor," Morris said.

Sabonjian will not be able to run City Hall as before with an army of patronage employees and is going to face some surprises, Morris said. "Obviously, Sabonjian was not elected because of his ability to manage but because of his personality," Morris said. "He had 20 years of favors to call in."

Morris, 39, a former radio and newspaper reporter, hopes to find work as a government consultant. "In the next week I probably will register as a lobbyist," he said. "I'll be a consultant. That's what my résumé will list me as at 8 a.m. tomorrow morning so I won't have a hole in the résumé."

How to Tell a Joke

An expert's secret formula

Condensed from This Week Magazine

JACK BENNY

WELL... I guess it was funnier the way *he* told it...

That's been the lame obituary of an awful lot of jokes that get dead on the carpet. How come? I think it's usually a matter of knowing a few easy rules about joke-telling. In the interest of a lot of storytellers—and their long-suffering friends—I'd like to pass on a few of the pointers I have picked up in 30 years of public jesting.

Let's put last things first, because the last word you speak is often the most important:

1. Polish that punch line. People laugh with surprise. A perfect example of the effect is in Adlai Stevenson's great evening line to the Gridiron Club after losing the Presidential election:

"A funny thing happened to me on my way to the White House."

An experienced speaker like Stevenson didn't have to practice that line in front of a mirror before unveiling it in public. Neither do you have to go that far. But it won't hurt to say your gag line to yourself a couple of times, to make sure you've lined up the most effective combination of words.

2. Tailor your material to the audience. "My uncle takes a drink now and then, just to steady himself. Sometimes he gets so steady he can't move."

George Gobel told that one, and the audience screamed. But how would it have gone at a temperance meeting?

Remember, too, if everybody at the party is a doctor, they may enjoy jokes about quacks; but picking on the only doctor in a crowd makes

him a victim and you a bully. That's not a funny situation.

3. **Your humor should match the situation.** Anything funny is funnier if it "fits"; if it touches on something the audience is interested in at that moment. If everybody in the room is arguing about the Cleveland Indians' chances against the Yankees, it's the wrong time for a talking-dog story. If you must tell it right then, at least try to make it a dog who can play shortstop.

Slide into your story subtly, picking up the thread of conversation and twisting it in your direction; or focus attention on something your friends are experiencing right now. Every living room is full of props which can be a springboard for a story: the curtains, the fireplace, somebody's new squirrel-dyed mink. For instance, after a telephone interruption:

"A friend of ours was waiting for an important call. She'd left the baby in the play pen, and told his five-year-old brother, Jimmy, she'd be back in a minute. Well, of course, the phone rang while she was gone, and Jimmy answered it.

"'Hello?'

"A man's voice said, 'Hello . . . uh, is your mother there?'

"'No.'

"'Well, will you tell your mother Mr. Baker called?'

"'What?'

"'Mr. Baker. Write it down. B-A-K-E-R.'

"'How do you make a B?'

"'How do I make . . . listen, little boy, is there anybody else with you? Any brothers or sisters?'

"'My brother Billy is here.'

"'Good. Let me talk to him, will you please?'

"'Okay.' Jimmy took the phone to the play pen and handed it to the baby.

"When their mother returned a few minutes later, she asked if there had been any calls. 'Yes,' Jimmy said. 'Some man called, but he just wanted to talk to Billy.'"

I threw in that long anecdote just to show it isn't only the "one liner" which fit smoothly into a topical humor situation. All that's needed is a bridge from the real living room you're in, to the setting of the story.

There are many other tricks to the comic trade which you can learn by practice: how long to stretch out the story, how long to pause before the punch line, what gestures to use, intonation, etc. These must be shaped to your own personality, and the only way to find what fits you is by trial and error.

4. **If you can't make other people laugh at your jokes, laugh at their instead.** Not everybody can be a good comic, but everybody can be a good audience; and that's an even bigger social asset. All you need is an interest in others and the ability to *listen*—instead of just waiting for the other fellow to finish talking so you can do this, you'll have more fun at a party, and be much more fun, than if you delivered four memorized jokes and spent the rest of the evening peeping at your watch.

The Squeeze on the Unions

Once all-powerful, the giant labor unions now find themselves in a period of steadily diminishing membership. The force—automation—which is thinning their ranks is labor leaders slow to use the strike threat

Condensed from The Atlantic Monthly   A. H. RASKIN

DISQUIETING feeling of impotence besets many who sit behind lordly desks in the glass-and-marble headquarters of giant labor unions. True, they still control huge treasuries and billions of dollars in pension and welfare funds; their strike calls can plunge vital industries into idleness; their political machinery can influence the democratic process. Yet each day brings compelling reminders that labor's strength is on the downgrade and that its leaders may soon be presiding over the dismantling of their empires unless they find new approaches to challenges thrust upon them by automation, intensified foreign competition and a dramatic shift in the composition of the work force.

What may be the wave future for all labor already over John L. Lewis's United Workers, the union that set the pattern for unionizing the production industries and for collective bargaining and technique. The miners are rich in territories and money. They have million dollars in their treasuries, 100 million dollars more in pension and welfare reserves. But the industry has become one of hard not of men. Employment in the soft-coal field has gone down from 700,000 to fewer than 200,000 since World War I. In hard coal the drop has been even more precipitous, 180,000 to 13,000.

Lewis, once the embodiment of class warfare, now sits with the operators as a director of coal

The Atlantic Monthly (April '61), © 1961 by The Atlantic Monthly Co., 8 Arlington St., Boston 16, Mass.

Flashing their million-dollar smiles with the newly wealthy Andrew Tegerides are, from left, daughter Dena, wife Christina, son Peter and daughter Maria.

'That's Me, Baby,' He Yelled, And Collected His $5 Million

NEW YORK (UPI) — Greek immigrant Andrew Tegerides puffed a huge cigar as he was named the winner of the state's $5 million lottery and explained his winning system, which owes a debt to Jack Benny.

"Now is the time to enjoy," Tegerides, 51, said Wednesday.

Tegerides, who landed alone in the United States in 1948 with "not even a penny" to his name, said he was a bit less restrained Sunday when he realized the six numbers he picked out on his $1 ticket hit the $5 million bonanza.

"That's me, baby," he said he whooped, and did a little dance with his wife, Christina, to celebrate. The couple waited until Tuesday to alert officials just to make sure they had won.

"We were very nervous," he said. "I still don't believe it. It's unbelievable."

Tegerides's winning numbers were 7-12-15-18-34 and 39.

Mrs. Tegerides explained the system: seven was a lucky number; 12 and 18 were the month and day her husband was born; 15, his age backwards; 34 her age backwards, and 39, "because that's Jack Benny's age."

At a presentation in state Lotto headquarters in the World Trade Center, Tegerides was accompanied by his daughters, Maria, 22, Dena, 16, and son, Peter, 24.

"He worked hard all his life," said Peter. "It's a blessing."

Tegerides went into semi-retirement in April, selling his interest in a restaurant to his brother after 21 years of work.

Tegerides said he will donate part of his winnings to the Greek church to fulfill a vow made many years ago that he would help if he was successful.

He also said he would remember his relatives who lost their possessions when the Turks overran his hometown of Karavas, Cyprus, during the 1974 war on Cyprus.

Despite his new wealth, he says his retirement is only temporary.

"I'm a working guy," he said. He doesn't "feel like staying home and do nothing."

He has no plans to buy a new home.

"Why should I move?," he shrugged. "I like it where I am."

Like Louis "Louie the Lightbulb" Eisenberg, a Brooklyn maintenance man who won the $5 million prize Nov. 14, Tegerides will receive a first payment of $236,625.20 in two weeks. Twenty annual payments also will be sent to him, each for $238,168.74.

By law, the government takes 20 percent of the checks for taxes.

The Jack Benny Times

Vol. 5, No. 4   INTERNATIONAL DISTRIBUTION   July-Aug. 1985

§PRESIDENT'S MESSAGE§

WELL...Jell-o again folks. July and August have been truly busy for me in every way!!! Not only have I been preparing for my move, but we have had an enormous upswing in inquiries and memberships. Just a reminder: anything mailed after August 26 should be addressed to me at:

   15430 Lost Valley Drive
   Ft. Wayne, Indiana 46825

Yet, if your hand absolutely refuses to write that, you may address it to the one in Grand Rapids. I'll be in Ft. Wayne during the week for college and Grand Rapids on the weekends for my Friday night show. In fact, a member already sent the same letter to both addresses, and I picked up both copies personally!!! A big THANK YOU goes out to those of you who answered my plea for mail. I've really enjoyed hearing from you. Now on with the show!

μμ NEW MEMBERS μμ

****JOYCE SHOOKS--An avid fan of Jack Benny, she is tremendously enthused about collecting all sorts of memorobilia on him. If you have any lists of tapes, books or the like, write her at: P.O. Box 307, Sparta, Michigan 49345.

****JAMES DIESTLER--No information available at this time.

****TODD R. HILL--This young man is only twenty, yet he is a big fan of Burns and Allen and Jack. He has video tapes of selected programs of both. He also wants to be a director.

****RON BROWN--No information available at this time.

****EDWARD FEDOR--No information available at this time.

****JAMES E. TREACY, JR.--This gent is seventeen, yet he is also one of the few young people who greatly enjoys old radio. He will be a senior in high school next year and is involved in the soccer team. Keep up the good work!!!

>> INTERVIEW <<

For you Grand Rapids area members...
A couple of weeks ago I had the pleasure and honor of interviewing Frank Nelson, a familiar member of Jack's cast. That interview will be broadcast on August 23 at 8 A.M. on my final Laughs From the Past show. Along with it I am going to play Jack's last show on radio. When I played the interview on Moments to Remember, the phone lines lit up with positive comments. "Fascinating," "Involving," "Great!" and "What fun!" were just a few of the words that people used to describe it. Tune in to WEHB, 89.9 F.M. !!!

Copyright 1989, Laura Lee

¥¥ AUCTION ¥¥

The deadline on the auction has been extended to October 15. The current bids are $15 on either magazine and $10 on either. Descriptions of the items appeared in an earlier issue of the Times, but if you can't find it, just write me. Winners will be announced in the next Times unless otherwise requested.

£ STILL MORE VIDEO TAPES £

GEE!!! What a response to this article in the last Times!!! I recently acquired a copy of Love Thy Neighbor starring Jack and Fred Allen at the height of the Benny-Allen feud. Amusing ending. (Not to say that the rest of the picture isn't!) I also got a couple of shows from the early 50's. One is the famed show with George Burns and Bing Crosby in the "Goldie, Fields and Glide" skit. The other is the last show of the 1953-54 season with Bob Hope, Dean Martin and Jerry Lewis. For information on tapes, just write me. I'll write up a list for you and then get a quote on costs for copies.

ß UPCOMING NEWS ß

In coming issues we'll have news on a Jack Benny exhibit in California sponsored by the Westwood Savings and Loan. Also on June 19, there was an archival screening of a Jack Benny Show by the Academy of Television Arts and Sciences.

Ø ARTICLES Ø

Enclosed with this month's Times are two articles. One is the information about Jay Hickerson's convention, and the other is an article from the Sunday Record of Bergen county, New Jersey. The latter was sent to us by John Schlamp. Thanks!!! If any of you happen to find any articles on Jack, please send me a copy so that I could print it in the Times.

Well, that looks like it for this month. Hope to hear from some of you soon!!! Please send mail to either the preceding Ft. Wayne address or to the International Jack Benny Fan Club Offices, 1620 Old Town Dr. SE, Grand Rapids, Michigan 49508.

The Jack Benny Times

Sep-Oct 1985 INTERNATIONAL DISTRIBUTION Vol. 5, No. 5

PRESIDENT'S MESSAGE

WELL!!! I never thought that the Times would be so late, but my life has been quite out of whack too, as many of you know. I've promised to write to so many people, but I just haven't gotten around to more than three letters. Anyhow to save time, for the several inquiries that I received I am simply giving the background on the fan club as a section of the newsletter this time. Usually it isn't as short and sweet as this, but next month will be very good...I guarantee!!!

§A BRIEF HISTORY OF THE IJBFC§

The International Jack Benny Fan Club officially started on January 1, 1980. We now have members all over America, Canada and Europe. There are no dues or obligations, but all donations are accepted! (They are also tax-deductible.) Many members are reputed to have all available Jack Benny shows for sale and/or trade. The Jack Benny Times is (usually) the bi-monthly newsletter of the fan club. Some of our more well-known members are George Burns, Fred de Cordova, Itzhak Perlman, Isaac Stern, Irving Fein, Mickey Rooney, Norm Crosby, Ronald Reagan, Bob Hope, Frank Nelson and George Bush. As most of you know, I founded the fan club on the basis that no one is dead until they are forgotten, and if I have my say, Jack shall never die.
If you would like to join the fan club, then just drop me a line, and I'll send a membership certificate asap. Laura Lee, Jack Benny Fan Club Offices, 15430 Lost Valley Dr., Ft. Wayne, Indiana 46825.

¥ INFORMATION, PLEASE ¥
or, The Benny Classified

WANTED--A copy of the first broadcast of Laughs From the Past on WEHB. Please contact Laura Lee at the above address.

WANTED-SUBSCRIBERS!--Richard Allyn publishes a small magazine dealing with old radio. It contains many features, including a "lending library" of shows. For more information, write him at: 1579 Elm Drive, Vista, California 92084.

WANTED--Any information on a Fred Allen Fan Club. He said it, I didn't! Contact Ken Weigel, 7011 Lennox Ave., Apt. 126, Van Nuys, California 91405.

AVAILABLE--Stationery personalized with a pencil portrait of your favorite star. Send a SASE to Christine Myers, 23712 Twin Oaks Place, Hidden Hills, California 91302.

WANTED--A transcript of the segments on Jack Benny from the

Copyright 1989, Laura Lee

the <u>Johnny Carson Anniversary Special</u> and <u>Entertainment Tonight</u>. Please conatact Either Laura Lee or James E. Treacy, Jr., 5395 Petersburg Rd., Dundee, Michigan 48131.

WANTED--"good books on OTR itself." Please send names and authors to James E. Treacy at the above address.

WANTED--78 r.p.m. records. Will be given a good home. Contact Laura Lee.

DO YOU WANT--a Benny classified ad? Send a request to Laura Lee!!

SPERDVAC

Are YOU interested in preserving and encouraging radio drama, variety and comedy? Then SPERVAC (The Society to Preserve and Encourage Radio Drama, Variety and Comedy) is for YOU. Enclosed is a copy of the press release on the Jack Benny exhibit in Los Angeles, an event with which SPERDVAC was involved. They put out a beautiful monthly newsletter called the <u>Radiogram</u> which has proved fascinating reading for any person interested in old radio. For more information contact: Barbara J. Watkins, P.O. Box 561, South Pasadena, California 91030.

...ONE LAST NOTE...

For those of you that have been in the club for a while, you probably have heard me talk about a purpose that I wished for the club to serve one day: to provide a vehicle for Jack Benny fans to obtain shows and other various material which would promote apprieciation of the comedy of Jack Benny. Well...it has been almost six years now, and up until the past year or two, I felt that I was beating my head against a brick wall. However I am now receiving letters from many members telling me that they are receiving letters and packages from other members who are interested in trading shows with them. It truly makes me proud to see that the IJBFC is finally serving this purpose. Thank you.

By the way, does anyone think that our name should be changed to the International Jack Benny Society?

If you have any announcements, requests or inquiries, write me!!! Laura Lee, 15430 Lost Valley Dr., Ft. Wayne, Indiana 46825.

And thanks, Rusty, for the other articles!

WESTWOOD
SAVINGS AND LOAN ASSOCIATION

June 10, 1985　　　　　　　　　　　　　　　　　Contact: Bernie Roswig
FOR IMMEDIATE RELEASE　　　　　　　　　　　　　　(213) 836-4381

CAST AND STAFF OF FIVE DECADES OF JACK BENNY SHOWS
TO ATTEND UNVEILING OF FIRST-EVER JACK BENNY EXHIBIT JUNE 18

(LOS ANGELES) -- The cast and staff of Jack Benny's radio and television shows dating back to the 1930s will be special guests at a VIP unveiling of the first-ever JACK BENNY EXHIBIT, a prized collection of the famed comedian's memorabilia, Tuesday, June 18.

Sponsored by Westwood Savings and Loan Assn., the display will be previewed by many of the actors, writers and backstage staff that made major contributions to one of the most successful comedy runs of all time. The by-invitation-only event will be held at Westwood's new headquarters office (10899 Wilshire Blvd.) from 5:30-8 P.M.

One of Benny's favorite charities, SHARE, will benefit from the unveiling reception through a direct contribution from Westwood Savings.

Among those expected to attend are Joan Benny and her daughter, Joanna Blumofe, Benny's only surviving family; Dennis Day, the Irish tenor who forever was trying to sing on the show; Phil Harris, the show's bandleader; Mel Blanc, who was the voice of uncountable characters; Sheldon Leonard, who played the racetrack tout for about 20 years; Frank Nelson, Jack's "nemisis" beginning in the 1930s; Veola Vonn, the "femme fatale"; and George Balzer, Benny's head writer from 1943-65.

Others include writers and friends Milt Josephsberg, Sam Perrin, Al Gordon and Hugh Wedlock; actor/songwriter Ned Miller; Elvia Allman and

(more)

2001 South Barrington Avenue, Suite 316, Los Angeles, California 90025 (213) 477-3021

Benny Celebs
Page 2

Sandra Gould, who played various character roles through the 1940s, '50s and '60s; Shirley Mitchell, who played telephone operator "Mabel" through the end of the tv series in 1965; Dorothy Ohman, Benny's personal secretary for 18 years; Jeanette Barnes, his scriptgirl for 20 years; and Gloria Chappell, one of his violin teachers.

Westwood Savings, which obtained the memorabilia on loan from the Jack Benny Estate, will display the exhibit - free to the public - beginning June 19 (at 10899 Wilshire Blvd.), through the next two months before it is permanently donated to the University of Wyoming.

The exhibit features audio tapes from Benny's radio shows; one of his violins; awards from the Television Academy, Friars Club and Carnegie Hall; documents including the one that changed his name from Ben Kubelsky to Jack Benny; and scores of historic photographs dating back to his vaudeville days.

The memorabilia, in storage since Benny's death in 1974, will be shown June 19-July 2 at 10899 Wilshire Blvd. in Westwood. It will then be displayed at Westwood Savings' Fairfax district office (369 N. Fairfax Ave.) July 3-16; the Rancho Park branch (10531 W. Pico Blvd.) July 17-30; and the Santa Monica office (1231 Wilshire Blvd.) July 31-Aug. 14.

***

"KODAK UNVEILS "JACK BENNY'S NEW LOOK"

DIG IT.

STARRING
JACK BENNY
WITH HIS GUEST STARS
GEORGE BURNS
NANCY SINATRA
GARY PUCKETT
AND THE UNION GAP
ROCHESTER
SPECIAL GUEST STAR
GREGORY PECK

WEDNESDAY, 9:00 PM
CHANNEL 2, 3, 41

close up

JACK BENNY ⓒ
9:00 ❷ ③ ㊶

JACK BENNY & FRIENDS IN HOLLYWOOD

Special: Jack's new hour features Nancy Sinatra, George Burns, Gary Puckett and the Union Gap, and a TV newcomer, Gregory Peck.

A sketch shows how Jack landed Gregory for tonight's show. Then it's time to unveil a new act: Jack, George and Gregory as Two Bushels and a Peck, a song-and-dance team that may—or may not—bring back vaudeville.

Also: cameos by Lucille Ball and Eddie "Rochester" Anderson, and Floyd, the penguin that was on Jack's last special (and is still waiting to be paid).

Highlights . . . Nancy: "Here, There and Everywhere," "The Best Is Yet to Come." Gregory: "The Shadow of Your Smile." Gary, Union Gap: "The Beggar." Nancy, Gary: "Spinning Wheel." Jack, George, Gregory: "Steamboat Whistles Blowing," "Come Along My Mandy." Jack (on violin): "Zigeunerweisen." (60 min.)

Nov.-Dec. 1985　　INTERNATIONAL DISTRIBUTION　　Vol. 5, No. 6

PRESIDENT'S MESSAGE

I'm still running back and forth, but life is now a bit quieter thanks to a wonderful invention: Christmas vacation!!! On January 1, 1986 we celebrated our sixth anniversary... quite a feat. I'm quite pleased. As I said in the last Times I am happy to see the club finally serving its purpose: providing a vehicle for Jack Benny fans to obtain material on him. The Jack Benny Fan Club Family Album is becoming a beautiful book. For those of you who are unfamiliar with the Family Album, it is a book contaning articles on each of the members. If you haven't already done so, please send a paragraph of information that you would like included and a photo if possible. WELL...I would like to wish you all a very happy, healthy and prosperous 1986. Now on with the show!!!

§§ NEW MEMBERS §§

****BILL OLIVER--Bill has been a tremendous help to me in several ways...I cannot even begin to repay him. In the future many of the articles that come with the Times have been provided through his courtesy. He has been a big fan of Jack Benny for most of his life, and he has been a joy to correspond with as his interest has spanned many years. (See also "Tapes")

****ANDREW HASKELL--This gent is 18 years old and often wondered if there were any other people that enjoyed OTR as much as he does. He is interested in corresponding with anyone that would like to discuss OTR. (See also "Tapes")

****GEORGE W. LILLIE--George is reputed to have one of the world's largest collections of OTR shows. His main interests include both Jack Benny and Lum and Abner. He is presently working on bringing L&A to television in puppet form. Keep watching...I'm sure it will work!!!

****ARI DORROS--Ari is just beginning to discover Jack Benny. I'm sure we'd be able to help him out in this endeavor!!! 8130 North Beach Drive, Fox Point, Milwaukee, Wisconsin 53217.

*****FRANK NELSON--Need I say more?!

¥ AUCTION ¥

Okay, okay. The absolutely, positively last date that bids will be accepted is February 28, 1986. Once again, the two items up for auction are two Look magazines. The first is May 15, 1945, and it has Jack on the cover. It is in excellent condition and has about six pages of pictures and text on Jack, plus many other interesting articles and ads. The other is November 1, 1955, and it also has Jack on the cover.

Copyright 1989, Laura Lee

It is in good to very good condition. It has a four-page article on Jack with plenty of text plus an article on Clark Gable and various other tidbits. Winners will be announced in the Jan-Feb issue unless otherwise requested. No, prior bids have not been forgotten. Send bids to Laura Lee at the address at the end of the newsletter. I personally think that the covers alone are so great that I have had them proudly displayed in my otherwise fairly empty room here in Ft. Wayne for the past several months.

µµ LOOKING FOR TAPES µµ

Several members are interested in trading and/or purchasing tapes from other members. Here are ones that have contacted me about it in the last three months or so:
Bill Oliver, 516 Third St. NE, Massillon, Ohio 44646
Andrew Haskell, 160 W. 39th Ave., Vancouver, British Columbia V5Y 2P2, Canada
Rob Cohen, 2680 Cannon Pt., Apt. 3D, Columbus, Ohio 43209
Joyce Shooks, P.O. Box 307, Sparta, Michigan 49345
James E. Treacy, 5395 Petersburg Rd., Dundee, Michigan 48131

If you are not listed here but are interested in buying or trading tapes, drop me a note.

£ BIOGRAPHIES £

By popular request, I am including a list of the biographies written on Jack. They are:

Jack Benny: An Intimate Biography, Irving Fein, G.P. Putnam, New York, N.Y., 1976.

The Jack Benny Show, Milt Josefsburg, Arlington House, New Rochelle, 1977.

Jack Benny, Mary Livingston Benny, Hilliard Marks and Marcia Borie, Doubleday, New York, N.Y., 1978.

My suggestion for finding these books is first to try your local used bookstores. If these fail, I have two nearly fail-proof companies. First is Renaissance Book Shop, 834 North Plankton, Milwaukee, Wisconsin 53203; it is the second largest used book shop in America. The other is Crabtree's Collection, 115 South Main St., Eaton Rapids, Michigan 48827. They have connections with stores all over America for finding books; they have found me some that I have searched for for years. Please mention the IJBFC if you write them.

* PERSONAL CONGRATULATIONS *

ATTENTION!!! The International Jack Benny Fan Club would like to send its sincere congratulations to Donnie Pitchford who is willfully giving up his freedom this June. In other words, he's getting married. Ain't love grand? I hope you will all join me in wishing him the best of luck.

¥ FOTR ¥

The Friends of Old-Time Radio had its 10th annual convention on October 11th and 12th of 1985. Many celebrities were on hand, and there were many interesting presentations. For more information on the convention itself, write Jay Hickerson, Box C, Orange, Connecticut 06477. For audio tape information write to Joe Webb, Box 268, Glen Cove, New York 11542. Video tape information is available from Ken Piletic, 705 South Oltendorf Rd., Streamwook, Illinois 60103.

ARTICLES

You'll find four articles enclosed with this issue (I hope). The first is a clipping from the Chicago Tribune, February 21, 1985 contributed by David Spangler. The second is an article from The Plain Dealer, December 28, 1974.* The third is information on a publication I have received entitled The Sounds Of Yesterday. Finally Jay Hickerson has sent me a list of organizations and publications that I thought might interest some of you.

If you have any announcements, requests or questions, write me!!! Laura Lee, c/o International Jack Benny Fan Club, 15430 Lost Valley Dr., Ft. Wayne, Indiana 46825.

*from Bill Oliver

A hometown tribute to Jack Benny
To loyal fans, comedian's wit remains a timeless treasure

By Laura Kavesh

After Jack Benny died a few days after Christmas in 1974, David Spangler, a 15-year-old Chicago textbook author, received condolence calls from his friends, so certain were they of his sadness over the comedian's death.

"I felt that I lost a close family member," Spangler said. "In fact, I was considering at the time going to California, to Jack's funeral, but I didn't."

Last Sunday, on a stage in the Jack Benny Junior High School in Waukegan, where the entertainer lived until he was about 16, Spangler imitated what he called Benny's "affectionately effeminate" walk and, with arms loosely folded and one hand cutting the air in Benny's famous wrist flutter, launched into a brief Benny routine for the approximately 400 people in the audience.

"Tonight's show is being billed The Jack Benny Special," Spangler said. "However, there's nothing special about it. It's simply two half-hour shows put into one. To me, a special is when coffee goes from $1.29 a pound to 87 cents. Now that's a special."

When the votes were in, Spangler lost the look- and act-alike contest to Bob McEvilla, a plumber who caught Benny's trademark voice nearly precisely and who was—he swears this is true—celebrating his 39th birthday the very day of the contest. Spangler didn't care, though; his love of Benny brought him. He entered another contest—again he didn't win—in which he was given the chance, in no more than 30 words, to discuss why he loved Benny. He used 31 words.

"I loved Jack Benny," he told the crowd, "because he was a beautiful human being and a tremendous role model for me. He was my favorite comedian, an extremely generous person and a true lover."

The second contest was won by Beatrice Sherman of Chicago, 58, who said she would be celebrating her birthday the day after the Benny party. She said she loved him because by sheer coincidence she, too, was going to be 39 forever.

Were he alive, Jack Benny would have celebrated his 91st—make that 39 plus 39 plus 13—birthday on Valentine's Day. That, together with the Waukegan connection, was excuse enough for hundreds of Benny fans to board a chartered train at Chicago's North Western Station and travel north for a day-long Benny-fest, hosted by old-time radio personality and nostalgia-guru Chuck Schaden (on WAIT AM 820, 7-11 p.m. weekdays; and WNIB FM 97.1, 1-5 p.m. Saturdays) and sponsored by the 20th Century Railroad Club.

"Sunday afternoons my father would bring home cream soda and vanilla ice cream and we would listen to Jack Benny; Charlie McCarthy came on after him, as I remember," said Jim Christen of Naperville, who brought along his 8th-grade son Jim, also a Benny fan.

The day included a quick look at Benny's white-frame home, but reminiscing was what it was mostly about. Apart from the train ride—an hour each way—the event took place at the junior high

Continued on page 3

Waukegan's favorite son, Jack Benny, in 1974

Jack Benny breaks up during a rehearsal for his radio program in 1954.

Fans pay tribute to Jack Benny's wi

Continued from first Tempo page

school that Benny himself dedicated in 1961.

"Waukegan's other two high schools are named Thomas Jefferson and Daniel Webster," he said at the time. "Both were better students than I." Benny flunked out of Central High when he was 16.

Special guests at the party were Frank Nelson and Veola Vonn, now married, who appeared on radio and TV with Benny. (Vonn was the resident "sexpot" with the silky, suggestive voice; Nelson, whether a railroad ticket seller or a waiter, always gave Benny a hard time, leading off with his trademark "yesssssssss?")

It turned out, fortuitously, that there was not a single entry in the bad violin playing contest. In another showdown, audience members were invited to compose advertisements for Jell-O, one of Benny's sponsors.

John Thimios of Skokie sang an ode to the product to the tune of Lionel Richie's "Hello," but was beat out for top honors by Chicagoans Jeri Jamieson, a pharmacist, and Joel Rothman, a 29-year-old lawyer who has been listening to Chuck Schaden's show for 15 years. They penned a Nelson-Benny routine, with just the right amount of insult. (Nelson, signing autographs at the back of the room, quickly looked at the sound of his "yesssssssss?" coming from someone else, and smiled.)

The party guests who grew up in the radio era recalled the delight of being able to use their imaginations while listening to Benny's shows. There were also those who were raised during Benny's transition from radio to TV, and still others who had never experienced him at all during his lifetime but who learned from their parents about a bygone era.

"He's funny. He tells good jokes," said 8-year-old Ryan Fredrickson of Joliet.

"Discovering this kind of radio was really a revelation to me because my parents never listened to it," said Pat Daley, 37. "But the literacy of the scripts compared to what you get on TV is incredible. Here have been given a whole family; I know what they look like and can create the scenes in my head."

After the show, Spangler said he wouldn't have missed the day. "His [Benny's] mannerisms have actually become a part of my personality," he said. "I don't really walk that way, but his personality really shaped mine. His was clean humor, and it always made me feel good. I never missed a show. It's probably the last regular series I ever watched."

PUBLICATIONS and ORGANIZATIONS

OLD-TIME RADIO PROGRAMS:
- HELLO AGAIN (Jay Hickerson) Box C, Orange, Ct. 06477, bi-monthly, $8/year
- NARA NEWS (Steve Ham) 4418 Irvington, Fremont, Cal. 94538; quarterly; $14/yr; Journal of North American Radio Archives.
- GOLDEN YEARS OF RADIO & TV (Linda & Ron Downey), Rt. 3, Box 263-H, Waynesville, N.C. 28786; quarterly; $10 yr.
- OLD-TIME RADIO DIGEST (Bob Burchette & George Wagner) 4114 Montgomery Rd., Cin., Ohio 45212, bi-monthly, $12.50/yr.
- NOSTALGIA DIGEST (Chuck Schaden) Box 421, Morton Grove, Ill. 60053, bi-monthly $10/yr.

OLD RADIOS AND PHONOGRAPHS:
- OLD TIMERS BULLETIN (Bruce Kelley) Main St., Holcomb, NY 14469; quarterly: $5.00/yr; Journal of Antique Wireless Association.
- HORN SPEAKER (Jim Cranshaw) 9820 Silver Meadow Rd., Dallas, Tx. 75217; monthly; $4.50/yr.
- REPRODUCER (George Potter) Box 19406, Dallas, Tx 75219; Journal for Southwest Vintage Radio and Phonograph Soc.

NOSTALGIA:
- WORLD OF YESTERDAY (Linda & Ron Downey) Rt 3, Box 263-H, Waynesville, NC 28786; 6 times a year; $12/yr.

RECORDS:
- KASTLEMUSICK BULLETIN (Robert Hill) 901 Washington St., Wilmington, Del. 19801; monthly; $18/yr.

MISCELLANEOUS:
- NOSTALGIA BOOK CLUB, Box 10654, Des Moines, Ia. 50336; monthly offering of nostalgic books.
- RERUNS (Richard Thorp) Box 4537, Clearlake, Cal. 95422; bi-monthly; $12/yr. (TV History & Nostalgia)

CLUBS: (Many have Newsletters)
- INDIANA RECORDING CLUB (William Davis) 1729 E. 77th, Ind., Ind. 46240 (Tape Squeal)
- MILWAUKEE AREA RADIO ENTHUSIASTS (Ken Pabst) 4442 N. 77th St., Milwaukee, Wisc. 53218
- NORTH AMERICAN RADIO ARCHIVES (NARA). See NARA NEWS above.
- OLD TIME RADIO CLUB OF BUFFALO, 100 Harvey Dr., Lancaster, NY 14086 (Illustrated Press, Memories), $15/yr.
- RADIO HISTORICAL ASSOC. OF COLORADO (John Lloyd) 2667 E. 99th Ave., Thornton, Col. 80229 (Return With Us Now) $15/yr.
- SOCIETY TO PRESERVE AND ENCOURAGE RADIO DRAMA, VARIETY & COMEDY (SPERDVAC) Box 1587, Hollywood, Cal. 90028; Los Angeles area, $15/yr.
- SOUTHERN TIER OLD-TIME RADIO CLUB (Gary Yoggy) Bonady Garden Apts., Onondago #11D, Corning, NY 14830.
- NATIONAL BROADCAST MUSEUM (William Bragg), 2001 Plymouth Rock, Richardson, Tx.75081
- VINTAGE BROADCAST SOCIETY (Lewis Krieger) 3000 Bronx Park East, Bronx, NY 10467, (On The Air)

Jack Benny — nation's best-loved comic

C. *New York Times Service*

BEVERLY HILLS, Calif. — Jack Benny, the comedian who brilliantly turned a gift for self-deprecating caricature into a 40-year coast-to-coast laugh on radio and television, died in his home here yesterday morning. He was 80.

Irving Fein, Benny's manager and associate for many years, said the comedian died of cancer of the pancreas. The cancer was not discovered until it appeared on X-rays Dec. 20. Fein said that Benny's physician said the case was inoperable.

Benny's death was particularly saddening to the world of show business on the West Coast and to old friends in entertainment and broadcasting in New York. He had been visited at his bedside before he died by Gov. Ronald Reagan, Frank Sinatra, Bob Hope, Danny Kaye and George Burns, who was his friend for 50 years.

Funeral services have been scheduled for noon tomorrow at Hillside Memorial Cemetery in Culver City. A special tribute to Benny will be televised by CBS tomorrow from 7:30 to 8:30 p.m.

Other comedians told funnier jokes. Other comedians projected their own personalities into stage situations that made an audience hysterical with laughter. Other comedians were much more effective in displaying their own wit. Where Benny told one joke, Bob Hope or Milton Berle could tell three in the same time.

Yet, Benny was perhaps the most constantly funny of America's funny men. He was adored by the public and even the most sophisticated critics appreciated him as an outstanding comedian. The late President John F. Kennedy once recalled that his father used to herd the family into their home's library every Sunday night to hear The Jack Benny Show on radio. No one was ever excused from listening. So it was with much of America.

His carefully developed character as a tight-fisted, somewhat pompous fellow who walked with a mincing, almost effeminate gait, and often expressed exasperation merely by resting his chin in his hand and

Just as Charlie Chaplin represented the "little fellow," Benny also caught the frustrations of the average man, maybe a middleclass American, whose aspirations were always being leveled by family, friends and servants.

One of his most famous bits had him being held up by a bandit who asked "your money or your life." Silence. More silence. Silence punctuated with laughter from the audience. Then, desperately: "I'm thinking, I'm thinking."

Jack Benny had one credo: "Never laugh at the other fellow; let him laugh at you."

If paid him well. In millions of American homes in the heyday of radio, Sunday night was not complete until the droll "kid from Waukegan" had extricated himself from some dilemma, an assignment that earned him radio's highest weekly fee — $27,500. He paid the other artists on his program from this. He later managed to translate his humor into equally effective television. In mercurial Hollywood he reached the top in 1933 and for a decade averaged two starring pictures a year, later becoming his own producer.

He was the first to admit that it was hard work and he had the reputation for being a worrier. Unlike some of his colleagues, he frankly acknowledged that he needed the help of professional gag writers to be amusing week in and week out. It was a task not made easier by his refusal to lean on the off-color joke. His private life was reserved and often of a serious mien.

Benny was born on Feb. 14, 1894, in Chicago, but grew up in Waukegan, Ill., which for purposes of comedy, he often mentioned as his birthplace. His real name was Benjamin Kubelsky. His father, Mayer Kubelsky, was a merchant in Waukegan.

The son attended Waukegan High School and, while still in his teens, evidenced a liking for the violin. Before long he was playing for the town's dances. In 1912 he entered vaudeville.

The vaudeville booking offices were hardly swept off their collective feet by Benny's efforts and the young violinist was confined to one-night stands. With the outbreak of World War I he joined the Navy and was assigned to the "Great Lakes Review," a sailors' road show.

It was while he was with the Navy production that Benny first interrupted his violin playing to give a spoken line. The resulting applause led him to decide to abandon the violin act after the war. He embarked on the highly competitive field of the ad-libber, where perhaps his greatest asset was an instinct for the proper timing of a joke.

It was this talent that literally stopped the show in whatever medium Benny was performing. His silence was eloquent and mirthful; his double-takes were the envy of his profession.

Although he had hard going at first, he got his first big chance in 1926 with a part in a Broadway musical, "The Great Temptations." This led to the most coveted assignment of all for a connoisseur of the extemporaneous quip: Master of ceremonies at the Palace Theater, a citadel of the two-a-day.

Benny's success was assured from then on. Hollywood quickly engaged his services, then the burgeoning radio industry. In 1932 Benny joined NBC, beginning a career in radio that was to last for 23 years. From 1934 through 1936 he was the champion in the radio popularity polls. Although he was in and out of the No. 1 position in later seasons, he always held a position among the first 10 radio offerings.

"I try to make my character encompass about everything that is wrong with everybody," Benny once said. "On the air I have everybody's faults. All listeners know someone or have a relative who is a tightwad, show-off or something of that sort. Then in their minds I become a real character."

He developed these stage personality traits to the limit. As the skinflint who couldn't quite make up his mind about the thing's ultimatum, "your money or your life," as the man who could not confess being older than 39; and as a character who took inordinate pride in his "baby blue eye," Benny became the amiable butt of his own jokes for his mass audiences.

He encouraged regular characterizations for others on his show. His wife, Mary Livingston, whom he married in 1927, portrayed "the little fresh dame." One of Benny's greatest finds, Eddie Anderson, developed into a star in his own right as Rochester, the valet.

During World War II Benny took his radio troupe on five worldwide trips, during which he entertained troops in all major combat areas. He repeated this in 1951, during the Korean hostilities.

A major change in his career took place in 1948 when he left NBC after 16 years and was signed by CBS. The transaction cost the latter network $2,260,000. Benny received $1,356,000 of this for himself but had to pay more than $1,000,000 in income taxes when he was unable to sustain his contention to the government that the money fell into the capital gains category.

Although CBS retained his radio show until 1955, it had its eye on television. Benny was considered a fine catch at a time when the TV field was wide open and the stations had ample time before them to choose the network with which they wanted to affiliate.

On Oct. 28, 1950, he made his long-awaited television debut. It was a disappointment in the eyes of the critics, who felt that it still relied too heavily on the radio tradition and had little visual attraction.

However, Benny made the grade with his third telecast the next April — he was doing only six shows a season — when his performance received general praise. That autumn he drastically altered his old routines and hit upon a TV presentation that was acclaimed widely.

"Mr. Benny has the best format — no format at all," a critic observed in explanation of his success.

In 1954 Benny initiated a regular half-hour show on alternate Sundays. A year later he also was made host of the monthly CBS color variety series, "Shower of Stars."

Among the motion pictures made by Benny were "Hollywood Revue of 1929," this first film, "Chasing Rainbows," "The Medicine Man," "It's in the Air," "College Holiday," "Artists and Models," "Transatlantic Merry-Go-Round," "Buck Benny Rides Again," "Charley's Aunt," "To Be or Not to Be," "George Washington Slept Here," "The Meanest Man in the World" and "The Horn Blows at Midnight."

THE SOUNDS OF YESTERDAY

Old Time Radio's New Publication

Now there is a new Old Time Radio Publication for all to enjoy, THE SOUNDS OF YESTERDAY. And if your a fan of Old Time Radio, you can't pass this up. THE SOUNDS OF YESTERDAY is an Old Time Radio Journal for all. Issue number one was released at the RHAC Old Time Radio Convention in Denver, Colorado, on July 27th, and it was very well received, everyone who saw it subscribed and commented on the amount of information it contained. So far response has been excellent! Now it is time for you to subscribe to THE SOUNDS OF YESTERDAY, as any serious Old Time Radio collector shouldn't be without it. Look at what the first issue contains:

- AIRWAVES The column on Old Time Radio
- Two Old Radio Quizzes - With prizes
- I CAN'T STAND JACK BENNY BECAUSE A new look at an old contest
- A HISTORY OF EARLY RADIO For the beginner
- THE DEBUT OF DONALD DUCK On Radio
- OZZIE AND HARRIET NELSON LOG Never before compiled
- LUM EDWARDS LETTERS Entertaining look at Lum and Abner
- AIR PLAYS Revive today's drama on Radio?
- Crossword Puzzle on Old Time Radio
- A look at Censorship on Old Time Radio
- And much much more, including, Old Radio Trivia, cartoons, articles on Will Rogers on Radio, Collecting Radio's Golden Age, Jack Armstrong, The Lone Ranger, Ripley's Believe it or Not, old Program Reviews, Joe Penner, Quotes from the Past, and even more.

Your probably thinking, How much is this going to cost me? Well, for just $5.00, you can receive a two issue subscription to THE SOUNDS OF YESTERDAY, that will include issue number one, (which will be sent immediately), and issue number two, which is due out in early December. So, if your a fan of Old Time Radio, then support THE SOUNDS OF YESTERDAY, for only with your support can this new publication survive, so please subscribe now. Make your check payable to THE SOUNDS OF YESTERDAY and send it to: THE SOUNDS OF YESTERDAY, P.O. Box 749, Laramie, WY 82070. And remember, support THE SOUNDS OF YESTERDAY.

The Jack Benny Times

Volume VI, Number 1 — INTERNATIONAL DISTRIBUTION — **January-February 1986**

~ PRESIDENT'S MESSAGE ~

Here's a big hello to all members, new and continuing. We have more new members for this issue than for any previously; this is mostly due to two organizations: the National Lum and Abner Society and WMT in Cedar Rapids, Iowa. I would like to express my sincerest thanks to both of them for their time. For those of you who don't know, I was interviewed on WMT radio on February 17, a station which plays Jack's shows every Tuesday night (thanks George!!!). I have received many notes saying that publishing names of those who are interested in buying, selling and trading tapes has helped immensely in opening communication channels, so we'll publish another one in the next issue. If you wish to be listed, just write me at the address at the end of the newsletter. Now on with the show!!!

▼ NEW MEMBERS ▼

Because of the number of members and lack of short bios, we'll borrow a technique from FOTR of listing everyone.

GERALD WALLACE...RICHARD ALLYN...ALAN GROSSMAN...ROBERT OLSEN...DOUG WOOD...HAROLD SOLES...BRUCE BAKER...BOB WEIGEL...CARLENE MEIER...STEVE SZEJNA--He is interested in finding Jack's radio and TV shows, 3334 South 15th St., Milwaukee, Wisconsin 53215....CAPTAIN D. SALVATORE....LEWIS A. PEARSON--This gent is also interested in tapes of Jack's radio shows...KEN WEIGEL--No. 1 won't say it...WILLIAM STEWARD... MICHAEL POINTON.

Sorry...I forgot: Lewis Pearson, 240 Ridge Drive, Marion, Iowa 52302.

JACK BENNY STAMP

Hey!!! The campaign is still on for those of you who didn't get around to writing before now. Norm Crosby and George Burns (two of the nicest people I know) are leading a campaign for a commemorative stamp in Jack's honor. I'm sure we all support it whole-heartedly, and so you can do your part, too! Send a letter of support to:

Jack Benny Commemorative Stamp Committee
P.O. Box 4N799
Los Angeles, California 90048

Of course if you favor Fred Allen, write anyway. As an anonymous member of the IJBFC says in true Fred Allen style, "I'm voting for it because...I'd rather have benny where I can see him."

▶▶ JACK BENNY MUGS ◀◀

With the increased membership, I'll put this in again for your perusal. Memory Mugs Company produced a Jack Benny mug four

Copyright 1989, Laura Lee

International Jack Benny Fan Club
15430 Lost Valley Drive
Ft. Wayne, Indiana 46825

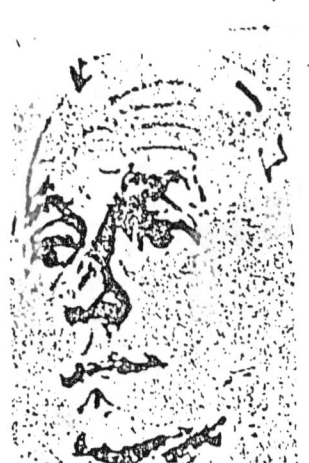

WEBL!

years ago with a chariacature of Jack with "Coffee isn't cheap" written by it. I have a picture of the mug from MMC, and it would definitely be a handsome addition to anyone's JB collection. There is a minimum order of 144 guaranteed at $5.50 each plus shipping. Yes, that is a lot of mugs, but if we all put our heads together, perhaps we might be able to arouse enough interest to get a new order made. Please help us out! If you and/or someone you know would be interested, please drop me a note.

¢¢ TAPES!!! ¢¢

Our very own Billie Brehm invites you to enjoy old time radio on cassette!! She has a 30-page catalogue for $3.00 cash or postal. Please note that these are one-hour cassettes with TWO programs each!!! Cassettes are $3.00 plus 35¢ for first class postage. For more information write:

Ms. Billie Lee Brehm
11402 Leibacher Avenue
Norwalk, California 90650

BACK ISSUES 99

Many of you have expressed an interest in obtaining back issues of the newsletter. Newsletters prior to June 1984, are unavailable for circulation, but the rest are!!! The dates on the issues are June, July and July addition 1984. They and then every two months beginning with Sep-Oct 1984. They are 50¢ apiece. Here's another reason to send me a letter!!!

AUCTION

At last! At last! The auction of the two Look magazines is finally done. The two winners will be notified by mail shortly.

HAPPY BIRTHDAY

Here's wishing a happy 39th birthday to those of you who informed me that you were born in the January or February. Notably, member George Burns turned 39 for the 41st time. my 39th birthday was celebrated for the 12th time even though I just turned 17, and outshining us all, Jack's 39th. came around for the 43rd time.

Thank you to all those who contributed articles to this issue of the Times.

Say k...Fred Allen would support the Jack Benny stamp because he always said he could lick Benny. Now he really could!! Can you top that?

HERE IT IS: Laura Lee, International Jack Benny Offices. 15430 Lost Valley Dr., Ft. Wayne, Indiana 46825.

write me for any reason you like, but please friends, send no bombs.

Funny business
Vintage radio shows to be syndicated

By JEFF PRYOR
Staff reporter

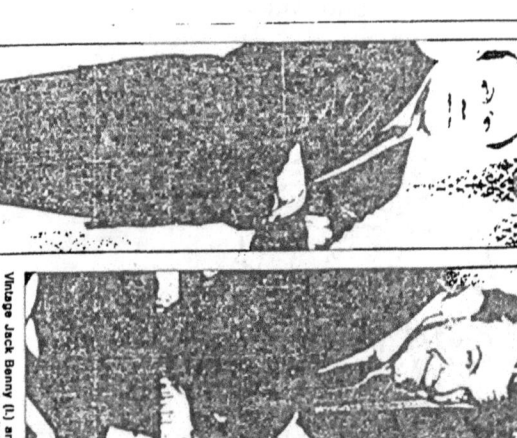

Vintage Jack Benny (L) and George Burns and Gracie Allen radio programs are being distributed by the Michelson organization.

Los Angeles—Jack Benny and Burns & Allen, two of the great comedy acts of all time, are back on the radio airwaves after more than a 20-year absence.

The two vintage programs— "The Jack Benny Show" and "The George Burns and Gracie Allen Show"— ended their original radio network runs decades ago and have seldom been heard since.

But now the Michelson Organization, a radio syndication outfit operated by Charles Michelson, who runs Beverly Hills, Cal.-based Charles Michelson Inc. and his son Robert, who runs New York-based Robert Michelson Inc., has optioned the rights to syndicate the two programs.

These are original episodes of the two classic comedy series, says Charles Michelson.

"All stations are using them as part of their regular A.M. format. We are in all the top 10 radio markets," he says.

Some of the nations airing the programs include Minneapolis' WCCO-AM, St. Louis' KMOX-AM, San Diego's KSDO-AM, Philadelphia's WCAU-AM and Chicago's WBBM-AM.

Charles Michelson says he approached the Jack Benny estate and George Burns and offered to distribute the old shows. He got the green light from both parties.

Most of the revenues will go directly to Mr. Burns and Mr. Benny's estate, which provides some educational funding. Charles Michelson is collecting a standard distribution fee.

"The Jack Benny Show" began in 1932 on NBC and from 1934 to 1936, it led in the popularity polls. CBS hired Mr. Benny away in 1948, he continued on radio until 1955, before taking his act to television.

Mr. Benny, who died of cancer in 1973 at the age of 80, played the role of a pompous, penny-pinching bachelor who quipped with an ear-wrenching version of "Love in Bloom."

"The George Burns and Gracie Allen Show" was a CBS comedy series on TV from 1950 to 1958. Mr. Burns was the consummate straight man to Ms. Allen's ditzy observations and antics.

In 1958, Ms. Allen retired from show business, but Mr. Burns starred in a sitcom about himself on NBC that ran a single season. Ms. Allen died in 1964, Mr. Burns remains active in TV.

Warren G. Bodow, the president and general manager of WQXR-AM, the musical station owned by The New York Times, says the programs are worth interrupting the flow of music his station usually broadcasts.

Mr. Bodow began airing "The Jack Benny Show" on Sunday at 7 p.m. on Dec. 1. He's already told of that the block of commercial time to a local municipal bond house.

As a special bonus, Mr. Bodow says he's convinced Isaac Stern, a well-known violinist and good friend of Mr. Benny, to talk with the audience about his fondest memories of the comedian at the premiere of the show.

Charles Michelson, who also syndicates a number of other old-time radio shows including "The Lone Ranger," says there are 52 half-hour programs each of "Jack Benny" as well as "Burns & Allen."

Newark, New Jersey 2-6-86

Honoring the 'pin-up girls,' post haste

DEAR EDITOR:

There is a movement afoot, endorsed by prominent politicians and show-biz people, to have the U.S. Postal Service issue a commemorative stamp honoring the late great comedian Jack Benny. "Pinchpenny" Benny truly deserves this honor and I am looking forward to adding the Jack Benny Stamp to my collection.

However, there is a neglected group of show-biz people who also are deserving of the honor. I hereby request the Postmaster General to consider bestowing long over-due recognition upon the "pin-up girls" of World War II, and other conflicts, by issuing a series of commemorative postage stamps in their honor.

Surely Betty Grable, Rita Hayworth, Marilyn Monroe and others deserve being honored for their obvious contribution to America's war efforts. They, most certainly, took some of the "hell" out of war, and made it a bit more tolerable for the fighting men involved.

Chet Dobkowski,
Belleville

JACK BENNY CHANGES HIS TUNE

A sour note in his relations with CBS sends him back to his old NBC podium

BY LESLIE RADDATZ

TV GUIDE MAY 9th 1964

A World War I Navy buddy of Jack Benny's once described him as "kind of helpless." Cleveland Amory, in a 1948 magazine article, said that the comedian was "rather childlike." And one of his former writers said, "Benny is the most naive and unsophisticated person I know."

This helpless, childlike, naive, unsophisticated person will return to NBC in the fall some $5,000,000 richer than when he defected to CBS in 1949.

But where his motive then was money—his share of the profits from the $2,260,000 which CBS paid for his corporation, Amusement Enterprises, Inc.,—today it is pique. The network dared to interpose Petticoat Junction between Red Skelton and himself and refused to move it when he asked. Benny was indignant when this move was planned last spring, and at the time his complaints were loud. Now that Petticoat Junction is a hit, outranking both Benny and Skelton in the ratings, he has quieted down. But the decision to change networks had already been made.

Although no money is involved in the current switch, in 1961 MCA, the former giant talent agency that is now a giant TV and movie producing company, bought a second Benny corporation, J&M Productions, for half of the $5,000,000 which the unsophisticated comedian has stashed away since he left NBC.

NBC fought hard to keep Benny 15 years ago and deeply resented his departure, throwing loot-laden giveaways and star-studded extravaganzas at him in a desperate attempt to dislodge him from his secure place in the public favor. But now the network, which usually has only one or two programs in the Top 10, is glad to get him back. NBC's board chairman, Robert W. Sarnoff, said, "We look forward with pleasure to another long association with Jack."

No word has yet come from Sarnoff's father, the board chairman of RCA, Brig. Gen. David Sarnoff, but his feelings were strong back in 1949. Heads fell at NBC after the wholesale exodus of NBC talent to CBS which was triggered by Benny's switch. At that time, Sarnoff père attended a correspondents' dinner where Benny entertained. Afterward, as the general stood talking with a group of NBC executives, Benny walked up and said hello. Everyone responded—except Sarnoff. There was a moment of embarrassed silence. Then one of the NBC vice presidents said, "General, you know Jack Benny." Sarnoff looked at Benny coldly and said, "Who?"

But this was only a minor tactical victory in a major war against Benny, waged not only by NBC but also by the Internal Revenue Service.

At first NBC tried to delude itself that listeners would continue to tune in at 7 o'clock Sunday evening to hear whatever the network had to offer, rather than switch over to CBS, which was carrying Benny at this hour, for years traditionally Benny's. NBC moved Horace Heidt's amateur program, which had been doing well at 10:30 Sunday night, into what it began to advertise as "The No. 1 Spot." Heidt bought space in the trade papers to say, "Thanks, Jack" for giving him the opportunity to be heard at such a popular hour. His gratitude was short-lived. The first ratings of 1949 showed that the No. 1 spot had moved to CBS, along with a certain unsophisticated comedian.

Next, NBC embarked upon what the Hollywood Reporter called "a giveaway show that will make existing competition look like Bingo . . . a top setup that will whip the radio public into a frenzy, with a fortune in prizes"—this despite the fact that NBC, also according to the Reporter, had asked the Federal Communications Commission to stop giveaway shows because of what "Stop the Music" had done to Fred *continued*

Jack Benny / continued

Allen. But the NBC program, a mishmash entitled "Hollywood Calling," did not make a dent in Benny's rating—nor did any of the other programs the network threw into the breach until television finally took over.

Meanwhile, the Internal Revenue Service had been working on the "capital-gains deal" by which CBS—with MCA in the background—had lured the helpless Benny away from NBC. If the comedian's profits on the sale of Amusement Enterprises, Inc., were regarded as personal income, they would be taxed at 77 percent; but if they were capital gains, the tax would be only 25 percent. Since the Government estimated that Benny himself had received all but some $200,000 of the $2,260,000 CBS paid for the corporation, the difference would be considerable. Commissioner George J. Schoeneman made the IRS position clear: "Proposals of radio artists and others to obtain compensation for personal services under the guise of sales of property cannot be regarded as coming within the capital-gains provisions of the Internal Revenue code . . ."

Since paying the lower capital-gains tax was the keystone of the whole deal, the naive and unsophisticated Benny decided to do battle with the United States Government. Testifying in Tax Court in 1954, he said that he considered himself "a fictional character" and that Amusement Enterprises, Inc., was not founded merely to be sold but was "a business with a great future." Kind of helplessly, he testified, "I was hesitant. I was reluctant to sell. I really didn't want to sell." The court apparently shared Benny's childlike faith in the future of Amusement Enterprises, Inc., and his belief in the fictional nature of his public personality—the hard man with a buck. The case was decided in his favor. It was estimated that this saved him at least $1,000,000 in taxes.

Whatever became of the "business with a great future," which CBS paid $2,260,000 for in 1948? The network will say only that it was "sold" six years later in 1954, the year before the tax suit was settled. It will not say to whom it was sold or for how much; and the transaction does not appear in the CBS annual report for 1954. Amusement Enterprises, Inc., is listed as a CBS subsidiary in 1954 by Moody's Industrial Manual, but it had disappeared from the CBS listing the next year. "I think CBS dissolved it," says Irving Fein, former CBS executive, now president of J&M Productions, the Benny corporation which MCA bought with 45,000 shares of its own stock in 1961.

Neither this sale nor Benny's decision to come back to NBC caused anything like the flap of 15 years ago. James T. Aubrey, president of CBS Television, who has kept the network in its present position, did not even deign to respond to Benny's criticism of him. An anonymous spokesman for the network merely pointed out that Benny was 70 years old and then, rather unkindly, added, "That's the kindest way to put it."

Concerning his return to NBC, Benny says, "It will be like going home." But, whatever the network, he goes on doing what he has been doing for more than 30 years—putting on a program which, on radio and television, has always been close to the top, while the Cantors, the Bergens, the Caesars and the Gobels come and go. There are days when he looks every one of his 70 years. At rehearsal he often sits by himself, silent and staring vacantly into space, apparently unconscious of the activity around him. He appears lonely then, and his face sags and is sad. But, morose during a rehearsal or "up" for a performance, there is something childlike about him.

Just don't let it fool you.

After 45 years, he's still 'Bee-yammy' to Benny

A SENTIMENTAL FAREWELL

The weekly 'Jack Benny Show' has ended, but the memories linger on.   By Benny Rubin

I had just finished doing The Jack Benny Show, and there was a lump in my throat as big as a tennis ball. Not that I'm an especially sentimental man—after all, I've done I'd guess 500 shows with Jack—but this was different. This was the last show, the end of an era, the climax of 33 incredible years on top of the radio and television heap. When this one was locked up, there would be no more regularly scheduled weekly Jack Benny show. For me this was like saying the sun would not rise tomorrow.

As I looked around the huge Universal City soundstage, I wondered what Don Wilson, the Smothers Brothers (who were guests that week), director Norman Abbott, producer Irving Fein and some of the others were thinking. Every one of the 50-odd members of the cast and crew knew it was Jack's swan song as a regular performer. Yet, like a pitcher working on a no-hitter, no one mentioned it.

When it was time to go home, there was a sudden stillness. I sensed that if anybody made a sad speech I couldn't stand it. So I ran backstage, where the makeup man was waiting to remove the beard I was using to play the Viennese psychiatrist. My only thought was to get out the door as fast as I could without running into anyone, especially Jack.

Naturally I ran into him. Only then did I notice waiters wheeling in a long table loaded with goodies. A voice said, "Aren't you going to stay for my party, Bee-yammy?"—that's what he's called me for 45 years.

Now I'm known as a guy you can just say hello to and he'll tell you 10 jokes. I can talk more in 10 minutes than Milton Berle can in an hour. But not then. Instead I was thinking, Jack, what are we going to celebrate? That you got yourself into a bind with Jim Aubrey [the now-departed head of CBS Television] over a time slot, that when you had the temerity to switch networks your old bosses clobbered you by flooding the market with your reruns, that because of this, audiences are to be deprived of one of *continued*

TV GUIDE — AUGUST 30th 1965

The Jack Benny Times

Volume VI, Number 2 INTERNATIONAL DISTRIBUTION March-April 1986

PRESIDENT'S MESSAGE

WELL...Jell-o again. Hey, gang, thank you for your nice letters these last two months. It's really true that I have gotten to know some of my best friends through the fan club. Even the Fred Allen fans are nice...believe it or not. Here's something funny that happened last Friday. I don't get to see Jack's shows on CBN too much, but last Friday I settled back to enjoy one. With a collection of about 65 JB shows on tape, it happened to be one I didn't have!!! Wonders never cease. Now on with the show!!!

¥¥ LOOKING FOR TAPES ¥¥

Here it is...the list you have all been waiting for...the tape interest list. If you would like to be included, just drop me a line. I understand that this has proved quite beneficial to many members.

Jack Bloom, 8618 Stansbury Ave., Van Nuys, California 91402

Rob Cohen, 2680 Cannon Pt., Apt. 3D, Columbus, Ohio 43209

Andrew Haskell, 160 W. 39th Ave., Vancouver, British Columbia V5Y 2P2, Canada

Laura Lee, 15430 Lost Valley Dr., Ft. Wayne, Indiana 46825

Bill Oliver, 516 Third St. NE, Massilon, Ohio 44646

Lewis A. Pearson, 240 Ridge Dr., Marion, Iowa 52302

Joyce Shooks, P.O. Box 307, Sparta, Michigan 49345

Steve Szejna, 3334 South 15th St., Milwaukee, Wisconsin 53215

James E. Treacy, Jr., 5395 Petersburg Rd., Dundee, Michigan 48131

WELCOME

"Last February I was lucky enough to have on my television show two of the zaniest and most refreshingly funny guys I've ever known. When they first bounced onstage that night in their bright red blazers--shoebutton eyes shining and faces freshly scrubbed--I was sure they had mistaken the studio for an eighth grade dancing class. But the minute they opened their mouths it was clear that I had just hired myself the funniest comedy team around. Thier viewpoint is absolutely unique. Their material is theirs alone. And, as if that wasn't enough to shake the foundations of a fellow performer, they sing too...And, once you've heard them I'll wager they'll rub off on you just as they did on me.

Copyright 1989, Laura Lee

When that television show was aired last spring my wife, Mary, told me that she thought it was one of the best shows I'd had in years...And you can bet she wasn't talking about my violin playing."

Those words were written by Jack Benny himself (as if you hadn't already guessed) about two of our newest honorary members. If you don't believe me, you can read it for yourself on the back of any <u>Mom Always Liked You Best!</u> album. I had the great pleasure of seeing these two in concert in Warsaw, Indiana; it was definitely one of the best shows I have seen in years. If you still don't know who they are, then you must take some time to listen to the music and comedy of the Smothers Brothers.

If you have Nickelodeon from your local cable company, be sure to tune in for their comedy shows on Sunday nights at ten. I had a rather brief but extemely pleasurable conversation with Dick Smothers about Jack and the old comedy shows. I'm certain that we all would like to extend a warm welcome into the fan club for Dick and Tom Smothers.

?? WHAT DO YOU KNOW ??

I was ecstatic to make a certain find at an estate sale a few weeks ago. It was a package from Des Moines containing an insurance plan called "Americare 39" from American Republic Insurance Company. Included was a large package of information covered with color pictures of Jack. Also included was a virgin, blue sound-sheet (in other words, one that has never been played). I haven't had the heart to play it yet, but it says that it's Jack with an "all-star" cast (probably members of the show). Supposedly Jack was going to promote this plan on television shortly thereafter. Has anyone heard of it or know anything about it?
(The rates are good...perhaps we should make a mass enlistment for it.)

MUGS

The last issue included information on a Jack Benny mug that might be available. Perhaps it wasn't too clear that Memory Mugs needs to make a minimum order of 144 mugs to start production of them again. We would have to get about half that many orders for ANY to be sold. Right now, we have about ten. It sounds like a lot, but I still think that we could do it. As one member said, "They would make GREAT gifts!!!" Please let me know if you're interested.

££ STAMP ££

Have you written a letter in support of the Jack Benny stamp yet? Stand up for your rights!!! You couldn't do this in Russia!!! **YOU**, yes you, have the right to demand

a stamp in honor of one of the greatest comedians of the 20th century!!! Go forth and proclaim it...Duke Ellington had his stamp, and now JACK'S TIME HAS COME!!! Send your letters to:
> Jack Benny Commemorative Stamp Committee
> P.O. Box 48799
> Los Angeles, California 90048

Gee...perhaps I should go into politics.

§§ LEST WE FORGET §§

March 14, 1947--Benny-Allen feud officially ends
March 17, 1956--Fred Allen passes away.

MARCH 23-- JACK BENNY DAY

March 29, 1932--Jack's radio debue on Ed Sullivan's show.
April 26, 1982--Don Wilson passes away.

On a lighter note, the Jack Benny Fan Club's own Donnie Pitchford will tie the knot on June 7. The last was a square knot, so perhaps this will be a double-half hitch and will earn him his eagle scout medal. All kidding aside, he will marry a lovely lady named Laura Pearson. With a name like that, she can't be all bad!!! Send any notes of congratulations to: 202 Alta, Longview, Texas 75604.

Our tanks to Brad Ashton for his contributions to this issue. Er, that's THANKS. Brad's in London and Britain is on our side at the moment!!!

Laura Lee, 15430 Lost Valley Dr., Ft. Wayne, Indiana 46825
Send any questions, additions, announcements, or articles to me that you would like added to the next issue. Please friends, send no bills (except green bills), animals or bombs. Good night, folks!!!

OH, YEAH, AND...

The long-lost August 1984 issue of the _Times_ has just been found. If anyone would like a copy of it, just write me and I'll send it free of charge.

COMING UP: ONE JACK BENNY —WELL DONE

The Friars Club roasts the comedian in a TV dinner

Emcee Johnny Carson turning the heat on happy Jack Benny as long-time friend George Burns chuckles.

Milton Berle: "Jack Benny is one of the most exciting men in California. His idea of a thrilling evening is to make obscene phone calls to Hermione Gingold."

Alan King: "Jack's so loved, revered, respected—I don't know how to compare this man. Perhaps St. Joseph—which is a small, dull town in Missouri."

Vice President Spiro Agnew: "I don't know how old Jack is. I only know that the Treasury Department sent me Jack's income-tax return, and his Social Security number was 1."

Question: What in tarnation is the Vice President of the United States doing tossing out one-liners about Jack Benny with the likes of Milton Berle and Alan King? Answer: Agnew, along with a gaggle of nonpoliticos —George Burns, Dennis Day, Don Wilson, Phil Harris, "Rochester," Ed Sullivan, Johnny Carson—is throwing a TV dinner saluting the famous 39-year-old. The testimonial feed will be on Music Hall Jan. 21 (9-10 P.M., ET).

Whatever compliments fly Jack's way are likely to be as left-handed as a Jerry Koosman pitch. That's because the comedy at this meal is being catered in the acrid tradition of a Friars Club "Roast." The Friars, a hang-out for troupers, have for years barbecued select brothers at luncheons in their New York and Los Angeles clubhouses. Of late, however, the "Roasts" have been transplanted to TV. Carson had one in '68 and Berle was raked over the coals in October of '69. Now the joke's on Jack—and in spades.

The taping took place on Sept. 11 of last year. Now, Friar tradition dictates that before any "Roasting," the "Roasters" gather to "loosen up," as the show's producer, Gary Smith, put it. Hence, at 7 P.M. on taping day, the good brothers were scheduled to appear in a makeshift Green Room one floor up from the studio. There they would partake of a ceremonial spirit.

Here are our notes, taken on the spot:
If it weren't for the two white-jacketed bartenders stuck off in an alcove, the place could pass for a rural PTA meeting hall. Metal bridge chairs hug the walls and plywood boards on sawhorses display the party's hors d'oeuvres: pretzels and peanuts. ("Since Kraft is sponsoring this show," snips a hungry public-relations girl, "you'd think they'd at least have some Velveeta.") The first Friar to show comes in at 7:15. It's Phil Harris. Somebody asks, "Wanna drink, Phil?"—which is tantamount to asking Joe Namath if he likes girls.

The room—packed as a witch's wake till now—begins swelling with humanity: brass from J. Walter Thompson—Kraft's advertising agency—friends and friends-of-friends of said brass, Kraft execs, their friends and friends-of, plus a slew of spouses fresh from Mr. Kenneth. Amid the crush of bodies, Ed Sullivan—who's been standing in silence—suddenly questions a neighboring couple with, "When's this show gonna be on the air?" Told Jan. 21, the man Don Rickles calls "Mr. Fascination" pauses, ponders and then volleys, "What day is *this*?" Somebody says it's Thursday and Ed zips his lip. Whispers Mr. to Mrs.: "He won't have to be *that* stimulating again until Sunday."

At 7:25, Johnny Carson appears, brandishing a nailed-on grin. Carson likes crowds as much as Howard →

The Benny crew swung into England for performance at the London Palladium in 1950. Striding decks in Southampton were (l. to r.) Alice Faye; her husband, Phil Harris; Mary Livingstone; Benny; Mrs. Eddy Anderson, and her husband, Rochester.

Hughes likes photographers. Plus, the night before, his dressing-room-office, stacked with wardrobe and personal belongings, had been reduced to a bucket of ashes. "Oh, material things don't *really* matter," Carson will bromide to someone's condolences, adding an arch, "Where do I pick up my money for this gig?" Meanwhile, the guest of honor, Jack Benny, has arrived and is greeting the pretty daughter of some friends with a hug and kiss that's only half-paternal, mooning, "I'm not that old *yet!*" Henny Youngman, the comic specializing in one-liners, works his way to Benny and tries for a yock: "Hello, Jack—and thank you for your last bad check." Mr. Benny doesn't laugh.

The room, by the way, is so dark you could develop film. The main stream of light leaks in from the hall just beyond the door. This source of illumination is suddenly corked, however, by the presence in the entrance of a half-dozen men—each wearing a plain, Sunday-meeting suit and a face that would stop a clock. Nobody sees their I.D.'s. But, then, you don't have to be mauled by a cougar to know you shouldn't get in one's way. Secret Service is written all over their unsmiling faces.

The suspicion is confirmed by the appearance of the Vice President and Mrs. Agnew. (This was unscheduled. Previously, Mr. Agnew had asked to meet with only Benny and Carson in his dressing room.) Flashing a smile to shame Helios, the Vice President distributes a dozen campaign-type handshakes and then heads for Benny. As their palms meet, Jack reaches for a laugh: "Mr. Vice President, this is the greatest thing that's happened in my life since they named a school after me in Waukegan." Mr. Agnew doesn't laugh.

It's picture-taking time. Just outside the room there's a closet-size studio where networks shoot—for newspapers and Sunday-supplement covers—the kind of stills that make everyone look as if they're made of plastic wood. In go the Agnews. Outside stay the Secret Service. And they steadily scrutinize the line of in-going stars—making such as Carson, Benny and Berle as nervous as high schoolers caught sneaking smokes at lunch. To relieve the tension, Berle is asked if he has met the Vice President. "No," replies Milton. "But I hear he and Ed Sullivan had a brilliant conversation. They stood and stared at each other for 10 minutes."

At 7:52, Mrs. Agnew emerges from the cubicle. At 7:55, the Vice President ducks out. With the grace of linemen guarding a quarterback, the Secret Service surround the Second Family and run interference for them ("They don't ask you to move," observes one watcher, "they move you") down a stairwell and into the studio. There Benny, a chronic worrier (his nails are bitten to the skin) is pacing off his preshow nerves. As is most everybody else. "If you don't have feathers in your stomach," Berle remarks, "there's something wrong with you." Testing his theory, Berle inquires about the state of the Vice President's nervous system. "Nervous?" replies Mr. Agnew. "What the hell about?"

Which, at 8:10, brings us up to showtime. The cameras begin recording the carryings-on. . . .

And now—months later, the shenanigans are on the air. What you'll be seeing is an edited version of a 90-minute gagfest. It's shorter because some of the wisecracks fizzled and—more important—a few of the ad libs would send NBC's *Priscilla Goodbody* into cardiac arrest. You see, when the Friars "fry" at home, the repartee is, to put it demurely, risque. And, during taping, some of the funnymen turned bluer than Mr. Benny's eyes.

TV GUIDE JANUARY 17, 1970

By BARBARA MERLIN   Aug. 31, 1976

One of the Comedian's Closest Friends Reveals...

Jack Benny's Amazing Psychic Experience on His Deathbed

Jack Benny dramatically lost his fear of death when a former vaudeville partner — dead for nearly 45 years — appeared to the dying comedian and gave him a glimpse into a beautiful life beyond the grave, reveals one of Benny's closest friends.

Only days before cancer took his life, Benny whispered to his aide, Eddie Villery: "I just saw Lyman Woods and spoke to him. He is going to help me through. He showed me the way . . . and it is beautiful."

Villery, 28, was the late comedian's friend and confidant during the five years before Benny's death. But Lyman Woods — Benny's vaudeville partner from 1912 to 1917 — had been dead almost 45 years!

"Jack had a terrible fear of death," Villery told The ENQUIRER. "He would become melancholy and deeply depressed whenever he heard of friends dying or even being ill. He feared death because, as he used to tell me, there was nothing after death — no family, no friends, no laughs and no audiences . . . just a great big black void."

Villery — Benny's chauffeur, valet and jack-of-all-trades — was also one of his closest friends, according to another good friend, comedian George Burns. "Eddie's a very nice fellow and a very honest man," Burns told The ENQUIRER. "He was very close to Jack."

The young aide was in constant attendance at Benny's bedside as the comedian lay dying in December 1974.

Under heavy sedation to ease the terrible pain of cancer of the pancreas, Benny kept repeating a name from the past — the name of Lyman Woods.

"The repetition of the name puzzled me," said Villery, now an actor and production assistant.

"And there was such a strange tone in his voice. 'Who is Lyman Woods?' I asked.

"Jack did not answer me. But several hours later, he mentioned the same name again — 'Lyman Woods.'

"Then Jack whispered: 'Didn't you see him?'

"There was a momentary silence. Suddenly Jack's pain-ridden face took on a look of pleasure. He opened his

JACK BENNY relaxes with a cigar in the company of his aide, Eddie Villery, and Villery's friend, Diane Gillis, in a Las Vegas hotel in 1973. Benny described his psychic experience to Villery, who was the comedian's confidant during the five years before Benny's death.

eyes and softly told me he'd just seen and spoken to him. Jack said Lyman was going to help him through 'into a beautiful hereafter.'"

Villery later found out that the late Lyman Woods was a musician who had been Benny's vaudeville partner from 1912 to 1917.

Shortly before Benny's death the name Lyman Woods again came to the comedian's lips, says Villery. "At first his voice was indistinct, then he began to speak more clearly. 'I was with Lyman,' Jack said. 'He told me it was beautiful — and it was . . . it was!'

"The significance of what Jack was saying dawned on me. As Jack was nearing death, his old and good friend Lyman Woods was helping him make the transition from life to death. He was guiding him home, helping dispel Jack's lifelong fear of that 'instant end' he talked about.

"Through his deathbed vision, Jack at the very end discovered that it was not a still, silent void of blackness he was entering, but a beautiful place to which he was being led by his old and dear friend of long ago."

Norman Abbott, for years producer and director of Benny's TV shows, confirmed that "Jack was always afraid of death and dying.

"Whenever anyone would compliment him about the picture he was most proud of, 'To Be or Not to Be,' he would immediately get moody and remark that he and Robert Stack were the only stars who played in the movie still left alive."

Abbott said Villery "was Jack's best friend during the last years. He was with Jack when Jack was dying and at that time he told me that the name of Lyman Woods kept coming to Jack's lips. I think you can genuinely believe Eddie. He has no reason to fabricate. I have always found him to be an honest person."

George Burns told The ENQUIRER: "Eddie was very close to Jack. He was always there during those last 5 years. The day Jack died, Eddie was in the room with Jack every time I went up to see how he was doing. Eddie was there — Eddie was always there."

Oh, good grief! You gotta read this one.

VAUDEVILLE PARTNERS: Young Benny with Lyman Woods, with whom he performed from 1912 to 1917. On his deathbed, Benny said that Woods, dead almost 45 years, showed him a beautiful life beyond the grave.

Holding candy-coated cards, Mary "proved" that she was a mere 21 during her '63 birthday party in Las Vegas.

A Jack Benny radio show in 1942. From left: Mr. Benny and his wife, Mary Livingstone; Phil Harris, leading the band; Dennis Day, singing comedian; Eddie Anderson, as Rochester, and Don Wilson, the announcer.

International Jack Benny Fan Club
5430 Lost Valley Drive
Ft. Wayne, Indiana 46825

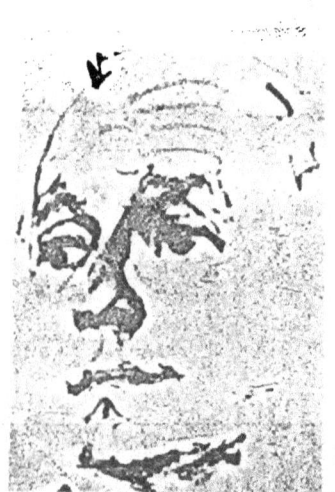

WELL!

The Jack Benny Times

Volume 6, Number 3   INTERNATIONAL DISTRIBUTION   May-June 1986

PRESIDENT'S MESSAGE

Well...Jell-o again folks!!! Another two months have passed, and I hope that this issue finds you all with a smile on your face and a song in your heart. If not, then drop me a note and I'll send a good song title for your heart and a good dentist for your smile. Otherwise, smile anyhow! As one member suggests, "Get up and read the obituaries. If your name is not there, have breakfast and start your day!"
I must thank Ken Meyer of WEEI Radio for having me on his show last month. Hopefully we will have some new members from the Boston area. Thanks again. My organ concerts in Colorado went very well. Also, I have just turned in my resumé to a local radio station, so hopefully I will be back in broadcasting here in Ft. Wayne. Now on with the show!

* NEW MEMBERS *

****BARBARA WATKINS--Barbara is the secretary of SPERDVAC, an organization with which many of you are familiar. Their Radiogram newsletter is quite interesting for any person interested in old radio. For more information write: P.O. Box 561, South Pasedena, California 91030.
****ROBERT DUNCAN--This gent is do dedicated that he has lived in both Anaheim and Cuc...amonga. He was introduced to Jack through his television shows, and is now discovering him on tape from radio programs. He is presently passing on his taste to his two children. Let's help him out with his collection! 2739 West Yale, Unit #D, Anaheim, California 92801.
****JACK ABIZAID--Jack has the honor of beating J. Bloom (see below) to be our first member whose name is "Jack." It was a narrow victory, though. He has been collecting OTR for ten years. He presently has nearly 300 of Jack's shows. He also collects OTR magazines. An aspiration of his is to write a book on OTR. 16 Hampshire Rd., Peabody, Maryland 01960.
****JACK BLOOM--This Jack has the honor of being our first member whose initials are "J.B.!" He has expressed an interest in trading tapes of Jack's radio shows. Jack--please note my street address. His is: 8618 Stansbury Ave., Van Nuys, California 91402. Thanks for "SKTB." I listened to it in the room in Colorado before the concert!
****BOB BURNS--No information at this time.

¥¥ ANNOUNCEMENTS ¥¥

The International Jack Benny Fan Club proudly makes the following announcements:

Two of our members were presented the Medal of Liberty on July 3 for outstanding achievements as naturalized citizens.

Copyright 1989, Laura Lee

They are: Itzhak Perlman and Bob Hope. Congratulations. Also congratulations to another member, Ronald Reagan, for being on the cover of TV Guide and George Bush for making a fine speech during the closing ceremonies.

Laura Pearson Pitchford has put up with...er...been married to Donnie for over a month now. Our condolances...er...congratulations to her. Exercise your right to vote! THE ISSUE: Should Donnie grow a moustache or not? Send ballots to: The Cedric Weehunt Moustache Society, 202 Alta, Longview, Texas 75604. Please, friends, send no bombs.

Let's also give a rousing round of applause to *Rex Riffle* for looking like Lum, *Jim Treacy* for graduating from high school, *Rusty Wolfe* for grilling chicken and hot dogs, *Star Roman* for designing our new letterhead (have you seen it?) and *Joyce Shooks* for having nice hair (or so *Lu* tells me).

JOB OPENING

Webster defines "vice president" as, "An officer next in rank below a president, acting in his place during his absence or incapacity." In all seriousness I feel that we should elect a Vice President to serve as a consultant to the President and to assume the position of President if I should ever become incapacitated. I'm not planning on being incapacitated, but you know how those things sneak up on you. Please send nominations to the address at the end of this newsletter.

JACK BENNY ITEMS

I'm still taking requests for Jack Benny mugs. Presently we have approximately twenty. Give the gift that keeps on giving until until you finish the drink in it. (Then refill it and it will give again.)
A few years ago, Editions Limited printed note cards with the Hirschfeld charicature of Jack on the front. They are approximately 7 1/8 by 5¼ inches and cost $9.00 per dozen. They are no longer printing the cards, but if there is sufficient interest, I will see if they are willing to reprint them.

FAMILY ALBUM

Attention new members: we have an official Jack Benny Fan Club Family Album which is to include all members with a brief biography so that milleniums from now, our posterity will be able to look back and see who the members of the IJBFC were and know their background. Please send a photograph if possible.

FOR THE TERMINALLY CURIOUS

Yes, the trash article in the last newsletter was from the National Enquirer. These articles are from Family Weekly, 2-24-74; The Plain Dealer, 2-20-76; Daily News, 11-29-85;

and The Illustrated Press, 6-85. They are printed in this order.

Send any announcements, advertisements, etc. to:
Laura Lee, International Jack Benny Fan Club Offices,
15430 Lost Valley Drive, Fort Wayne, Indiana 46825.

and remember - Weebles wobble but they don't fall down.

Star Chat
By Peer J. Oppenheimer

Jack Benny, 80 Talks About Jack Benny, 39

Jack Benny and his wife Mary, whose "knowledge about show business," he says, "is absolutely amazing."

The last time I saw Jack Benny was in his beautifully furnished, immaculate Beverly Hills mansion. This time I faced him across his cluttered desk in his Beverly Hills office. He turned 80 on Valentine's Day, and we began talking about his proposed retirement.

FAMILY WEEKLY: Tell the truth now —could you ever think of yourself as not working?
BENNY: Let me put it this way. I could retire up to a certain point. And I'll tell you what that point is. If I made a business of my concerts—and you know I give concerts for charity all the time—if I could do enough throughout the year, then I could probably retire. You see, I LOVE to play the violin. But I also love to get laughs. And I love to talk. So when I give a concert, I can do everything I do in Las Vegas. The dif-

> "Everybody knows my stinginess is a joke. But in order to compensate, it costs me a bloody fortune!"

ference is, the people who come to concerts are pretty sophisticated—the same people who maybe come to hear Isaac Stern, or Heifetz. In fact, Isaac Stern acts as an agent for me because he tells me where they need the money. I always say he gets ten percent of nothing.
FW: What do you think of today's permissiveness—particularly in movies?
BENNY: It's too bad. Producers are taking the easy way out. And the fact that the films are rated means nothing to me. I mean, either a picture should be permitted to be shown, or not, and not have an X rating or a G rating, or however they rate them.

FW: During the last election there was a Proposition 18 in California that, if passed, would have prohibited the showing of a lot of films. What did you think of that?
BENNY: I voted no because while I don't like obscene films, I don't want censorship. Of any kind, anywhere. Otherwise someone can suddenly say, "Well, we don't want this Jewish joke!" or "We don't want this Italian joke." If a proposition like that went through, there's no telling how far censorship would go!
FW: As you grow older, are you growing more conservative?
BENNY: Not if conservative means stingy, careful with money. This I have never been. Neither has my wife. If I had, I should be the richest actor in show business. But politically—well, I am not a party man. I've never been a Democrat or a Republican. I don't want to get hooked, I guess—I just want to vote for who is right.
FW: You say you aren't stingy. How did that joke start?
BENNY: By accident. In one of my old shows there were a couple of jokes about my being stingy. The audience laughed. A little later, when I did a weekly show, we used the same gag and it worked again. All of a sudden I became a stingy character. And then I realized how humorous it was, an element that is easy to laugh at. It's easy to relate to.
FW: Has this ever gotten out of hand?
BENNY: Sometimes when I do guest shots, they plan on doing too much, and I'll say, "Hey, wait a minute, fellas! I can't be stingy throughout the entire show! There must be other things to do." I'm so identified with it now that I don't have to spell it out anymore.

For instance, on the Dean Martin show I walk into a restaurant and a reporter comes out and says there's a big comet in the air and it's going to hit the earth in about five minutes and the earth will be destroyed. I don't say a word, but I go to the phone, and I say to the operator, "Who do I see?" I just put a dime in the phone box...." I don't have to go any further. Just my going to the phone gets the laugh.
FW: Did anyone ever take your stinginess seriously?
BENNY: No. Everybody seems to know it's a joke. But in order to compensate, it costs me a bloody fortune! Even with charities, I'm forced into giving a lot more than I can afford sometimes.
FW: How about your insistence that

> "I don't give a hoot how much people liked me on radio or in vaudeville. That's gone."

you are 39 years old? How did that get started?
BENNY: I kept the year 37 for a couple of years. When I was 38, I kept that up for about another three years. Then when I got to be 39, for some reason or other we thought 39 was a funny number. Also, a lot of little kids think that when you are 40, you are an old man. And who wants to be old?
FW: Did anyone ever object to your growing older than 39?
BENNY: Well, once we decided, for the publicity, to have a big 40th birthday. You can't imagine the letters I received, including one from The Christian Science Monitor, begging me not to do it. The Monitor's letter wasn't humorously written, it was serious. They said that most people know my

right age [Jack was born Benny Kubelsky on February 14, 1894]; but the people say, "Well, if Benny stays 39 and keeps working, I can keep on working, too!" So I stayed 39. But we don't play that bit much anymore. Or the Maxwell car joke. That's old stuff now —it's become corny.
FW: You don't look much older now than you did 20 years ago. How do you manage to stay in such good shape?
BENNY: Luckily I don't care much about eating. I love breakfast, but after that I can go on practically nothing. And I play golf—not as much or as well as I used to. But I think the most important thing is to do things mentally. I love to work.
FW: You once told me that one of the reasons you stayed young was because your grandchildren kept you young. Is that still the case?
BENNY: Maybe that was right at the time, but today I feel it's my work that keeps me young. I like practically everything I do, and I don't delve into myself. I don't give a hoot how much people liked me on radio or in vaudeville. That's gone. And when somebody asks me, "What did you like best, radio or television?" I say, "When I was in radio, I liked radio. But I couldn't wait to get into television. If there is something after television, that's what I will like!" You don't live for yesterday or even today. You live for tomorrow.
FW: Did the fact that you and Mary worked together for such a long time help your marriage?
BENNY: Yes. But you know, it was quite by accident that we became a team. When I met her she was selling ladies' hosiery at the May Company. In those days a lot of comedians would bring a girl out onstage to work for them. They were supposed to be dumb girls. All the comedians had dumb girls. Well, one day the one working for me became ill and Mary knew the part, and I said, "You know, you could do this beautifully!" And she did.
FW: After that, did you teach her a lot about the business?
BENNY: Mary's knowledge about show business is absolutely amazing. She claims she learned certain things from me, which she probably did, but there are certain things that you instinctively have to do correctly to succeed. Like she would know enough not to try hard for jokes, that if it was written correctly on paper all she had to do was read it. That's why Ronald Colman and his wife were great on my show. They were dramatic actors, but all they did was read the comedy lines exactly as they were written.

10 ■ FAMILY WEEKLY, February 24, 1974

The house that Jack's wit built
Benny's genius payed off

In this excerpt from the book "Jack Benny," Mary Livingstone (Mrs. Jack Benny) talks about the mansion they built in Beverly Hills that would become a major stop for sight-seeing bus tours. The book is written by Benny's widow along with his brother-in-law and long-time comedy writer, Hilliard Marks and Marcia Borie.

In 1937, the Jack Bennys were involved in the biggest domestic project of their married lives when they hired architect and builder Carlton Burgess to oversee the construction of a home in Beverly Hills.

While radio audiences conjured up an image of Jack Benny living in penurious squalor — befitting his public cheapness — the elegant mansion was under way.

The home, Benny's residence for 25 years, soon became a landmark on those movie-star maps sold by canny old women who stood on selected street corners of Beverly Hills, Brentwood, and Bel Air. In fact, 1002 N. Roxbury Dr. was a twice-daily stop on regular sightseers' bus tours.

Occasionally, tourists got a glimpse of Jack or Mary, but there was one special day and one special group which Jack would talk about and laugh over for years to come.

On this particular day, he had dressed up as a strolling gypsy, complete with bandana around his neck and funny hat on his head. Then, fiddle in hand, he went out the back door, slamming it shut, and began playing away as he crossed his lawn.

Serenading his neighbors, Lucy and Desi Arnaz, and dressed in a funny costume, Jack did not bring about the laughs he had anticipated. Feeling slightly foolish, as Lucy endearingly loved to make Jack feel (as all his friends did when he tried to be funny off camera), Jack walked back across the lawn in his weird getup.

But when he got home, he found himself locked out — and, on a rare day, the house empty. Mary was in

Jack Benny in the 1940 Paramount film, "Buck Benny Rides Again."

Palm Springs. The servants were off. Joanie was away at school.

So there he stood, fiddle in one hand, trying desperately to get into his front door.

At that precise moment, the tour bus came down Roxbury Dr. Jack could hear the driver over the PA system announce "And on your right, the home of..." Without even thinking, Jack turned toward the bus.

The driver sputtered for a moment, then continued, "The house of...why, there he is now, Jack Benny!" Within seconds, the bus had emptied, and several dozen tourists ran across the front lawn to get his autograph.

Jack started to explain his getup...his predicament...signing autographs and shaking hands. The fans were so excited, no one even remarked on Jack's strange outfit.

Benny was nonplussed by the experience until he realized that for tourists to see him dressed as a gypsy, violin in hand, vainly attempting to get into his own house, was nothing unusual — his "image," rather than being diminished, had been confirmed.

Jack's house cost a quarter of a million dollars to construct, decorate and furnish during days when that sum was an enormous fortune. It was a two-story home of the Georgian period, with a red brick exterior and an expansive lawn out front.

Mary, who had a reputation for giving the most elegant and charming parties of any hostess in town, frequently utilized the backyard-pool area, in addition to the living room, dining room and drawing room — especially for her larger parties.

Years later, daughter Joan can still vividly recall some of the "extravaganzas" that took place in the Benny household.

"My parents gave the most lavish parties. When we were kids, Sandy Burns, or my other best friend, a girl named DeeDee, used to spend the night at my house whenever we knew a Benny gala was in the works — especially Mother's New Year's Eve parties.

"We would get ready for bed, dressed in our robes, then we'd hike down on the top stair of the landing, look over the railing and watch as each new guest arrived.

"The parties were always big and fancy in what was the 'golden era' of Hollywood. Usually, they would have a huge tent put up in the backyard and hire an orchestra. There were flowers everywhere. The men came in black tie and the women in gorgeous formals. It was such fun watching. Every big star in town came, and we were as impressed by them as any kids from Ohio might have been...

Continued on Page 3-C

It's Bach, Beethoven & Benny

11-29-85

THE "JACK BENNY SHOW" on classical music station WQXR? Better believe it. Starting Sunday at 7:05 p.m., 'QXR will interrupt its broadcasts of Bach and Beethoven each week to present "The Best of Benny," culled from the famed comedian's 1948-55 CBS radio broadcasts.

The initial program will be introduced by violinist **Isaac Stern**, who was instrumental in convincing Benny to appear in a gala fund-raiser at Carnegie Hall 25 years ago

"I consider the Benny show to be the best comedy program ever produced in radio history," said **Warren Bodow**, president of WQXR. "We have selected 52 of the best from the 200 half-hour shows that were made available to us. This is the first time the station is departing from its musical format to present a comedy series."

Appropriately enough, the series will air in Benny's old, familiar time slot. The star began his radio career on NBC in 1932. CBS hired him and other big NBC stars in 1948 and Benny continued on radio until 1955. He was one of the few radio stars who made a successful transition to TV.

His shows were very meticulously planned and executed. The programs were never built around one-line gags or fast quips. Each broadcast began with a funny premise and then the dialogue was written to fit. A critic once wrote that Benny was not "one who said funny things, but one who said things funny." He was known for his excellent timing, mannerisms and expressions of disbelief and frustration, as well as utterances like "Well!!," "Hmmm!!" and "Now, cut that out."

Supporting players included his wife, **Mary Livingstone**, announcer **Don Wilson**, singer **Dennis Day** ("oh, just sing, Dennis"), bandleader **Phil Harris** and **Eddie (Rochester) Anderson**. Only Harris and Wilson are still living. Benny died in 1974.

"We expect the show to appeal to two different audiences," said Bodow, "those who were fans and remember the original series from their youth, and others who only know him from legend and will be able to hear him for the first time." Bodow stressed that the Benny show is not a harbinger of things to come for 'QXR. "This is the only show of its type that we will present," he explained. "We don't plan

JACK BENNY and his violin

to air any 'Fibber McGee and Molly' or 'Great Gildersleeve.'

"No show can match the consistent high quality of the Benny outings, and that's the reason we chose to put them on." Bodow said that there are other classical music stations around the country which have run dramatic shows, such as "Sherlock Holmes," but he has no plans to follow suit.

"We will try to peg the Benny show to an appropriate holiday," added Bodow. "A Christmas show will run at Christmas and so on. This week's program takes place right after Thanksgiving and deals with Jack taking violin lessons from Monsieur LeBlanc, played by one of Benny's regulars, **Mel Blanc**. Who better to introduce the segment that Isaac Stern?"

—George Maksian

Jack Benny rehearsing in 1967 for a violin performance at the inauguration of Ronald Reagan as Governor of California. He could play well, but often played for laughs.

Wit put Jack Benny on the map

Continued from Page 1-C

"We'd ooh and ahh at Clark Gable, Jimmy Stewart, Robert Taylor...the whole Hollywood's Best 10 Box Office names. We even collected autographs.

"Invariably, Mother would ask us which few celebrities we especially wanted to meet and talk to," she continued. "Always we would name two or three, and Mother would bring them upstairs.

"I'll never forget the first time she brought up Frank Sinatra. He was the bobby-soxers' delight then, and we practically died!"

For close to three decades, 1002 N. Roxbury Dr. was a showplace the Bennys loved and shared with their family and closest friends. In the late '60s, they sold the home and moved at first into a penthouse apartment, which they hated, and finally to another mansion, this time in Bel Air.

All his life, Jack was such a very simple man. The home on Roxbury Dr. was the place he loved the best. In fact, every once in a while, even after he had lived there for 20 years, he would look around and shake his head. Then he'd say, with wonder and pride, "Gee, it sure is a long way from Waukegan!"

* * *

Late in the fall of 1948, Jack Benny made headlines. After 15 years with the National Broadcasting Co., he was changing networks. Amos 'n' Andy, Burns and Allen, Edgar Bergen and Red Skelton were also involved in the move.

Perhaps because Jack was so readily identifiable as "the owner of the 7 p.m. Sunday spot on NBC," his was the name which headlined the story of the massive switch to CBS in the Hollywood trade papers.

William Paley, president of Columbia Broadcasting System, had instigated the move. In anticipation of television's vast future, he had accomplished the single biggest talent coup in the history of radio.

By hiring this block of comedic giants, Paley had assured himself that, when TV became a household word, the word — and the stars — would belong to CBS.

The executives needed some questions answered. For instance, how would Jack look on the small screen? What format should he follow?

Isaac Stern, Bob Crosby, Margaret Whiting, the Andrews Sisters, Lum and Abner, and Rochester had been signed to guest-star The writers came up with a top-notch script.

What happened next was remarkable. Jack sauntered on stage simulating his usual breezy manner, and instantly, his instinctive inner confidence took over.

The applause which greeted him was overwhelming. From the moment he began his opening monolog, it was clear Jack Benny would be a natural in this new medium!

JACK: "Ladies and gentlemen, I want to introduce myself...I'm appearing here tonight through the courtesy of a 10-inch tube...However, I do want to apologize for my appearance here this evening as I know that most of you prefer wrestling.

"Had I known that wrestling was going to be so popular on television, I would've stuck to it...because that used to be my business, and I was very good at it, too.

"As a matter of fact, Gorgeous George got his idea from me. I was known as 'the Body Beautiful Benny'...When I stepped into the ring and took off my robe...WELL!...I made Frank Sinatra look like a nickel...

"And one thing I must say in all seriousness...that is that I'm not a bit nervous. I know that most comedians are nervous about television... like Bob Hope...Eddie Cantor...Red Skelton...but not me. I figure this way: If I'm a success tonight, all right...If not, I'll kill myself.

"Of course, there's one comedian I'm sure will have a little trouble on television ...and that's Fred Allen. I don't know whether you've seen him in person or not...but with those bags under his eyes, he looks like a short butcher peeping over two pouches of liver."

On that night, in 1949, before anyone else had ever seen Jack on the small screen, it was Mary who was the first to realize his enormous potential. When the show was over, she came up on stage, kissed Jack and said, "Doll face, you'll just be sensational on television!"

Tomorrow: Jack Benny's contributions to symphony orchestras in particular and the world of entertainment in general.

ED'S WANAT CORNER

Remember back in 1969 when you could pick up a news paper and read about your favorite comedians. We'll return with back to Yesteryear Comedians Talk About Comedy - Part 2. Jack Benny & Fred Allen.

Monday, February 17, 1969

COMEDIANS TALK ABOUT COMEDY—II

Benny's Time-Tested Formula for Success: Know What's Funny, Make Best of It

By Larry Wilde

This is the second in a series of 12 articles excerpted from a new book of interviews in which a group of the funniest people of our time tell what they find as funny. Jack Benny is being interviewed.

FROM a Jack Benny monologue:

Last week I woke up in the middle of the night with the most wonderful idea for a joke. I couldn't go back to sleep. I worked on it all night. The next day I came to the theater and did four shows... and in between each show I worked on that joke. That night, I stayed up all night trying to perfect the joke. And finally, the next day I got it. I went out on the first show—and it was such a wonderful joke — I started to tell it right in the middle of the joke... I fell asleep.

WILDE: Jack, has what people laughed at changed much through the years?

BENNY: I don't think so. I think they laugh at the same things. Years ago you could do some corny things and be funny. I can look over what I used to do today, many years ago and pick out things of us were.

THE ONLY thing is if you are working on characterizations, things that were funny 30 years ago have to be embellished. You have to be smarter, wilder. Like, if I do zingy jokes I can't do an ordinary joke about leaving a guy a nickel tip — that's not funny anymore. Now you have to leave me a dime or the waiter leaves me a dime. Maybe the waiter would have to be that cheap, you see, in order for it to be funny. Today, it has to be actually funnier.

WILDE: Many comedians earn an excellent living doing club dates, conventions — some as much as twenty-five thousand dollars or more but few of the world will never hear of them. Same are very content with this anonymity while others are still striving to reach the top. Was it always your goal to become a star?

BENNY: I would think so, and I think nearly every comedian wants to be just like a politician would like to be President of the United States. And it don't care who the politician is...

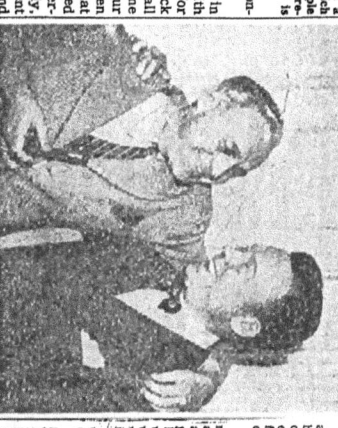

REMEMBER WHEN?—Jack Benny, left, and Fred Allen were buddies in this 1943 photo. The two comedians later developed a long-standing radio feud, as Jack explains in today's installment.

he might be the mayor of Carson City, but if he's in politics, he would like to end up to remain a star all these years?

BENNY: I think I have had, through my years of radio and television, almost always a very good show; got combined among the top half-dozen. But I've been considered very good, but the best editor, which is important — almost always a better editor. Most of the comedians gave me credit for being not the best comedian in the business, but the best editor, which is important — as important as being a comedian. It's not that I am such a particularly funny man. It's the things I do in routines. People will say to me: "Did you laugh at the pauses in the tape?" This all comes as you go along, but when I got to the point where I was getting four hundred and fifty dollars a week, brother, then I was quite a rich man. I started to move in the best circles. I felt it came about as a result of editing and analyzing yourself and your material?

WILDE: Were you born with it is it?

BENNY: The latter — I don't think I was born with it. I have been given more credit than I deserve, in that, because I have a superhuman in every joke I do. The right off the reel, good timing, anything like that. The reason other comedians feel that way, and maybe the public, is are gradually getting to know about timing, they know that words now and talk about it very slowly and I talk like I am hesitate to... I might think.

WILDE: Could you pinpoint the special steps you've taken to remain a star all these years?

BENNY: I think I have had, through my years of radio and television, almost always a very good show; got combined among the top half-dozen. But I've been considered, of course, but I think that I am basically... the comedian, because most of the comedians gave me credit for being not the best comedian in the business, but the best editor, which is important — as important as being a comedian. It's not that I am such a particularly funny man. It's the things I do in routines. People will say to me: "Did you laugh at the pauses in the tape?" This all comes as you go along, but when I got to the point where I was getting four hundred and fifty dollars a week, brother, then I was quite a rich man. I started to move in the best circles. I felt it came about as a result of editing and analyzing yourself and your material?

WILDE: So you really didn't wake up one day and say: "I want to be a great comedian"? It was a step-by-step process?

BENNY: Yeah, but I think everybody does feel that way because if they don't, it's not good — it's better to feel that way. But some fortunate so, not only in recognition but in improvement in what I was doing. If you get up to the top, Was it step-by-step, you don't drop so fast.

BENNY: I answered him, and it went on and on. We never got together. If we did, the feud would have dropped, because we would have been conceived, so to speak, and it would have been considered no feud with Fred Allen was an accident.

WILDE: Was Fred Allen considered the comedian's comedian?

BENNY: Because he was a great writer, Fred was a wonderful humorist. He wrote funny letters. He wrote great books. He wrote great shows... I don't know whether altogether somebody was great because he had so many audiences. Many of the sometimes they wouldn't be at all. They would tune from it. I always blame it on editing.

LET'S TAKE your... you are preparing this book, you gotta edit it, right? They say a play is never written, it's rewritten. Well, the same goes for an article in the paper, or a monologue for writers and myself sit down and argue and discuss whether the word "but" here or hurts a joke. That's how important editing is.

WILDE: How did "Love in Bloom" become your theme song?

BENNY: Quite by accident. "Love in Bloom" is not a theme song, I particularly with a comedian. It happened that I was looking with that number thirty years ago, and before I could do anything about it... it was an avalanche, and it became my theme song.

WILDE: Mr. Benny, Jack, you are considered to have the best timing among comedians. Was exactly is timing?

BENNY: Sometimes I tell have been given more credit than I deserve, in that, because I have a superhuman in every joke I do. The right off the reel, good timing, anything like that. The reason other comedians feel that way, and maybe the public, is are gradually getting to know about timing, they know that words now and talk about it very slowly and I talk like I am hesitate to... I might think.

BENNY: All these things happened by accident... with one very slight reminder about your show as I did...

REMEMBER WHEN?

Benny trademarks come about? Thriftiness, bragging, playing straight to the people you work with, etc.?

WILDE: How did all the Jack...

BENNY: Some jokes about my being stingy...

OTHER PEOPLE have a great timing but they talk very fast. It would be tough for them to talk slowly and it would be tough for me to talk fast.

WILDE: Could you define timing?

BENNY: It's tough to define "rhythm"... "pause"...

WILDE: Do words like describe it?

BENNY: WELL, my pauses — fortunately when you're on radio, when you couldn't see me. The audience felt the same pauses and same laughs that I might do... monologue three or four nights and not change a word and an audience sitting out front will get back into the swing and rhythm. It's a necessity. It's something everybody has to have.

A GOOD JOKE without timing means nothing and a bad joke with good timing means nothing — except you can help a bad joke with timing where you can help a good joke with bad timing. That's why you gotta know how to drive it...

WILDE: It is a question of an easy flow?

BENNY: That's right — one word or one syllable too much or one too little completely. I can show it. I was playing Las Vegas, a wonderful audience every night and I knew that my very opening — I would come on the stage and my first line was something, and every night it got a good laugh. Then one night I would come out, and I knew but I was tired. I had not put on the laugh was not as big and not so long or as big good but not as long as the performance. I would know the next day at the performance. I was knocked me off my timing for about two minutes, I couldn't get back into the swing and rhythm.

WILDE: Can anyone learn timing?

BENNY: I think so, but in nearly the cases he has to have something.

WILDE: Jack, which medium — radio, television, movies, night clubs, or the stage — do you prefer to work in?

BENNY: They're all charity concerts. I enjoy playing with nearly by the Carnegie Hall. A lot of these times background... comes from a hundred and eight musicians — Leonard Bernstein, George Szell, or William Steinberg, Alfred Walensteen, or some like that would be Heifetz. I would be pretty nearly thirty of them. Yesterday and Carnegie Hall, I've had...

NEXT: — A chat with Joey Bishop.

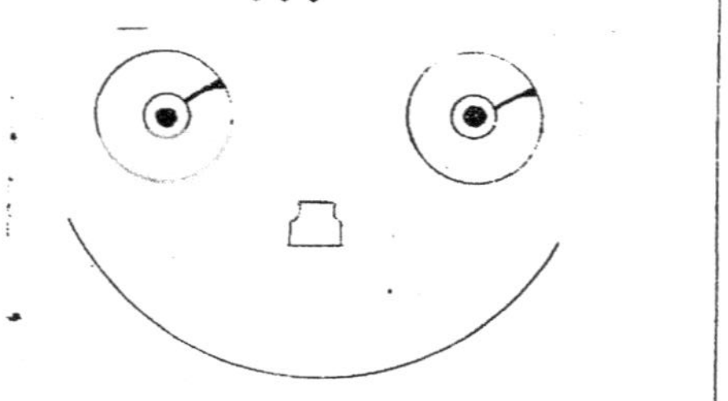

REEL—LY SPEAKING

Well summer's now upon us. There are no more club meetings now until September but our old time radio listening still goes on. Some of the shows in the club library are really great, they bring back fond memories of days gone by. When we listen to them. I can remember myself and a couple of my boyhood friends rushing home after school at St. Mary Magdalean school on Fillmore Avenue in Buffalo, our pockets full of baseball cards, marbles, a pocket knife, a real genuine Boy Scout kind, a hand ball, to be hit against the school's brick wall at lunch time. We'd hop, skip and jump over the fire hydrants while running homeward hoping to get there in time for the beginning of Jack Armstrong, (we all knew Jack's school song by heart. We all use to sing along at the introduction of the program. After Jack Armstrong we'd listen to Terry and the Pirates, Dick Tracy, Little Orphan Annie and finally Don Winslow of the Navy. After that it would be

outside for sand lot baseball till my Mom called us for supper, when dad came home from work, we'd all sit down to supper. After supper my sister and I would clear the table and start our homework while dad had that second cup of coffee and a cigarette. When the homework was done either dad or Mom would check it to see if it was all done and neatly. They didn't make us do over our error, for they was two grades ahead of me and her work was always harder. Who ever got done first got their choice of radio shows. Dad had bought us a new Zenith radio for Christmas last year and that was our family Christmas present and not much else because money was scarce then. When we got up Christmas morning and saw the radio for the first time and heard its wonderful sound, we didn't mind not getting much else! I heard the King of England give his Christmas message. Wow I really heard a king, even if it was on short wave. Anyway, back to after supper too. I even heard some of the waves early evening radio programs, and thrilled to the tune of the William Tell Overture played before the story and still do. The next day at school I knew all the guys in my class would be talking about the Ranger and his wonderful horse Silver. I don't really remember what shows came next but there was Flashgun Casey, Red Skelton, Ozzie and Harriet and how many of the shows now long forgotten? Remember The Ghost of Benjamin C. Sweet? Wow I brought that out from

CONTINUED ON AGE 15

International Jack Benny Fan Club
15430 Lost Valley Drive
Ft. Wayne, Indiana 46825

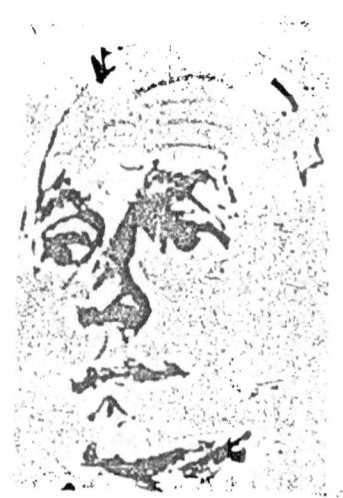

WELL!

The Jack Benny Times

Volume VI, Numbers 4-5   INTERNATIONAL DISTRIBUTION   July-October 1986

IN MEMORIAM:

Frank Nelson 1911-1986

IN MEMORIAM

I regret to inform the members that one of our most honorable honorary members, Frank Nelson, passed away on September 12. I know that many of you had met him at various OTR conventions, and I'm certain that we all feel a certain personal loss. I was fortunate enough to interview Frank for my radio programs, and found him to be a most fascinating person. I must admit that shivers went down my spine when he said, "YESSSSSS? Welll...look who's here! It's Laura Lee!" I have received many notes from various members saying how much they enjoyed talking with Frank and getting to know him. I would like to invite anyone who had known or met him to jot down a few words on your rememberances so that I may publish them in an upcoming _Times_. I'm sure I speak for the entire fan club in sending our deepest condolances to his widow, Veola Vonn; and the International Jack Benny Fan Club would like to dedicate this issue of _The Jack Benny Times_ to his memory.

PRESIDENT'S MESSAGE

Jell-o again...As usual, I have been swamped with homework, etc., and when I finally was ready to put the July-August _Times_ together nearly a month late, I was notified that Frank had passed away. I then wanted a good picture of him for the cover which delayed the issue further. When I was ready then, I realized that by the time I got _that_ issue out, it would be time for the next issue. Hence, you are receiving a "double issue" covering July to October. I hope you all will bear with me, as usual. Let me know what you all are doing these days--that's half the fun of the club!!

$$ AUCTION $$

Lately, I have received several auction lists from Paul Riseman. These auction lists contain sheet music, books, magazines, and many other paper collectibles. I have noticed several fine Jack Benny items in the lists of popular music, and I felt that some of you that are interested in that vein of Benny memorabilia would find these lists beneficial. JUST DON'T OUTBID _ME_! Write to: Paul Riseman, 2205 South Park Avenue, Springfield, Illinois 62704. Please mention the IJBFC.

¥¥WANTED¥¥

Jack Benny Christmas radio special, 45 minutes, Frances Bergen as a guest star, done in 1954 or 55. Rusty Wolfe, P.O. Box 21428, Chattanooga, Tennessee 37421.

Radio stations interested in possibly handling slowly materializing radio show with nostalgia music and OTR. For more info write Laura Lee at the address at the end of the nl.

Copyright 1989, Laura Lee

Old crayons for upcoming movie poster designer--"Rhapsody In Bloom." Jack Bloom, 8618 Stansbury Ave., Van Nuys, CA 91402.

Any tapes of The Goon Show or Bob and Ray. Yes, this one is serious even though it's not JB. What the heck...I challenge you people to find ten Goon Shows. Steven Phipps, c/o IPFW, Dept. Communications and Theatre. 2101 Coliseum Blvd. E. Ft. Wayne, Indiana 46805

μμ CONGRATS! μμ

Our condolances...er...congratulations to two members who have decided to tie the knot. Dick Smothers was married last month to a Washington socialite (does anyone know her name? I can't find it), and Rex Riffle is to be married on November 26 to a woman about whom we know nothing. Pretty sneaky, eh Rex?

Anyone else being born or getting married or anything? Is Rusty Wolfe still barbecuing ice cream? Here's a good one I heard recently. I was always taught that a woman is born, you go to school, you grow up, you get married, you die. I am not getting married--I'm not dying!

££ LENDING LIBRARY ££

Some time ago there were a few rumbles about a lending library of Jack Benny tapes. One member has already offerred to donate his shows to the library. Right now I still can't copy video tapes, so that's in suspended animation. However, I would like to get some feedback on starting such a library. What do *you* think? What could you contribute to it?

$ CONTRIBUTIONS $

Every once in a while I get a little surprise check in the mail for a donation...and I thank you most sincerely. Very often they are made out to the IJBFC. I checked into opening an accout for the fan club, however it would cost nearly as much to maintain it as the checks I would put into it. Jack Benny would surely not approve of such a move, so I must ask that if you wish to send a check, please make it out to Laura Lee instead of the fan club. Sorry for any inconvenience this may cause--our bank's a real crab.

...AND LAST BUT NOT LEAST...

If anyone has any articles on Jack that copy well, please don't hesitate to send them in for possible publication in upcoming Times.

I heard Xmas music on the radio the other evening...I'm not ready for that yet!!!

Write me!   Laura Lee, c/o   *Int'l Jack Benny Fan Club*
15430 Lost Valley Drive
Ft. Wayne, IN 46825

ain't that pretty?

"This Is Jack Benny — Who Cares?"

Condensed from Redbook

Frederick Van Ryn

How a would-be violinist became radio's most popular — and most worried — comedian

ONE EVENING in 1932 a pale, trembling man who looked as if he might faint any moment, stepped to a mike in a New York radio studio, took a deep breath, closed his eyes, and said: "Ladies and gentlemen, this is Jack Benny. There will be a slight pause while you say, 'Who cares?'"

Today, at least 30,000,000 persons care enough to listen to Jack Benny every Sunday night. About to celebrate his 11th anniversary on the air, he is the possessor of one of the best-known voices in the world. No other American, with the exception of President Roosevelt, can boast such a steady radio following. And probably most of his followers can name the leading members of the Benny cast: his heckling girl friend, Mary Livingston; his valet, Rochester; his gullible tenor, Dennis Day; his *non compos mentis* boarder, Mr. Billingsley; and his playful polar bear, Carmichael, who exists only in the imagination of Benny's script writers.

Their goings on are taken quite seriously by numbers of his listeners, who frequently volunteer advice, suggestions and help. An Iowa farmer was so touched by the plight of Rochester, who could not cure Benny's horse of the lamentable habit of sitting down in the middle of the street, that he mailed in a gadget which he described as a "cow-kicker." "I guarantee," read the accompanying letter, "that this invention of mine will make even a mule get up." Benny fans have donated cans of grease and decorative gadgets for his imaginary 22-year-old Maxwell car; even the War Production Board, presumably a hardheaded outfit, once wrote Benny asking him to contribute the Maxwell to the scrap campaign. The comedian had the dickens of a time locating a car of the right make and age, which he duly presented to the WPB while notables cheered and newsreel cameras whirred.

Success and money (he gets $17,500 per broadcast and $125,000 per picture) have brought Benny lots of things, but not what he needs most seriously — freedom from worries. He is the greatest worrier in show business. To quote his wife, Mary Livingston, Jack "lives on a steady diet of fingernails and coffee."

No sooner is one program over than Benny begins fretting about next Sunday's bill. He foresees all kinds of pitfalls and prophesies disaster. When his associates point out that a practical business concern like General Foods, his present sponsor, thinks well enough of his program to spend a lion's share of its advertising budget on it, he shakes his head. "That's what those other guys used to say," he replies, "and now you've got to put on a diving suit to find their Crossley rating."

Bright and early on Monday morning he telephones his writers, Bill Morrow ($2000 a week) and Eddie Beloin ($1000). "Any ideas, boys?" "None," they reassure him cheerfully. "Just gags." "I'm not interested in gags," says Jack irritably. "Gags die, humor remains."

He hangs up and begins biting his nails. Then he goes for a long walk. He recognizes nobody, sees nothing. Once in a while he stops and, to the amazement of passers-by, bursts out laughing. He has thought up a "situation." Unlike other laugh-provoking programs, Benny's shows are never built around gags but always around a "situation." "If your basic situation isn't amusing and believable," he says solemnly, "no amount of gags will save you."

What he calls a "situation" is really the plot. That is why his half-hour program is a short story instead of a mumble-jumble of wisecracks and smart repartee. A basically true short story, at that. When it deals with his frantic preparations for a trip to New York, he is actually about to take an eastbound train. If it's a birthday party, he is actually about to give one. "I just elaborate and exaggerate a lot," he explains. The elaboration and exaggerations invariably make Benny the butt of the remarks of all the other members of the cast.

With "the situation" determined upon, Morrow and Beloin lock themselves in a room and start work on the script. By Wednesday they have the first draft ready. Benny reads it slowly, frowning. He gets up, goes to the window and chews his unlighted cigar. The silence is unbearable. Finally Jack speaks up. He suggests changes. "He is the best editor I ever met," says Morrow. "He knows the characters in his show so well that he can put his finger on a false note at once."

At the first rehearsal, on Friday, Benny hears the actors read their lines and decides what's still wrong with the show. After that, Morrow and Beloin start rewriting the script again. They never stop polishing and blue-penciling until the program goes on the air.

Rochester's role and Jack's perennial feud with Fred Allen — two features of Benny's show of which his audience can never have enough — were both unplanned additions to

Copyright 1943, McCall Corp., 230 Park Ave., N.Y.C. (*Redbook*, May, '43)

"THIS IS JACK BENNY — WHO CARES?"

the program. About six years ago, Jack decided that he needed a colored actor to play the part of a Pullman porter on his next show. A chap named Eddie Anderson was engaged for that one performance. But Jack's public clamored for more "Rochester," and after his second radio appearance he was signed up for keeps. True to his formula, Benny always keeps Rochester in the same role. The public expects Rochester to be a valet, so a valet he is.

The Fred Allen-Jack Benny battle began just as spontaneously. Several years ago Allen decided to stage a take-off on Major Bowes' amateur program. He rounded up singers who couldn't sing, actors who couldn't act, musicians who couldn't play. One of the performers, a boy in short pants, told Allen that he was a violinist, and wanted to play *The Bee!* While the boy was scraping away, Allen recalled that the piece was Benny's specialty. At the end he commented, "Only eight and you can already play *The Bee!* Why, Jack Benny ought to be ashamed."

On the following Sunday, Benny produced four people who supposedly knew him when he was a child in Waukegan, Illinois, and who testified that he could play *The Bee* when he was six. Allen came back with some disparaging remarks about Waukegan. That started the ball rolling. Soon Benny and Allen realized that inadvertently they had stumbled across something big. But even today **they never tell each other what they are going to say.** They sometimes appear as guests on each other's programs, and Allen, an ad libber par excellence, generally gets the best of these encounters. One night when Allen took a particularly vicious verbal swing at Jack, the latter gasped: "If my writers were here with me you wouldn't dare talk to me like that!"

A silent, shy man, Benny admits that by no stretch of the imagination could he be described as the life of the party. He laughs — uproariously — at other people's jokes, but makes no attempt to top them. The fact that he is the nation's leading comedian still puzzles him greatly. He cherishes a clipping concerning his first vaudeville appearance in New York, in 1921. It says, succinctly, "We would like more violin and less chatter."

Jack, the son of a Waukegan storekeeper, started out to be a musician. While still in his early teens he played the violin in small orchestras at school dances and policemen's balls. He tried to get a job in the local theater, but the manager didn't think he was good enough and hired him as a doorman instead.

Eventually — Jack was 17, then — he teamed up with a pianist named Cora Salisbury and toured small Illinois towns in a "dumb" act — neither of them said a word.

In 1918 Jack, then 22, joined the navy. He visualized himself in an admiral's uniform. Much to his disgust, **he was assigned to play in** "Maritime Frolics," a show put on by the Great Lakes Naval Training Station. He played his violin between the acts to raise money for navy relief. For a while he was notably unsuccessful. But one night he came across with a gratifying contribution to the relief fund.

That started Jack thinking. By the time war was over he had reached two drastic decisions: he changed his name from Benjamin Kubelsky to Jack Benny and gave up his ambition to be a great violinist in favor of becoming a vaudeville performer.

There followed 14 years of vaudeville all over the country. Then one day Ed Sullivan, the Broadway columnist, bumped into him in a New York restaurant and said, "Jack, will you appear as a guest on my radio program tomorrow night?" "But I don't know a thing about radio," Jack protested. "Nobody does," said Sullivan. Mary Livingston recalls that the night preceding his air debut Jack couldn't sleep a wink and kept repeating, "Am I going to flop! Am I going to flop!"

Nine years later, on May 9, 1941, 1000 screen, stage and radio stars, producers, and heads of advertising agencies paid tribute in Los Angeles to the man they described as "the greatest radio personality in the navy world." Niles Trammel, president of NBC, announced over a coast-to-coast network that his company had decided to make Jack Benny the only individual in the history of radio "to own his own time." Seven to 7:30 p.m. on Sunday was to belong to Benny for the remainder of his life. He might change sponsors at his pleasure, but the half hour he had made the most valuable on the air was to be his for keeps.

At 49, Benny has one ambition and one fear. He would like to wind up his career as a motion-picture director and he is deathly scared lest he miss hearing a good story. Recently he entertained a few people at his home and went to bed at the stroke of midnight, pleading an early rehearsal. The others stayed up, swapping yarns. About four o'clock in the morning, somebody made a remark that provoked loud laughter. Immediately Jack burst out of his bedroom. "What was that?" he asked anxiously. "What got that laugh?"

¶ To the first contributor of each accepted item of either Patter or Picturesque Speech a payment of $5 is made upon publication. In all cases the source must be given. An additional payment is made to the author, except for items originated by the sender. Contributions cannot be acknowledged or returned, but every item is carefully considered. Address Patter Editor, Box 105, Pleasantville, N. Y.

(Patter and Picturesque Speech on pages 18 and 104)

"Could I get you to tell me the secret of your success?"... "Oh! It's a secret, eh?"

JACK BENNY GRILLS HIMSELF

By Jack Benny

HELLO, again! This is Jack Benny, the famous journalist, just returned to his typewriter after an interview with Jack Benny, the famous radio comedian. The interview? Let me set it down in detail:

"Pardon me, sir," I said, "I'm Jack Benny, the famous journalist."

"I never heard of you," he replied. "What do you want? And what do you mean butting into the studio here while I'm broadcasting? Can't you see I'm on the air?"

"I've heard of you," I replied. "You're the guy who tells the jokes on Frank Black's Sunday night program."

"Pardon me," said the great Mr. Benny. "Let me get this straight. Are you the comedian, or am I?"

"Mr. Benny," I said, "RADIO GUIDE has asked me to interview you... First, could I get you to tell me the secret of your success?"

"Oh! It's a secret, eh?" he replied. "My good man, don't you know I have five million listeners every Sunday night?"

"But Jack Pearl, the Baron Munchausen of the Air, says you have only three."

"Why, the low—— You mean he says I have only three million listeners?"

"No," I informed him. "He meant three listeners—three people."

"Hello, again!" said Benny. "This is Jack Benny speaking to you from obscurity."

"Now, Mr. Benny," I continued, "let's get down to facts."

"How far down?" he asked, "you mean you must have the low-down?"

"No," I told him, "we must keep this interview clean. Now let me explain—I'll use one syllable words so you can understand. I want facts about your life."

The blank look on Benny's face disappeared.

"I getcha," he cried.

"Well, how old are you, Mr. Benny?" I asked him.

"Off the records," he said.

"Where were you born?" I asked next.

"Waukegan, Ill."

"Do you ever think of going back there?"

"Yes!" he exclaimed, "I'm going back tomorrow! I just got a wire that my tailor's dead."

"I've heard that one before, Mr. Benny."

"I've heard that one before, too," he replied. "Wait a minute. Are you criticizing me or interviewing me?"

"I'll ask the questions," I told him. "You just answer them."

"All right," he agreed, pulling a cigar from my vest pocket. "Ya gotta match?" he asked then.

"Mr. Benny," I said, handing him my lighter, "I understand you were in show business a long time before you became a radio comedian. Tell me, what was the first role you ever played?"

"I once played the role of a sailor."

"What was your next success?"

"Well, after playing comedy in the Navy, I was booked for a vaudeville circuit on the West Coast. I was terrific. I was sensational. I was marvelous—colossal."

"What do you mean by that, Mr. Benny?"

"I mean that my act was fair."

"Well, Mr. Benny," I insisted, "it has been rumored around that you have some talent as a violinist. Did you really play the violin on the stage?"

"Sure," he declared. "Why, that's all I did."

"Why didn't you continue fiddling?"

"Well," he said, "Heifetz, Fritz Kreisler and Spalding were playing too, and the field became overcrowded. So I quit."

"According to the recent poll conducted by a New York newspaper, you are the most popular of all the radio comedians in the United States. How does it feel?"

"It's stupendous! Colossal! Terrific!"

"Oh, you're using that line again, eh? What do you mean now?"

"Just that. I really mean it. Can't I be serious once in a while?"

"How long have you been on the air?"

"Two years."

"What was your funniest and most popular show during that time?"

"The dramatic skit, 'Grand Hotel,' which is a satire on the movie, 'Grand Hotel.' Why, we had to repeat it four times by popular request."

"You mean," I said to the comedian, "that the people demanded that you repeat it four times—FOUR TIMES, Mr. Benny?"

"Must you insist on knowing the truth?" he asked.

"I must have facts," I told him.

"Well, Mr. Benny," he said with a sigh, "I see I'll have to come through and tell all. Actually, one of those Grand Hotel repeats was made because I ran short of material for a broadcast."

"What are you going to do when your broadcasts for the automobile sponsor are through?" I asked him.

"Haven't you heard? Why, *(Continued on Page 19)*

NEXT WEEK'S RADIO GUIDE

SPECIAL FEATURES

Edition will Contain a Group of Striking Articles Including

THE TRUTH ABOUT RADIO ADVERTISING

A Frank, Striking Presentation of Interest to all Listeners

BEN BERNIE'S OWN "LOOK BEHIND ME"

The Great Maestro's Whimsical Review of Milestones He's Passed

STARTLING FACTS IN CENSORING OF RADIO PROGRAMS

Revelations of Astonishing Taboos and More Astonishing Permits

AL JOLSON'S STORY OF HIS OWN HOUR

The Great Entertainer Tells About "That Ol' Debbil, Radio"

GEORGE GERSHWIN'S "SECRETS OF SONGS"

(WEDNESDAY CONTINUED)

5:20 P.M.

CBS—Jack Brooks, tenor; Eddie Copeland's Orchestra: WABC

5:25 P.M.

WRVA—Rhythm Parade

5:30 P.M.

NBC—To be announced: WEAF WTIC WLIT WGY WCSH WRC
CBS—Jack Armstrong, All American Boy: WABC WNAC WDRC WCAU WOKO WJAS WJSV
NBC—Singing Lady, children's program: WJZ WBZ WBZA WBAL KDKA WHAM
WOR—Easter Egg Dying

5:40 P.M.

WRVA—Sports Review

5:45 P.M.

NBC—Wizard of Oz, dramatization: WEAF WTIC WEEI WGY WCSH
CBS—Brooke, Dave and Bunny, songs: WABC WAAB WDRC WJAS WOKO WCAU
NBC—Little Orphan Annie: WJZ WBAL WBZ WBZA KDKA WHAM WMAL
WNAC—The Cosmopolitans, novelty quintet
WOR—Sylvia Clyde, soprano; Orchestra

NIGHT

6:00 P.M.

NBC—Xavier Cugat's Orchestra: WEAF
CBS—Buck Rogers in the 25th Century: WABC WOKO WAAB WCAU WJAS WJSV
NBC—Westminster Choir: WJZ WBAL WBZ WBZA
KDKA—Evensong
WCSH—News Flashes
WEEI—The Evening Tattler
WGY—Evening Brevities; News Items
WHAM—Sportcast
WLW—Jack Armstrong, sketch
WNAC—News Flashes; Weather
WOR—Uncle Don
WRVA—Evening Meditations

6:15 P.M.

CBS—Gene and Charlie: WJSV
NBC—Westminster Choir: WHAM
CBS—Bobby Benson and Sunny Jim: WABC WAAB WDRC WCAU WLBZ
KDKA—Sports; Program Preview
WCSH—Al Buck's Sports Review
WEEI—Gene and Glen, comedy sketch
WGY—Hank Keene's Radio Gang
WLW—Joe Emerson, tenor
WNAC—The Merry Go-Round
WRVA—Musical Program

6:20 P.M.

WCSH—Studio Program

6:30 P.M.

NBC—George R. Holmes, talk; News: WEAF WMAL
CBS—Enoch Light's Orchestra: WAAB WDRC WJSV WLBZ WJAS WOKO
NBC—Irene Beasley, contralto: WJZ WBAL
CBS—Music Box: WABC WCAU
KDKA—Studio Program
WBZ-WBZA—Old Farmers Almanac
WCSH—Randall and McAllister Program
WEEI—Musical Program
WGY—Musical Program
WHAM—Hughie Barrett's Orchestra
WLW—Bob Newhall, "Mail Pouch Sportsman"
WNAC—Jack Fisher's Orchestra; Bette Brooks, soloist
WOR—Harold Stern's Orchestra
WRVA—Current Events

6:40 P.M.

WEEI—Organist

6:45 P.M.

NBC—Your Folks and Mine, drama: WEEI WCSH
CBS—Ye Happy Minstrel and Tiny Band: WABC WCAU WDRC WNAC
NBC—Henry Burbig and the Rhythm Boys: WEAF WFI
CBS—Tito Guizar, Mexican tenor: WIP
NBC—Lowell Thomas, today's news: WJZ WBZ WBZA KDKA WLW WBAL WHAM WMAL
WGY—Musical Program
WJSV—Frank and Jim
WRVA—Dance Period

7:00 P.M.

NBC—Martha Mears, contralto; orchestra: WEAF WRC
CBS—Myrt and Marge, drama: WABC WOKO WDRC WCAU WNAC WJAS WJSV
NBC—Amos 'n' Andy: WJZ WBAL WBZ WBZA KDKA WLW WRVA WHAM WMAL
WCSH—Gene and Glenn, comedy sketch
WEEI—The Whittlin' Club
WGY—Through the Looking Glass
WOR—Ford Frick, Sports.

7:15 P.M.

NBC—Billy Bachelor, sketch: WEAF WGY WCSH WEEI WRC
CBS—Just Plain Bill, skit: WABC WNAC WCAU WJAS WJSV
NBC—Gems of Melody; John Herrick, baritone; Harold Sanford's Orchestra: WJZ WBZ WBZA KDKA WBAL WHAM WMAL
WLW—Henry Thies' Orchestra
WOR—Harry Hershfield
WRVA—Quartet

7:30 P.M.

NBC—Shirley Howard; The Jesters, Red Wamp and Guy; Milt Rettenberg, pianist; Tony Callucci, guitar: WEAF WTIC WGY WCSH WRC
CBS—Music on the Air: WABC WOKO WNAC WDRC WJAS WJSV WCAU WLBZ
NBC—Ramona: WJZ WBAL WMAL
KDKA—Charley Agnew's Orchestra
WBZ-WBZA—"Fire! Fire! Fire!" Commissioner Edward F. MacLaughlin
WEEI—After Dinner Revue
WHAM—Three of Us, girl's trio
WLW—Prairie Symphony
WOR—Jack Arthur, baritone; Orchestra
WRVA—Kiddies Radio Club

7:45 P.M.

NBC—The Goldbergs, comedy sketch: WEAF WEEI WCSH WLIT WGY WRC
CBS—Boake Carter, News: WABC WNAC WCAU WJAS WJSV
NBC—Irene Rich in Hollywood, skit: WJZ WBZ WBZA WBAL KDKA WMAL
WHAM—Blue Blazers
WLW—Studio Program
WOR—True Stories of the Sea
WRVA—Smoky and Poky

8:00 P.M.

CBS—Phil Duey; Frank Luther, Jack Parker with Vivien Ruth: WABC WNAC WDRC WJSV
NBC—Jack Pearl, the Baron, comedian; Cliff Hall; Peter Van Steeden's Orchestra: WEAF WTIC WEEI WCSH WLIT WGY WRVA WRC
NBC—Crime Clues, mystery drama: WJZ WBZ WBZA KDKA WLW WBAL WMAL
WCAU—Love Making Incorporated
WHAM—Lavender and Old Lace
WOR—Josef Ranald Hand Analyst

8:15 P.M.

CBS—Edwin C. Hill; The Human Side of the News: WABC WOKO WNAC WDRC WCAU WJAS WJSV
CBS—Irene Thompson and the Three Naturals: WIP
WOR—"The Old Theater", A. Winfield Hoeny
WRVA—Melody Mart

8:30 P.M.

NBC—Wayne King's Orchestra: WEAF WCSH WLIT WGY WTIC WRC
CBS—Albert Spalding, violinist; Conrad Thibault, baritone; Don Voorhees' Orchestra: WABC WOKO WNAC WDRC WCAU WJAS WJSV
NBC—Dangerous Paradise, dramatic sketch: WJZ WBAL WBZ WBZA KDKA WLW WHAM WMAL
WEEI—"Lady Lillian and Chet"
WOR—Lavendar and Old Lace; Musical Program
WRVA—Souvenirs

8:45 P.M.

NBC—To be announced: WJZ WBZ WBZA WBAL WHAM
KDKA—Studio Program
WEEI—Musical Comedy
WLW—Radio Court
WRVA—Forum

9:00 P.M.

NBC—The Hour of Smiles; Fred Allen, Portland Hoffa, Jack Smart, Lennie Hayton's Orchestra: WEAF WCSH WLIT WGY WLW WRVA WTIC WRC WEEI
CBS—Dramatic Guild: WABC WNAC WDRC WCAU WJAS WJSV WLBZ
NBC—Raymond Knight's Cuckoos; Mrs. Pennyfeather; Mary McCoy; Robert Armbruster's Orchestra: WJZ WBAL WBZ WBZA KDKA WHAM WMAL
WOR—"Italics"

9:30 P.M.

CBS—Guy Lombardo's Orchestra; Burns and Allen, Comedy Team: WABC WOKO WNAC WDRC WCAU WJAS WJSV
NBC—John Charles Thomas, baritone; William Daly's String Orchestra: WJZ WBAL WBZ WBZA KDKA WHAM WMAL
WOR—Harry H. Balkin, character analyst

9:45 P.M.

WOR—Willard Robison's Orchestra

10:00 P.M.

NBC—Corn Cob Pipe Club of Virginia, barnyard music; male quartet: WEAF WTIC WCSH WLIT WGY WLW WEEI WRVA WRC
CBS—Old Gold Program; Ted Fiorito's Orchestra; Dick Powell, master of ceremonies: WABC WOKO WNAC WDRC WCAU WJAS WJSV WLBZ
NBC—Vincent Lopez' Orchestra; Ed Sullivan, columnist; Frances Langford, songs; Three Scamps; Guest Stars: WJZ WBAL WHAM WBZ WBZA KDKA WMAL

10:15 P.M.

KDKA—Art Farrar's Orchestra
WOR—Harlan Eugene Read

10:30 P.M.

NBC—Tourist Adventures; Irwin Talbot's Orchestra: WJZ WHAM WRVA WLIT WRC WMAL
NBC—Ghost Stories by Eliot O'Donnell: WEAF WGY WEEI WTIC WRC
CBS—Freddie Rich Entertains: WABC WDRC WOKO WJSV WIP WLBZ WJAS
KDKA—Romance of Dan and Sylvia
WBZ-WBZA—Eventide Singers
WCAU—House Warming
WCSH—Studio Program
WLW—Zero Hour
WNAC—Will Dodge's Orchestra; Charles Cossen, tenor
WOR—A Quarter-Hour in Three-Quarter Time

10:45 P.M.

CBS—Freddie Rich Entertains: WAAB
KDKA—Nancy Martin
WBZ-WBZA—Sammy Liner's Orchestra
WCSH—Ghost Story (NBC)
WNAC—Larry Funk's Orchestra

Jack Benny Grills Himself

(Continued from Page 3)

Mr. Benny, I thought everyone knew I have had offers from two motion picture producing companies to make talkies. One was from Metro-Goldwyn-Mayer and the other was from Paramount."

"What!" I exclaimed. "You mean you haven't had an offer from Warner Brothers?"

"No," he said sadly. "I made a picture for them once."

"But radio seems to be the most important thing in your life, Mr. Benny," I continued, "and your program is the most important part of your interest in radio. What kind of humor do you think is appreciated most by your audience?"

"New," he replied simply.

"Have you tried that type, Mr. Benny," I asked.

"Oh, yes," he said. "I frequently run out of old jokes. Why, most of the time I have to write new material for my broadcasts."

"Do your studio audiences always applaud your performances?" I continued.

"Oh, yes, as a general rule. But once in a while we have to remind them. You know, audiences are apt to let their minds wander from the comedian they're listening to."

"Oh, another thing about your program, Mr. Benny. I'm sure the readers of RADIO GUIDE will be interested in this one. Is Mary Livingstone really your wife?"

"Yes, but don't you dare print that!" he cried. "It might hurt my woman fan mail."

"All right, Mr. Benny," I said. "I won't. And now, Mr. Benny, excuse me if I become personal. You set yourself up as a comedian, don't you?"

"Well—" he began.

"Don't interrupt," I cut in. "I want to know if you're really the merry fellow the people believe you are . . . the man with the trigger-action wit?"

"Absolutely," he declared. "Why, I'll bet you'll be surprised to learn that I can tell the *funniest* jokes without rehearsing more than three times."

"What are your ideas for future programs, Mr. Benny?" I asked.

"Well," he said, "I think maybe I'll do 'Way Down East'."

The interview was interrupted at this point by the appearance of a stranger.

"Better not do that one," said the stranger.

"Why not?" asked Benny. "Saaay, who are you anyway, barging in here like that?"

"Name's Harry W. Conn," said the stranger. "And I think you had better do 'I'm No Angel,' because it would be more appropriate."

"Very poor," said Benny.

"Well, you know Mary Livingstone loves to do impersonations of Mae West."

"So what?" said Benny, "I should ruin my program just to give Mary experience?"

"Well, I don't think the Down East idea is any good, either," continued Mr. Conn. "In fact, I won't have anything to do with it."

"Now, wait a minute, Conn," Benny said. "Who asked you to have anything to do with it?"

"You did," said Conn, "two years ago. And here's my contract with your signature on it. I cost you money."

"So it is . . . so it is," said Benny. "Why, now I recognize you . . . you're . . . ."

"I am," Mr. Conn said, "the only radio script writer you ever employed."

"PLAY, FRANK!" said Benny.

11:00 P.M.

NBC—Angelo Ferdinando's Orchestra: WEAF WTIC WCSH
CBS—Nick Lucas, songs; Freddie Rich's Orchestra: WABC WOKO WIP WAAB WDRC WJSV WJAS
NBC—Pickens Sisters, vocal trio: WJZ WBAL WMAL
KDKA—Sports Review
WBZ-WBZA—Weather; Sports Review
WCAU—Boake Carter, talk
WEEI—William Scotti's Orchestra
WGY—Happy Felton's Orchestra
WHAM—Recital Program
WLW—Press Flashes
WNAC—News Service; Correct Time; Local News
WOR—"Moonbeams"
WRVA—Dance Orchestra

11:05 P.M.

WLW—College of Music Concert Ensemble

11:15 P.M.

NBC—Press-Radio Bureau, News: WEAF WGY WRC WCSH WTIC
CBS—Press-Radio Bureau, News: WABC WJAS WJSV WIP WDRC
NBC—Reinald Werrenrath, baritone: WJZ WBAL
KDKA—Around the Cracker Barrel
WBZ-WBZA—Joe Rines' Orchestra
WCAU—Ben Greenblatt
WHAM—Dance Orchestra
WRVA—Ray Knight's Cuckoos (NBC)

11:20 P.M.

NBC—To be announced: WEAF WTIC WCSH WGY WRC
CBS—Little Jack Little's Orchestra: WABC WDRC WJAS WJSV WLBZ WIP WAAB

11:30 P.M.

NBC—Rubinoff's Orchestra: WEAF WTIC WCSH WGY WLIT WEEI
CBS—Little Jack Little's Orchestra: WABC WNAC
NBC—Jules Stein's Orchestra: WJZ WBAL
KDKA—Lloyd Huntley's Orchestra
WBZ-WBZA—Kay Fayre, soloist
WCAU—Louis Russel's Orchestra
WOR—Ozzie Nelson's Orchestra

11:45 P.M.

NBC—Press-Radio Bureau, News: WJZ WHAM WBAL WBZ WBZA
CBS—Dick Messner's Orchestra: WABC WDRC WNAC WJSV WIP WLBZ WOKO
KDKA—News; Orchestra
WCAU—Harold Knight's Orchestra
WLW—Rubinoff's Orchestra

11:50 P.M.

NBC—Ben Pollack's Orchestra: WJZ WHAM WBZ WBZA WBAL

12:00 Mid.

NBC—Ralph Kirbery, baritone: WEAF WTIC WGY WEEI WLIT WMAL
CBS—Claude Hopkins' Orchestra: WABC WOKO WNAC WCAU WJAS WJSV
NBC—Carlos Molina's Orchestra: WJZ WBZ WBZA WBAL WHAM
KDKA—Marty Gregor's Orchestra
WLW—Dimmick's Orchestra
WOR—Bide Dudley Reviews the New Play

12:05 A.M.

NBC—B. A. Rolfe's Orchestra: WEAF WTIC WMAL WLIT WEEI WGY
WOR—Sam Robbins' Orchestra

12:30 A.M.

NBC—Clyde Lucas' Orchestra: WEAF WTIC WEEI WLIT
CBS—George Hall's Orchestra: WABC WCAU WOKO WNAC WJSV
NBC—Harold Stern's Orchestra: WJZ WBZ WBZA WLW
KDKA—Art Farrar's Orchestra
WGY—Johnny Johnson's Orchestra
WHAM—Cato's Orchestra

1:00 A.M.

CBS—Enoch Light's Orchestra: WABC
[illegible]

. . . Discard your Aerial . . . Attach a $1 Du-Wa . . . Then, Listen to the Difference!

No static or disturbing noises, clearer reception, greater selectivity. No ugly wires to mar your room or hang out your windows. DU-WA Aerial Eliminator assures perfect reception on both long and short wave lengths. Ends all dangers of lightning storms, short circuits. Fully guaranteed.

Easy to Connect

No fuss. No bother. You can connect a DU-WA Aerial Eliminator in two minutes. Just hang it from the back of your radio. No tools are needed. Size only 8"x8¼".

SEND NO MONEY

Try It 5 Days at Our Risk

Mail the coupon. No money is necessary now. When delivered pay the postman $1, plus few cents postage. Try it out. If you're not delighted, return it in 5 days—your $1 will be refunded at once.

HENRY GOLDSMITH CO., INC.
[illegible] W. [illegible] St., New York City
Please send DU-WA Aerial Eliminator, with instructions. I will pay postman $1, plus few cents postage. If I am not delighted, I will return it in 5 days for $1 refund.
Name
Address
[illegible]

Mary Livingstone and Jack Benny celebrate is annual 39th birthday. This particular 39th, is in 1951.

Jack Benny and Mary Livingstone at the heighth of Jack's radio success

Jack Benny as a youth (above) was better on the violin than Benny the man.

Jack Benny aghast on "I've Got a Secret."

BENNY DELIGHTS IN LAUGH CHARACTERS which have been developed on his show—among the newest of which is "John L. P. Sivony," a portrayal excellently drawn by youthful comic Frank Fontaine. (CBS-Braslaff photo.)

"BENNY'S BACK!" WAS THE JOYOUS CRY heard everywhere when Jackson and his happy crew returned to their old stand at CBS. With him for his opener were Mary, TV's Alan Young, CBS vice president Howard Meighan—and, far right, "Blue Eyes."

The Secret of Jack Benny's Success

Is a Blending of the Old and New—the Anticipated Topped by the Unexpected

Sunday, 4:00 p.m., 9:30 p.m.
CBS-KNX, KCBQ, KCBS

"BENNY'S BACK!" That was the by-word around radio this fall when Jack Benny and his familiar team of laughmakers returned to the mikes for their nineteenth season. It is, at the same time, Benny's first of what will probably mount up to a comparative string of successful seasons in the new video medium. (KTTV, Channel 11, check TV logs for time and day.)

Benny is back, as always, in his familiar role of the balding, penny-pinching patsy, but his CBS Jack Benny program, as in the past, will be replete during the coming year with riotous new laugh skits, new characterizations, new guest surprises.

This indestructible quality of the great wit's character creation and a show format flexible enough for a perennial infusion of fresh idea material and talent point to the secret of his enduring and inimitable success. As radio critic John Crosby once wrote: "Benny hasn't, as is so persistently rumored, been doing the same thing for eighteen years. He wouldn't have lasted that long if he had."

Comedy situations in a Benny program season have, year after year, been marked by freshness and originality. New characterizations, his own and those of an odd assortment of fellow actors and actresses, have paraded across the script in endless procession. His guests, too, have been spectacularly impressive, as witness the case of the Ronald Colmans, who appeared sixteen times on the show.

But the program personalities, including the whimsical portrayals of regular cast members, are probably the most memorable highlights of the Benny saga. Among those who turned up last season was Frank Fontaine, a new comedian, playing a mentally retarded sweepstakes winner named "John L. P. Sivony." Mel Blanc, a regular, did a week-by-week impersonation of Al Jolson. Benny himself added another facet to his characterization, that of the naive treasurer of the Beverly Hills Beavers, a boys' club.

"Hiya Buck!"

Who doesn't remember the famous Buck Benny of the long-running "Buck Benny Rides Again" sequence? Andy Devine, whose entrance line was "Hiya, Buck!", was the chief stooge of this comedy turn. The skit ceased with the release of the Paramount film "Buck Benny Rides Again," in which Benny and most of his ribbers appeared.

Mr. Billingsley was a quaint character dreamed up and played by Ed Beloin, a former writer. A subnormal self-appointed house guest, Mr. Billingsley consistently made wry comments at the wrong time in a dry voice. Beloin, never an actor, always had Benny worried that he'd miss his cues or fluff his lines.

Another witty specimen knocked on the Benny door announcing "A telegram for Mr. Benny." The role was played by Harry Baldwin, Benny's secretary, who would glow over his laconic line with Barrymore-like pride at the end of each performance.

Mr. Kitzel, a current fabrication, is played by Artie Auerbach, former New York newspaper photographer. His "peekle in the meedle with the mustard on top" and his baseball stories are laugh toppers. Mabel Flapsaddle and Gertrude Gearshift, the Benny telephone operators, enacted by Sara Berner and Bea Benaderet, tie the program in knots with their saucy badgering of the boss.

Off and on the show have been
(Please Turn to Page 38)

November 10, 1950

Page Five

NOVEMBER 10, 1950 — RADIO-TELEVISION LIFE

Radiomites
By Norma Jean Nilsson

The proud one this week is Donna Jo Boyce, whose recent radio appearances have been on "Dr. Christian" and "Life With Luigi." Donna is still breathless with excitement as she tells of her trip back to her home town, Fairmont, West Virginia, where she made a personal appearance in connection with the Warner Brothers film, "The Breaking Point," in which she had a prominent role. Mayor Albert T. Robinson presented Donna with the key to the city, and there was a big parade in her honor, and Donna had her name on the marquee in golden lights. Even some of the big stars don't get keys to cities. Lucky Donna!

Jill Oppenheim, "Sharon Ann" on "One Man's Family," had a thrilling experience too. Jill, who will probably be a famous ballerina herself some day, was one of the privileged guests of Semon Seminoff at an "after-the-show party" which he gave for the entire Sadler's Wells Ballet. What a thrill it was for Jill to meet personally Margot Fonteyn, Moira Shearer and Robert Helpmann. It was wonderful enough to see this exquisite ballet, but to meet the stars in person and at a private party!

Gloria McMillan, who does such a grand job as "Harriet" on "Our Miss Brooks," did a different kind of a role when she was featured last week with Vincent Price in "The Saint." Gloria tells me that she's practicing real hard preparing for her very own piano concert this winter at the Assistance League. I certainly will be there to hear her play, because Gloria is a real artist at the piano.

I almost fell flat on my face when I bumped into Jerry Farber the other day. He was doing the title role of "Huckleberry Finn" on the "NBC Theater." I did a double take when I realized that this handsome six-footer was really "little" Jerry Farber. I had seen him only recently in Orson Welles' Macbeth and he looked like a little boy to me. But I guess I forgot to remember that this picture was made a couple of years ago. All you understanding directors and producers, take notice! Jerry is now willing and ready for "young man" parts, and if his past credits mean anything, you won't be taking any risks with him, that's for sure.

Jimmie Ogg, who has been in show business practically all of his young life, is really making a name for himself at the Players' Ring Theater. He is cast in all of their plays from comedy to drama to musical comedy, and turns out some top-notch performances. But Jimmie isn't the only actor in his family. His little brother Sammy makes his radio debut this week as "Little Beaver" on the "Red Ryder" show. Johnny McGovern, who was such a darling "Little Beaver" for so

Page Thirty-eight

What's New With Mel Blanc?

(Continued from Page 3)

who turn out the lyrics.

In time, Mel hopes to supplement his already crowded work schedule of radio, cartoon and record assignments with that "just right" TV role. Meanwhile, video viewers can catch him occasionally on interview shows and maybe soon again on Mike Stokey's "Pantomime Quiz."

But, however busy he is—or the busier he gets—there's one thing sure. Mel will continue to set aside his summers for Big Bear, where he keeps busiest of all—skimming the waves on water skis or in his eighteen-foot Mercury speedboat, and pulling in a handsome season's catch of trout, bass, crappie, and blue gill —a catch that proves as satisfying as the landing of any full season's choice mike roles.

The Secret of Jack Benny's Success

(Continued from Page 5)

Sheldon Leonard, Sam Hearn, Frank Nelson and many other stooges. Leonard is the racetrack tout with the soft, patronizing voice. Hearn played Mr. Schlepperman, whose greeting, "Howdy, stranger," stirred a ripple of chuckles. Nelson is often heard as the haughty floorwalker, the butler or some generally nasty type, with a mocking "yeahus" when addressed.

Benny's main foils, of course, have come in for equally hilarious typing. Tenor Dennis Day is the timid mama's boy who is always asking for his salary, and Phil Harris is ribbed as a lady-killer with a predilection for word-mangling and liquid refreshments. Rochester as the extrovert valet and chauffeur constantly befuddles the harassed Benny. Mary Livingstone is the heckling girl friend whom Benny constantly threatens to send back to the hosiery counter at the May Company department store.

The Benny-Allen Feud

Practically every important figure in show business has guested on the Benny funfest, but Fred Allen's visits have been among the most notable. Benny and Allen carried on a feud for years on their own programs. Every once in a while they crossed over for mutual calls, letting

many years, is now fourteen years old and too big for the part. Cheer up, Johnny, we all have to grow old, and there are bigger and better things just around the corner for you.

So long kids, see you next week, and remember, when there's news on your bean, call NORMA JEAN.

the quips and sparks fly at close range. "If I had my writers here," Benny once exploded, "you wouldn't talk to me like this."

To his sheer delight, the fabulous funnyman has taken the worst beating from his stooges of any comedian in radio history. Everything about him is mercilessly lampooned —his thinning hair, his baby-blue eyes, his age (thirty-nine years), his romantic attractiveness, his Maxwell, his money vault, his thriftiness and his fiddle. A few years ago his writers even dreamed up a contest in which listeners were invited to send in letters of twenty-five words or less dwelling on the theme "I can't stand Jack Benny because. . . ." More than 450,000 letters poured in. Benny reveled in the scheme.

That's why Jack Benny is the indestructible comedian, who never changes himself but keeps his show ever fresh with fun and funsters.

Worth His Weight

(Continued from Page 4)

grams, what Smart really wants is the opportunity to make "one good picture a year—exclusive of 'The Fat Man!'"

This isn't too much to hope for, particularly after more than two successful decades in the theater. On this thought Smart becomes quite positive because, in all modesty, he knows he is a good actor. (Surprising was his other admission that he didn't like his voice . . . for no reason except that he doesn't care for the sound of it).

His weight, albeit an important factor, is quite another story. Granted that it has made him a recognizable figure, J. Scott confesses the extra poundage has been a detriment to his career. Smartly, he has never played up the obvious grossness, but has relied on his acting to execute for him credits on "Theatre Guild," "Mr. District Attorney" and "This Is Your F.B.I."

Ladies' Man

Socially, he admits to being every bit as much a success as the next fellow. "I get just as many come-hither smiles from all weight divisions of the fair sex," he says with a twist of the moustache, "and my advice to women is to forget dieting and concentrate on developing personality instead." If this be the counsel that Smart himself has followed, then he most certainly has developed personality . . . a bit on the eccentric side but quite enchanting.

★ ★

CINDERELLA

Ilene Woods wears on her right shoulder a small gold slipper, the mate to which is owned by Mrs. Walt Disney. That's because Ilene's voice was "Cinderella" in the Walt Disney production.

By Shirley Gordon

"ROCHESTER'S" FRIENDS are always betting on his horses—and losing. Then "Lijero" came along. The comic's chums called him up for a tip on the horse. "He don't look so good," advised "Rochester", so his pals passed that one up. "Lijero" came in the winner, paid $65.20 on a two-dollar ticket!

Meet Eddie Anderson, Who Has Been Trying For Years to Get Jack to Put His Money on a Horse

OFF-MIKE, BENNY'S man is Eddie Anderson, a versatile fellow with a yen for sports. He's enjoying this chat with Joe Louis. (Note the champ's trunks, the Jack Benny sweater on Rochester).

Sunday, 4:00 p.m.
9:30 p.m.
NBC-KFI

"ROCHESTER!" shouts Jack Benny into an NBC microphone.

"Comin', boss!" comes the sandpaper-voiced reply of Benny's gentleman's gentleman to end all gentleman's gentlemen—"Rochester Van Jones."

At the microphone is Eddie Anderson, dusky-skinned counterpart to the rib-tickling character he portrays on the air. Your Radio Life reporter attended the Sunday afternoon rehearsal of the Benny crew one recent afternoon and, when the opportunity came, cornered actor Anderson for a chat about himself.

In an idle interval during the preliminary script readings, "Rochester" joined us in front of the footlights, settled down in one of the studio's sea of empty theater seats, squirmed restlessly and tapped his dancing feet as we plied him for a few vital statistics—such as the fact that he is local boy, born in Oakland California, on September 18, 1905.

He smiled fondly on the subject of horses, his pet off-mike interest. He has trained thoroughbreds, owns several horses running at Bay Meadows, has a twenty-acre ranch in the valley on which he keeps a half dozen mares and a stallion imported from South America. He has been trying for years to persuade Jack Benny to be a horse-owner.

Is Hobbyist

In addition to his skill with horses, Anderson is a clever mechanic and carpenter. He has a workshop in back

(Please Turn to Page 31)

Benny's Man Sunday

(Continued from Page 30)

of his home where he builds model railroads, planes and miniature racing automobiles.

"My model railroad's been packed away since the war, though," he told us. During the war, Eddie financed a friend's parachute factory. "I got a lot of publicity about it," he remarked then, "but it wasn't my idea at all."

He does have ideas of his own, however, and is holder of several patents for mechanical contrivances he has invented. His wife comments proudly, "There just isn't anything Eddie can't do."

The Andersons (Mrs. "Rochester" is Mamie Wiggins, a non-professional) live in Los Angeles with son Billy, whom Eddie says is "quite a sportsman."

Eddie himself enjoys all sports—fighting and football as well as horse-racing and raising. He goes to the movies and listens to the radio infrequently, has a phonograph collection ("that contains classics as well as hot numbers"), and likes to read ("mostly books about horses"). He has little taste for nightclubbing. "I worked in them too much," he reasons.

In school, Eddie had been encouraged to join the band. He took up the alto and had become proficient enough to play marches, but by the time he was out of school his love of rhythm and music had gone to his feet.

Was Dance Instructor

He became a dancer, and during one time he taught the art. "It's only necessary to learn the fundamentals from a teacher," he explains. "After that, you should get in front of a mirror and work up your own steps and routines. In five minutes, I can tell a real dancer from one who's been taught to dance."

Anderson's family was in show business. His mother was one of the few Negro women tight-wire artists; his father sang with the Richards and Pringle Minstrels, Howe's Greater London Circus and with Fordham's Medicine Show.

Eddie was in his early 'teens during World War I and with his brother, Lloyd, sang and danced wherever soldiers were gathered. They were spotted by Edith Sterling, cowgirl and wife of Art Acord, movie cowboy. The Acords got the Anderson boys a job in a company that was trouping from San Francisco to San Diego and back. Eddie's contribution to the show, believe it or not, was a Russian dance!

Later, Eddie's other brother, Cornelius ("Corny" for short) joined them and together the boys billed themselves as the "Three Black Aces."

It was in 1924 that "Rochester"-to-be had his first chance to read a comedy line, in a show called "Stepping High" in the town of Sapulpa, Oklahoma.

In 1935, filmgoers will remember seeing Eddie as "Noah" in "Green Pastures." A series of screen successes followed including a lead role in "Cabin in the Sky." Anderson's forthcoming film appearance is with Phil Harris in "Everybody Loves a Bandleader."

How "Rochester" Born

"Rochester" came into being when the Benny scripters wrote an episode taking place aboard the San Francisco Chief, during which Jack exchanged dialogue with a Pullman porter. An audition was held to cast the part. Eddie Anderson was the second actor heard, and the remaining four were never auditioned. Benny listened to Eddie's "Rochester" delivery, turned to his writers and decreed, "He's got it. Get him."

The listeners felt the same way about Eddie's "Rochester." The Pullman porter became Benny's "man Sunday."

Coming in on cue, at this point in our chat, Benny bellowed, "Rochester!"

"Comin', boss!" smiled Eddie, and "Rochester" stepped to the microphone again.

The Moment That Seemed Like a Year

(Continued from Page 26)

first time recently, nothing went right with the show. The theme somehow got put on in the middle of the program; the records were spun at the wrong speed; and Ruben, who is supposed to ring a gong, found he'd forgotten to put it where he could reach it. He finally managed to get to it—swung—and missed!

Often the times that an announcer wants to be particularly silk-hat turn out to be his worst moments. Jim Thomas, now producing "Rogue's Gallery" and "Murder Is My Hobby" among others for Mutual-Don Lee, will never forget the time he was once announcing a classical musical program and presented Smetanoff's "Battered Bride." And Bob Freed once ad-libbed an introduction for a very famous group of concert musicians. He got as far as "We are most fortunate to be able to present at this time the So-and So salon . . ." and then his mind blanked out. For the life of him, he couldn't think of the proper word. The seconds were ticking by and he had to say something . . . anything . . . so of all words he picked on "bunch!"

Sometimes the forces that get shows tangled up are beyond control. On a recent "Red Ryder" program, Red and Little Beaver were supposed to be in a deep, dark cave, danger lurking around every stalactite, with a dank, unearthly quiet over everything broken only by their hushed whisperings and the faint re-echoings of a few pebbles they were desperately trying not to dislodge. The scene was building itself up to a terrific climax when through the speaker in the control room came the unmistakable beat of a piano hitting out eight-to-the-bar. Engineers and producers went gray before they discovered that Harry Zimmerman and the Four Lyttle Sisters were rehearsing for "California Melodies" in the room next to the echo chamber, and the sound was leaking through.

Bloody Episode

Elliott Lewis, who plays "Archie" on "The Amazing Nero Wolfe," will never forget the time a sound man raised up suddenly under a brake drum which was being used as a gong on the program he was working. The man hit the drum such a crack that he cut the top of his head open. He stood there, dazed, the blood streaming down his face and covering his clothes. Someone stepped over quickly and took him off the stage, and the cast had to continue with the broadcast not knowing whether he was dead or alive.

Forgotten scripts can be quite a problem. Lois January got so flustered by a New York air raid that she left hers in her apartment. There was no time to go back after it; she ad-libbed her entire hour-long show, and had the pleasure of hearing fans afterward tell her it was one of the best she'd ever done.

Forgotten appointments can be a problem too. The Andrews Sisters once gave Hollywood commentator Erskine Johnson a bad time by not showing up until the program had been on the air five minutes. But the worst time Johnson ever had was when he was broadcasting on another Los Angeles station. The program preceding his had ended, Johnson was cued on by his producer, and was well into the script when he was suddenly stopped cold by the voice of the producer who had come out of the booth and into the studio.

"I can't stand this stuff night after night!" he screamed.

Johnson's eyes nearly fell out of his head, but he kept on reading.

"How can YOU read it every night?" the producer demanded.

Johnson, sure the man had gone mad, kept on, waiting for the announcer to lead him away to the wagon which must be waiting. But the announcer instead took up where the producer left off, and between them they out-screamed Johnson into the worst time he ever hopes to have. Finally, bested by their shouting, Johnson laid down his script, his radio career ended. It wasn't until they both burst out laughing that Erskine realized that the date was April first.

Mary Vs. Mrs. Jack

By Mary Livingstone Benny

MARY AS MRS. JACK BENNY, with Jack and their daughter, Joan.

WAY BACK IN 1932, shortly after my lawfully wedded spouse, Jack Benny, started to broadcast, he and his writers dreamed up a new female character for his program.

The gal was to be a Benny fan from Plainfield, New Jersey—one who was inspired by Jack's ether personality to write "pomes." She was to corner Benny, recite her poetry, tell him in a dizzy, but unabashed manner about her family, particularly about Mamma, a character who didn't share the daughter's enthusiasm for the comic.

Arrangements were made for several radio actresses to audition for the part, but none of them quite made it. Then Jack suggested I try. But I wanted no part of his radio career and no part of the microphone for myself. The mere thought of that little box frightened the living daylights out of me. I was very happy not to approach it.

"But, Doll," Jack insisted, "you've worked with me in my vaudeville act. It's not much different. Try it."

Tank Personality

He and his writers explained that unwittingly they had custom-tailored this particular gal to me. The reading they wanted was that of a fresh kid and they had always figured me a fresh kid. I didn't know whether to be flattered or insulted, but I was so darned scared I didn't have a chance to give it too much thought. Before I knew it I was playing Mary Livingstone, the "pome"-writing brat from Plainfield, with a Mamma who had a personality like a General Grant tank.

I don't think in the beginning they figured this kid would stay on the program very long. She would come in from time to time and that would be it. But somehow or other Mary Livingstone has stayed with the Benny show throughout Jack's thirteen years of broadcasting.

Things haven't changed much with that character. She is still a fresh, brash kid who heckles Benny. The poetry has disappeared except on very, very special occasions. As far as the program is concerned, Plainfield, New Jersey, is still her home and she still gets phone calls from Mamma who still has no use for Jack and who calls him a penny-pinching, no-good four-flusher. Through phone calls and letters Mary learns and tells the radio audience all about her family; about Mamma, about Papa and his various jobs, about her sister, Babe, who got her nose caught in a vacuum cleaner, and about her numerous brothers and cousins who are always in and out of jams and scrapes.

But more important, Mary-on-the radio is the slightly cynical, wise-cracking female who puts Benny in his place when he starts feeling too cocky. Also, Mary is a kind of girl friend of Jack's, certainly not his wife, because he still has his other sweethearts, like Gladys Zybysko. And Mary-on-the-radio is not above flirting with good-looking men.

Still Nervous

I was nervous when I first stepped up to the microphone. I'm still nervous. I'm all right once the broadcast starts, but I have lost none of that mike fright that first attacked me back in 1932.

I really do have a sister Babe. She's Mrs. Myrt Blum, the wife of Jack's business manager, and Jack and the writers use her name to represent that female Li'l Abner character radio sister of mine more or less as a rib. I hope nobody ever confuses my own mother with the fictitious Mrs. Livingstone of Plainfield, New Jersey, however. My own mother is not a breaking-down-doors, name-calling Amazon. She's a quiet, warm person who, contrary to Mrs. Livingstone of Plainfield, is crazy about her son-in-law, Mr. B., an attachment that is extremely mutual.

As Mary Livingstone, I function two days a week: Saturday when we have our first rehearsal, and Sunday when we broadcast. I don't work in Jack's pictures, and other than appearing with him when he goes on hospital tours and entertains at the Canteen, I am no other part of professional life.

But as Mrs. Jack Benny, I function seven days a week. I am mother to Joan, now aged eleven, who, in the process of growing up, gives us many of those nice normal problems which most parents have. She stimulates

(Please Turn to Page 9)

MARY AS MISS LIVINGSTONE, the "Pome-Reading" gal on Jack's Sunday program.

The Jack Benny Times

Volume VI, Number 6 — INTERNATIONAL DISTRIBUTION — Nov.-Dec. 1986

To all of you:

From: L. "B." L.

§§ PRESIDENT'S MESSAGE §§

WELL...after many moons, here are the _Times_ you have all been waiting on for so long! As of this writing the July-October edition is still not back from the printer's, however as you have probably already discovered I'm sending all three editions together. I hope it was worth the wait!

Now for our big blow-out issue of the year, I was fortunate enough to be able to interview one of our first honorary members, Irving Fein. I would like to thank Mr. Fein again for his time--I very much appreciate it. I hope you all get as much enjoyment from reading it as I did. Now on with the show!

*** REMINISCING WITH IRVING FEIN ***

L: ...You started out...as a publicist with several movie studios. Could you tell us a little about that?

I: Well, I was a publicist and head of publicity for various companies like Warner Brothers, Columbia and Samuel Goldwyn, and then I joined Jack Benny's company. ...I joined him as director of publicity and advertising, and we did the Jack Benny radio program, plus we did other outfits. We did a movie...and then that company was sold to CBS, which was when Jack made his historic move from NBC to CBS, and in that move...CBS at the time used to have one out of the top ten shows. Jack moved over and moved the whole rating picture over to CBS. Within a year, CBS had nine out of the top ten shows. Everybody followed Jack: Bing Crosby, Red Skelton, Burns and Allen, Edgar Bergen and Charlie McCarthy, and suddenly CBS became the big network and NBC was the smaller network. Then I became Vice-President of CBS, and I left Jack for a little while to go to New York. Jack kept calling me every two days. We talked and finally Jack said, "How would you like to come back?" I was very happy in New York, this is after about three months, and he said, "I'm sending my agent to see you to start a new company called J and M productions." He offerred me a job as President of the company. So I accepted, I left CBS and rejoined Jack--I was only away from him six months total...So I became President of his company and we produced the Jack Benny program and a lot of other programs. We were in business, and finally as Fred (de Cordova) had a company that also started to run the Benny program when I became executive producer of the Benny program on television. In 1961 we sold our company to MCA who owned Universal studios. We still had four years to go on both our contracts, and we ended up working for MCA for four years until 1965 doing the program as employees of MCA. In 1965 we left the weekly show...and we went on our own and I became his manager. Then we did a lot of specials, a special every year, plus we did public appear-

Copyright 1989, Laura Lee

ances, theatres, Broadway and so forth, and we did this until he died twelve years ago.

L: Just to backtrack a bit, you were with him since 1947, so how did you make the switch from radio to television?

I: Jack was a very careful fellow--he never jumped at things. He did it very gradually. The first year in 1950 radio was still the big thing. Television was not lucrative. Television was a losing proposition at that time. So we still had our weekly radio show where Jack was number one. We kept the radio show going every week, and the first year we did four shows for television. In those days, there was no cable across the country. In order to do the shows we used to have to fly to New York. We used the cable (there) so you could see it in four or five cities. Then they used to make kinescopes of the show and play it around the country...The second year we did six shows. We kept doing the radio show. The third year we did nine shows and still did the radio show. In order to do this, we'd do it on a hiatus. We'd film two or three films so we'd have film to break in. Then we did thirteen shows-- we were on every other week. We'd alternate with shows. We alternated with Ann Southern, and then we alternated with a show called Bachelor Father with a young fellow by the name of John Forsythe (ever hear of him?). And then after about 1960 we started to do a weekly show. We did twenty-three shows, then we did twenty-four shows, and we ended up doing twenty-eight shows.

L: So did you have many crossover scripts?

I: Oh, sure. What we did was we took some of the great radio scripts--it was silly to waste them, the great shows we had done in '47 or '49, and we reproduced them. Some of the radio scripts didn't work on television, but a lot of them were perfect for television. When we did the vault show, we went down in the vault...The Ronald Coleman show that we did on radio we did with Mr. and Mrs. Jimmy Stewart instead of Ronald Coleman.

L: So what exactly was the weekly routine for putting together a radio or a television show?

I: Well, the routine is that the writers work on the show, they'd tell Jack what they were doing and they'd kick around the idea, then they'd write the show, and then they would meet after the show was written and approved by Jack, Jack was a great editor, Jack would change some things, add some things, make rewrites and things, we would start reading it on Monday, rehearse it on Tuesday, Wednesday and Thursday and we would tape them on Friday (for television). While we were doing the rehearsing and all that, the writers were writing the next show...Then we would meet on Monday and do the final editing on the show. We had the script...written in advance, and then on Monday we would polish the script...

L: As you look back on the show itself with all the wonderful cast--Dennis Day and Phil Harris, Frank Nelson and so on...could you give us a few words about the major cast members?

I: Mary didn't like television too much, so by that time

Mary wanted to quit, so we didn't use Mary too often. She didn't do any of the live shows--she did some of the film shows. Rochester...out of the 28 shows we would use him fifteen or sixteen times. Dennis Day...(was used) five out of nine shows. Don Wilson was in every show of course, he was the announcer--even if he didn't have a role, he was the announcer. Frank Nelson was used to play certain characters when we needed him. Sometimes we'd go five or eight times without using him and then have him two or three times in a row. He played that nasty man when Jack would go in and buy something and he would turn around and say, "Yessss?" Mel Blanc we used as often as we could--he played a lot of characters. Mel played the Mexican--the "Si, sy" routine, and Mel did the French violin teacher (Professor Le Blanc), and he did the train announcer--"Train leaving on track five for Anaheim, Azusa and Cuc..amonga!" Benny Rubin used to play a lot of bits...Sheldon Leonard we used not so much in television as in radio. Sheldon Leonard played the tout...he always touted Jack on which elevator to take...

L: How were some of them...to work with?

I: Eddie...was a character...Jack Benny was one of the early guys who had no problem with race relations...In the forties, we would...play a city and the hotel wouldn't take Rochester because the hotel didn't take blacks. Jack wouldn't stay at those hotels; he'd move to another hotel...Eddie was the kind of guy who squandered his money tremendously...He had race horses...and he lost a fortune on his race horses. Then he went into boats, and he had a boat and he had a captain which cost him a lot of money. Then he started with racing cars...He wanted to race a car in Indianapolis. He spent a fortune on racing cars, so he spent an awful lot of money. When we finished the Benny show he had a stroke...and he couldn't speak as well as he used to, and he couldn't remember his lines as well--they didn't come out quite right. We usually had to cut his lines down to short sentences. We had a lot of difficulty getting him to do his roles, but he complied. After the Benny show he didn't work too much, and he ended up in not such good shape financially because he spent his money all those years.

L: Do you have any particular anectdotes that stick out in your mind from the show or any particular show?

I: Well, we had some wonderful shows...Everybody else talks about the famous, "Your Money or Your Life" routine when the hold-up man held up Jack and said, "Your money or your life." Jack didn't say a word for a while, and the guy repeated, "Your money or your life," and Jack said, "I'm thinking it over!" which was a classic line. We had one with Jimmy Stewart where Jack and a girl took Jimmy Stewart out to dinner and when the check came...Jack made a half-hearted attempt at the check, and Jimmy Stewart grabbed the check and said, "I'd feel better if you'd let me pay the check," and Jack said, "Well, if your health is concerned."...Jack Benny was going out on stage and he took his clothes off and handed them to Rochester, "I have some money in my pocket, so watch my clothes." When...Jack was out rehearsing...a telegram was delivered, and Rochester didn't have any change, so he went to Jack's pocket and took out a quarter and gave it to the telegram boy. Jack came back and reached for his pants and just held them up, shook them a little bit, turned to Rodchester and said, "Rochester, someone took a quarter out!" That was one of the biggest laughs we've ever gotten--the fact that he had all this money in his pocket and he could tell that a quarter was missing by the weight!

L: That was also rescripted for television with...Joe Besser.

I: Joe Besser did this...character, an effeminate character, and in the early days of television, the censors... asked us not to use him because of that character. They felt it was offensive...Joe Besser was a very funny guy.

L: ...Many times I'm asked by...young people, "Who is Jack Benny?"...

I: Well, he was a wonderful guy. He was the antithesis of the movie star. He was not a big person, he was just another guy. I travelled the world with him...and there was never the feeling that he was the star and I was just the little guy. We were equals, just two fellows going out. My wife used to come with us sometimes, and we'd get a bedroom and a suite, and the star would take the best bedroom, but Jack would always say, "Look, you take the good bedroom because there's two of you and I'm only one. I don't care where I sleep." One time we did a concert with the Victoria Symphony... near Vancouver. Jack raised over six million dollars for symphony funds. We played practically every city in the United States...We played with the London Philharmonic and in all the Canadian cities. When we were in Victoria, they put us up at their number one hotel...and the Queen of England had been there just the week before, and she had had the...Royal Suite...It was the most beautiful suite I've ever seen...My wife and I and Jack were ushered up to the suite, and the living room was sixty to eighty feet long. The master bedroom was...a combination of two rooms, a bedroom and a sitting room. The bathroom was a tremendous bathroom with gold fixtures...The other bedroom was on the other side of the dining room. It was a small, regular bedroom. Well, they ushered Jack into this suite and it was just magnificent. Jack looked around and said, "Where is Mr. Fein going to be?"...We all went down to our room which was fine (fein?). We were happy, but Jack said, "No, you two take the Royal Suite and I'll take the other bedroom." They were horrified. The governor of the island and the officials of the symphony wanted Jack to have that since the Queen had been there just the week before, and they kept pushing, "Jack, you should have that other one." Jack said, "No, I don't care." We ended up with the Royal Suite and Jack had the bedroom! He was just that kind of a guy.

L: Now you're working with George Burns...Any projects on the horizon for him?

I: We have about seven movies being readied, and hopefully one will come through soon. We're working on Oh, God IV, and we have a lot of other things. Jack and George were best friends for fifty-five years. That's because George never criticized Jack's violin playing, and Jack never criticized George's singing. Jack and George were completely opposite kinds of fellows. Jack Benny was sort of a sloppy guy in the sense that we'd check into a hotel and within six hours, Jack's bedroom would look like he'd been there for two months. The Kleenex would be on the floor, the newspapers would be all over the floor. His pants would be on one bed, his shoes would be on the floor, his socks would be on a chair, his shirt would be on another chair and telephone messages would be all over the place... George can be in a room for months and you'll think he just checked in. George is immaculate. George is NEAT. It's funny because I've travelled with George the same way and they are so different. Yet they grew up the same way. They were in vaudeville together, the same small towns, the same background. Total opposites of each other.

Ed. note: I'm not usually that impressed with celebrities when I meet them, but I had the great pleasure of meeting both George and Irving in 1982. I must say that of almost any person I've ever met, George Burns truly impressed me most of all. Once again, my thanks to Irving Fein, and happy birthday to George Burns!

μμ WANTED μμ

Wanted--any magazine articles such as Radio Guide and ½ hour shows on Lum and Abner. Contact: George W. Lillie, 112 - 29th St. NE, Cedar Rapids, Iowa 52402. That is what you wrote, isn't it, George?

Still wanted--first Laughs from the Past show on Jack Benny from WEHB. Contact Laura Lee at address at the end of this, and every, newsletter.

Wanted--more hours in the day. Contact Laura Lee.

DO YOU WANT--a Jack Benny classified ad? Just drop, who else, Laura Lee a note and state your classifications! *

Our thanks to Bill Oliver for a member and this issue's article.

Please send announcements, questions, requests, rumor, scandal and gossip to: Laura "Benny" Lee
Int'l Jack Benny Fan Club
15430 Lost Valley Drive
Ft. Wayne, IN 46825

Please friends, send no bombs. Thanks!

*Just don't drop,
Laura Lee!*

Beyond the deadpan: a comic confe...

By JUDSON HAND
Books Editor of The News

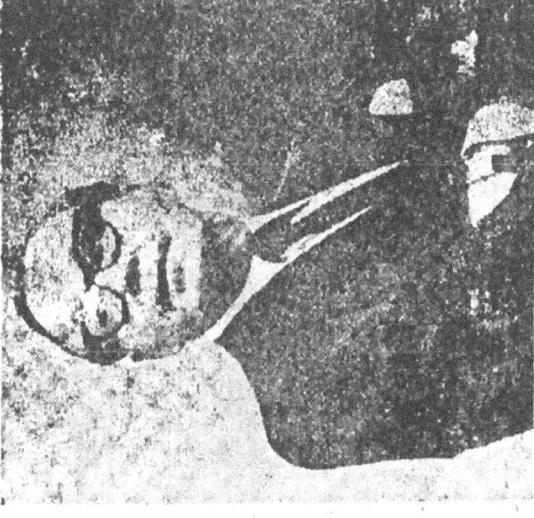

Jack Benny: the only waves in his life were ah...

PAPERBACKS

DURING THE 1930s and 1940s, you could stroll down any residential street in America at 7 p.m. on a warm Sunday, and, wafting from dozens of radios through open windows, you'd hear the same thing: The Jack Benny Show. In those days, Jack ruled as the absolute monarch of family comedy.

He always came on like a petulant tight-wad, a loser's loser, the butt of everyone's jokes. His whining delivery on radio was as familiar to most Americans as President Roosevelt's voice.

Jack's real personality, everybody knows, was far different from the one he projected in showbiz, as Irving A. Fein, for many years Jack's friend and business associate, makes clear in his biography, JACK BENNY (306 pages. With an introduction by George Burns. Pocket Books. $1.95).

In real life, Jack was generous to a fault, a shrewd businessman who always made it in the cutthroat world of show business and a perfectionist who thought about how to improve his comedy routines to the exclusion of almost all else. Once he had to ask Fein what the Watergate scandal was all about, but he never had to ask about the fine tuning of a joke or how to build Phil Harris, Rochester or Dennis Day into a comic personality on his show.

Fein's book is a comprehensive and warmhearted one because, during the 25 years he worked as one of Jack's righthand men, he was also Jack's friend. Still, in stretches, the book becomes a bit tedious because Jack had few real ups and downs in his long life. He lived a series of successes in vaudeville, radio and TV. He was married only once, happily. And, for the most part, he seemed happy with what he'd achieved. He was a comic who, apparently, never seriously yearned to play Hamlet.

Benny fans from the old days should love the book, though. It's comprehensive and full of little anecdotes which bring the man alive.

For example, in the early days, Jack faced a hooting audience at the old Academy of Music theater on Manhattan's 14th Street (today it's called the Palladium and features rock music).

"Hello folks," he said as he galloped on stage. A couple of ripe tomatoes were thrown at him. "Goodbye folks," he said immediately and disappeared off the other side of the stage and through the stage door of the theater.

Another time, he played a vaudeville show after the Marx brothers. He got no laughs and was discouraged until Minnie Marx, the mother of Groucho & Co., explained to him that her sons were so funny that no act could follow them. Jack had to agree.

Jack made the transition from vaudeville into radio with a minimum of defeat, being assisted along the way by Ed Sullivan, then a columnist for The News. On radio he achieved his finest hours.

Gradually, he and his writers built up the characters in the radio show:

Mary Livingston, played by Jack's wife as a dizzy, naive girl; Phil Harris, who pretended to be a drunken bandleader; Dennis Day, a boy tenor who was even more naive than Mary; Rochester, Jack's servant who generally outwitted him; various farout characters played by Mel Blanc and others. For all of these characters, Jack was the perfect foil.

Jack also entered into a fake feud with his pal and fellow radio comic, the late Fred Allen. On the air, the two comics would revile each other, but, whenever Jack was in New York, Fred was one of the first people he'd visit.

Not surprisingly, Jack made the transition from radio to television with little anguish. After all he'd served his apprenticeship in putting over al gags in vaudeville. His peculiar, min... alone was enough to draw laughs. People ... up to see him in person at Las Vegas ... where.

Jack never became a big movie star, though. cinema just wasn't his medium. Once he ... a standing joke on radio about how bad ... films, "The Horn Blows at Midnight," was ...

On Dec. 29, 1974, Jack Benny died. He ... 80 years old, but to his fans he would always, a young man of 39.

Fein's book is... a distinguished bio... long shot, but, like all of Jack Benny's ... lots of fun. Every real Benny...

ON RADIO

WAAT	970	WHOM	1480
WABC	770	WINS	1010
WBNX	1380	WLIB	1190
WCBS	880	WMCA	570
WEVD	1330	WMGM	1050

WNBC	660	WOV	1280
WNEW	1130	WPAT	930
WNJR	1430	WQXR	1560
WNYC	830	WVNJ	620
WOR	710	WWRL	1600

1:25—Baseball: Giants vs. Chicago Cubs—WMCA; 7:55—Yankees vs. Baltimore Orioles—WINS; Dodgers vs. St. Louis Cardinals—WMGM.

8-8:45—Watkins Committee Testimony concerning Senator Joseph R. McCarthy, as reported by newsmen (Recorded)—WABC.

8:05-9—Symphony Hall: Featuring George Gershwin's Piano Concerto in F—WQXR.

8:30-9—Walk a Mile: Quiz, with Bill Cullen—WNBC.

8:30-9—Nightmare: "Bread and Butter," superstition is the solder that binds a failing business partnership; Peter Lorre, narrator—WOR.

9-9:30—The Best of Groucho Marx (Recorded)—WNBC.

9-9:30—Crime Photographer: Casey sees through a girl's fraudulent scheme contrived "For the Family Honor," with Staats Cotsworth—WCBS.

9:30-10—The Big Story of Gene Lindsey, who unearthed clues leading to the brutal killer of a widow, with John Larkin—WNBC (Premiere).

9:30-10—Paul Whiteman Varieties: With Shirley Harmer and Bill Derpell, vocalists; Dizzy Gillespie, trombonist, guests—WABC.

10-10:30—Psychologically Speaking: "Do We Know How to Give Sex Education?"—Dr. Hugo Beigel and Otto Schlesinger, guests; Mrs. Lee R. Steiner, moderator—WEVD.

10:05-11—Gala Performances, by Arturo Toscanini, Kirsten Flagstad, Walter Gieseking, Zino Francescatti, Arthur Fiedler, Enrico Caruso—WQXR.

DAYTIME

7:00-WNBC—News; Allyn Edwards
WOR—News Reports
WABC—News; Jack Gregson
WCBS—News; Jack Sterling
WNYC—Sunrise Symphony
WQXR—New York Times News
7:05-WQXR—Bright and Early
7:15-WOR—Gambling's Musical Clock
7:28-WQXR—Weather Report
7:30-WNBC—News; Allyn Edwards
WABC—Charles M. McCarthy
WCBS—News; Jack Sterling
WQXR—Breakfast Symphony
7:35-WABC—Jack Gregson
7:45-WNYC—News
8:00-WNBC—News; Allyn Edwards
WOR—News Reports
WABC—News; Bob Haymes
WNYC—Around New York
WQXR—New York Times News
8:05-WQXR—Breakfast Symphony
8:15-WOR—Dorothy and Dick
WABC—The Fitzgeralds
WCBS—Want Ad Column
8:30-WNBC—Tex and Jinx
8:45-WNYC—Food Talks

8:55-WNYC—News Reports
9:00-WOR—News Reports
WABC—Breakfast Club
WCBS—This Is New York
WNYC—Masterwork Hour
WQXR—New York Times News
9:05-WQXR—Just Music
9:15-WOR—Gambling's Breakfast
9:30-WNBC—News; Jim Coy
WOR—The McCanns at Home
WCBS—Joan Edwards Show
WQXR—Piano Personalities
9:45-WQXR—Composer's Varieties
10:00-WNBC—Bob Smith Show
WOR—News; Martha Deane
WABC—My True Story
WCBS—Arthur Godfrey Time
WQXR—New York Times News
10:05-WQXR—Morning Melodies
10:25-WNBC—Whispering Streets
10:30-WNYC—You and Your Health
10:45-WABC—Break the Bank
WABC—When a Girl Marries
10:55-WOR—News Reports
11:00-WNBC—Strike It Rich
WOR—Florida Calling
WABC—Modern Romances
WNYC—For the Ladies
WQXR—New York Times News
11:05-WQXR—Mid-Morning Concert
11:15-WABC—Ever Since Eve
11:25-WOR—News; Queen for a Day
11:30-WNBC—Phrase That Pays
WABC—Dean Cameron
WCBS—Make Up Your Mind
Dr. Lyman Bryson, Guest
11:45-WCBS—Second Chance
WCBS—Rosemary
WQXR—Luncheon Concert
12:00-WNBC—News; Jack Lalelle

WOR—Guest Time
WABC—News Reports
WCBS—Wendy Warren
WNYC—Midday Symphony
WQXR—New York Times News
12:05-WQXR—Capital Comments
12:15-WOR—Aunt Jenny
12:20-WOR—Tall Tales of the West
WABC—George Archer
12:25-WABC—Jack Berch
12:30-WABC—Maggi McNellis
WOR—News Reports
WCBS—Romance of Helen Trent
12:45-WOR—Answer Man
WCBS—Our Gal Sunday
12:55-WNYC—News; Famous Artists
1:00-WOR—News; Jim Coy
WABC—Ray Heatherton Show
WABC—Frank Farrell Show
WCBS—Road of Life
WQXR—New York Times News
1:05-WQXR—Midday Symphony
1:15-WCBS—Ma Perkins
1:30-WABC—Boy Next Door—Music
WCBS—Young Dr. Malone
1:45-WCBS—Guiding Light
2:00-WNBC—News; Herb Sheldon
WOR—McCanns at Home
WCBS—Second Mrs. Burton
WNYC—Chamber Music Time
WQXR—New York Times News
2:05-WQXR—In a Lighter Vein
2:15-WCBS—Perry Mason
2:30-WCBS—This I Believe
WNYC—Radio Playhouse
WNYC—Symphonic Matinee
WQXR—Alma Dettinger

2:35-WABC—Martin Block's Make-Believe Ballroom
2:45-WCBS—The Brighter Day
3:00-WNBC—Welcome, Travelers
WCBS—Hilltop House
WQXR—New York Times News
3:05-WCBS—Symphonic Matinee
3:15-WCBS—House Party
3:30-WNBC—Pepper Young's Family
3:45-WCBS—Right to Happiness
WCBS—Mike and Buff's Mailbag
4:00-WNBC—One Man's Family
WOR—In the Mood
WCBS—Edward R. Murrow
WCBS—Galen Drake
WOR—News Reports
WQXR—New York Times News
4:05-WQXR—Stella Dallas
4:15-WNBC—Young Widder Brown
WCBS—Lanny Ross Showtime
4:45-WNBC—Listening—Jacques Fray
5:00-WNBC—Woman in My House
WQXR—Just Plain Bill
WOR—Bobby Benson Show
WCBS—John Henry Faulk
WNYC—Music From the Campus
WQXR—New York Times News
5:05-WQXR—Cocktail Time
5:15-WNBC—Lorenzo Jones
5:30-WQXR—Front-Page Farrell
WNYC—London Column
5:45-WNBC—It Pays to Be Married
WNYC—Air Warden Service
Report; News
5:55-WOR—Cecil Brown—Comments
WCBS—This, I Believe

EVENING

6:00-WNBC, WOR, WCBS—News
WNYC—Little Symphonies Concert
WQXR—New York Times News

6:05-WQXR—Dinner Concert
6:15-WNBC—Sports Daily; Mel Allen, Russ Hodges
WOR—Dorothy and Dick
WCBS—Curt Massey Time
6:25-WQXR—Time for Music
6:28-WQXR—Weather Reports
6:30-WOR—News Reports
WCBS—Herman Hickman Show
WNYC—French Press Review
WQXR—Dinner Concert
6:40-WCBS—Weather Report
6:45-WNBC—Three-Star Extra
WOR—Sports; Stan Lomax
WABC—Sports; Bill Stern
WCBS—Lowell Thomas
WNYC—Weather; U. N. News
7:00-WNBC—Intermezzo
WOR—Fulton Lewis, News
WABC—John W. Vandercook
WCBS—Tennessee Ernie Ford
WNYC—Masterwork Hour
WQXR—New York Times News
7:05-WQXR—On Stage
7:15-WOR—Today's Business News
WABC—Quincy Howe, News
7:20-WOR—The Answer Man
7:25-WQXR—Weather Report
7:30-WNBC—News Reports
WOR—Gabriel Heatter
WCBS—The Choraliers
WQXR—Switzerland—Music
7:45-WNBC—One Man's Family
WOR—In the Mood
WCBS—Edward R. Murrow
WOR—News Reports
7:55-WABC—News Reports
8:00-WNBC—Treasury of Stars
WOR—Squad Room
WOR—Watkins Committee Testimony (See Box)
WCBS—F. B. I. in Peace and War—Drama
WQXR—Symphony Hall (See Box)
8:15-WNBC—Frank Sinatra Show
8:25-WCBS—News Reports
8:30-WNBC—Walk a Mile (See Box)
WOR—Nightmare (See Box)
WCBS—21st Precinct: With Everett Sloane
WQXR—Alice Morgenthau Collection Program
8:45-WABC—Jack Gregson
8:55-WCBS—News Reports
9:00-WABC—The Best of Groucho Marx (See Box)
WOR—News: The Man From Times Square
WABC—Sammy Kaye's Serenade
WCBS—Crime Photographer; With Staats Cotsworth
WNYC—Mission to the Middle East—UNESCO Series
WQXR—New York Times News
9:05-WQXR—Panorama: The Measure of Ernest Bloch; An Illustrated Appraisal
9:25-WOR, WABC, WCBS—News
9:30-WNBC—Big Story (See Box)
WABC—Paul Whiteman Varieties (See Box)
WCBS—Jack Carson Show
9:55-WCBS—Robert Trout, News
10:00-WNBC—Fibber McGee and Molly
WABC—Harry Flannery, Comments
WCBS—Mr. Keen
WNYC—Municipal Concert Hall
WQXR—New York Times News
10:05-WQXR—Gala Performance (See Box)
10:15-WNBC—Heart of the News
WOR—Spotlight Story
WABC—Helen Hall Show
WCBS—Lenny Herman Orchestra
10:25-WQXR—Weather Report
10:30-WNBC—News; Stan Freeman
WABC—The Cisco Kid
WABC—G. H. Combs
WCBS—Melody in the Night
WNYC—Sports—Harry Wismer
WQXR—Sports (FM to 3)
10:55-WOR—News Reports
11:00-WNBC, WOR, WABC—News
WQXR—The Choraliers
WQXR—New York Times News
11:07-WQXR—Music for Orchestra
11:15-WNBC—Joe Hazel—Sports
WOR—John Gambling Show
WCBS—Dwight Cooke's Guest Book
11:20-WNBC—Tex and Jinx
11:30-WCBS—Galen Drake
11:45-WOR—Air Lane Trio
WCBS—Waner Orchestra
11:55-WNBC—News Reports
12:00-WNBC, WOR, WCBS—Dance Music
WCBS—Music 'Til Dawn
WQXR—New York Times News
WQXR—Walk a Mile (See Box)
12:05-WQXR—The World of Music
1:00-WOR—Mr. Midnight

FM Schedules

WFUV	90.7
WNYC	93.9
WABC	95.5
WQXR	96.3
WNBC	97.1
WEVD	97.9
WMGM	100.3
WCBS	101.1
WQHF	101.9
WWRL	105.1

The New York Times NEWS BULLETINS every hour on the hour 7 A.M. to midnight over WQXR (1560 on your dial) WQXR—FM 96.3 mc. (on FM set)

New York Times Wed. Sept. 8, 1954

For Immediate Release:
January 19, 1987

Media Contact:
Lynn Breger - 312/623-1040

TAKE THE TRAIN TO THE TRIBUTE

For several generations, Americans were entertained by Jack Benny, the perpetual 39 year old comedian from Waukegan, Illinois. Now Benny's hometown will celebrate his Valentine's Day birthday weekend: February 13-15, 1987.

The 3-day celebration will feature a variety of entertainment for young and old. At the Waukegan Public Library, Benny fans can enjoy Benny films, audio and video tapes, and a Benny memorabilia exhibit. The Lake County Camera Club will also sponsor a "Benny Blue Eyes" contest with prizes in three age categories: under 12, 13-38 years old, and 39ers (no one in Waukegan is over 39!!).

At the YWCA, you can attend a Benny radio-listening party hosted by Carl Amari of WJKL/94.3 FM. The Valentine bake sale by the Waukegan Woman's Club will include an auction of "man-made" pastry. And don't miss the "Model-T" versus the Maxwell - a vintage fashion show and afternoon tea!

Only Waukegan area McDonald's restaurants will offer the regular hamburger as a 39¢ special "Benny burger" on February 13-15, 1987.

Benny Boosters ($39 donation) will receive a "39 Again Birthday" button to wear for admission to the gala reception on Saturday night for Joan Benny, Jack's only daughter. Entertainment will be provided by the Benny String Ensemble and the Waukegan Chamber Singers.

Benny fans from Chicago and Milwaukee should take Metra to the Tribute. A roundtrip from Ravenswood station is just $3.90 roundtrip for groups of 25 or more. And Benny Center violin students will provide a musical welcome. So for an "Anaheim, Azuza & Waukegan" adventure, take Metra to the Tribute.

SCHEDULE OF EVENTS

Location

Friday, February 13

12:30 P.M.	Press Conference for Joan Benny with community representatives	County Building 18 N. County St.
2:30 P.M.	Opening of Benny Memorabilia Exhibit	Waukegan Public Library 128 N. County St.
3:30 P.M.	Benny Film: "Horn Blows at Midnight"	Waukegan Public Library
8:00 P.M.	Commemorative service for Jack Benny	Cong. Am Echod 1500 Sunset Ave.

Saturday, February 14

10:00 A.M.	Benny Film: "To Be Or Not To Be"	
9-5:00 P.M.	Videos of Benny TV appearances	
9-5:00 P.M.	Benny Memorabilia Exhibit	Waukegan Public Library 128 N. County St.
1-3:30 P.M.	"Benny Blue Eyes" Contest by Lake County Camera Club	
2:00 P.M.	Benny Film: "Horn Blows At Midnight"	
10-1:00 P.M.	Valentine Bake Sale by Wkgn. Woman's Club "Man-made" pastry auction (Noon)	
1:30 & 6:30 P.M.	Radio-listening Party with Carl Amari	YWCA 445 N. Genesse St.
3:30 P.M.	"Model-T" vs the Maxwell (Vintage Fashion Show)	
7:30 P.M.	Reception for Joan Benny ($39 donation) Entertainment by Benny String Ensemble and Waukegan Chamber Singers	Benny Center Bowen Park

Sunday, February 15

10, 2 & 5:00 P.M.	Benny Film: "Charlie's Aunt"	Cong. Am Echod 1500 Sunset Ave.
1-5:00 P.M.	Benny Memorabilia Exhibit Benny Audio & Video tapes Benny Film: "To Be Or Not To Be"	Waukegan Public Library 128 N. County St.
1-5:00 P.M.	"Benny Blue Eyes" photo exhibit Judging at 3:00 P.M.	Waukegan Public Library 128 N. County St.
1:30 P.M.	Radio-listening Party with Carl Amari	
3-4:30 P.M.	Valentine Bake Sale by Wkgn. Woman's Club	YWCA 445 N. Genesee St.

FOR MORE INFORMATION: Lynn Carol Breger, Tribute Coordinator
515 West Madison St. Waukegan, Il 60085

The Jack Benny Times

Volume 7, Number 1   INTERNATIONAL DISTRIBUTION   January-February 1987

Festival *Happy birthday, Jack!*

39 Again?!   Issue!

PRESIDENT'S MESSAGE

Jell-o again and welcome to another issue of the <u>Times</u>. As most of you know, the International Jack Benny Fan Club celebrated its seventh anniversary on January 1. Applause to each and every member; <u>you</u> are the ones that give the club meaning and the spirit to keep going.

As you have probably already noticed, we have slightly altered our printing format to cut the cost to you. Unpaid members please note the enclosure--it is quite important.

This issue is devoted to the "39 Again Jack Benny Festival" which took place in Waukegan on February 13-15. It was quite a surprise to me, but that's another story (see Festival Summary). On a different note, I, as many, was saddened by the news of the passing of Liberace. What does this have to do with Jack, you ask? Well, if you ever happen to see a copy of Liberace's book <u>The Things I Love</u>, turn to page 193-- there is a hilarious picture of Jack. The rest of the book is also fascinating.

Anyone looking for a particular Benny item? If so, drop me a note for a Jack Benny classified ad in an upcoming issue. Now on with the show!

NEW MEMBERS

Welcome all you new members! Because of the large number of newcomers and lack of bio information, we will simply list the names. Please refer to TTL for addresses.

ELLEN BARKERWILSON E. RYDER***TIM "WHATZISNAME" HOLLIS
KEITH SCOTTJOHN SHORES***JOHN DiFRANCESCO
STEVE SCALZOYOSEF BRAUDE***HAL BOGART***BRUCE BOGART
MAYNARD NEWMANJACK MELCHER***JOHN MALONE
HARVEY STARKOFFSTEVE SMITH***KIMBERLY SMITH
HOWARD JOYCEMARY JOYCE***RICHARD H. EVERILL
DEANA EVERILLJAMES EVERILL***RICHARD B. EVERILL
LeROY F. FILLENWARTHMARILYN FILLENWARTH

<u>New Honorary Members</u>

****PHIL HARRIS****DENNIS DAY****MEL BLANC****JOAN BENNY

!! TAPE TRADING LIST !!

Yes, here it is--the one for which you have all been waiting. If you are not on this list or would like to be, or if you are on this list and would not like to be, er...uh...whatever, write and let me know!

Ellen Barker, P.O. Box 1402, Reseda, California 91335; also looking for Lone Ranger

Copyright 1989, Laura Lee

Jack "Picasso" Bloom, 8618 Stansbury Avenue, Van Nuys, CA 91402

Hal Bogart, 2029 Aldersgate Drive, Lyndhurst, Ohio 44124

Yosef Braude, 25 Longhorn Road, Providence, Rhode Isand 02906

Rob Cohen, 655 Brice Road, Reynoldsburg, Ohio 43068

Richard H., Deana, James and Richard B. Everill, 1558 Knox Dr., New Haven, Indiana 46774

Andrew Haskell, 160 West 39th Avenue, Vancouver, British Columbia V5Y 2P2, Canada

Howard and Mary Joyce, 1050 Locksley SW, Grand Rapids, Michigan 49509

Laura Lee, 15430 Lost Valley Drive, Fort Wayne, Indiana 46825

John Malone, Rural Route #2, Wee-Ma-Tuk, Cuba, Illinois 61427

Bill Oliver, 516 Third Street NE, Massillon, Ohio 44646

Lewis A. Pearson, 240 Ridge Drive, Marion, Iowa 52302

Michael Pointon, 11 Kings Court, Kings Road, London SW19 8QP, England

Keith Scott, 4 Bellbird Crescent, Forestville 2087, N.S.W. Australia

Joyce Shooks, P.O. Box 307, Sparta, Michigan 49345

Steve and Kim Smith, 1945 Coit NW, Grand Rapids, Michigan 49505

Steve Szejna, 3334 South 15th Street, Milwaukee, Wisconsin 53215

James E. Treacy, Jr., 5395 Petersburg Road, Dundee, Michigan 48131

WOW, whatalist!

FESITVAL SUMMARY

One snowy day about the middle of January I was just getting ready to plow out the driveway. Then I got a collect call from Waukegan. Surprise! Did you know that there is a festival going to be held? No, really?! Thus with a quick bit of shuffling about, material on the fan club was donated to the JB memorial exhibit, and the schedule of events was enclosed with the last newsletter.

A whirlwind weekend in Waukegan was just the thing for the winter blahs. Press conferences, exhibits, movies, a talent show, a memorial service and many other events helped to make the three days eventful ones. Thanks to those members who were able to make it there.

For me, the highlights of the weekend were speaking at Am Echod, the synagogue which was founded by Jack's father, and presenting an honorary membership to Joan Benny, Jack's daughter (contrary to the press release which stated she was his sister!). I was fortunate enough to spend some time chatting with Joan about her current activities and, of course, about her father.

Did anyone hear All Things Considered on Feb. 14th? They (National Public Radio in Washington) spent about a half hour interviewing me for that show, but nobody, including me, seemed to hear it. The Los Angeles Times also interviewed both Joan and me, but I haven't seen that, either. Did anyone else? If so, I'd like a copy.

We stayed at the TravelLodge in beautiful downtown Waukegan. All nice people--(312) 244-8950 for reservations if you happen to be dropping by (or 800-255-3050). As ever, it is impossible to thank everyone properly, so let's give it the once-over. Thanks to: Jim for the super tour of the Genessee, another big higlight! The pictures are great-- you'll get copies soon! Lynn S. for the tour of JB Junior High--I'll write as soon as I get your address! Dave for flying all the way from Arizona, Mike for being a good kid, Lance for keeping me from eating Saturday (REALLY thanks--ask my mother--she did eat), Joan again for being a great gal, Carl for your help--let me know if any stations are interested!, Carl's fiancée for putting up with my chatter, the YWCA for helping us in many ways, all the reporters who made me feel important (as if I wasn't egotistical enough), the woman who kissed my hand, Judge Breger for dating my mother, the "residents" at the TravelLodge for being patient with us at 12:15a.m., Mike's parents for a great cup of tea, the librarians for not yelling when I threw the phone in the trash can, the cute baby for being photogenic, the car for breaking down, Am Echod congregation for making my talk so enjoyable to do, the waitress who wouldn't bring our dinner, the wind for freezing Mom's diet Coke, and all those who helped make it so enjoyable for me! THANK YOU!!!

§§ WATCH THIS SPACE §§

Watch this space for the first big undertaking of the IJBFC which will require everyone's help--including YOURS!

μ ARTICLES μ

In this issue are two articles: one from the News-Sun of Lake County and the other from the Chicago Sun-Times. There were so many articles written on the festival that it would be impossible to print them all. However, many of you know that there was an extensive article on me sent on the AP teletype. If anyone is interested in it and has not seen it, send me a letter and I'll send a copy. Thanks Andrew! You did a great job!

Back issues are 50¢ as always.

Send questions, comments, corrections, additions, etc. to:
Laura "Benny" Lee, c/o ⟶ *Int'l Jack Benny Fan Club*
15430 Lost Valley Drive
Please, friends, send no bombs.   *Ft. Wayne, IN 46825*

OH, AND...

We have a VERY LIMITED QUANTITY of buttons and flyers from the festival. If you would like to have one (button and flyer), they are $1.50 each. Please send monies to the above address.

Also, we would like to thank Irving Fein for providing us with a copy of the letter below as the coordinator of the festival refused us a xerox of the original. Thanks, kid!

GEORGE BURNS

December 18, 1986

TO THE JACK BENNY FAN CLUB

I understand you kids are paying a tribute to Jack, so I thought I'd drop you a little note.

Jack and I were friends for 55 years, and I miss him. Not only I miss him, we all miss him. And I'll let you in on a little secret, he was really older than 39 -- much. And I'll tell you something else, he wasn't the cheapest man in the world. Jack Benny threw money around -- not very far, but we won't go into that.

Jack Benny was a great comedian. He made the whole world laugh, and I made him laugh. Like we were having lunch once at the Brown Derby restaurant, and Jack said, "I'm going to have cream of wheat", and I said, "I'm having bacon and eggs."

Jack said, "I hate cream of wheat," and I said, "Then don't order cream of wheat."

He said, "But Mary said cream of wheat is good for me."

I said, "Then let Mary eat cream of wheat."

Jack said, "I love bacon and eggs," and I said, "So order bacon and eggs."

"Mary said bacon and eggs are bad for me."

"Tell Mary not to eat bacon and eggs."

Then the waiter came up, and I ordered bacon and eggs. Jack said, "I'm going to have bacon and eggs, too."

So I said to the waiter, "After we have our lunch, give Jack Benny the check."

Page -2-

Jack said, "Why should I take the check?", and I said, "If you don't take the check, I'll tell Mary you had bacon and eggs."

That's when the world's greatest comedian laughed so hard he fell on the floor.

Another time I was at the country club having lunch, and Jack came in. Instead of saying, "Hello, George," he said, "I didn't sleep last night."

I said, "Jack, how did you sleep the night before?", and he said, "The night before I slept great."

I said, "Then sleep every other night."

The world's greatest comedian was on the floor again.

Everybody looked up to Jack Benny. I couldn't, he was always on the floor.

Well, kids, I'm sorry I can't be with you, but I hope your festival is a big success.

Best,

George Burns

News-Sun 2-14-87

Autographed, no less!
Joan Benny

Still '39'
Benny love in bloom again

By Tony Gordon
Staff Writer

Jack Benny's daughter, Joan Benny, opened the weekend-long "39 Again Birthday Celebration" Friday afternoon at a press conference in the Lake County Building in Waukegan by donating mementoes of her late father's career to Jack Benny Junior High School.

Benny gave Robert Tabor, principal of the school, a brass plaque stamped with the comedian's name that had once marked his dressing room at the London Palladium and a collage of theater lobby cards advertising four films he appeared in. The items will be displayed at the school.

She told a crowd of about 20 people at the press conference she hopes to add items to the school's collection, such as a copy of a letter to her father from President John Kennedy, thanking the comic for his efforts as the emcee of a birthday party held for the president at Madison Square Garden in New York, and one of the four Emmys he was awarded by the National Academy of Television Arts and Sciences.

Also at the conference, Joan Benny was given resolutions passed by the Waukegan City Council and the Lake County Board recognizing her father's fame and the events set for this weekend. She was also made an honorary member of the International Jack Benny Fan Club by that group's president, 17-year-old Laura Lee of Fort Wayne, Ind., who has legally changed her middle name to Benny. ✱

The tribute was organized by Lynn Breger, a publicist from San Francisco
Continued on Page 7

✱ not my legal

New column begins in Sports

A new column makes its debut today in the Sports Weekend section.

"Offside" features notes, quotes and anecdotes from the Lake County sports scene.

Offside is a Sports Department contribution to the newspaper's family of popular columns which include Inside and Sunny Side.

Jack Benny's daughter, Joan Benny, opened this weekend's "39 Again Birthday Celebration" in Waukegan.

News-Sun Photo by Jonathan Daniel

Jack Benny fan looks at old clippings of the comedian at the Waukegan Public Library.

News-Sun Photos by Jonathan Daniel

Joan Benny licks some icing off her fingers from the "39 Again" birthday cake.

Benny

Continued from Page 1

who once lived in Waukegan. Breger said she expected thousands of out-of-town visitors to attend the events this weekend, which marks what would have been Benny's 93rd birthday today.

Breger said Benny was a man who, "regardless of how high his star rose or how much his fame grew, always had a part of himself in Waukegan," where he lived until he was 17 years old.

Showings of Benny's films, receptions for his daughter, bake sales and radio listening parties are among the events scheduled for the weekend at the Public Library, the YWCA and at the Benny Center in Bowen Park.

A Jack Benny exhibit at the library was unveiled Friday following the press conference. It contains reproductions of letters to the comic from George Burns and others, copies of The News-Sun from June 1936, when the world premiere of the Benny film "Man About Town" was held at the Genesse Theater in Waukegan, and items from Benny's days in the city.

2-13-87

Benny's '39 again for Waukegan gala

By John Jeter

"The show itself is the important thing. As long as people think the show is funny it doesn't matter to me who gets the punch lines." Jack Benny

Like the man being honored this weekend, Lynn Breger deflected questions yesterday about herself. She preferred to talk about the comedian, violinist, cheapskate and Waukegan's favorite son.

Jack Benny, who was born Benjamin Kubelsky in 1894 and who died in 1975, at 39 because that's the age he kept telling people, will be honored throughout the weekend at the Breger-produced "39 Again Birthday Celebration."

Breger is, uh, 39 years old.

"Gee, I'm from Waukegan," said the San Francisco-based publicist and die-hard Benny fan who owns the Write Image, a copywriting and publicity firm.

"My grandfather worked for Jack's dad, my dad took violin because Jack took violin. Jack's humor still sustains me," she said. She just hopes it will sustain the eventful weekend.

The kickoff is 12:30 p.m. today, the day before Benny's Valentine's Day birthday, and will feature the comedian's daughter, Joan, of Beverly Hills, Calif., arriving at the Lake County Building in a 1941 Packard.

The celebration, which ends Sunday, promises to be a good one for Benny's adopted daughter. She will be inducted into the 200-odd member International Jack Benny Fan Club and will be the honored guest at a Benny-

gala reception. It's at 7:30 tomorrow night in Bowen Park, with entertainment by the Waukegan Chamber Singers, and it will be open to those who donated, uh, $39 or more.

Laura Lee, a 17-year-old sophomore at Purdue University's Fort Wayne, Ind., campus, can't wait. She is fan club president.

In a telephone interview from Fort Wayne, she spoke of Benny as if he were still 39.

"The popularity of the show was really because Jack's character had so many different facets that you could either see in yourself or you could see in a friend or a relative," she said. "He enabled you to laugh at those facets of your character."

"I'm happy to see something come up like this with Jack Benny," she said of the event, which some quarters of the city aren't as happy about.

A woman who answered the phone at one organization asked that neither her name nor her agency be used because neither wanted anything to do with the whole thing.

Dana Domerchie, administrative assistant to Waukegan Mayor Robert Sabonjian, said of Breger, "We found her rather difficult to work with, and the profits were going to her. ... She couldn't tell us where the money would go."

Breger says she stands to lose the $5,000 she sunk into the project, but she doesn't want to lose any friends.

"When you cause local trouble, that's not a good thing," said Breger, who added that in high school she once interviewed Benny.

Int'l Jack Benny Fan Club
15430 Lost Valley Drive
Ft. Wayne, IN 46825

WELL!

The Jack Benny Times

Volume 7, Number 2   INTERNATIONAL DISTRIBUTION   March-April 1987

A Picture's worth a thousand words!

** PRESIDENT'S MESSAGE **

Jell-o again...better late than never. There are several reasons why the <u>Times</u> is a little late, but who cares. It's here now! Hopefully lots of things will happen in the coming month and there will be lots to write about in the May-June issue. Anyhow, first let me give the biggest <u>THANK YOU</u> possible to all you members out there who responded to the notice in the last issue for the subscription fee. The response was even more than I had expected, and I hope that the following issues will make it worthwhile. By the way, I can't locate two members. (Sounds fishy, eh?) If anyone has current addresses for either Pat Mechling or Phil Baird will you please let me know? Thanks.

I feel that this issue will be the one that really will start things in motion (I hope!). We have two major projects in the works, and we need <u>everyone's help</u>. These will be described in detail in a few minutes. Also, we are enstating a new "column" in the newsletter for your favorite scenes. In SPERDVAC's radiogram someone recommended that people send in their favorite jokes from old radio to share with the other readers. We thank Ken Weigel for sending us his to start it.

Two more "thank yous" before we start. I gave a talk on OTR comedy at the Indiana Historical Radio Society annual banquet on May 2nd, and the audience was magnificent. Thanks folks, I couldn't have done it without you! Also this evening, Dave Hinman from WMT interviewed me for his show. Thanks, kid...I really enjoyed it! Thanks also to George for all the kind words. If I'm back on the air, you probably won't even have to pick up the phone to hear me when I find out about it! Now on with the show!

¥¥ WE WANT YOU!!! ¥¥

Thanks Jay for all the help and advice. Now let's see if we can put these things over with a bang! The first activity should be credited to Mike Kirsling in Waukegan who loaned me the UCLA Jack Benny Checklist. This list was made around 1970 and lists radio and television shows that Jack did, plus books and magazine articles written about him. Being that this list is seventeen years old, it is quite out of date and incomplete. What we need is an up-to-date list which is as complete as humanly possible. This would include as perviously mentioned, radio and TV shows of Jack's and books and magazine articles on him. This list could be sold to interested parties with the funds going to financing future endeavors of the club (perhaps a convention!). I have the ultimate JB radio log and two television logs to meld together for the first parts, but we need your help for the magazines, etc. If you have a small pile of articles on Jack around, it would be very helpful if you could take a minute to copy down either the title or author or each article. If it is a large pile, then just drop me a note we will see what information we need. Even if there is only a chapter of a book on Jack, we need that, too. Also, any radio and TV shows that Jack guested on outside of his regular series should be noted. In short we want EVERYTHING!

Here is the second endeavor. I know that many of you have been awaiting this announcement for some time, so here it is. I think I only need to say two words: tape library. Yes, at long last we are going to start a tape library. I now have some access to dubbing equipment. Firstly I must say that for the moment, we only need audio tapes. You needn't run to your players and start madly taping shows right now...too much possibility for duplication. All I need are the dates of the show or a short description of the plot. Tim, I already have yours somewhere! Anyhow, as before, if you have a minute, just jot the dates and drop them in the mail--we'll consolidate these and contact you. The actual practice for loaning out tapes has not been established in stone as of yet, but as soon as all the bugs are worked out, we will give you the full report. (Bugs... could that possible be the bee?!) (Or the ant, Jack?) Any questions? Just write to the address at the end of the letter.

§§ TRINKETS §§

We have had three generous offers for Jack Benny memorobilia. Firstly, Tristar, Inc. manufactures "39 and holding" buttons, magnets, keychains, mugs, balloons and cards. They are white prining on a black background. The buttons, magnets, keychains and mugs are self-explanatory. The balloons say "Happy 39th and Holding," and the cards have "39 &" on the front and "holding" inside. Being that we don't have a retail license, we must pay the retail for these. However, that's alright because there is a minimum order of $75.00 and we get there faster! SEND NO MONEY NOW.

The Lioness Club of Waukegan has a lovely pin with a Maxwell on it. It says "Waukegan, Illinois...Birthplace of Jack Benny" around the perimeter. They are very handsome and well-made. They are $2.25 apiece--let me know if you are interested and I'll contact them.

The Collectors' Book Store in Hollywood has a few press books that are uncut and original scripts from some of Jack's movies. I'd give my arm for these myself, but they are $90.00 apiece. My heartiest congratulations to the takers of these.

As ever, we have the Jack Benny festival buttons and flyers for $1.50 per set. If you are interested in any of the above except the CoBS items, contact me at the address at the end of the newsletter. (The prices vary on the Tristar items, so just ask for a price list. They are quite reasonable, though.) For the press books and scripts contact:

Malcolm Willits, c/o The Collectors' Book Store, 1708 North Vine Street, Hollywood, California 90028.

!! FAVORITE SCENES !!

From K.W.:
One of my favorite Benny "bits" is the one where a panhandler (played by Frank Fontaine) asks him for a dime and Benny gives him half a dollar. Back at the house Rochester is putting away dishes and Jack tells him about giving the bum 50¢ and crash! go the dishes on the floor.

Jack: Rochester, why'd you drop those dishes? All I said was I gave a man 50¢. (sound of dishes crashing to the floor)
Rochester: I didn't touch 'em! They jumped off by themselves!

Later as Jack retires for the night he writes in his diary:
Jack: Dear Diary, April 9, 1950¢. Today I did a wonderful thing. A needy person asked me for a dime for a cup of coffee and I gave him 50¢. (distant crashing of dishes) Rochester! What happend in the kitchen?
Rochester: (off) I don't know, I'm in bed!

Jack falls asleep and dreams that the man he gave the 50¢ to puts it on a sweepstakes ticket and wins $150,000.

Jack: $150,000! That $150,000 is mine! I gave you that 50¢! I paid for that ticket! It's mine! It's mine!
Rochester: (coming on) Boss! Boss!
Jack: It's mine! I paid for it!
Rochester: Boss! Wake up!
Jack: I paid--! Huh? Huh?
Rochester: What were you dreaming about, Boss?
Jack: About giving that man 50¢. (sound of dishes crashing) Oh for heaven sakes, there go the rest of the dishes! (Music up and out)

RADIOFEST

The Antique Radio Club of Illinois and the Antique Wireless Association are proud to announce Radiofest '87 at the Holiday Inn Holidome and Convention Center in Elgin, Illinois. There will be several persentations on the history of radio and a talk entitled "The Rise and Rall of Radio Magazines." I hope to be able to make it myself. How about this...visit the Radiofest and go another piece down the road to see Waukegan!!! That should be enough wild frivolity for a day or two! No, really, I'm sure the fest will be both interesting and informative. Drop by and look around! (Alright, so I ended with a preposition. Who cares.)

LILLIE OF THE VALLEY

Ahem...the aforementioned George Lillie could really use some help. He has a dream to bring Lum and Abner to television with "the world's most beautiful puppets." These puppets (resembling L&A, of course) will cost between five and fifteen thousand dollars each. In his own words, "We hope to start doing thirty second commercials and later a half hour show. Anyone making it successful will receive the first $1000.00 and own ten percent of Lum and Abner Puppets Television Productions." Just think...these puppets could be guest hosting the Tonight Show someday. If anyone is interested in helping him with this venture, write to him at: 112 29th Street NE, Cedar Rapids, Iowa 52402.

Send all comments, questions, suggestions and various information to:
Laura Lee, c/o International Jack Benny Fan Club Offices, 15430 Lost Valley Drive, Fort Wayne, Indiana 46825.

Please friends, send no bombs.

Inventing Jack Benny
He Created the First Sitcom— A World We Believed Was Real

By Gary Giddins

I BECAME INTERESTED in Jack Benny in the early 1970s, when I saw him live. The occasion was a New York concert appearance by George Burns, who, after several years of relative inactivity, was embarking on his highly successful comeback. Benny came along to introduce him. It took him about 10 minutes and I don't remember a word he said. But I've never forgotten that as soon as he walked out—body bouncing, arms swinging to breast-pocket level, eyes glazed with stoic chagrin—I was convulsed with laughter, an effect his TV appearances had never had on me. If Burns was good, Benny was magical.

That I can't recall anything Benny said in concert is germane, since he may be the only great comedian in history who isn't associated with a single witticism. He got his biggest laughs with two exclamations—"Now cut that out!" and "Well!"—and impeccably timed silences. When he died in 1974, I watched the news stories for samples of his jokes. There weren't any. The one bit they frequently played came from radio: Benny, out for a stroll, hears footsteps behind him. A holdup man says, "Your money or your life." Benny says nothing—for a very long time. That's the joke. But it isn't the topper. The holdup man repeats his threat and Benny shouts, "I'm thinking it over!" On the original radio broadcast, he followed through with yet a third variation on the theme: The holdup man gets abusive and Benny, a model of agitated innocence, responds, "If you wanted money, why didn't you just ask for it?"

Needless to say, none of this is funny if you don't know the character of Jack Benny. What an arduous exercise it would be to try and explain Benny's unprecedented and unequaled success in American comedy to an audience unfamiliar with the sound of his voice or the pan on his face. Happily, that task is not yet necessary.

Everyone I know knows Benny, though the degree of knowledge depends on age. Those over 40 remember him from TV; those under 40 remember him chiefly from radio (specifically, a Sunday-night-at-seven ritual so widespread that in 1943 NBC declared the time slot his, no matter what sponsor bought it). Benny was a comic institution for about 40 years and

Gary Giddins, a staff writer for The Village Voice, is the author of the forthcoming "Celebrating Bird: The Triumph of Charlie Parker." This article was adapted from Grand Street.

THE WASHINGTON POST
AUGUST 3, 1986

A Pompous Skinflint Who, at 39, Became an Idol

apparently had no detractors—though Benny wouldn't have been too sure. In his later years, an insecure group eager to use him in its newspaper ads hired a market-research group to measure his popularity. The company was elated by the results: He was loved by 97 percent of the American public—a higher number than for anyone else. "What did I do to that 3 percent?" Benny wanted to know.

Yet the character he created and developed with inspired tenacity all those years—certainly one of the longest runs ever by an actor in the same role—was that of a mean, vainglorious skinflint: a pompous ass at best, a tiresome bore at near best. Incredibly, many listeners believed that Benny was "Benny," a phenomenon that amazed the actor. A lawyer once dunned him with outraged letters for refusing to pay Rochester his piddling back wages (a plot contrivance on radio); the exasperated Benny finally wrote him, "I only hope you're making in one year what Rochester makes in one month."

Many of the veteran entertainers who pioneered on radio, exchanging a string of vaudeville theaters for millions of living rooms, were surprised by the new audience's credulity and the implications. A fan once asked Gracie Allen if Benny was really cheap; she responded, "Am I stupid?" Yet Benny courted trouble by injecting just enough reality into his work to confuse the issue, and by sustaining his conceit—this, perhaps was his greatest achievement—through all the fashions that attended the Depression, the Second World War, the affluent society and the switch to television.

Once he established his image, he remained intransigently loyal to it. No, but-seriously-folks closers or nice-guy apologias for him. Unlike every other comedian you can name, he never stepped out of character. He seems to have sensed early on the new medium's potential as a mirror for the more commonplace foibles of a mass audience. In any case, he emerged over the decades as a comic staple who could bind the sensibilities of several generations.

Benny's fictions evolved so humanly that the actors who incarnated them ended up adopting the names of their roles. Eddie Anderson had many credits before he joined the Benny crew, but was thereafter known in private life as Rochester, Owen Patrick McNulty legally changed his name to Dennis Day after his first with Benny; his family convinced him to change it back, but he performed exclusively as Day. Sayde Marks, Benny's wife, assumed the name of a shopgirl she played and remained Mary Livingstone Benny even after retirement.

Benny also underwent a name change, though not to suit a script. During his apprentice years in vaudeville, his real name, Benjamin Kubelsky, prompted two law suits—the first from a violinist named Kubelik who thought a violin-playing Kubelsky would confuse

FIRST PERSON

The Benny Magic

people; the second from Ben Bernie, who complained that the resulting pseudonym, Benny K. Benny, was a deception designed to cash in on Bernie's fame. ("Now Jack Osterman is suing me," Benny used to tell friends, referring to a comic of the day.)

He was born Benjamin Kubelsky on St. Valentine's Day, 1894, in Waukegan, Illinois, the son of Russian immigrants and Orthodox Jews. At six he began violin lessons and at eight was acclaimed a local prodigy; at 12, he persuaded a friend to get him a job from ticket taker to usher to musician in the pit orchestra. He must have been pretty good, because Minnie Marx tried to hire him as music director when her sons played the theater, an offer his parents made him decline.

In 1912, Benny was expelled from high school and went on the road with a flashy pianist and veteran performer named Cora Salisbury. When she retired after the season, he teamed with another pianist and in 1916 the act of Benny and Lyman played the Palace Theater at $250 a week. They did 11 minutes of musical parody and, although Variety called it a "pleasing turn for an early spot," they

stopped. Benny returned home when he learned his mother was dying, a year later he joined the Navy, where he devised a routine with the famous novelty composer and pianist Zez Confrey. More significantly, he also did his first monologue in a Navy show that eventually toured the Midwest.

By the time he returned to the civilian circuit, Benny was concentrating on getting laughs while holding on to the violin as a prop. He was billed "Benny K. Benny: Fiddle Funology," then "Jack Benny: Fun with a Fiddle," and finally "A Few Minutes with Jack Benny."

Robert Benchley praised his cool bravado and subtlety when Benny returned to the Palace in 1924, but others panned him for what they construed as egotism and aloofness. Benny was studying other comics to learn how to sustain narratives and raiding joke books for one-liners, including occasional "cheap jokes"—e.g., "I took my girl to the Great Temptations, on which tour he courted and married 18-year-old Sadye Marks. Never a major vaudeville star, Benny appeared in three unsuccessful movies and worked mostly as an encee during the next few years. Yet he was making good money in 1930—at least $1,500 a week—as the comic faced up to the fact that vaudeville was through and began looking beyond it.

In 1934, at age 40, Benny saw the promised land. His guide was a writer George Burns had introduced him to named Harry Conn, who seems to have played Orson Welles to Benny's Herman Mankiewicz. Accounts differ about Conn's contribution, since they parted bitterly a few years later, but there is no doubt—Benny himself was emphatic about it—that Conn was instrumental in conceiving the brainstorm that revolutionized radio: situation comedy based on the lives of the performers, complete with sophisticated sound, effects.

Instead of revue skits and strings of jokes, each show would be a vari-

ation on a constant theme: life with Jack Benny. It was Conn's misfortune to underestimate the importance of Benny's delivery, timing, personality, and script-editing in making the initial concept work. Once the idea was established, writers could be replaced, as Conn was when his demands grew unreasonable. But before that happened, he and Benny came up with many of the motifs that would become the star's trademarks: the scenes set in his home, the Irish tenor, the cheerful announcer, the dumb girlfriend, the obnoxious band leader, and the reductio ad absurdum of shows that depicted only a mock rehearsal for the show on the air.

It was not an immediate hit; in 1934, the New York World-Telegram named Benny the most popular comedian on radio, but two sponsors dropped him. Not until 1936 and 1937, when Rochester and Phil Harris joined the cast, did the Benny phenomenon take hold.

When Benny supplanted Eddie Cantor in the ratings in 1937 as the most popular comedy star on radio—a position he maintained for most of the next 15 years—he rang the death knell, symbolic and real, for vaudeville. Cantor later remarked, "He made all the other comics throw away their joke files." His popularity had no equal in radio, then or ever. Ultimately stymied by Benny's success on NBC, CBS produced an ambitious series of topical dramas for the Sunday-at-seven slot, because no sponsor would buy the time. (The notion of combating popularity with quality seems rather quaint today; CBS, which bought Benny's radio show in 1948 and made a fortune with it, canceled him on TV in 1964, when "Gomer Pyle" beat him in the ratings.)

As Fred Allen told Maurice Zolotow in 1950: "Practically all comedy shows on the radio today owe their structure to Benny's conceptions. He was the first to realize that the listener is not in a theater with a thousand other people but is in a small circle at home. . . . Benny also was the first comedian in radio to realize that you could get big laughs by ridiculing yourself instead of your stooges. Benny became a fall guy for everybody else on the show." Or as Benny put it, "The whole humor of Jack Benny is—here's a guy with plenty of money, he's got a valet, he's always traveling around, and yet he's strictly a jerk."

Some jerk. Everyone knows a few things about radio's Jack Benny: he was eternally 39, bald, self-admiring, drove a dilapidated Maxwell (is there any other kind), lived alone with a valet named Rochester, and had irresistibly blue eyes. With the possible exception of the last, none of this was true of the real Jack Benny; in fact, he had to eliminate the bald jokes when he moved to television. Henri Bergson wrote, "The comic comes into being just when society and the individual, freed from the worry of self-preservation, begin to regard themselves as works of art."

Of course, his most fertile subject was his stinginess, an angle that produced countless variants. Here is a small garland of them:

He pays his agent 9 percent.

He keeps Mary's fur in his refrigerator: it's "a better deal than the storage company."

He plays a $100 Stradivarius—"one of the few ever made in Japan."

For 15 years, he drove a 1927 Maxwell—sound effects by Mel Blanc—which he reluctantly sacrificed to the wartime need for scrap metal. Reborn as a bomber, it made the same sputtering noises.

When traveling, he pawns his parrot rather than leave it at the pet shop at 75 cents a day.

He stays at the Acme Plaza in New York—the basement suite, which "underlooks the park."

The act of pulling a dime out of his pocket produces suction.

He discovers his tux is stained. Rochester: "That's what you get when you rent a dress suit." Benny: "Well, let's be careful who we rent it out to."

When Fred Allen visits him in the 1945 movie "It's in the Bag," Allen finds a hatchet girl in the closet and a cigarette machine in the living room. "This guy wouldn't give you the parsley off his fish," Allen mutters.

Benny's secretary calls a cab for him, and is told it'll take two hours. "Are they that busy?" he asks. "No, they say they'd like time to think it over."

A terrorist throws a rock through Benny's window with a note that warns, "Get out of town before it's too late." "Hmmm," Benny mused, "just a note, no ticket."

At the race track, Benny says, "I hope I win, I can sure use the money." Mary: "Why? You've never used any before."

Benny's cast of characters was fine-tuned by the same hit-and-miss system that produced his most enduring conceits. Some performers remained with him for decades. The most celebrated was Eddie Anderson, a vaudeville star whose appearance as a Pullman porter in a 1937 episode was so successful that he was brought back as Benny's valet. He continued as Benny's long-suffering but shrewd and frequently impertinent sidekick until he retired 21 years later.

As Rochester Van Jones, Anderson delivered a brazenly hoarse counterpoint to Benny's spry chatter, and usually got the best lines. On his day off, Rochester might don an outrageously gaudy smoking jacket, sprawl on a chaise sipping mint julep and smoking a cigar, refusing even to answer the phone. But he earned those days. Rochester had to dip his typewriter ribbon in grape juice because Benny wouldn't replace it. When Benny tried to talk him out of installing his own phone, assuring him he could use his, Rochester said, "I know, boss, but look at it this way. Suppose the house is burning down and I haven't got any change?" They didn't quite love each other; but they were thoroughly at home in each other's company.

Yet his public image was utterly nonpolitical. Indeed, his refusal to link his comedy to serious issues made him especially valuable in the 1960s, when everyone else made a show of taking sides. Benny continued to fulfill the comedian's contract to focus on manners rather than morals. I've been able to find only one instance of his making a political statement: "I am neither a Democrat nor a Republican. I'm a registered Whig. If it was good enough for President Fillmore, it's good enough for me. Now don't laugh about President Fillmore. After all, he kept us out of Vietnam."

I don't imagine there will ever be another generation of entertainers who can sustain the loyalties of successive generations as Benny and a handful of his contemporaries did. President Kennedy is said to have been eager to meet Benny because he recalled the Sunday evening ritual in the 1930s when his father made the whole family sit through the radio.

The tempo of life, the dissolution of family entertainment, and the increasing disposability of popular culture have imposed new imperatives and standards. Does this mean that Benny himself will simply fade away? Will the very character-induced economy that enabled him to get laughs simply by staring into the camera undermine the effectiveness of his programs when the character is no longer widely known?

One innovative cultural critic, John A. Kouwenhoven, has suggested that the strengths of American art lie in its open-endedness, in its fulfillment of Emerson's dictum that man is great "not in his goals but in his transitions." Situation comedies, like other American variations in high and low culture—including skyscrapers, jazz, Leaves of Grass, comic strips, the Constitution, and soap operas (to use some of Kouwenhoven's examples)—derive their integrity not from a notion of finalization but from process and continuity. They are designed with interchangeable parts, to be altered and disposed. What survives is the motivating idea, the germinal core.

Benny himself was a remarkably adaptable figure in the entertainment world, taking every techno-logical twist and popular fashion in stride and refusing to wallow in sentimentality and nostalgia. Yet his radio shows are largely inaccessible to contemporary tastes, as are virtually all radio shows from the pre-TV era—except to satisfy those same maudlin longings Benny rejected.

The TV shows are another story, chiefly because we still live in a television age. Ironically, despite the visual humor and the irresistible physical presence of Benny, they are not as richly made as the radio series. But they will suffice to keep Benny from becoming primarily a show-business metaphor—much as films kept Will Rogers and W. C. Fields from becoming mere metaphors respectively of cracker-barrel wisdom and inebriated impudence. In the relaxed ambiance of Benny's TV skits, a singular clown holds his ground—"completely relaxed, and not a worry in the world."

Jack Benny's Widow in Rare Appearance

Making a rare public appearance, Jack Benny's widow Mary Livingstone (right) joins Gregory Peck and his wife Veronique at a recent March of Dimes benefit at the Century Plaza Hotel in Los Angeles. The still attractive Mary has become a virtual recluse since Benny's death more than three years ago.

PIX! or is that Bix?

International Jack Benny Fan Club
15430 Lost Valley Drive
Ft. Wayne, Indiana 46825

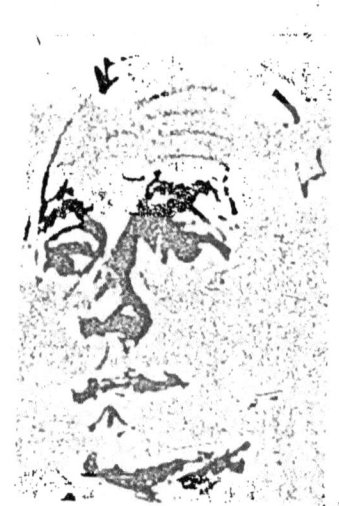

WELL!

The Jack Benny Times

Volume 7, Number 3   INTERNATIONAL DISTRIBUTION   May-June 1987

** PRESIDENT'S MESSAGE **

Hello again, folks! Usually I take this opportunity to tell you about all the wonderful and whimsical things which have happened since the last publication of the <u>Times</u>. Well, to be perfectly honest, absolutely nothing has happened. Well, that's not completely true. Teddy the dog was altered a few weeks ago, they are serving omlettes the size of throw rugs at Amish restaurants in Ohio, they (whoever <u>they</u> are) are building a bank in Charm, my divorce from the secretary of the Lum and Abner Society has been finalized and a subsequent proposal of marriage has been offerred by a Russian banjo player who is about 4'8 (I'm 5'11), and the cotton pickin' radio stations in this town have not yet accepted my show because the program directors only like rock and fusion jazz. Other than that, nothing has happened.

Being that we have just completed the first half of 1987, the income statement for the IJBFC is now available for any interested members. This obviously covers financial activity of the first half of the year and leftover acrued expenses prior to the time that dues were instituted. If you wish to receive a copy, just send a SASE to the address at the close of this newsletter.

I understand that Dennis Day may be in poor health--I will update you on this situation as I receive word from either him or his family. By the way, did anyone really receive the last <u>Times</u>? I expected some sort of small avalanche of letters for info on some of the activities, but I have received veritably nothing.

Now the one for which you've all been waiting. Here's the complete listing:

       Big Clip Society - Bob Burnham, Rob Cohen, Phil Evans
                     Tim Hollis, Tom Mastel, Rex Riffle,
                     Steve Szejna, James Treacy, Rusty
                                         Wolfe
    Rub Club - Jay Hickerson, George Lillie, Donnie Pitchford
    Super Big Clip Society - Jack Bloom

And now on with the show!!!

!! BLASPHEMY !!

having just completed reading fred allen's book entitled <u>much ado about me</u>, i have found it to be an entertaining chronicle of his early years and career in vaudeville. if anyone is interested in getting a true feeling for the life in vaudeville as well as an in-depth look at the early life of fred allen, pick up a copy at your local used book store. this section is comparable to a dandelion--to some it is a lovely flower, but to others it is just a "lifeless reed" in need of removal. greetings to ken.

TALKS WITH JOAN

As you all know, last February in Waukegan (of all places) I had the great pleasure to meet Joan Benny, daughter of you-know-who. I captured some of the interviews on tape, and here is the transcription of the results:

J: At some point, either Sunday or Monday, either my father or them together--I don't remember who the idea came from--I would say more often my father who was really totally responsible for the shows...and he would then say, "Next week we'll do the Christmas shopping show where Mary and I go to the May Company. Then the opening part of the show would be assigned to one writer, then we'll do a segment on a counter with Nelson giving me a hard time, then we run into Dennis...and then we finish the show with whatever and I do the wrap-up." then each one of the writers would write his segment, and then they would meet probably Tuesday or Wednesday--back in the old days of radio it was at our house in the library with the secretary whose name was Jeanette--so it would be the four writers, my father and Jeanette. They would simply go over the show from beginning to end, starting at the beginning and then all of them, the writer who wrote it...would have the script of what he had written, and then they would just do line by line by line, changing it, doing whatever they thought. My father was ultimately responsible--he was really the editor. They would get it together, and he was the one who always OK'd it. He'd say, "Well, I don't think that's good enough, let's change it." Then they'd have a final script...by the end of Friday because Saturday there was a rehearsal...Sunday they simply showed up at show time...I used to love sitting in on those sessions--they were very funny.

...the next day...

J: I am very pleased...being Jack Benny's daughter. On the other hand, I live my life. I've been married, I have four kids and I've just been Joan. As a matter of fact I remember having an absolutely wonderful dog. The neighborhood loved this dog, and everyone in the neighborhood knew him. He arrived when my oldest was a baby and lived to be fifteen years old...and I remember thinking, "My God, I went from being Jack Benny's daughter to Wolfgang's mother! When am I going to be me?!"

Q: ...When you were just hanging around with you parents, was your dad funny?

J: ...When I was a little girl, he loved to try to make me laugh, but he would do very silly things. He would dress in silly clothers, he would make funny faces, (editor's note: makes the mind run wild, doesn't it?) that kind of humor that you do for a three-year-old.

I used to love it. I remember sitting at the table having dinner, probably with my nanny, and in the breakfast room which looked through the dining room, and there were double doors to the dining room out in the hall, and he would walk by and...he used to pretend that he was walking down stairs, and then he'd come back pretending he was walking up the stairs.

Q: Did he ever joke with you about turning thirty-nine?

J: No. That was a professional joke...That was the public persona as opposed to the private. He was a very kind man, he was very wrapped up in his work. He had a couple of hobbies: he loved baseball, he loved to play golf... He was basically a very egocentric man without being egotistical. It was like blinders, it was a routine for next week's show, or who he was going to get as a guest, and he would be talking about baseball, my children or whatever, and it was interesting to see how quickly the conversation came back to something related to [the show]. I think maybe that's why he was as professional and as good as he was, because he cared so much about it. He wrote with the writers, he edited, he was a part of everything, he never left it to...[showing] up on the show date and [reading] the script...He wrote the show with the writers--it was ultimately a token responsibility.

Q: Did aging bother him?

J: Yes, it did...That was the private persona as opposed to the public...I think that that's simply human foible. There are people who are much more bothered about aging than others. Others take it rather casually...He took care of himself. Of course, when he was away from my mother he cheated [e.n.:ON HIS DIET, FOLKS!!!]. He was a very casual person, he loved to walk, and he loved to drop in on friends. He walked all over and he dropped in on his next-door neighbors or Jimmy Stewart who lived a few doors down and Lucille Ball who lived next door, and then later when I had my own house, he'd drop in on me--frequently. It was always, "Oh, Daddy, I just made some cookies. Have some cookies." "Well, I shouldn't really..." I said, "Daddy, they're not going to hurt you." He'd say, "Okay," and of course he would, he just needed a little reassurance that that was okay...

[e.n.:Go for it, Jack!]
Once again, many thanks to Joan for all her time. I'll write soon!

§ AND IN CONCLUSION... §

I forgot to say that I purchased a one-man band. I can now call myself "the big noise from Grand Rapids." Did you know what McChicken sandwiches are called in Canada? Seriously, folks, they're called McPoulets. What does this have to do with Jack Benny? Nothing, really.

As ever...
Laura Lee, c/o International Jack Benny Fan Club offices, 15430 Lost Valley Dr., Ft. Wayne, Indiana 46825

P.S. August 14 and 15 is Elgin Radiofest!

The gasman gag—could you make a million with that? Radio's No. 1 comic says go ahead and try

Jack

READING TIME ● 13 MINUTES 50 SECONDS

IN the late summer of 1939, after having mulled over his grievances for four years, Harry W. Conn, a writer, went to his lawyer and sued Jack Benny for $65,000. Conn said that during thirty-nine weeks of working for Benny, starting in September, 1935, he had concocted jokes and japeries which Benny had continued to use and from which Benny had made the tidy sum of $1,170,000. Five per cent of this, Conn said, ought by rights to be his.

The methods Mr. Benny used to settle this little difficulty out of court are not of interest; that $1,170,000 figure is, however, since it represents the fortune you can make if, like Benny, you can go on the air for a half hour once a week and make America laugh. According to latest reports, he turned down a $25,000-a-week offer to accept $17,500 from the National Broadcasting System and the dessert manufacturer who sponsors him. In addition, he was given a unique joint contract with Paramount and Twentieth Century-Fox in which he is to be available to either or both parties and for which he will receive a typical star's salary.

Radio's number one artist got that way and stays that way through the employment of a formula he creates himself and which he zealously improves but never changes. It is by no means a secret one. The extremely literate Mr. Benny will analyze it for you upon request, and if you think you can make anything of it you have his permission to try.

Benny is a clown, as distinguished from a jester—that is, you do not laugh with him at a joke he tells; you laugh at him because the joke is always on Benny.

Benny's fabricated comedy character did not evolve into the richly complete buffoon his fans now know and delight in until he developed it for his radio shows. To be able to turn every type of gag and every variation of a situation on himself, he was forced to endow the character with all the harmless weaknesses an ordinary man can have, and exaggerate them.

In character, Benny is the greatest tightwad in modern history; he is a braggart, forever boasting about his conquests of women, his ability as an actor, and his intimate social relations with Blue Book and movie colony celebrities. Yet it always turns out that he is lying about the women, that he is a punk actor (he is perfectly adequate when he plays himself on the screen), and that none of the celebrities knows who he is.

More important than these failings, Benny feels, is the old-womanish quality he has—fussy, eternally hurt and irritated over some petty annoyance or fancied slight. Things are never going right, and everybody is always perfectly horrid to him. His anger every year because he has not been voted the Academy Award is an example.

All the other members of the show have characters just as carefully established as Benny's, and just as carefully maintained. Mary Livingstone, who is his wife, plays Benny's girl friend, a hard-boiled, straight-thinking girl who is stuck with him emotionally but knows him thoroughly and who keeps asking, in exasperation and in effect, "What's the matter with you, for Pete's sake? Whatta ya wanta be like that for?"

The most successful gag Mary was ever given to read was an excellent example of her affectionate but tough attitude toward Jack. She announced at the beginning of the program that she wanted to recite a poem, and he told her she couldn't. All through the show she kept begging him to let her read her verse and each time he said, "No, Mary, there's no time. And besides, it's probably a *lousy* poem."

Finally she told him in desperation, "Listen, Jack. You let me recite my poem, or I won't buy my Christmas cards from you next Christmas!" This is a classic variation on his tightwad propensities, Benny explains, because it shows that, not satisfied with his present job, he would plan and work for such meager pickings.

Phil Harris, the orchestra leader, is a man about town, a great guy with the ladies, who likes to drink, stay up all night, and shoot his wages on the horses. Phil picks on Benny, too, bearing down heavy on the sarcasm.

Even better than Mary's Christmas-card gag, in Benny's opinion, is the one about the oranges, with Phil in the spot. Jack has bought a house in Florida and Phil has come to visit him. As Benny is proudly showing his guest around the place, Phil reaches up to pick an orange off a tree, and Jack immediately grabs his arm. "Hey," he

Benny's Ten Best Gags

BY HOWARD SHARPE

A Liberty Classic 1941

yeus, "none of that stuff! Don't you see that sign—no fair stealing the fruit?"

Sometime later, when Benny is in the house, an alarm bell goes off. "Oh-oh," says Benny, rushing to the window. "Phil, you put that orange right back where you got it!"

The gag got a good laugh when Jack was too stingy to let Phil have even one orange, but when the audience discovered he had gone to the immense trouble of wiring every orange in the grove with a burglar alarm, it let loose with the longest roar ever clocked on a Benny program.

The rotund announcer, Don Wilson, does the commercials, takes a bit of teasing because of his size, and likes everybody, smoothing things over when the others wrangle too long among themselves. Dennis Day, who sings romantic ballads in a good tenor, is the show's ingénu, wide-eyed and innocent as Little Annie Rooney. He replaced Kenny Baker when Baker left the show about two years ago. Like Baker, he has been given a naïve character, and is one person in the cast who is not as bright as the boss. He appears in such situations as this:

(It is Dennis' first trip to New York with the program.)

JACK: Hey, Dennis!
DENNIS: Yes, please?
JACK: Take a bow, kid. *(Applause.)* Well, here you are in the big city, Dennis. . . . Been having any fun?
DENNIS: Have I! . . . I've been to the Eltinge, and the Apollo, and the Gaiety, and the Republic. . . . *Wow!*
JACK: Why, Dennis, those are all burlesque shows.
DENNIS: Boy, I whistled myself silly!
JACK: Now, Dennis, I won't have this. I promised your mother I'd take care of you and see that you behaved yourself.
DENNIS: But I wanta get circles under my eyes like Phil Harris.

When Benny first began broadcasting he played his comedy fairly straight, in the accepted fashion, but shortly he began to grow a little cocky, kidding not only himself and his gang but the show, the script, and, to the initial horror of every one, the sponsor and the product. Ed Wynn had previously begun a practice of butting into the commercials on his show, saying, "Well, well," and "You don't say?" at every claim made by the announcer. Benny went further, writing comedy twists and whole gags to serve as the commercial.

One of the first concerns to buy his time manufactured a best-selling ginger ale, which the Benny program was supposed to plug. Benny told the audience a little story about a salesman of this product whose territory was the Sahara Desert. The fellow had been traveling across the Sahara for weeks and finally came upon a caravan which had been blown off its course many days before by a sandstorm and which was dying en masse of thirst. To each parched Arab the salesman gave a glass of his ginger ale—"And when he asked them what they thought of it," Benny concluded, "not one of them said it was a bad drink."

In deference to the public whose slave he necessarily is, Benny gives unrelaxing attention to the character of Rochester (real name: Eddie Anderson), his Negro valet, chauffeur, and houseman extraordinary, and incidentally the most popular of the Benny radio family. Rochester is always playing tricks on his employer, arguing with him, and making wisecracks, an attitude certain portions of the country would resent if it were not established that, after all, Rochester works his head off for Benny and Benny never pays him. A typical situation designed to remind listeners of this (and incidentally a prize Benny gag) had Rochester complaining about not getting his salary, and asking when he could have the eighty dollars Jack had just lost to him at casino.

JACK: Now, don't forget about that old blue suit I gave you last week. That was worth at least twenty dollars —and I'll only charge you sixty dollars for teaching you to play casino. So we're even; I don't owe you a thing.

ROCHESTER *(resignedly)*: I knew that's how it would end up, but I was wondering just how you were going to figure it out.

Rochester's troubles are chiefly concerned, however, with two of the other constant characters: Carmichael, the polar bear some one sent Jack for a Christmas present, and Mr. Billingsly (played by Ed Beloin), a crazy but harmless old crackpot who lives at Benny's house. During each show Rochester telephones Jack at the broadcasting studio and makes his report on the activities of these guests, whom he hates but whom Benny tolerates. It is a Benny characteristic that he doesn't care if Mr. Billingsly is nuts, so long as he doesn't bother him and pays his board. Most recent of the Rochester-Carmichael situations revolved around the gasman, who, according to Rochester, went downcellar, where Carmichael lives, to read the meter and didn't come back up again. Rochester claimed Carmichael had eaten the gasman, with Benny saying that was ridiculous and that the fellow must have gone out through a window or left when Rochester was looking the other way. This situation lasted for weeks, but the best tag of the lot came at the end of a telephone conversation, when Benny was about to hang up:

ROCHESTER: Say, boss . . .
JACK: Yes?
ROCHESTER: The gasman's here.
JACK: *There*, now! You see? What did I tell you? Carmichael didn't eat him after all. What does he want?
ROCHESTER: He wants to know where's the other gasman?

Benny, after appearing on a radio program as a guest of Ed Sullivan, determined, in 1932, to take six months off from vaudeville and concentrate on radio. The show was not by any means an overnight triumph. Sponsors did not pursue him nor respond to his wooing until it was discovered that his slowly won audience was constantly growing in size and devotion and that listening to Jack Benny was becoming a household institution.

With such nonsense, satirical and exaggerated, as the Buck Benny Rides Again routines, in which Jack played a blustering but scared-to-death Western sheriff, his lengthy feud with Fred Allen, and sly gibes at all current news topics and popular personalities, the program grew in appeal until it had the highest Crossley rating on the networks. Then Paramount signed him, whereupon he fortunately turned out to be just as funny in the movies, which is not inevitable with radio comedians.

Forte of the Benny program is the running gag. Some are in the short-run classification, which means they wear out after a few weeks; others survive to become an integral part of the show, along with the established characters. All are accidental in origin, meant as one-program situations and retained because they naturally fit into the pattern or are too successful not to milk so long as the public

JACK BENNY'S TEN BEST GAGS

will have them. Carmichael was one of the latter happy accidents, and so was the Maxwell, Benny's incredibly ancient bus which he will not relinquish so long as it will run at all and which he always defends. Benny takes all of his trips in the jaloppy and makes his crowd go with him. After they have used it for a trip to Palm Springs, for instance, Mary complains that Jack was too stingy to buy them any food on the journey.

JACK: Now wait a minute, Mary. What about that delicious pressed chicken we had?

MARY: It *had* to be pressed—you ran over it.

JACK: All right. I didn't mean to do it; it was an accident.

MARY: An accident?

JACK: Yes.

MARY: Then why did Rochester yell Tallyho! and chase it clear through a cornfield?

Later on in the program Rochester makes his regular phone call:

ROCHESTER: I'm over here in Pasadena to pick up the Maxwell, but you didn't give me enough money.

JACK: Rochester, I gave you twenty dollars to have that motor fixed, and that's plenty.

ROCHESTER: I know . . . but complications have set in.

JACK: What do you mean?

ROCHESTER: You remember how the motor used to backfire just before it would blow up?

JACK: Yes.

ROCHESTER: Well, now it whistles eight bars of There I Go—and boom!

Holidays and seasons provide Benny and his writers with basic settings in which to stage situations, which in turn breed their own twists and gags. On the first day of spring the program opens with Jack planting seeds in his garden, Dennis mowing the lawn, Rochester kibitzing, and Mary making wisecracks. "Say, Jack," she says, "look at the cute little swallow over there."

JACK: Oh yeah? How do you know it's a swallow?

MARY: He's got a sign on his back—Capistrano or Bust. . . . Oh-oh, here comes your boarder.

JACK: Oh, yes. I wonder why he's wearing that turban. Hello, Mr. Billingsly.

BILLINGSLY: Good afternoon, Mr. Benny. Digging in your garden, I see. I do hope you plant pistachios—they're delightful.

JACK: But, Mr. Billingsly, pistachios are nuts!

BILLINGSLY: Well, who isn't?

JACK: Oh, I didn't look at it quite that way. . . . H'm. By the way, you look just like a Hindu. Is that a turban wound around your head?

BILLINGSLY: No, that's a bed sheet. I slept like a top last night.

Most Benny programs include a satire on a recent movie, in which the entire gang is apportioned parts and which, as routines, have become noteworthy commentaries on certain entertainment formulas practiced as a habit by Hollywood. The best of these, Benny feels, was his take-off on The Women, in which he cast all the men as the various female characters and told Mary she could be Don Wilson and announce the play. With Jack playing Norma Shearer's role, Phil in the Rosalind Russell cat part, Don as Joan Crawford, the home-breaking actress, Dennis as Denise, Jack's five-year-old daughter, and Rochester playing Jack's maid, Rochelle, the little drama proceeded merrily.

Rochester, told he must play the maid, asks why he can't be Benny's valet.

JACK: Because I don't want a man in my room when I'm dressing. . . . Now, fellows—

ROCHESTER: *I ain't gonna wear no dress!*

JACK: *You are, too.* Now, fellows—

ROCHESTER: *I ain't gonna put on no mascara!*

JACK: *You are, too.* Now, fellows—

ROCHESTER: *It ain't gonna show!*

The opening scene takes place in Jack's boudoir. He calls for Denise.

DENNIS: Yes, mumsie?

JACK: We're having dinner alone, darling. Daddy's working late at the office.

DENNIS: Oh, mother, when are you going to wake up? When are you going to realize that men are only snakes in the grass?

JACK: Denise! . . . I will *not* have you talking that way about your father.

DENNIS: But gee, mumsie . . . father hasn't been home for dinner in over five years.

JACK: Well, maybe he isn't hungry. . . . Hand me my foundation cream. I must get made up.

DENNIS: Aren't you going to shave first?

In the luncheon scene, when all the girls are catting about each other, a knock-down drag-out hair-pulling fest occurs, during which the sound fades and Wilson does a commercial; in the end, while Jack is packing for Reno, her husband, J. Updyke, comes home at last, replying to Jack's frenzied welcome that he is just after a clean shirt. Jack says they're in the bottom drawer and is off to a train as the music signals the tag.

Situations and these plays create the kind of happy laughter which sustains for minutes at a time; but for the periodic belly laughs which every comedian must produce if he wants to be great, Benny depends on two- or three-line punch jokes. Thus, when Jack is organizing a football team:

JACK: Now, Mary, we're short of men this year and you'll have to be one of the players. Here's your equipment. Put it on.

MARY: O. K. . . . Oh, Jack, do men wear these?

JACK: Put 'em on! Those are *shoulder* pads. . . .

THE END

"By the way, how are all your folks?"

International Jack Benny Fan Club
15430 Lost Valley Drive
Ft. Wayne, Indiana 46825

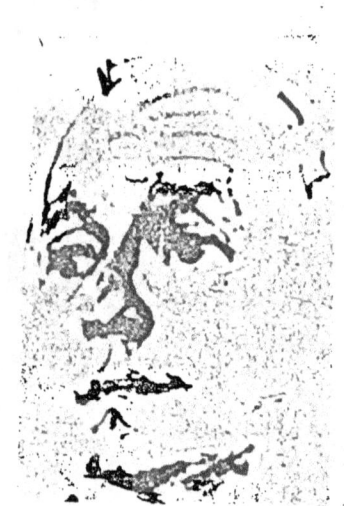

WELL!

The Jack Benny Times

Volume 7, No. 4 — INTERNATIONAL DISTRIBUTION — July-August 1987

§§ PRESIDENT'S MESSAGE §§

Yup...

      IT'S TRUE!!!

      IT'S TRUE!!!

The Jack Benny Junior High School is now the first official branch of the International Jack Benny Fan Club. Rah, rah!! Lynn--I had a certificate all made, but I'm not satisfied with it. I'll make another one asap and send it. I also found the mags. Hopefully in the near future we will be able to do an issue on the background of the school and their present activities. In the meantime...GO 39ers!!!

As several of you know already, honorary member Dennis Day has been diagnosed as having Lou Gehrig's disease. I thank the members who notified me of this; never take it for granted that I know! Anyhow, Mr. Day, "isn't giving up or giving in," according to spokeswoman Kitty Davis. Please include him in your prayers...Heaven knows we still need him! Now for some bright news on the same subject...last Tuesday I had the <u>great</u> fortune and pleasure of interviewing Mr. Day. We usually save lengthy interview transcriptions until the end of the year, but in lieu of the length and quality of the interview (all credit given to Dennis!), I would like to print it in two parts; the first installment will appear in the next <u>Times</u>, and the conclusion will be in the Nov-Dec. issue. I am very excited--I'm certain you will all love it.

If anyone is in the NE Ohio area, call Bill Oliver for the complete tour. (Oh, that music room!) My thanks for his time and patience with me! You really must see some of the great sights if you're ever travelling through the Akron area--the scenery is magnificent. Of course the official greeting when one IJBFC member meets another goes as follows: one queries the other, "Hark! Who goes there? Friend or foe?" The other, being a member replies, "Friend." The response: "What's the password?" The password is, naturally, "Now cut that out!" followed by current status, if any (Big Clip Society, etc.). I hope this alleviates any confusion.

I suppose everyone who subscribes to <u>RD</u> has seen the article on Fred Allen. I'd say more, but my writers aren't here. Also, someone (was it you, Bill?) wanted to know the address of an OTR dealer named Dick Judge. Anyone know? Finally I just received word that Jack Bloom drained his pool and re-filled it. Did you find the monster?

I know. You're saying this is a darn long <u>PM</u>. Well, yes. Lastly, thanks to Billie for the cover, and to the rest who wrote letters that I haven't answered yet. I'll get to it soon! Now on with the show!

Copyright 1989, Laura Lee

****NEW MEMBERS****

First, a bio sent in by Jack Melcher.
****JACK MELCHER - "I am a Jack Benny fan who likes the video shows and older radio tapes. I work here in Waukegan for the post office, and until the last few months, I delivered to the house that Jack Benny lived in on Madison Street. I also write articles and am the associate editor for Box Top Bonanza, which deals mostly with old radio premiums and the giveaway items for kids' shows." 2717 Sallmon Avenue, Waukegan, Illinois 60087

If anyone else would like a bio, send me the info you would like included!

****GARY MOLLICA****GARY A. DUNN****NEWELL LONG
****LAWRENCE PREUSS****KELLY MALONE****BONNIE M. SPANGLER
****BENJAMIN SPANGLER****Mrs. CHARLES E. PERRY****MARY E. GRIGG
****JOHN W. WEIK****PHYLLIS WEIK****JEANETTE THOMAS
****JOEL RASMUSSEN****ALLAN KIENZLE****PATRICIA S. CONN
Thanks and welcome!!!

$$ FUND RAISER $$

Dennis Day will soon be releasing a record to help fund the research of ALS. We will have more information on that in the next issue. However, we should do our part too. In a previous issue, we mentioned a set of "39 and Holding" items. This included key chains, buttons, cards and the like. There is a minimum order of $75.00 worth of material on my part. Therefore, in a following issue we will list prices of the available items. ALL PROFITS will go to ALS from the International Jack Benny Fan Club in honor of Dennis Day. If you are interested in such items, please drop me a note. If anyone has any further ideas, feel free to let me know.

¥¥ JACK BENNY LOGS ¥¥

Yes, it's made out of a lazy lagoon blue wood and burns for 39 minutes; you can cook a steak to perfection over it as long as you like it "well!" Now seriously folks...the JB log is coming together beautifully. Once again if you have any dates of appearances on radio other than regular shows or info on tv specials, books or magazine articles, we would truly appreciate your help!!!

£ FAVORITE SCENES £

Here's another member's favorite scene:

From 3-13-55 --Jack is assigning parts for his radio play, "The Murder of Malcolm Smith, or He Had an Appointment with the Dentist In the Afternoon, but He Was Drilled In the Morning"...

Jack: Now Mary, you're going to be the widow, Mrs. Malcolm J. Smith.

Mary: A widow?

Jack: Yes. Your husband has been killed, leaving you three million dollars, an estate in Santa Barbara and a yacht. and you're all broken up.

Mary: Why? Does the yacht leak?

(k-did i ever send you the ap article?)

FAMILY ALBUM

Yes, this is still alive. To preserve the "heritage" of the IJBFC, we have what we call the Jack Benny Fan Club Family Album. Each member that wishes to be included should contribute any of these three things: 1) a photograph of themselves (not their cats, Jack) 2) written bio or 3)desired information (I'll write the bio). Son of a gun, we'll have big fun on the bio.✻

KONTEZT

The first official contest of the _Times_, and YOU WERE THERE! George W. "Lillie of the Valley" has drawn up the enclosed word search containing the listed words. No words are repeated in the puzzle (except "Don." There are two of those). Once all correct words are circled, the leftover letters in their remaining order will spell out two complete sentences pertaining to Jack Benny. To enter, simply send the two correct sentences to the address at the end of this newsletter. Six of the correct responses will be chosen by a random drawing. DUH PRIZE: For the six lucky winners, George Lillie will personally record a surprise tape which he assures me is the _best_ selection in his vast collection! Pencils ready? CIRCLE!
GOOD LUCK!

Word List (in no particular order)

Anaheim		Davis	Harris
Azusa	Faye	Bea	Dennis
Cucamonga	Blanc	Dix	Radio
Sullivan	Joan	Don	Day
Canada Dry	Rochester	Don	Comedy
Fred	Daughter	Verna	TV
Lum and Abner (?)	Eddie	Ted	Mabel
Allen	Yeeees	Eyes	Gertrude
Waukegan	Andy	39	LeBlanc
Illinois	Max	Jack	Maxwell
School	Sam	Mary	Frank
Jello	Milt	Vault	Fontaine
Sportsmen	Bill	Benny	Gladys
Quartet	Ed	Livingstone	Parker
Alice	Joel	Wilson	Baker
Mel	Sara	Phil	(continued)

Word List (continued)

Stevens	Flapsaddle	Green
Chevrolet	Kitzel	Nelson
Basement	Well	
Carmichael	Emily	
Sheldon	Martha	
Leonard	Crosby	

```
G A N D Y J C N A L B E L S A R A A
E D C Y R D A D A N A C D C K G B E
R I N R A D I O N Y A E B H N M A D
T X L E H B E N N Y R A M O L L E J
R I E N I A T N O F S W M O R A D L
U S A S I M I E H A N A A L I C E E
D U H I S I N N E D C U T L U A V Z
E L C O E D W O K U D K 3 9 S A T T
I L I N L R I R C J O E L U R N E I
D I M I D A L E A B U G Z T E R T K
D V R L D N S N J E G A D L T E S T
E A A L A O O B Y N R N A I S V H E
S N C I S E N A O O E L V M E L E L
Y A D N P L F D O N E M I P H I L O
D O T M A H E N E B N E S D C V D R
A J S A L U T A A L N L L I O I O V
L V A S F E E M N E B A K E R N N E
G S H O T W D U L Y L I M E L G E H
T U M R S S B L A N C H T Y E S L C
P L A A K N A R F S U H R E A T Y S
A U X L L E W B E U G I L E H O B I
Q L W D T V H Y M U E J A E T N S R
C L E K B E E P A R K E R E R E O R
E I L N N T Y D X L I B R S A A R A
R B L B A S E M E N T Y D E M O C H
N E M S T R O P S N O S L E N Y ! !
```

Hint: The 2 "Dons" start with the same "D."

PLEASE, I'M BACK!

By Betty Mills

Dennis Day Comes Home to All of The McNultys, Jack Benny—Plus New Fall Ether Show of His Own

Sunday, 4 p.m.—8:30 p.m.
NBC—KFI—KFSD

"DENNIS DAY'S back," we smiled — "And nobody's got me!" he concluded.

"But how about Jack Benny and the sponsor of your own fall show," we quizzed. "Don't they count?"

"Shurrre," answered Eugene Dennis McNulty in his best Irish brogue. "I was only joking—and pretty badly at that."

If it was a coincidence that likeable Dennis made his return to the Benny show on St. Patrick's Day, it was a lucky one. For what better time could the McNultys celebrate their good fortune at having Dennis back than on their annual day of good cheer. For all of the McNultys are *that* Irish, and Dennis is no exception.

Green His Favorite

As a matter of fact, the young tenor met us with a brand new album of Irish melodies in his hands. They were his first recordings since his recent discharge from the Navy. From a huge shamrock on the cover smiled the face of Dennis Day, and when we congratulated him on the attractiveness of it, he modestly replied, "The green is pretty, isn't it? It's my favorite color."

"I just bought a large home in the Los Feliz district and am playing interior decorator. If I had my way, every room would be green, but I suppose you can overdo a good thing."

Mama and Papa McNulty and Dennis' two brothers are coming to California within the next few months to share the new home with him. "What a time I'm having," laughed the singer. "You should see me acting like a housewife and trying to decide what color goes with what and which material looks good with which material. How do you women do it?"

"But playing housewife is an easier task than playing sailor, isn't it?" we asked.

"Hmm," grinned Dennis in a noncommittal way. "You forget I worked for Jack Benny. I had to join the Navy. I needed the money."

Civilian readjustment isn't too difficult a problem in Dennis' life. "Gosh, no," he agreed. "I was around town with the Armed Forces Radio Service for four months before I was discharged. Everybody got used to seeing this face."

"Is that why there wasn't any vacation before returning to your duties on the Benny show?" we questioned.

Anxious to Return

"Guess I didn't need one," he agreed. "I was too anxious to return to work. I hadn't exactly been idle, because overseas, after I was transferred to the entertainment unit, we played 300 shows and covered 100,000 miles. Old friends like Tommy Riggs, Claude Thornhill and Jack Cooper were along, too."

Asked if people always mistake him for the type of character he portrays on the Benny program, Dennis admitted that they did. "Biggest surprise to them," he averred, "is that my voice isn't as high as it appears on the radio. And that I'm not such a dope!" When he appears on his own fall show, Day will build it around himself with an abundance of songs and comedy situations. "It's a dream I've always had."

Apparently the eligible young bachelor intends to remain that way, as there seems to be no "steady" at this writing.

"Gosh," he shyly grinned, "that new house is going to be pretty full as it is, don't you think?"

JACK BENNY —

"Benny's From Heaven"

By Bob Crosby as Told to Mildred Ross

THE MOMENT Bob Crosby returned from his summer vacation, we barged in on a hectic recording session to ask him one question: "How do you feel about your association with Jack Benny?"

"Benny's from heaven, as far as I'm concerned. He's the elite in comedian ranks," enthused Bob. Although Bob is an established successful entertainer—motion pictures, radio, records and club engagements—he seemed genuinely delighted with his new association.

Not even by the wildest stretch of one's imagination is Bob replacing Phil Harris. Their personalities are poles apart. Bob's first TV appearance with Benny was purely coincidental. They appeared together on KNXT's inaugural ceremonies last spring. The pair immediately struck a harmonious balance.

"It's rather speculative at this point (late August) just what character, if any, Benny has in mind for me," said Bob. "But Benny has always created successful types . . . 'Rochester,' Dennis Day, and 'Mr. Kitzel,' I'm sure he'll do all right by me. There's one thing I'm certain of, however," beamed Bob boastfully. "I'm beating brother Bing and nephew Gary to the punch as a television regular."

Vacation

Before Bob dashed back to the recording studios, he took the time to tell us about his "Swiss Family Robinson" vacation:

"I've just returned from the Northwest, where I've had a most gratifying experience. I took my two eldest boys, Chris and Bob, Jr., to the wild bush country to teach them fly fishing. The boys were impatient at first because the art of casting took a little time to learn. However, after they acquired the technique they were in the stream from sunup to sundown.

"Their smiles of achievement matched my smile of parental pride. Watching their skill develop was a real thrill. They learned how to throw a lure, making it appear as a real fly. The quickness of their reflexes set the hook at the precise moment a fish rose to the bait. I don't know of anything else that will teach boys self-reliance like being on their own in rugged territory.

"After leaving the wild life and bush country behind we headed for Montreal. While there, I became interested in a proposed summer camp for underprivileged boys. Feeling the way I do about the influence of camping on character development, I volunteered to raise money for the camp. We staged a five-hour radio marathon, raising over $10,000 for the project. The boys and myself are planning to return to Montreal next summer to witness the camp's first season."

Busy Schedule

Bob's pleasant reminiscing was abruptly called to a halt. He was reminded that after his recording date he had a "Club 15" rehearsal scheduled. In addition to the Benny shows, Bob continues as head man of CBS's "Club 15" for the seventh year.

As Bob dashed out he called over his shoulder. "Incidentally, you might like to know that my children would show more enthusiasm if I were going to become a regular 'Space Patrol' member rather than a regular of the Benny gang."

WHERE BOB CROSBY GOES, stacks of music go too. The Head Man of CBS's "Club 15" is assisted on that show by Gisele MacKenzie, The Modernaires and Jerry Gray's orchestra.

SCHOOLBOY CROSBY excelled as an all-around athlete at college. However, the maestro confines his love of sports to fishing and golf these busy days.

THE TEAM OF BENNY and Crosby delights televiewers as well as diehard radio fans. Established showman Crosby is genuinely enthused and appreciative of his association with Benny.

International Jack Benny Fan Club
15430 Lost Valley Drive
Ft. Wayne, Indiana 46825

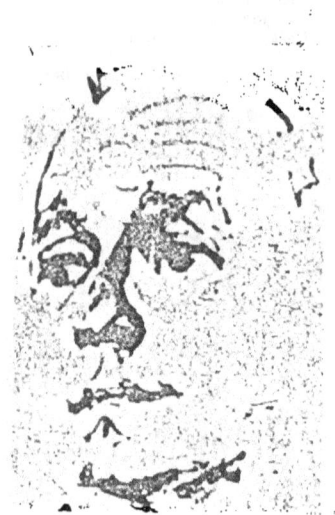

WELL!

The Jack Benny Times

Volume VII, Number 5   INTERNATIONAL DISTRIBUTION   Sept.-Oct. 1987

ßß PRESIDENT'S MESSAGE ßß

Jell-o again! This is Laura Lee talking...er, writing and Don...well, you know the rest. Welcome to one of the (if not the) best issues of The Jack Benny Times in its entire history. I hope I'm not bragging too much, but this issue is definitely something about which to brag. Immediately following the PM is the first installment of a two-part transcript of the Dennis Day interview. Yes, it's definitely the one for which you have all been waiting!!!

READ THIS

On that note, we now have a special Dennis Day offer for you. From the tape library (also see below) we have compiled a special Christmas tape of Dennis singing all your favorite Christmas carols from both records and actual Jack Benny shows. Plus as a special IJBFC exclusive (as of this writing), Dennis discusses his upcoming record release for the benefit of the study on Lou Gehrig's disease. In the spirit of this cause, to obtain this tape, just send a blank 60 minute tape and $1.00 to the fan club offices (whose address, as always is at the end of this newsletter). 100% of the profits will be contributed to fund the study on Lou Gehrig's disease in the honor of Dennis Day. Spice up your Christmas with the voice of Dennis Day and support his cause!!!

Our heartfelt thanks to Jack Bloom for supplying the above idea. Jack has been a bit under the weather lately, but he is now recovering at a rapid pace. He has also been extremely helpful in supplying information to the JB log and shows to the JB library. Get well soon, Jack!!! Send any cards or such to: 8618 Stansbury Ave., Van Nuys, CA 91402. Used crayons will also be accepted.

Have you been working on the Jack Benny search-a-word in the last Times? We have had only two correct responses, and we will accept up to six. George assures me that the prize is the best half hour in his vast collection, so give it a shot! Oh, yes. The deadline is December 25, 1987. All you have to do is send in the two sentences from the leftover letters when all correct words are circled. Go for it!!!

Speaking of the JB log and library, a target date has been set for the co-release of both: February 14, 1988, Jack's 94th birthday. Much thanks to Alan Grossman for his contributions of early Benny material. If you have anything that you'd like to donate to the library or information to round out the log, please contact me. By the way, does anyone know DEFINITELY the date of the show where Jack showers with a peeled potato?

Well, I suppose it's about time for me to shut up and let Dennis do the talking. I have to pant bubs anyhow! Now on with the show!!!

And happy belated birthday to Fred de Cordova!

AN EVENING IN THE LIFE OF DENNIS DAY

Once again, I would like to express our most heartfelt gratitude to Mr. Day for his time.

L: Oh, Dennis!
D: Yes, please?
L: Oh, that kid drives me nuts!
D: Now cut that out!
L: Well! Say, getting down to it, what were some of your first performances before you actually went on the Jack Benny show?
D: Well, before I went on the Jack Benny show, I had graduated from Manhattan College in New York City about nine months...before the Benny show--before I auditioned for it...I had always loved singing--I was in the glee club--I was President of the college glee club, and I had won a contest in New York among the metropolitan colleges for performing. There were instrumentalists, there were all kinds...I was a singer and I was chosen...The prize was to sing with Larry Clinton and his orchestra, who was then a very popular orchestra. He had written the <u>Dipsy Doodle</u> among other things...and several other classical songs that were adapted from Tschaikovsky, and he had adapted them into a popular mood...It was a great challenge to me, and I got on that program with Bea Wayne, I remember distinctly at the time. I did two songs and I took an air check of it...an acetate, because we didn't have tape at the time. Of course radio was the only thing we had--we didn't have television, it was just radio. I took an air check of the two songs, and I suppose that it would be about six months later--Kenny Baker was my predecessor on the Jack Benny show, [he] left the program, I suppose had a little disagreement with Jack Benny, I think it was about money or something.
L: That figures.
D: Whatever it was, he left the program and Jack and his agents were looking for a new singer to replace him, and somebody suggested I send it over to his agent because I was told after I got the program that Jack had auditioned or at least listened to records or people who had said, 'This is a great singer,' and everything. About 500 singers throughout the country, and I sent the record over thinking that nothing would ever happen, and by good fortune--God rest her--Mary Livingstone, Jack Benny's wife, she happened to be in the agent's office one day listening to a lot of audition records, and she heard mine and she was the one. She liked it, she went to Jack, and she persuaded him to audition me in person. Well, I did. I went down, I was called to audition and I nearly went through the floor. I'll never forget when I first went down to the agent's office to meet somebody--they didn't tell me who--and I walked in and there was Jack Benny sitting behind the desk. Now, you remember that Jack Benny was the number one program on radio at that time, and here I'm

face to face with Jack Benny which I never in my wildest imagination ever dreamed of just meeting the man. So here I walk in and meet him, and he said, 'Dennis, I heard your recording and Mary played it for me, and would you like to audition?' And I said, thinking it was maybe another week or so, I said, 'Oh, sure.' He said, 'Well, how about tomorrow?' There again I nearly went through the floor, too because this meant I had to get hold of someone to accompany me and go over a whole repertoire of songs to sing for him. So I did and after the meeting, I was to go the following day to NBC, up to the eighth floor, I believe it was, at Rockefeller Center and they had a studio there. So I rushed over and worked with a man who was a song plugger, really. He worked for Chappell Music Company--Billy Bruce, and Billy was a wonderful, wonderful little man who coached me and worked with me--I was nobody at the time--and that's the way you got songs. You went around to the publishers, you know, and they had people who played piano, mostly for people who were stars or budding stars on radio who had their own programs. Well, I didn't have my own program, but he took a liking to me and was very kind to me, and he coached me a lot. So I went over to him and I said, 'Would you play for me for my audition?' So we worked for an hour or two or so getting songs together and we then went to the audition the following day...I sang for about fifteen minutes--Jack Benny, his director, and a few other agency people, the agent...were all in the control booth, and I was on a stage with a mike and a piano and my pianist. So I sang for about fifteen minutes, then I heard a voice say, Dennis take a break, so I took a break for about a few minutes and I was talking to my accompanist and my back was turned to the control booth, and I was talking about what songs we were going to sing next and everything else...Then I heard the loudspeaker say, 'Oh, Dennis!' and I turned and said, 'Yes, please?' That was the thing Jack Benny told me months and months later, he said, 'You know, that was one of the things that sold me on you,' and the fact that I was kind of naïve to say...instead of...'Yeah, what do you want?' I turned and I said, 'Yes please?' In an Irish household, you never were impolite to your parents or your betters. Here he told me this months later, 'You know, that helped me decide that I kind of liked you.' Well, then shortly after that, I guess after I finished the audition a couple days later, Jack Benny gave me a round trip ticket to go out to California to audition for his writers and producer out there. I went out on the train, on the Golden State Limited, I'll never forget and...my mother and dad came down to see me--I'd never been west of the Mississippi--to me, there were still Indians in Chicago... I was twenty-one, and I got on the train and who was on the train...and I ran into Irene Ryan--God rest her--who was on the Beverly Hillbillies as the grandmother, and Irene was so wonderful to me, knowing I was a scared kid and was going out to Hollywood. She was only going as far as Chicago, because there I had to change trains...and then went on to Hollywood, and then I auditioned for the writers and producers when I got out there...I was told to wait around because Jack Benny hadn't come back from San Francisco. He was up at the World's Fair, which was then being held at Treasure Island--this is in 1939--September of 1939. Well he came back maybe a week or so later, and I stayed at the Hollywood Athletic Club which it was at that time, and I had a lovely time there, but of course I didn't have any money--they didn't give me any money, and I had to wire home to my folks to send me some money so I could eat! So I did stay there, and then I got a call to come down to Jack Benny's office after he got back down, and it was at that meeting that I knew I was going to be the new singer on his radio program--you know it wasn't when I signed the contract, mind you, but when Jack Benny took back the other hand for the train ticket! He <u>did</u>! I kid you not!...But here I signed the contract, and it had a two-week option in it. If I didn't make good in two weeks, he had the option of dismissing me and looking for somebody else. So then I lasted for the first thirteen weeks, because those options came up every thirteen weeks on the first year, and then after that it would be on a yearly basis. So I lasted for the first full year, and then I was picked up again, so I must have been doing <u>something</u> right, because that two-week option and everything else stretched all the way to over twenty-five years with Jack Benny--and they were wonderful, wonderful years, because I owe everything that I ever have...my place with Jack Benny, he gave me my break, my start--everything I have I owe to Jack Benny. And I'd say that even if I didn't know it was good for me! Honestly, Jack Benny was a wonderful man...You know, the things that were portrayed about him on radio, newspapers, magazines and the like as being a cheapskate, tightwad and a miser up close with the dollar--that wasn't Benny at all...He only seemed that way...because so many other people spent money. Benny was a generous man. He had to bend over backwards when he would go anywhere to have a bite to eat or anything like that, he'd have to overtip. Instead of leaving a dime, he'd leave a quarter! But he was a beautiful man. You see, all of that was built up. He got all his laughs on character--not on jokes, out-and-out set-up jokes and then boom. It was all on character, because people could relate to Jack Benny because first of all he was a nice man, he was a gentle man, he was a beautiful man, he had a good heart, and a very sincere man. But everybody could relate because he played the part of a cheapskate. Well, there's one in every family, and also we're all vain. When they'd ask him his age, he'd say, 'Thirty-nine,' and the color of his eyes. He said, 'Blue. Bluer than the lips of a schoolboy at forty below!'

L: And bluer than the thumb of a cross-eyed carpenter!
D: Exactly...These are things that are part of human nature. So here I was the brash...well, the silly, naïve kid. But

see, there was logic in everything silly or naïve or stupid that I might have said or did, and...the logic was simply to drive Jack Benny nuts, and I used to do this. Of course, I always had to go to his house in the first year or so, and rehearse the song that I'm going to sing on the following Sunday's program so that he would approve it because I couldn't do a song on the show without [getting] his approval--'Is this okay?'...and he was always very nice about it. He never would say, 'No, that's no good,' or 'Maybe you could get another song,' or something like that, but I always went over there. Well, this time I went over, and I sang the song I was going to do on the following Sunday's program and after I was through, Jack Benny said to me...'That's very nice, Dennis. That will be fine.' And I said, 'Gee, thanks, Mr. Benny! I gotta go now,' and he showed me to the door, and I was about to leave, and I turned and said, 'Goodbye, Mr. Benny! And have a nice trip!' and I left. You know, he went upstairs, he was halfway through packing before he realized he wasn't going anywhere! So that's the way I used to drive Jack Benny, these silly things that they would write for me, and...we stuck pretty much to the scripts. Every once in a while somebody would make a blooper, he was always fast to pick it up. I remember Mary Livingstone in one particular script where she was supposed to say, 'the grease rack,'--she saw the car on the grease rack. Instead she said 'grass reek.' And Benny...picked that up and carried that on, and I think we referred to that for about three or four shows then. So he was always very, very fast--he was not a slouch. He could respond to anybody. The only man, I think, that I saw get the better of Jack Benny, and I'll always remember that at the Paramount theatre, Jack Benny and Fred Allen. That was the man. They had made a picture... it might have been *Love Thy Neighbor*, yes. And this was a première, and they were on stage, you know, and here every time Jack would open his mouth, Fred Allen would have some spontaneous answer, and finally Jack Benny turned to him and said, 'You know something, Fred? You wouldn't say that if my writers were here!' He was so great. The man was, to me, I think not only a very human and wonderful friend of mine--a great heart--but you know, the thing about Jack Benny--he was a gentle man, and that's what they have on his tomb where he is buried: Jack Benny, a gentle man...which is true. He would never want to hurt anybody. I remember one instance where we had a bit player on our radio show, and he was reading the line at rehearsals, and Jack would try to correct him. He said, 'No that's not the way I want you to read it. Read it this way...', and we'd go over it again, and the fellow would read it wrong...Finally at the dress rehearsal, we went through it and he read it wrong, and Jack flew off. He said, 'No, no, dammit, I told you that's not the way, this is the way!" and the poor fellow was crestfallen. Well you know, twenty seconds later, Jack Benny went over to this man who was probably getting about $150 for his

spot on the program, and Jack Benny...said, 'I'm sorry.
I apologize. It wasn't you. It was something else that
was bothering me.' That's the sign of a man who has...
a bigness about him, to go over to a little bit player and
apologize. [He] wouldn't want to hurt anybody. See, he
never wanted to hurt anybody, and he felt by blowing
steam he had hurt this man...And it shows the true character
of Jack Benny.

                    TO BE CONTINUED!!!

(Ed. note: See? Isn't it terrific?)

Please send all TAPE ORDERS, information, inquiries and
so forth to:
Laura Lee, c/o Jack Benny Fan Club offices, 15430 Lost Valley Dr.,
Fort Wayne, Indiana 46825
Please friends, send no bombs.

International Jack Benny Fan Club
15430 Lost Valley Drive
Ft. Wayne, Indiana 46825

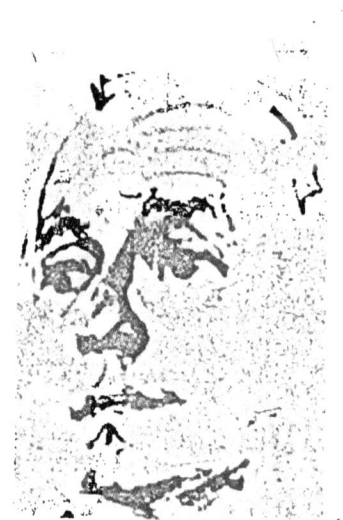

WELL!

The Jack Benny Times

Volume VII, Number 6   INTERNATIONAL DISTRIBUTION   November-December 1987

BAH, HUMBUG!

PRESIDENT'S MESSAGE

Not much happening in this department except final exams next week. This does not necessarily mean that I have had much time; my attentions have been focused on school.

My apologies for the delay in these issues; I have been trying to work out some wrinkles on the merchandise offers enclosed. Also please take note of the Dennis Day offer in the S-O issue. All best wishes to Dennis and his family--we are all still pulling for you!!!

Now let's just say Merry Christmas, Happy Channnukah and what have you. Now on with the show!!!

A CONTINUING EVENING WITH DENNIS DAY

L: (Jack) never really took too many of the lines in the show himself.
D: Well, no, he played straight for all of us. That was the whole secret of Jack Benny's success...Each of us: Phil Harris, Rochester, Don Wilson, myself, Mary Livingstone or anyone, we got a page and a half of dialogue, and he was playing straight for us. We got all the laughs, but it was dynamite material, because he had the best writers anyone could...buy, and that's one thing he insisted upon: good writers. You're only as good as your writers and the material that was given to you. And Benny...had four writers, and he payed them exceptionally well--he payed all of us really very well because we were exclusive to him, we could not work outside of the Jack Benny show unless we got his permission. I know my contract was exclusive, so was Rochester, so was Don Wilson, so was Phil Harris. You could not work outside of the Jack Benny show, on other shows, without his permission on radio...He was always very generous. He never would turn you down, but the reason he did that was to protect the characters that he was building...because lots of other shows would destroy or have you say something that would hurt that character. That's why he was very exclusive. We were exclusive, so he payed us very well. I didn't get the thirty-five dollars a week that was in the script--I got seventy-five! You know, actually I got $250...for the first thirteen weeks I was on with Jack Benny per program...To me I thought that was the end of the world! Remember...my first program was October (8), 1939, and...I remember I rented a house out in Studio City in San Fernando Valley, a furnished house, three-bedroom house and I rented it for $125 a month!
L: That's good!
D: That shows you the difference (with) what's happened with inflation, and what the value at that time was. So $250 was equal perhaps to $1,500 today, at least in today's dollars or maybe more. Still in all...before...I went in the Navy after four and a half years with Jack Benny, I was getting then $1000 a week, which was a lot of money then. Then after I came out, I had my own radio show...for Colgate-Palmolive, and then I went back with Jack Benny. My job was there.

Larry (Stevens) was the one who took over my place the two years I was in the Navy. So I was given my job back when I got out of the Navy, so I had two programs: my own radio program and the Jack Benny show. On the Benny show I was getting $2500 a week then, that was in 1946. So we stayed on radio through 1954 or 55, so that was quite a thing for us. What a career I had! Here I had a two-week option and it lasted all of those years.

L: Did you ever have a problem breaking out of that character since it was so set by the Benny program?

D: No, it's amazing that people even on the Benny program, being a silly, naïve kid, would separate the fact that I was a silly, naïve kid and accept the fact that I could sing a good song--that I was a good singer--that I was able to sing a legitimate, good song; I could do semi-classics, classics, whatever. So they accepted that. They separated the two characters. Of course, like Benny, the 39, after he was 60 he couldn't say that anymore because then it wouldn't be believable. When I did my personal appearances, I was able to refer to the Benny but not be the Benny character, particularly that silly, naïve and...stupid kid. Stupid things would not go, even with somebody else playing against me, and I'd say silly things, they wouldn't be funny. Only with Jack Benny they came to be because he was the perfect straight man for all of us.

L: Are there any particular anecdotes that stand out in your mind from any of the Benny programs?

D: Well, it's awfully difficult to pick out any particular anecdote about Jack Benny that you feel that...this is funny or funnier than the other or anything that may have happened. I know every time I went to a rehearsal when I first went with Jack Benny for the first five or four and a half years before I went in the Navy, it was always an excitement for me...because you knew it was going to be a funny script and it was going to be really funny just to hear and to listen to that...We always went out to his house or sometimes we would read it in the studio, but normally we would go to his house out on Roxbury Drive in Beverly Hills, and we'd sit around--we'd get the script and we'd read it just once. See, Jack wanted to get a reading; see, Jack wanted to get a reading and see how the...lines were going to play...We'd go out there, and I always get a tremendous charge out of the reading the first time because you didn't know what was coming, and Benny was the greatest audience because if something was funny, he could see. This man could see humor...this was his whole life; he had an intuitive sense of humor in reading this thing. He'd say, "Oh!" and fall right down on the floor laughing!...He was the greatest audience and intuitively, too, he knew if something in the script was not right, that it was not good for himself or for any member of the cast. He knew that intuitively, and out it would come. You know, after that first reading we would leave the house...which would be probably on a Thursday (that) we'd have that first reading, Wednesday or Thursday, normally on a Thursday, then we'd come back in on Saturday to the studio and we'd have another reading; and that script would, of course, then have been tightened up, they would have maybe taken out some spots and substituted others for them, and really that script would be fifty times better than the original that we first read...when we went out to his house...He was a great editor...and he knew instinctively what was good for Jack Benny, for each and every one of us in the show for the whole program. He knew instinctively what was good for us, and if anything wasn't, you knew it was out.

L: So you never actually sat in on the <u>writing</u> sessions...

D: No, I never did...I know that in...the first ten years or so that I was with him, Jack used to sit with the writers and they'd discuss what they were going to do on the following Sunday's program...He had four writers, so...one set like George Balzer and Sam Perrin would write this part of the program, and Tackaberry and Milt Josefsberg would write the other part of the program, and then they'd get it together...Jack was always the one who sat on top and said, "No, that's not good," or..."This is the way we're going to go," when they'd be editing the particular script, and then after the show was over what they were going to do for the following week. Because Jack never liked to reminisce a great deal, he always liked to talk about, "What am I gonna do next? Who am I gonna have on my program?" I just came back from Maui as a matter of fact, I was over there, my wife and I and some of my family, we have a condominium over there, and we just came back and I happened to go into Woolworth's over in Kahoolawe on the east side of the island, and here they have all of these video tapes, and there was a Jack Benny video tape with Humphrey Bogart, and I had to get that tape! I think that was one of the specials he had done in the early 50's for Chrysler [Ed. note: or Oct. 25, 1953 for LSMFT], and I bought that tape and ran it on the VCR, and it still holds up great today as it did at that time. That was the beauty of Jack Benny's humor. They show his TV shows now on the Christian network, and they run practically, I think a couple of times a week, and they also run his old radio shows, and that humor, even though it's forty or forty-five years old, is still as funny today as it was then. You see, he didn't have topical humor necessarily...(He) might refer to President Truman or somebody like that, but it was still funny then and it's as funny today. That's why a lot of the college kids and the younger group of people are saying, "Hey! This is funny stuff!" when they hear it or they happen to see it on video.

L: So which shows do you think were better--the radio shows

or the television shows?
D: Well, I think radio had a great deal more to it in the fact that you used your imagination. Each one of you were your own painter in your mind of what that scene and those people (looked like) and what was happening. In your mind--you could hear it over the radio. So that to me was very difficult for many of the people, Bob Hope was able because he was more or less of a stand-up comic, was able to transfer from radio to television, so was Jack Benny. But not to me, it didn't have the impact...I remember, just to give you an example...very famous on radio was Jack Benny's visit to his vault. Down in the cavernous depths, you know, and you could picture in your mind just from the way sound effects were and the dialogue where he was going, and you could picture, there was a moat there when you'd hear the chain clanking of raising the moat, and the sharks and then aligators and everything else, and you could all picture that in your mind. I remember the first time it was done on television. It was very funny, believe me. It was very funny when they did it on TV, but I remember after we did it...the next day probably, going down the street the next day going to the Brown Derby and people would come up, friends and just people, and they'd say, talking about the show, "It was a great show, but uh-uh, that's not the way I saw it." Then somebody else would say, "Uh-uh, that's not the way I saw it." Each one had their own picture of what it should be like. So this was the thing that's very difficult to do in television what had already been done, or what people's minds in their own imagination thought it was like in radio, because we did not have the boob tube, you know, television. We had only your imagination in radio. So I think that was probably...much better for us and certainly for Jack and for everyone else to do it in radio, although Jack still lasted a long, long time and had career not only from 1932 to 1955 or so on radio but also on TV. He started in about 1950, and he was doing television right up until the time that he passed away--he was preparing to do a show. He died (December) 26, 1974, and he was going to do a show February 14, 1975 which was his birthday. So he was just a few months short of being 81 years of age, and what a great life--what a beautiful life--and what joy and happiness that he gave to so many people throughout the world.
L: Just to sidestep a little bit away from the Jack Benny Show... I suppose this won't be exactly sidestepping it, but how did A Day In the Life of Dennis Day evolve?
D: Well, when I got out of the Navy, Ted Bates' agency...the advertising agency for Colgate-Palmolive...got a hold of Frank Galen who had been a writer with Burns and Allen, and they came up with the idea of the Dennis Day show, where I was living in a boarding house...Bea Benaderat was playing the woman who was married to Dink Trout, of course Mr. and Mrs. Anderson--that was their name, and they had a daughter (Mildred), and I was living at the boarding

house there in Weaverville, or whatever you want to call it. So that's how they came up with the idea was Frank Galen, and he had a couple of other writers with him, and they formulated on the basis of a Dennis Day character... that they knew from Jack Benny...I had that program for five years on radio.

L: Right. From '46 to '51 I think.

D: In television I had my own show...RCA Victor were my sponsors, and of course my last year they put me against I Love Lucy. That was 1953. They were then at the height of their popularity, and I could never get any kind of a rating. As a matter of fact, I've had requests now... I'm going to release on video to be shown on TV my Dennis Day show. So even though it's in black and white... the Lucy show is still on. The Real McCoys are out now... and an awful lot of shows. So I think I'm going to get that out.

L: So was it really kind of an extension of the Day in the Life show?

D: Not really, it was...a little bit, but not really. First I tried, more or less, one with my mother, Verna Felton, just trying to find a format. It was very difficult to do singing in a show--I did three songs in every show, usually, and then have a storyline...Really you only had twenty-six minutes of show because the rest would be commercials. So it was very difficult to try to find a real format. Then...Paul Henning (Petticoat Junction) was my writer, and that's when they had Charley Weaver, Cliff Arquette...and we had little Susie James (who) was the little girl who lived in the apartment (Susie Sterling played by Jeri Lou James) and Ida Moore played one of the older people in it. That's how this thing evolved, so... I guess it was two and a half years I was on TV. But I couldn't get a rating against I Love Lucy and that was it.

L: Well, if it's going to be rereleased, who knows!

D: Yeah, a lot of people never saw it then!

STAY TUNED FOR THE CONCLUSION!!!

As ever, if you have any comments, questions or requests, drop a note to:

Laura Lee, c/o the International Jack Benny Fan Club Offices, 15430 Lost Valley Dr., Ft. Wayne, IN 46845

Please, friends, send no bombs.

_____   If this box is checked, $5.39 is due for another year.

PACIFIC STANDARD TIME	CENTRAL STANDARD TIME		
	8:00	CBS: News
	8:00	NBC-Blue: Peerless Trio
	8:00	NBC-Red: Organ Recital
	8:15	CBS: Morning Moods
	8:15	NBC-Blue: Tone Pictures
	8:15	NBC-Red: Four Showmen
	8:45	NBC-Red: Animal News
8:00	9:00	CBS: Today in Europe
8:00	9:00	NBC-Blue: White Rabbit Line
8:00	9:00	NBC-Red: Turn Back the Clock
8:15	9:15	NBC-Red: Tom Terriss
8:30	9:30	CBS: Wings Over Jordan
8:30	9:30	NBC-Red: Sunday Drivers
9:00	10:00	CBS: Church of the Air
9:00	10:00	NBC-Blue: Morning Musicale
9:00	10:00	NBC-Red: Radio Pulpit
9:30	10:30	CBS: March of Games
9:30	10:30	NBC-Blue: Four Belles
9:30	10:30	NBC-Red: Children's Hour
10:05	11:05	NBC-Blue: Alice Remsen
10:15	11:15	NBC-Blue: Neighbor Nell
10:30	11:30	CBS: MAJOR BOWES FAMILY
10:30	11:30	NBC-Blue: Southernaires
10:30	11:30	NBC-Red: News
10:45	11:45	NBC-Red: Music and Youth
11:00	12:00	NBC-Blue: RADIO CITY MUSIC HALL
11:00	12:00	NBC-Red: Vernon Crane's Story Book
11:30	12:30	CBS: Salt Lake City Tabernacle
11:30	12:30	NBC-Red: On the Job
12:00	1:00	CBS: Church of the Air
12:00	1:00	NBC-Blue: Ted Malone
12:00	1:00	NBC-Red: Music for Moderns
12:15	1:15	NBC-Blue: Ted Malone
12:30	1:30	CBS: Grand Hotel
12:30	1:30	NBC-Blue: Metropolitan Moods
12:30	1:30	NBC-Red: From Hollywood Today
1:00	2:00	CBS: Democracy in Action
1:00	2:00	NBC-Blue: Great Plays
1:00	2:00	NBC-Red: Smoke Dreams
1:30	2:30	CBS: So You Think You Know Music
1:30	2:30	NBC-Red: University of Chicago Round Table
2:00	3:00	CBS: N. Y. Philharmonic
2:00	3:00	NBC-Blue: Norman Cloutier's Orch.
2:00	3:00	NBC-Red: I Want a Divorce
2:30	3:30	NBC-Blue: H. Leopold Spitalny
2:30	3:30	NBC-Red: News from Europe
3:00	4:00	NBC-Blue: National Vespers
3:00	4:00	NBC-Red: Glenn Miller Orch.
3:30	4:30	CBS: Pursuit of Happiness
3:30	4:30	NBC-Blue: Richard Himber Orch.
3:30	4:30	NBC-Red: The World is Yours
4:00	5:00	CBS: Hobby Lobby
4:00	5:00	MBS: Musical Steelmakers
4:00	5:00	NBC-Blue: Moylan Sisters
	5:15	NBC-Blue: News
4:15	5:15	NBC-Red: Bob Becker Dog Chats
4:30	5:30	CBS: Gen Barrie
4:30	5:30	MBS: The Shadow
4:30	5:30	NBC-Blue: Met Opera Auditions
4:30	5:30	NBC-Red: The Spelling Bee
5:00	6:00	CBS: SILVER THEATER
5:00	6:00	MBS: Listen America
5:00	6:00	NBC-Blue: New Friends of Music
5:00	6:00	NBC-Red: Catholic Hour
5:30	6:30	CBS: Gateway to Hollywood
5:30	6:30	NBC-Red: Grouch Club
6:00	7:00	CBS: European News Roundup
6:00	7:00	NBC-Blue: Dinah Shore
6:00	7:00	NBC-Red: JACK BENNY
6:30	7:30	CBS: SCREEN GUILD THEATER
6:30	7:30	NBC-Blue: Mr. District Attorney
6:30	7:30	NBC-Red: Fitch Bandwagon
7:00	8:00	CBS: ORSON WELLES
7:00	8:00	NBC-Blue: Festival of Music
7:00	8:00	NBC-Red: CHARLIE McCARTHY
7:30	8:30	NBC-Red: ONE MAN'S FAMILY (Jan. 7)
8:00	9:00	CBS: FORD SYMPHONY
8:00	9:00	NBC-Blue: Walter Winchell
8:00	9:00	NBC-Red: Manhattan Merry-Go-Round
8:15	9:15	NBC-Blue: The Parker Family
8:30	9:30	NBC-Blue: Irene Rich
8:30	9:30	NBC-Red: American Album of Familiar Music
8:45	9:45	NBC-Blue: Bill Stern Sports Review
9:00	10:00	MBS: Goodwill Hour
9:00	10:00	CBS: Ellery Queen
9:00	10:00	NBC-Red: Hour of Charm
9:30	10:30	NBC-Blue: Cheerio
9:30	10:30	NBC-Red: NBC String Quartet
10:00	11:00	CBS: Paul Sullivan
10:00	11:00	NBC: Dance Orchestra

Benny's Dennis Day . . . and Dennis' talkative "Mother."

Tune-In Bulletin for December 31, January 7, 14 and 21!

December 31: Here it is the last day of 1939, and nobody's sorry to see it go. The networks are doing their bit to send it on its way, with all-night dance programs chasing 1939 across the continent and clear out to Honolulu. . . . From 2:00 to 3:00 this afternoon, E.S.T., NBC-Blue broadcasts Headlines of 1939, a review of the year's news events. . . . The Rose Bowl Pageant in Pasadena is to be described on Mutual tonight. . . . Grace Moore is the guest star on the Ford Hour.

January 7: One of your old favorites returns today when Grand Hotel begins on CBS at 1:35 this afternoon. . . . And the Chase and Sanborn show, NBC-Red at 8:00, is cut to a half-hour beginning tonight—with One Man's Family in the other thirty minutes.

January 14: Today's your last chance to hear Paul Wing's Spelling Bee program over NBC-Red at 5:30. . . . Ted Malone makes a pilgrimage to Oliver Wendell Holmes' home in Boston at 1:15 over NBC-Blue. . . . Gladys Swarthout is the guest star on the Ford Hour.

January 21: Helen Traubel, soprano, is the Ford Hour's guest tonight. . . . Henry Wadsworth Longfellow's home is visited by Ted Malone at 1:15.

ON THE AIR TONIGHT: A new singer and a new comedienne—in fact, you might agree with lots of folks and call them the new singer and the new comedienne of the current radio season. They're Dennis Day and his "mother," heard on Jack Benny's Jell-O show on NBC at 7:00, E.S.T. and 8:30, P.S.T.

"Mother," Mrs. Lucretia Day, of course isn't really Dennis' mother at all. In real life she's Verna Felton, a veteran radio actress who has appeared frequently on the Benny show in the last three years. In fact, at one time or another, she has played mother to everyone in the gang. Besides her radio experience, she has a long and honorable stage career behind her too, for she made her theatrical debut in 1901, when she was nine.

Verna is married to Lee Millar, a former stage director who is now a radio actor too, and they have one son, fifteen years old. Young Millar followed in his mother's footsteps by appearing on the stage when he was nine, but since then he's decided that he likes music better than acting, and now is studying piano.

The Millars live on a ranch in San Fernando Valley, where, in spite of her heavy radio schedule, Verna manages to do most of the cooking for her family, and a good deal of the sewing besides. She and her husband always criticize each other's radio performances, and wouldn't think of going on the air without first rehearsing at home and getting suggestions from the other. "Mother" is Verna's favorite role of all time.

Her "son," Dennis Day, after three months of amazing success on the Benny show, is the same self-assured but unassuming kid he was when he first stepped up to its mike. He's entirely given up his early notion of being a lawyer, and is so definitely committed to a singing career that he refuses to drink or smoke because such things are bad for the voice.

He lives with his real mother in a small North Hollywood house surrounded by flower beds. This garden, next to his second-hand coupe, is Dennis' greatest joy, since he was born and brought up in New York City, where he never had a chance to cultivate anything more extensive than a window-box. He's no night-clubber, and his idea of a really good time is driving his car all over Southern California. He hasn't any "steady girl."

SAY HELLO TO . . .

BILL JOHNSTONE—who plays "The Shadow" on the mystery thriller of that name this afternoon at 5:30 on MBS. Bill was born in Scotland in 1908 and came to America as a boy, where he was first a reporter, then switched to acting. He owns a farm in Connecticut and spends his summers on it, living in a New York apartment in winter. His eyes are hazel, his hair prematurely gray.

'TIS THE SEASON!!!

Do you have friends that like Jack Benny who are not members of the fan club? Then give the perfect Christmas gift-- a membership to the International Jack Benny Fan Club!!! The membership is FREE!!! Simply send the name(s) and address(es) to the IJBFC offices, and we'll send them a membership certificate. If you so desire, the subscription rate to the Jack Benny Times is only $5.39, and you can give them the very latest news on Jack Benny memorobilia and his colleagues! So give the gift of laughter this year-- especially when it's free. Jack would probably say, "WELL! I couldn't pass up a deal like that!!!"

HAPPY THANKSGIVING!!!

Jack Benny FAN CLUB

15430 LOST VALLEY DRIVE
FORT WAYNE, IN 46825

FAN CLUB
15430 LOST VALLEY DRIVE • FORT WAYNE, IN 46845

Note zip code change!

December, 1987

Jell-o again, folks!

1987 IJBFC CHRISTMAS CATALOG

Perhaps a bit tardy, but as they always say, if you can't be prompt, be sanitary. Anyhow, the following is a list of the items that we are marketing for this holiday season. I already have some of these items, and I can personally vouch for their quality. Attached is an order form for your convenience. PLEASE NOTE: <u>100% OF THE PROFITS FROM THIS VENTURE WILL BE DONATED TO RESEARCH ON ALS (LOU GEHRIG'S DISEASE).</u> As most of you know, Dennis Day has been diagnosed with this ailment, so the IJBFC wants to do its share to aid the study for its cure. Here's the fun way to help because <u>you</u> get great merchandise in the bargain!
LET'S HEAR FROM <u>YOU</u>!!!

JACK BENNY JUNIOR HIGH
The following items will have "Jack Benny 39ers" printed on them as JBJH's sports teams are the "39ers." How appropriate!

<u>Tee</u>--Solid crew neck tee with set in collarette. Mid Weight. 50% cotton, 50% polyester............................$8.50

<u>Twill Shorts</u>--Twill boxer style shorts with elastic waistband and V-notch leg opening. 50% cotton, 50% polyester...$8.50

<u>Crew Neck Sweatshirt</u>--50% cotton, 50% polyester......$17.50

<u>Hooded Pullover</u>--50% cotton, 50% polyester..........$22.50

<u>Sweat Pants</u>--Leg print. 50% cotton, 50% polyester...$17.50

<u>Baseball Jacket</u>--Nylon taffeta shell, flannel lining, stand-up collar, reinforced pockets, front snaps, water repellant, machine washable.................................$28.00

<u>Satin Pro-line Jacket</u>--Nylon satin shell, flannel lining, stand-up collar, reinforced pockets, front snaps, water repellant, machine washable..........................$35.00

<u>Oxford Winterguard</u>--(Hey Michigan members!)Nylon oxford shell, fully lined with nylon quilted fiber fill, reinforced pockets, stand-up collar, front snaps, water repellant, machine washable...$39.00

<u>ONLY AVAILABLE TO JBJH ASSOCIATES AND IJBFC MEMBERS!!!</u>
<u>GREAT GIFTS!</u>

1987 IJBFC CHRISTMAS CATALOG (cont'd)

39 AND HOLDING

Tristar has provided us with these items for all who refuse to turn 40! White printing on black, all say "39 and holding" unless otherwise noted. Delcare your support for Jack's age combat with the following:

Button...$1.50

Key Ring..$3.00

Balloon--"Happy 39th and Holding"....................$2.00

Cup..$7.00

Card--Front:"39 &", Inside:"Holding"..................$1.50

(Similar items available such as card--front:"After 40 forget the natural ingredients...", inside:"what you need is artificial color and preservatives!" Write for further info.)

Please detach the order form and order lots of everything. Well, maybe not everything, but you know what I mean. Please enclose check or money order, as being stuck with unpaid-for merchandise is not my bag. PLEASE TRY TO HAVE YOUR ORDERS IN BY JANUARY 31, 1988. This will give me some idea of the order quantity, and no one will be sitting waiting around for their order to come some time in the distant future. You never know when someone will tap your shoulder and say, "Hey, bud. C'mere a minute. I really like that Jack Benny stuff you're wearin'," and hand you a bowl of Jell-o and a Lucky Strike.

Come on and help Dennis' cause! JACK BENNY FANS UNITE!!!

Laura Lee, c/o International Jack Benny Fan Club Offices, 15430 Lost Valley Dr., Ft. Wayne, IN 46825

(Hope you're enjoying Dennis' interview in the Times!)

FAN CLUB
15430 LOST VALLEY DRIVE • FORT WAYNE, IN 46845

1987 IJBFC CHRISTMAS ORDER FORM

Please send this order form and check or money order to the above address. THANKS!

Item	Price	Quantity	Total
JBJH Tee	8.50		
JBJH Twill Shorts	8.50		
JBJH Crew Neck Sweatshirt	17.50		
JBJH Hooded Pullover	22.50		
JBJH Sweat Pants	17.50		
JBJH Baseball Jacket	28.00		
JBJH Satin Pro-Line	35.00		
JBJH Oxford Winterguard	39.00		
39&H button	1.50		
39&H Key Ring	3.00		
39&H Balloon	2.00		
39&H Cup	7.00		
39&H Card	1.50		
		Subtotal	
	Additional ALS Donation		
		Total	

On JBJH items, please note size: Youth: S(6-8), M(10-12), L(14-16) or Adult: S(34-36), M(38-40), L(42-44), XL(46-48) An XXL(50-52) is available for an additional $2.00.

The Jack Benny Times

Volume VII, Number 1 INTERNATIONAL DISTRIBUTION January-February 1988

IN MEMORIAM:

Jack breaking up Milt Josefsberg, 1953. In background director Ralph Levy and music conductor Mahlon Merrick.

Milt Josefsberg 1911-1987

** PRESIDENT'S MESSAGE **

Jell-o again, folks. On January 1 of this year we celebrated our eighth anniversary. Thanks kids for helping this club grow better every year! As most of you know, this year we will be releasing our ultimate Jack Benny log and tape library, most of which is due to the activities of YOU. More about those later.

One of Jack's writers, Milt Josefsberg, passed away December 14th of last year. He worked with Jack for many years on his radio and early television shows, and later wrote a magnificent book entitled The Jack Benny Show. Check around your local used book shops for it--it's definitely worth the search! He was an honorary member of the IJBFC, and he is deeply mourned by many of us. We would like to dedicate this issue of the Times to his memory.

As some of you know, our target date for the log and library was Feb. 14th. Well, in the middle of January during the cold snap, one of our pipes froze and broke, flooding our first floor hallway and bathroom, and pouring Niagra Falls down on a ten-year collection of radios, victrolas, pump organ, etc. and lots of paper stuff sitting out everywhere. Folks, never go through this if you can help it. I am still putting the basement back together and thus am postponing the release of these two items until late May or early June. I hope you understand. By the way, if you have any Jack Benny material that you would like to include in the library, drop me a line at the address at the end of the newsletter. Also, does anyone have any info on shows between 1932 and 1935? We have filled in quite a bit, but still have some rather large gaps.

I received a Christmas card from Phil Harris, and he says to say "Hi!" Or is that "Hiya Jackson?!" Anyone interested in receiving an income statement covering the last year for the fan club, send a SASE to the IJBFC offices. Thanks also for the cards and letters commenting on the last two issues. I passed your kind thoughts along to Dennis on the phone last Sunday, and he sends his sincerest thanks. He is in great spirits and is "taking each day as it comes." Speaking of him...

IT AIN'T OVER UNTIL DENNIS SINGS...

SAY FOLKS! DENNIS DAY'S RECORD IS OUT!!! If you want a copy, send a check for $5.00 made out to Dennis Day to the offices of the IJBFC. These will be forwarded to him en masse, as he is personally publishing the record. ALL PROFITS GO TO ALS RESEARCH. JACK BENNY FANS UNITE!!!

L: Jumping ahead to today, what kind of music do you listen to now?
D: Oh, I listen to...(music) mostly in my era. You know my kids all...have the radios when they play...the tapes.

Parker Fennelly of Allen's Alley also passed away and is missed by many.

Copyright 1989, Laura Lee

They go for all the Madonnas and...things.
L: Heavens, there's rock in the Day household?!
D: Well, they like...the current things. So each generation finds their own. We had our own. There's no Jerome Kerns around or Cole Porters...
L: Or George Gershwin... (leave it to me!)
D: Or Oscar Hammerstein, and Rogers and Hart and all of those, so it's a little different today...But I think they find their own--what they like...To me, it seems...repetitious, kind of monotonous. It's a beat, really. I can't understand any of the lyrics half the time...
L: I'm sympathetic to that. I still play your records and Al Jolson...(So) you are still performing?
D: I was...As a matter of fact I went back to Holyoke. I performed...over St. Patrick's--that's my big time! And I performed in Cleveland and in Youngstown, Ohio, then I was also in Pittsburgh, then I went to Hiyanis (sp?), I was up in New Hampshire, and then...on the 21st and 22nd, I was given by the city of Holyoke, Massachusettes, the John F. Kennedy memorial award for distinguished Irish-American, and I was very honored to get that...I received that, and I marched in the parade almost three miles! But from that time on, I started having problems with my legs, and I thought it was part of growing old because I'm not 39 anymore! And finally...when I got home after I did a show on March 26th in New York...I came home and then I went to an orthopedic (doctor). He x-rayed my back and said I had deterioration of the lower spine and that physical therapy would do me some good. So he sent me to a physical therapist, and then we were leaving in May to go to Maui...While I was there I thought...I might get an adjustment. I went to a chiropractor--he did a little adjusting, and he said, "I don't think you need adjusting--I think you've got a nerve problem...Would you mind if I sent you to a neurologist?" So I went to a neurologist on Maui, and he examined me and gave me certain tests...He said, "Definitely you have a nerve problem in your neck and probably your back...You better have in attended to." So I made arrangements...when I got home to go to Scripps Clinic down in San Diego. They ran all the tests on me, the cat scan, the milogram (sp?) and the electromyogram and everything on me, and they came up with the diagnosis that I had motor-neuron disease and more than likely was ALS or Lou Gehrig's disease...I have a spastic walk, I can hardly walk now. I do walk with the aid of a cane. I'm afraid all my days of performing are in the past. I can still sing, and I love singing, but I'll have to do like Jane Froman used to do. When she was hurt flying on the transatlantic over on one of the clippers going to Portugal I guess it was, World War II, the plane crashed and she was paralyzed so she did all her performing from then on in a wheelchair. So God willing, I might be able to do that. So I hope to continue. I have a recording I did about six months ago--it's a 45...I believe Dick Clark is interested in releasing it...

_____ If this box is checked, $5.39 is due for another year.

L: Maybe you could be on <u>American Bandstand</u>!

D: Yeah! Well, all the money...that will come from it will go to the research center ALS, which is USC, Dr. King Engle... I'm now under his care--he's the head of research at USC for motor-neuron diseases, and he treated the late Senator Javits of...the state of New York, and all the monies...from the recording would be going to help him and research. I did the Jerry Lewis telethon here this past Sunday...and...I saw one portion of it when I was in Maui, but I understand they ran it three times, first with Sammy Davis, then with Jerry Lewis and also with Ed McMahon... So it was a short spot where I am walking with a cane and telling them what has happened to me, and it could happen to anybody. I never dreamt that it <u>would</u> happen to me. The good Lord has different ways of testing us...so that we can share in some of his glory, that we can share in the fact that He loves us all, He loves us eternally, and He's got an infinite love for us. He must love us an awful lot, when he allows us to share in the sufferings of Jesus Christ.

L: Well, you're definitely in all of our prayers...

D: Well, I appreciate that. I know I've had a...wonderful response from people all over the country since this was announced...

L: One last question I must ask out of personal curiosity. Some time ago, there was a Dennis Day bear that came out, wasn't there?...

D: Yes, yes...they did have it. It came out of Illinois... and the first bears were fine. My wife had a gift and antique shop in Santa Monica, and the first bears were made in the United States...They were very good and we sold out all...of what she had, because I had a little song on it about the bear. Then after that, I guess something happened with the American manufacturer...he was too busy to make them, so they went to Korea, and evidently the quality of the bears went down, and I pulled out of the whole thing. I said, "I'm sorry, I just can't have my name on it."...

L: ...Okay, well thank you so much for your time. It's been quite an honor.

D: Well, it was an honor for me to be able to talk to all of you wonderful fans of the Jack Benny Show, and those wonderful years that I had and was blessed to be able to be associated with a man like Jack Benny, and Mary Livingstone and Rochester and Don Wilson and Phil Harris...
Phil and I are the only two left...God knows how long either one of us will still be here.

L: Well, Mel Blanc is still around...

D: Yeah, well he was not one of the original starring cast-- he wasn't announced...The Jack Benny Show starring Jack Benny, Mary Livingstone, Phil Harris, Rochester, Dennis Day and...yours truly, Don Wilson! Actually... a featured player (who) was a wonderful man, too, who passed away not too long ago was Frank Nelson. YESSSS?! Oh yes, he was a beautiful man. Mel is still working.

He's had about seventeen operations since his automobile accident about twenty-five years ago...But Bea Benadaret used to be on there. I do see Sandra Gould every once in a while, she played one of the telephone operators on the program. There's still a number of them--Elliot Lewis who played...Frank Remley, and...Sheldon Leonard. He was the "Hiya bub!...C'mere. What elevator you takin'? Un-uh." Those were funny things.

L: Yeah, there were so many wonderful cast members.

D: ...I appreciate your talking with me, and as I say to be able to talk to you and to all the fans of the Jack Benny shows, and to all my wonderful friends.

L: Believe me, it's been an immense pleasure...

AND IT WAS! IT WAS!

Well, look at all this room now. Some of you asked about the exact beginnings of the fan club, so here is the updated official history as adapted from the release for the 1987 Jack Benny Tribute:

The International Jack Benny Fan Club officially started on January 1, 1980. Laura Lee, aged ten years, was the sole founder and President. The first newsletters were individually typed and included copies of articles on Jack Benny and his colleagues. Four honorary members were soon added: George Burns, Irving Fein, Fred deCordova and Itzhak Perlman. Membership grew slightly in thr first years, but the club was still in obscurity. Because of constraints on Laura's time, the newsletters eventually fell out of publication and the club became dormant.

In mid-1983, Laura discovered an article about a Jack Benny fan in Connecticut, Jay Hickerson. Laura contacted him about the small club and her desire for more members. Jay himself became a member and mentioned the club in his publication, Hello Again, named after Jack's immortal opening line. Laura received many letters of inquiry, and the small club began to expand. Seeing the renewed interest, in June of 1984 the newsletter was reinstated under the name The Jack Benny Times (oh really?). In September of 1984, it became a bi-monthly publication containing mews and articles about Jack Benny and information about gaining material on him such as tapes, books, and magazines. The fan club was then publicized in many other publications as well as in radio interviews with Laura.

In 1984, the word spread overseas about the club--with members in Europe, the club became international. In 1986, the Times was enlarged to encompass more articles. The Jack Benny Fan Club Family Album was established to make to club more personal; members sent in a photo and a letter giving a short autobiography of themselves to be immortalized in this special album for future generations of Jack Benny fans. The fan club has enabled contact between dozens of people who now trade tapes of Jack Benny's shows. A tape library of audio tapes is targeted to be released in May, 1988, and a video library is in the talking stages. Also in May, the club is planning the release of the ultimate Jack Benny log, containing listings of radio shows and appearances, television shows and specials, movies, books and articles concerning Jack Benny. Each member helps in his or her own way to perpetuate the memory of Jack Benny.

The members are now spread all over America, Canada, Europe and Australia. The club was founded on the philosophy that, "No one is ever dead until they are forgotten." The members of the International Jack Benny Fan Club firmly believe in the fact that...

    Jack Benny shall live forever.

Here's a list of all our honorary members in the order of their induction into the club:

    George Burns
    Irving Fein
    Fred deCordova
    Itzhak Perlman
    Ronald Reagan
    Bob Hope
    Isaac Stern
    Norm Crosby
    George Bush
    Mickey Rooney
    Frank Nelson
    Veola Vonn
    Jimmy Stewart
    Dick Cavett
    Dick Smothers
    Tom Smothers
    Phil Harris
    Dennis Day
    Mel Blanc
    Joan Benny
    Robert Sabonjian
    Milt Josefsberg
    Larry Adler
    Ernest Maxin
    George Balzer

Speaking of him, the next issue will be the start of the George Balzer interview, showing the program from a writer's point of view! Tune in next time, you all!

For those of you keeping score: the package I sent to Boris was returned to me, refused in Moscow because of "a tape." On top of that, one of the tapes was apparently stolen. Isn't that nice? Twenty bucks to send it, four-fifty to put the search on it, and eight bucks to get it returned. And all I got was a stolen tape. Oh well. We'll let you know what develops.

WRITE! Laura Lee, c/o International Jack Benny Fan Club Offices, 15430 Lost Valley Dr., Ft. Wayne, Indiana 46845.

Thought you might enjoy these clippings. Note the date on the Herman cartoon! (It came out on Jack's b-day!)

DENNIS UPDATE

As most of you know, Dennis took a bad fall shortly before St. Patrick's Day. They had to do some surgery, so I have been told, to release some pressure on the brain, but the latest news is that he is doing much better. If you would like to send a card, simply send it to the club offices and we will forward it right away. In the meantime, all our thoughts and prayers are with Dennis and his family. That probably sounds very much like a cliché, but I am certain that it is true from your letters.

COME ON, DENNIS!!! YOU CAN DO IT!!!

                                        Sincerely and with love,

                                        The members of the IJBFC

Jack Benny FAN CLUB

15430 LOST VALLEY DRIVE
FORT WAYNE, IN 46825

The Jack Benny Times

Volume VIII, Number 2   INTERNATIONAL DISTRIBUTION   March-April 1988

JACK BENNY ON "THE TONIGHT SHOW" STARRING JOHNNY CARSON

Jell-O Again!

PRESIDENT'S MESSAGE

Well, here it is at last. There are a million reasons why this issue did not come out at its appropriate time, the main ones being illness from February to late April, final exams in May and working on the log the rest of the time. At this moment, the log is 98 pages. We still have some verification and updating to do, so when it is ready for publication there will be a separate announcement mailed to all members with information on ordering. If you will indulge me, I must say that it looks like it is going to be fantastic.

Does everyone know that Jack along with Red Skelton, George Burns, Gracie Allen and a few others are being inducted into the Television Academy Hall of Fame in November of this year? Isn't it great? We will update you on this as information arrives.

Finally, yes the typing on the newsletter has changed. Larry Adler said that the other was difficult to read, so we went out and bought a computer just for him. Say, has that marriage come through yet? Anyhow if anyone so desires, our printer can rattle off a large-print version of this newsletter; so if you are blind, let me know. Now on with the show!

NEW MEMBERS

****JUDITH KENNEDY****JOHN BURNS****GARYDON RHODES****
LARRY VALLEY****DAVID L. ANDERSON****DONALD C. PALMER****
DONALD E. TAYLOR****VIRGINIA C. TAYLOR****MARION TINTORRI
****EVA TINTORRI****ROGER NELSON****J.E. GALLOWAY, JR.****
FRANCIS W. DALY****DON MARIS****SCOTT SEVERSON****
JAMES A. RAPPOLT****SARA T. RAPPOLT****BARRY HERMAN****
JAMES A. LINK****STEVE OUALLINE****JEFRY N. ABRAHAM****
RANDY SKRETVEDT****CHARLIE "CHUCKLES" WILLER****
RON "OH MISTER, MISTER" GREGORY****MARK J. BADE****
KATHLEEN S. PAPE****GEORGE T. PAPE****NORMAN GREENBERG****
JOHN DICKMEYER*****ROBERT SABONJIAN*****
MILT JOSEFSBERG*****LARRY ADLER*****ERNEST MAXIN*****
GEORGE BALZER*****SAM PERRIN

(Keep in mind that these have been backing up since before the Dennis interview.)

Welcome to all our (rather) new members!!!

TAPE TRADING LIST

Ellen Barker, P.O. Box 1402, Reseda, California 91335

Jack Bloom, 8618 Stansbury Avenue, Van Nuys, CA 91402

Hal Bogart, 2029 Aldersgate Drive, Lyndhurst, Ohio 44124

Yosef Braude, 25 Longhorn Road, Providence, RI 02906

Rob Cohen, 6635 Helm Ave., Reynoldsburg, Ohio 43068
"Would like to trade: Jack Benny, Amos and Andy, Bergen and McCarthy radio shows and videos of their movies. Also info on where to obtain actual radio shows that were put on video tape or film."

The Everills, 1558 Knox Dr., New Haven, Indiana 46774

Andrew Haskell, 160 West 39th Ave., Vancouver, British Columbia V5Y 2P2, Canada

Howard and Mary Joyce, 1050 Locksley SW, Grand Rapids, Michigan 49509

Laura Lee, 15430 Lost Valley Dr., Fort Wayne, IN 46845

John Malone, Rural Route #2, Wee-Ma-Tuk, Cuba, IL 61427

Bill Oliver, 516 Third Street NE, Massillon, Ohio 44646
(I promise! I'll write! Just as soon as I find a cassette! I'm so sorry! And thanks for everything!!!)

Lewis A. Pearson, 240 Ridge Drive, Marion, Iowa 52302

Michael Pointon, 11 Kings Court, Kings Road, London SW19 8QP, England

Keith Scott, 4 Bellbird Crescent, Forestville 2087, N.S.W. Australia (G'day!)

Joyce Shooks, P.O. Box 307, Sparta, Michigan 49345

Steve and Kim Smith, 1945 Coit NW, Grand Rapids, MI 49505

Steve Szejna, 3334 South 15th Street, Milwaukee, WI 53215

James E. Treacy, Jr., 5395 Petersburg Rd, Dundee, MI 48131

Is that everyone?

DENNIS' RECORD

Once again everybody, if any of you out there want one of Dennis Day's new 45's featuring "The Wind In the Willows" and "Let There Be Peace On Earth," please send $5.00 to the office address at the end of the newsletter. The proceeds from this record are going to the study for a cure for ALS, Lou Gehrig's Disease.

FAVORITE SCENES

Here's another of your favorite Jack Benny scenes:

From 1-23-49: Jack is having his teeth checked by Doctor Frank Nelson.

Dr. N: Open your mouth.
Jack :   (Wide open groan) Doctor! Why are you spinning my pivot tooth?
Dr. N: I used to be a disc jockey.
Jack :   A disc jockey?
Dr. N: And now I'd like to pull this next tooth for Sam, George, Milt, Tack and all the boys at Hickey's bar! And happy birthday to Jeanette!
Jack :   Now cut that out!

A moment later...

Dr. N: Nurse, grab the patient by the hair and hold his head back.
Nurse: Yes, doctor...oops!
Dr. N: Welll, then grab him by the ears!

Doctor Nelson's technician, Mel Blanc, brings Jack's x-rays. Jack is strapped to the chair...

Blanc: Doctor, I wanna have a word with you.
Dr. N: Excuse me, it's my technician.
Blanc: (whispers)
Dr. N: Really?
Blanc: (whispers)
Dr. N: Are you sure?
Blanc: Yeah!
Dr. N: Oh, then you've gotta help me! Nurse, hand me my forceps.
Nurse: Forceps!
Blanc: Novacaine.
Nurse: Novacaine!
Dr. N: Needle.
Nurse: Needle.
Blanc: Swab.
Nurse: Swab!

```
Dr. N:   Burrs.
Nurse:   Burrs!
Blanc:   Straight chisel.
Nurse:   Straight chisel!
Dr. N:   Saliva ejector.
Nurse:   Saliva ejector!
Blanc:   Drill.
Nurse:   Drill!
(tempo picks up)
Dr. N:   Coat.
Nurse:   Coat!
Blanc:   Hat!
Nurse:   Hat!
Dr. N:   Umbrella!
Nurse:   Umbrella!
Jack :   Doctor! Doctor! What are you doing?!
Dr. N:   Our lease is up - we're moving!!!
```

Send your favorite scenes to our address at the end of the newsletter!

FAMILY ALBUM

Yes, we still are assembling the Jack Benny Fan Club Family Album. All members who have not already done so are requested to send a photo (if convenient) and any information you would like included to us at...you guessed it, the address at the end of the newsletter.

Here it is! Send all questions, comments, etc. to: Laura Lee, c/o International Jack Benny Fan Club Offices, 15430 Lost Valley Drive, Fort Wayne, Indiana 46845.

Please friends, send no bombs.

KW sez this was one of Jack's plots to get back at Fred Allen!

Off Mike (Personalities)

Listener Collects From Allen!

Last week an alert radio listener took advantage of Fred Allen's program insurance — and collected. As

OCTOBER 24, 1948   RADIO

you know, Fred has taken out insurance to protect listeners who lose money because they are listening to his show when they get a prize-winning telephone call from a rival show. Well, one Allen listener wrote to the program and recounted how he had not answered his telephone because he did not want to turn off Fred's show. Later, he discovered that a friend had been calling to invite him over for dinner. Thus he felt that Allen was responsible for his missing one free dinner!

Fred sent the fellow three dollars and added, "Let me know if there's a tip involved and I'll send the money for that!"

After Television, Then What?

Jack Benny's Own Story of How His Friends In Show Business (Including a New Young Comedian Named Hope) Are Shaping Up for The Coming Trials by Television Camera

By Jack Benny

"TELEVISION?" says Jack Benny. "It's very interesting—I'm fascinated by it. In fact, I'm planning on staying home some night to watch it." (Bert Six photo.)

IT SEEMS that every radio comedian I bump into these days is worried sick about television. What will it be like? How will it affect them? What will be the reaction of the public when it can see as well as hear these comedians? For the actor, it means learning a new medium; mastering a different technique. No more reading from scripts; every line must be memorized. The sudden transition will not be easy. We few, who won't be affected by television, can't help but notice the fear in the faces of those less fortunate actors. It's like a Frankenstein monster that haunts them until they can't see or think straight.

Cantor Bears Up

Only recently, I had lunch with Eddie Cantor, a case in point. He spoke about Ida; his five daughters; the new picture he's producing; a play he has coming up on Broadway. He told me a few stories (which I had already heard from Jessel) and raved about some song he was doing next week on the air. But, *not once* did he mention what was uppermost in his mind—television. Cantor is always acting, but he couldn't fool me. I knew that underneath his apparent gaiety — the hand-clapping, the eye-rolling, the jumping up and down—he was trying to find escape —escape from the morbid fear that was sapping his strength and confidence.

Of course, with me, it's different. But, I couldn't help wondering how I would feel if I were in poor Eddie's spot.

As we left the restaurant, I tried to cheer him up. I shook hands with him and said, "Don't worry, Eddie."

He said, "Worry about what?" Pathetically, he pretended he didn't know what I was talking about. And as the chauffeur opened the door and little Eddie stepped into his big Cadillac, I knew that during that long drive to his forty-room home in Beverly Hills the one thing on his mind was that terrible dread of television.

Then, there's Burns and Allen. I played golf with George Burns and he pulled the same act as Cantor. He made out that he didn't have a worry in the world. He purposely played a better game of golf than I did, just so I wouldn't see how upset he was. On the way back to the club house, he kept laughing and telling me the same jokes Cantor told me (which I had already heard from Jessel) and all the while I knew his nerves were at the breaking point; that the specter of television gnawed at every fiber of his being. I kept thinking how fortunate I was —that I wasn't in the same position. Poor George, and Eddie, and Bob Hope, too.

Hope Is Brave

I met Hope at N.B.C. the other day, and he was carrying on worse than Burns and Cantor. Naturally, Bob is younger. He's just getting his break, and television will hit him harder than the others. There he was, standing in the lobby surrounded by a crowd of G.I's, signing autographs and cracking the same jokes that George Burns told me, that Cantor told me, (which I had already heard from Jessel). And when Bob called out, "Hello Jack, I'll be with you in a second," I knew immediately from the timbre of his voice that television was making a nervous wreck out him, too. But, I've got to hand it to Hope. In spite of the heartbreak, the fear inside of him, not once did he let down or allow his actions to betray his real feelings. He was brash and breezy, eyes sparkling, full of pep, but when I inadvertently mentioned what television would do to some radio comedians, that got him. His reaction was instantaneous. His face sobered. His manner softened. He put his arm around my shoulder, and for a brief moment I thought I saw a tear in his eye. At that instant I hated myself for having let those words slip out. How it must have hurt the boy!

He said, "Buck up, Jack. It'll work out somehow." Poor Bob. He didn't want me to worry about him.

Poor Allen

Then I got to thinking about the others. Fred Allen, for instance. What must be going on in his mind? In spite of what everybody thinks about Allen, we must admit he is intelligent. He realizes what television will mean to him. He shaves every morning. He *knows* what he looks like. I tuned in on his program accidentally one Sunday, and it was pitiful. He told the same jokes that Bob Hope told those G. I.'s, that George Burns told me after Cantor told me (which I had already heard from Jessel). I never felt so embarrassed for anybody in my life. The only thing that saved Allen's program was the audience. They were so sorry for him, they laughed continuously all through the show. You can't fool the American public. The people know television is just around the corner, and it was just their way of saying, "So long, Fred. You did a great job."

Last night, I went to bed, but I couldn't sleep. I kept tossing and turning. Every time I closed my eyes I saw poor little Eddie Cantor, Burns and Allen, Bob Hope, Fred Allen; and all those other radio comedians less fortunate than I. It was a never-ending parade. Fibber McGee and Molly, Edgar Bergen, Red Skelton, Jack Carson. Yes, even "The Great Gildersleeve." All of them potential victims of television. And as I lay there wide awake in bed, I knew what they were going through

(Please Turn to Page 32)

AUGUST 8, 1948

LIFELINES
BY EVELYN BIGSBY

Brunetta Mazzolini is a brunette to admire. She has a voice AND valor. At the last minute (7 p.m.), when the regular soloist was too ill to appear on the first show of Sigmund Romberg's NBC summer series, Brunetta stepped in and did such a commendable job that she became permanent. "If the fact that I was singing coast-to-coast with Romberg had registered with me, I would have been petrified," Brunetta told Radio Life.

She started singing at thirteen. Her brother was ill, so an uncle brought some operatic records to entertain him. Brunetta thought a Rigoletto aria so amusing that she worked up a take-off.

She understood and spoke Italian well, so was able to do the aria "straight" for an amateur contest and won. That prompted lessons and a two-year scholarship at Curtis Institute of Music in Philadelphia. She's been here in Hollywood three years, studying, working in small productions and radio.

At the Studio Club where she lives, Brunetta is now quite a queen. Other size 10 girls practically insist on Brunetta's wearing their loveliest evening dresses for the broadcasts. They attend the shows en masse. They're rooting for her to stay on radio come fall and to study in Europe next year. It was through a Studio Club girl who worked at NBC that Brunetta first heard about the Romberg auditions. Although she didn't win the berth at first, Brunetta kept spirits high.

She was busy sewing in the Club's utility room when the phone call summoned her to pinch-hit at Romberg rehearsal. "At first I thought it was a joke," Brunetta claimed. "I haven't been right ever since."

Her folks in St. Johns, Michigan, burst with pride when they heard her on the air. Due to being on a time-zone border, they burst doubly, tuning the show on both eastern and central times, one hour apart.

CALIFORNIA CARAVAN
THRILLING DRAMA!
SUNDAY at 3:00
ABC NETWORK
CALIFORNIA MEDICAL ASSN.

Page Thirty-two

GAGS OF THE WEEK

Mrs. Lael G. Street, 1113 Fair Oaks Avenue, South Pasadena, Calif.
Heard on "House Party":
Ken Niles: What is the definition of lumbago?
Small Boy: All I know, it's a famous composer.

Mrs. E. Peters, 2704 South Della Street, Garvey, Calif.
Heard on "Breakfast in Hollywood":
Garry Moore: What is the nicest place you have seen in California?
Visitor: The powder room in I. Magnin's in San Francisco.
Garry Moore: That's one place of interest I will never see.

Dorothy Thompson, 3111½ Hamilton Way, Los Angeles 26, Calif.
Heard on "Jack in All Trades":
Jack McCoy: Ladies, if your sewing machine is out of order, remember "Wishing will make it sew."

Lynn Mayer, 3039 Arrowhead Avenue, San Bernardino, Calif.
Heard on "Winner Take All":
Bill Cullen: From what animal does lynx fur come?
Contestant: A rabbit.

Mrs. Isabelle Noble, 4366 Westlawn Avenue, Venice, Calif.
Heard on "My Favorite Husband":
Lucille Ball: Oh George, that suit! You look like a banker.
Richard Denning: What's the matter with it, did I spill some money on it?

Mrs. M. G., Los Angeles 27, Calif.
Heard on "House Party":
Harry von Zell: Who is Lily Pons?
Schoolgirl: Lilies in the water.

After Television, Then What?

(Continued from Page 7)

—sleepless nights, tossing and turning, wondering what the future held in store for them. The uncertainty—the agony of waiting! The feeling of complete helplessness as, moving ever closer, television crept to engulf them and relegate them to the past.

It doesn't seem fair. Why doesn't science leave well enough alone? Radio is all right the way it is. Television can wait. Another twenty years won't make any difference. I'm willing to make the sacrifice. I'll relinquish my high place if it will help others less bestowed.

Let's not forget the human equation. Let's remember that the backbone of civilization is charity and kindness. So I say, hold off television. Science be dammed! Long live radio!

House Party Host

(Continued from Page 6)

court. With dotted pencil lines he traced the flights and bounce of the hard little rubber ball, showing how a served ball may sometimes bounce off the front wall, ceiling, and perhaps both sidewalls before the opponent can get a swipe at it. It's a wonder hundreds of heads and knuckles aren't ground to dust each day against the concrete or wooden walls and floors of courts everywhere.

But as Linkletter explained, "The requisites for becoming a player are safeguards against accidents. The game requires agility, timing, coordination, and vision. One of the most necessary prerequisites for a *good* player is his sense of 'anticipation' . . . that almost intuitive sense of what's to happen.

"It takes the average person several months to see any real improvement in his game. A beginner will learn to hit the ball immediately, but learning to hit the ball almost equally well with either hand is another story. That ambidexterity is what takes time.

"Another factor that makes handball a wonderful all-around game is the fact that it's extremely inexpensive. After you have shoes and a half dozen balls, you don't have to sink a lot of money into equipment. A ball usually lasts through eight or ten good hard games before it loses any of its elasticity or bounce."

Handball is by this time established in practically every gymnasium, indoors and out, all over the country, and whenever Art goes traveling with his shows, the General Electric distributors and dealers arrange matches for him in their home towns.

"One distributor in Detroit got a match set up for me, then got carried away and started laying out the bets, right and left, on my winning. I nearly let him down badly, and just scraped through to win. I would have felt like a dog. But I can't tell you how I welcome the sport and exercise those matches provide," Art thankfully reminisces.

The fact that Mr. Linkletter neither drinks nor smokes, that he makes a point of a good number of regular hours of sleep, holds his lunch-hour appetite in check, and deliberately enjoys as a hobby a game vigorous enough to supplant both his college swimming and basketball activities, doesn't mean he's preoccupied with health rules.

"I just like to feel good. Now I enjoy going to the 'House Party' and 'People Are Funny' shows. It's a real pleasure to greet those audiences, and see that they have fun. But if I ever cease to feel well, and going to the station becomes 'work' . . . it won't be fun any longer, believe me. Keeping in good shape is the only way I know of to insure enjoying my work completely. Handball is just the game to do it."

FAN CLUB

15430 LOST VALLEY DRIVE
FORT WAYNE, IN 46825

The Jack Benny Times

Volume VIII, Number 3 — INTERNATIONAL DISTRIBUTION — May-June 1988

IN MEMORIAM

Dennis Day 1917-1988

PRESIDENT'S MESSAGE

Well, we have some good news and some bad news. First, the good news. This issue will be our silver anniversary issue! Yes folks, this is the 25th issue in our "new" **Jack Benny Times** series. The **Times** was reinstated in June of 1984, and this is our 25th issue since then. (If this does not make sense by your calculations, just drop me a note and I will explain.) The newsletter has definitely grown in both size and circulation since then; in fact, the first issue was simply put in the memory of the typewriter and run off one by one. All the addresses of the recipients were hand-calligraphied by yours truly. That idea was quickly dispensed when I looked up at the clock and noticed that it was 5:45 a.m.! Anyhow I hope that you all have enjoyed reading the **Times** as much as I have enjoyed putting it together.

Now for the bad news. I suppose all or most of you know this already or have derived the meaning from the cover. Our most distinguished honorary member, Dennis Day, passed away June 22 at approximately 10:20 p.m. He had been released Sunday after a 17-day stay at St. John's Hospital in Santa Monica. I first spoke to Dennis last September, just shortly after he had been diagnosed with having amyotropic lateral sclerosis (ALS). Despite this grim discovery, he was in excellent spirits. He had said the day after he had been diagnosed, "I'm in good spirits and in the hands of the Lord." That was something that always amazed me in subsequent talks with Dennis; he had such faith in God--stronger than almost anyone I had ever known. This seemed to be the thing that "kept him going" without submitting to depression over his condition. Whenever I spoke to him on the phone, the anticipation of it made me rather jittery--just the thought, "I'm going to talk to DENNIS DAY!" Yet his voice always possessed such a gentle air that you felt as though you were just chatting with an old friend. It was rather that same innocence that came through his character with Jack; he could put you at ease with just a few words. The last that we talked, we were discussing my coming to California to visit them. I also mentioned that a relative of a member's friend had also just been diagnosed with ALS, yet reading the interview had helped so much. He said, "Just keep your chin up and don't give up hope! Simply be strong and God will take care of you." I am certain that God is taking good care of Dennis now...Heaven knows that he certainly deserves it for all the joy and music that he has given us. Our sincerest condolences to all of his family. Also, the day after he had passed away, I was listening to some JB shows while I was working in the back yard. The first song that I heard Dennis sing was

"Wish You Were Here." I think that the words are quite fitting:

> They're not making the skies as blue this year,
> Wish you were here.
> As blue as they used to when you were near
> Wish you were here.
> And the mornings don't seem as new,
> Brand new as they did with you,
> Wish you were here, wish you were here.
> Someone's painting the leaves all wrong this year,
> Wish you were here.
> And why did the birds change their song this year?
> Wish you were here.
> They're not shining the stars as bright,
> They've stolen the joy from the night;
> Wish you were here, wish you were here,
> Wish you were here.

God bless and keep you, Dennis. And thanks so much.

TALKS WITH GEORGE BALZER

This interview will also come in several installments, like Dennis' interview. Here is chapter one!

L: ...Exactly what makes a comedy writer? Were you always funny in school or come from a "comedic" family...?

GB: Well, what makes a comedy writer--I don't know whether they're made or...well, I don't think they're made. It's a talent, if you want to call it that, that from the day you're born you have it. A lot of people have it; they've just never discovered it and never had any chance to develop it, whereas others find out at an early age or sometime in life that they do and say funny things. Then as they think back whether there were any earlier indications, they find out that there were. So really being able to write comedy is not something which you can learn; it's an ability that you have, and you can improve upon it. But to just suddenly say, "Gee, I think I'd like to write comedy," and then start writing it...no, that doesn't work. I always feel that there (are) really three plateaus in people: the first would be anyone who has a sense of humor. Of course, that would include everyone because without it we couldn't live more than a couple months in this world. That's the ability to recognize humor. The other would be that if you hear or see something funny, you laugh at it. Then there is a way of seeing something on a rather serious side, and it makes you think funny about it. Then the last plateau would be where you can sit down at a typewriter or with a pencil and pad and see nothing funny and see nothing serious, have nothing at all to work with, but yet you can start out with that blank piece of paper and within a very short time you have developed something that's humorous, and that then becomes comedy. When you can do that, you're a comedy writer. When you have nothing to start with, nothing to think about to spark you into those thoughts, and you can just go and create something that turns out to be funny, why you are then a potential comedy writer.

L: Is that why the Jack Benny writers worked it twos more, that it was easier to work together to bring something funny from a twosome rather than from a single?

GB: No, we worked both ways. We used to work strictly two separate teams, and then when we would finish our halves of the show we would then get together with Jack and we would, all four of us, start from the very top and go over everything...When we had an idea for a show, it didn't make any difference who took what half. It just wasn't that important...We would kind of say, "Oh, this week we'll take the first half and you take the second," or "We'll take the second, you take the first."...What we would do was we'd kind of keep in touch by phone so that...let's say we, my partner and I, we took the first half. As we finished our assignment, we would call the others and say, "This is the line we're finishing with," and we'd give them an actual line that we finished with and say, "You just pick it up from there." That's the way the show was tied together.

L: Any fixed person that you usually worked with? I mean did you usually work with John Tackaberry or Milt Josefsberg?

GB: ...I always worked with Sam Perrin...Sam and I were together before we got on the Benny show, and then Milt and Tack were the other team. That's the way we wrote...Long toward the end, many, many years later... we had switched then, we had picked up two other (writers), Hal Goldman and Al Gordon, that we put on staff when we were doing both radio and television in the early fifties...Then there were six of us on staff. Then when we dropped radio and just did television, during that transition time, Sam and myself, we stuck to television while the others did radio. But we always got together with them to work on their radio show, and they would get with us to work on our television show. But after a period of about four years, or five, whatever it was, we dropped radio, and that meant the staff had to be cut back. So Sam and myself remained and Jack kept Hal and Al, and Milt and Tack moved on. They were there about twelve years...

we just continued on from there then with just the four of us. Now during that period or at the end of that period, we would work in a room, the four of us, with the script girl (Jeanette Thomas) and just talk the show out; and she could always tell what to keep by...whatever was said by whoever might say it--how it was received. I used to say to her after five (or) six minutes, "I'd say, "Jeanette, read back to us what you've got," and the lines she selected to keep were exactly the lines we wanted her to keep. She knew, she just had a feel for what we wanted to keep of all that was being said. It worked out very well.

L: She could almost be called one of the editors of the show...just as Jack.

GB: Very much, yes. Just take it all down in shorthand and then she would make copies of whatever we did that day, and then the next morning we would look it over, clean it up a little bit, and go on from there...

L: Were there any big problems with the transition from radio to television?

GB: No...you see, Sam and myself, we usually wrote more in picture, even though we were writing for radio at the time. We approached it where we created a word picture, and you may be able to notice this in some of the scripts, or in most of them. We create the situation in kind of a word picture and have our comedy work around that, whereas Milt and Tack worked a little more on the joke side. You know, where you would just bump into somebody, Mr. Kitzel or whoever it might be, or some character, and then get into kind of a joke routine, and then we'd go from there. So when it came time to turn the television problem over to two of us, Sam and I took that because we always wrote for pictures, even though in radio you do words, whereas in television you use sets and so forth.

L: Speaking of the word picture, was it you and Sam Perrin that...came up with the idea for the vault?

GB: No...See, I don't take credit for everything! That idea came from Milt and Tack...They came in one morning and said they had a routine which they had written for their assignment, using the vault under Jack's house. Well naturally, when we read it we said, "Gee, this is great!" So we started to use it, and we used it many, many times after that. If I may say, as long as we're talking about the vault, that was one thing that brought out the value of a viewer or listener using their imagination; because for several years we did the vault on radio...and it became very popular. Then we started television, and within the first year or two, we thought it might be very funny if we did the vault on television. So we got with the directors, producers, the set people and all, and we told them specifically what we had in mind and that they should build the set and so forth. They came up with a very, very good vault--excellent vault--we thought...We went on the air, and the next morning we would run into people, and they'd say, "Saw the show last night, but THAT VAULT! That's not the vault!" We'd say, "What are you talking about?" They'd say, "Well, to me, the vault is...", then they'd go into a long story of what had been their imagination for three or four years. Then we would run into others who would give us the same reaction. Everybody had a different picture of the vault and we proved the value of radio. You make everything the ultimate...That's just a little sidelight on the vault.

L: Probably the Maxwell with Mel Blanc doing it on radio also didn't carry over as well onto television.

GB: No, it didn't because in radio, much of the comedy... the studio reaction actually came from watching Mel in that coughing, gasping, wheezing stance that got such big laughs...As a matter of fact, most things were not quite as good on television, unless they were strictly visual material, as they were on radio.

L: So you think that radio was better?

GB: I think that Jack as a performer was better on radio. He had everything going; the voice...he was not so concerned then with trying to remember lines and movements and so forth. On radio you stood there with your script and you read your part. With the aid of sound effects, you could create anything you wanted to.

L: Somebody once asked me about Jack on television--how he would stand and stare at the audience in one of his famous "takes," and how that could have worked on radio as well as it did because you can't see Jack, actually see him doing a take at the audience... Probably...many of the listeners had never actually seen him. So just what...are your thoughts on how that worked on radio as well as it did on television?

GB: Well, actually radio, to a degree, cheats a little in that you have a studio audience, and when a particular line might be said, say against Jack, and there was reason for him to look, then he would just use the studio audience as if they were the television viewing audience. It was really the same kind of situation, and Jack always timed the laughs in that before the next party, actor or actress, was to start their line, Jack would always have a little "Hmmm" on radio. That just kind of...left the space and it was filled with laughter, then when that had died down, Jack would give that signal for the next line to be read.

```
             TO BE CONTINUED

If you have any questions or comments, please send them
to:  Laura Lee, c/o International Jack Benny Fan Club
Offices, 15430 Lost Valley Drive, Fort Wayne, IN 46845

Please friends, send no bombs.
```

Show world shocked by death of Benny

BEVERLY HILLS, Calif. (AP) — The show world reacted in sorrow and disbelief yesterday to the death from cancer of Jack Benny, whose gentle, self-effacing humor brought laughter to Americans for a half a century.

"I can't believe he's gone," said Mary Livingston to Benny's longtime manager Irving Fein. She had been the comedian's wife for 47 years and on radio played his wise-cracking friend.

"I didn't realize he was that sick, it happened so fast," said actor James Stewart. "It's almost hard to grasp. We'll miss him tremendously, as will everyone."

Fein said that doctors decided the cancer was inoperable because of Benny's age. During the final days he was in such pain that he remained heavily sedated. When news broke of his illness the day after Christmas, Walter Matthau, Bob Hope, Johnny Carson, Jack Lemmon, Danny Kaye, Edie Adams, George Bruns, Frank Sinatra and other stars paid visits to the Benny house. Another visitor was Gov. Ronald Reagan, a fellow star during Benny's years at Warner Brothers.

Benny was too ill to see any of the visitors. They gave their sympathy to Mary Benny and daughter Joan Blumofe.

"Everyone who knew him loved him," said Johnny Carson of the comedian who often appeared on the "Tonight" show. "I never heard him say an unkind word about anyone . . . I feel fortunate having my life touched by him."

Learning of Benny's death in a phone call from Burns, George Jessel said in Boise, Idaho, "If there is a place where good men live on, then there will be a place for Benny."

President Ford sent the family a telegram declaring, "If laughter is the music of the soul, Jack and his violin and his good humor have made life better for all men. We will remember you in our family prayer."

Eddie Anderson, who played Rochester, the Benny butler, chauffeur and all around jokester since 1937, expressed his shock and sorrow. "I can't explain the sadness I feel. I worked with many people in show business, but I don't know anyone to compare with Jack."

Said Edgar Bergen: "Jack Benny was a dear man and a great friend. The world has suffered a great loss but everyone can take comfort in the knowledge that he brought so much laughter into so many lives for so many years."

Added comedian Don Rickles: "I will miss him greatly and so will everybody. His dear wife Mary can take great comfort in the fact that no man was ever loved more than Jack."

Benny's type of cancer is hard to detect

WASHINGTON (AP) — Cancer of the pancreas, which claimed the life of Jack Benny, is one of the most difficult forms of cancer for doctors to find.

Once X-ray studies or other diagnostic methods conclusively confirm pancreatic cancer's presence, it is usually too late.

"By the time the diagnosis is made, the disease is far advanced. Survival is a matter of months, sometimes a matter of weeks," said Dr. Philip Schein of Georgetown University.

The pancreas is a gland that secrets digestive juices into the small intestine. Because of its location deep in the body and the peculiar nature of the tumors that grow there, detection is difficult.

Benny, 80, complained about stomach cramps in Dallas Oct. 19 while preparing for a benefit appearance. He wanted to perform but doctors forbade it. Hospital tests in Los Angeles disclosed nothing abnormal.

At a Dec. 8 appearance in Hollywood to accept an award, the pains struck again.

"The doctors still couldn't find anything wrong with Jack," said Irving Fein, Benny's manager.

"We all thought his pains were psychosomatic. But last Friday he had some more X-rays and the cancer was discovered."

International Jack Benny Fan Club
15430 Lost Valley Drive
Ft. Wayne, Indiana 46825

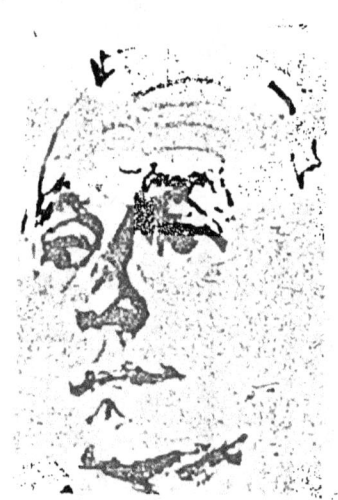

WELL!

The Jack Benny Times

Volume VIII, Number 4   INTERNATIONAL DISTRIBUTION   July-August 1988

JACK BENNY

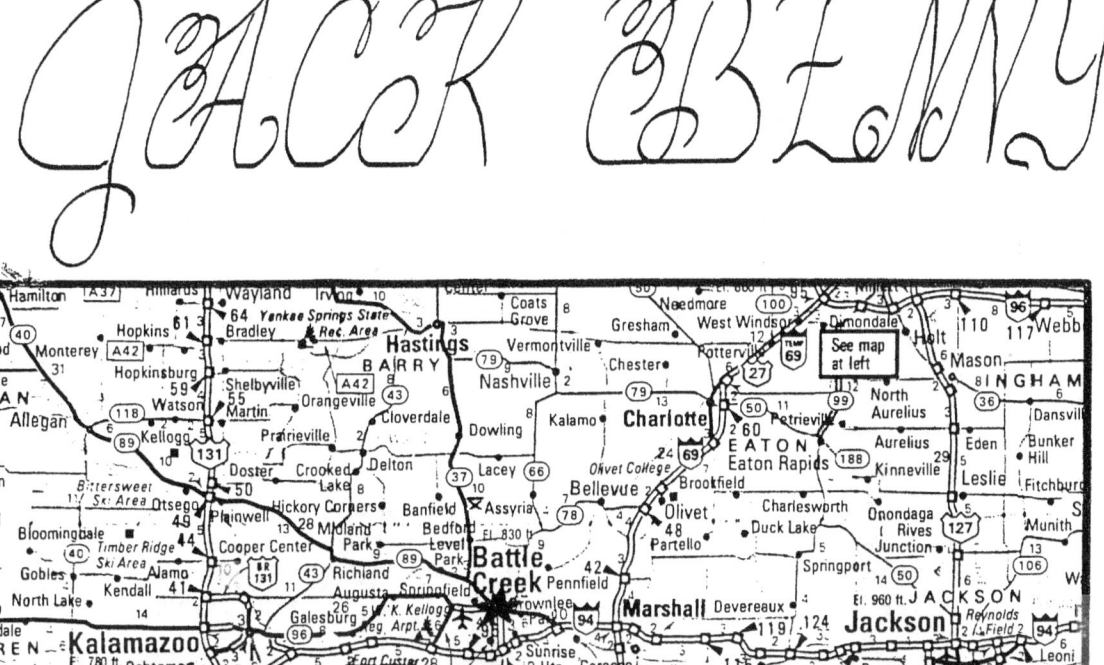

IS ALIVE!

PRESIDENT'S MESSAGE

Jell-o again! Well, just look at that right-hand margin. Larry Adler, upon seeing the type of the computer, insisted that the margin on the right be aligned. After reading the manual for several hours, I finally chanced upon the way to do it. Has that marriage come through yet? Is there even a chance that this is coming out on time? Wonders never cease.

It seems that the Television Academy Hall of Fame awards will be taped at a studio on the 20th Century Fox lot on November 13th, and will be broadcast on or around the 29th of November on (you guessed it) the Fox network.
Joan Benny will be accepting Jack's award. We will let you know more as information arrives.

How did the last two **Times** look? I think the halftones are a great improvement. Also, was there any problem sending them flat? Here is something for you to toss around; if I send the newsletter flat every other month (ho ho), it will be 35 cents. If I send it folded every other month, it will be 25 cents. If I send it flat every four months, it will be 45 cents. Let me know what you think the best solution is. I personally like the two-month format; it is small enough to just read through in one sitting. If we go with the flat, I think the membership will have to be raised to $6.39 (this also accommodates the halftone covers). Let-a me know.

Now on with the show!

DO YOU BUY CASSETTES?

Of course you do! And how much do you pay for those cassettes? That much? Well, read on friend! I have been sent some literature on Superior Tapes, Inc. in Monrovia. They have several different grades of cassettes in lengths from 12 to 122 minutes. Most of the people that I have spoken with have expressed an interest in the 62-minute cassettes for dubbing half-hour radio shows. The two most inexpensive grades are: pre-loads (assembled in Hong Kong) that are voice grade, and custom-loads (assembled in US), also voice grade. Pre-load 62 minute are **26 cents apiece** (yep, that's right), and c-load 62's are **29 cents apiece.** Even BASF chrome is available for 64 cents apiece in the 62 minute length. There are also two intermediate grades; if you want further information on these, let me know and I'll xerox it. Anyhow, the minimum order on tapes is 100. Soft poly boxes are 6.5 cents apiece in cases of 500, and clear Norelco boxes are 8 cents apiece in cases of 250. In lieu of the minimum order, if there is anyone out there who would be interested in joining in a bulk order of

Minimum order 1 case

Copyright 1989, Laura Lee

these cassettes and/or boxes (and grade desired), please write and let me know how many you would want. DO NOT SEND MONEY AT THIS TIME. I will keep tabs on how many everyone wants, and before ordering I will send letters to interested parties on totals due for their orders. At this time, I am quite certain that an order for 62 minute cassettes will be made, but orders of boxes and/or tapes of other lengths will be decided according to the response. Once again, if you want more information on this, drop me a card (ace!) and I will xerox the information for you.

JACK BENNY IS ALIVE!!!

Recently we received a call from Alexander Throttlebottom of Battle Creek, Michigan reporting that he had seen a man who resembled Jack Benny in his vicinity. He was playing a violin on the counter at the opening of a Stop-and-Go store and passing around a hat. He also reported that he was playing and singing a song entitled something to the effect, "When You Say Excuse Me Dearie Then I'll Return to Sorano." With this description, our reporters travelled as fast as their Maxwell could carry them to the home of Mr. Throttlebottom. He had this to say:

T: Yup, I was just goin' in thar for a big bottle of Bromo Seltzer when this guy in a toupee started playin' his violin. Then he took off his hat, and the label inside said, "Eat at Charlie's." So we all put some money in there, you know we just couldn't resist those blue eyes and all. Anyhow I went over to him and asked him if he was any relation to a comedian named Jack Benny. He put his hands on his face, hollered 'WELL!' and flew out. I ain't seen him since.

Q: Did you happen to see the make on his violin?

T: Yeah, I tried to see inside when he bent over to pass the hat, and I think it said Strad. Maybe Joe Strad.

Q: Can you describe more exactly the color of his eyes?

T: I'd say they were sort of a lazy lagoon blue.

Q: Bluer than the thumb of a cross-eyed carpenter?

T: Yeah, that's it. And bluer than the lips of a poor schoolboy at forty below.

Q: Well, Mr. Throttlebottom, it looks like you've found our man. Do you have any idea why he faked his death?

T: Well, I read somewhere that he said that being such a cheap guy cost him so much money cause he had to overtip. I guess he just got sick of doing it and wanted to be able to leave a nickel again.

Q: That's very possible. Do you remember anything else about him?

T: Well, when I dropped a quarter there in the store, he jumped around to see where it landed, jumped off the counter and grabbed it. But when I said that it was mine, he handed it back to me.

Q: Oh, I'm sorry Mr. Throttlebottom--that can't possibly be the one we're looking for. Sorry to inconvenience you...

Well, they can't all be gems.

JACK BENNY CLASSIFIEDS

WANTED - The Fred Allen show with Stuart Canin playing the "Bee" for the first time. Harry Goldman, RR6 Box 181, Glen Falls, New York 12801.

WANTED - 12-8-49 Jack Benny show where Jack buys Don shoelaces. Steve Oualline, 10214 Black Mtn. RD. #49, San Diego, California 92126 or Laura Lee.

WANTED - old records of any kind, Jack Benny shows for fan club library, etc. Laura Lee.

DO YOU WANT a Jack Benny classified? Send information to: Laura Lee, 15430 Lost Valley Dr., Ft. Wayne, IN 46845.

>>> MORE TALKS WITH GEORGE BALZER <<<

L: Since you say that your writing was so visual, how did you go into radio and not, say, pictures?

G: Well when I started, you see I was doing no writing at all. I just had reason to believe that I could write comedy, and luck and fate had much to do with my getting started and being successful. I actually got into the business with encouragement from Andy Devine...he played a part on the Buck Benny series on the Benny show. Andy was on the show about five years, I think...At the time I got interested in writing, I kind of thought to myself I could write, I thought I could write some of material like a Jack Benny show. So I wrote...four or five shows which were, in my mind, what the Benny show was all about. Talk about fate and luck, a man named Tom Devine bought a piece of property right behind our home out in the San Fernando Valley, and it turned out that Tom was Andy Devine's brother! So knowing this, when Andy was over there I made a point to be there visiting Tom! So I told Andy what I had in mind and whether he thought I should continue or not, and he said, 'George, radio uses material so fast--they use so much of it that if you think you can do it, just stick with it.' So I took his advice--I stuck with it, I got him to look at a few more things that I wrote, and then without saying anything to me he took them to Young and Rubicam advertising agency that handled the Benny show, and within a week or so I got a call from a Mr. Tom Harrington who was the head of the agency. He asked me to come in--he wanted to see me. So I went in, we talked about the show and so forth and they were encouraging, and while I was talking to them he said, 'How would you like to come to the Benny show on Sunday night?' I said,...'Oh, that would be just wonderful.' Now up to this point, I had never, never been inside a radio studio. So he picked up the phone, he called somebody and said, 'I want four tickets for Sunday night,' and the voice on the other end informed him that they were all gone. So he turned to me and said, 'There are no more tickets.' Well, of course I went right back down to the bottom...and he said, 'However, if you come to the artists' entrance and ask for me, then you can come back into the control room.' The first time I was in a radio studio ever, I was in the control room of the Jack Benny Show...Then for about two years, nothing happened. I picked up a little job here, a little job there...I don't know if you remember the character Bob Burns, Kraft Music Hall...I contributed to the writer who wrote that spot for a while. Then through another contact I had, I...went to eleven western states, a show called 'Circle Carnival' [Is that right? Can't find it in any books]. Then while I was on that, I got a call from Young and Rubicam who said, 'We want to put you on the Burns and Allen Show.' So Sam and I went...I met Sam [Perrin] on the Burns and Allen Show...and I was with George and Gracie for one season, and then the sponsor, Lever Brothers, wanted to put on what they call a summer replacement--that holds the time spot for the major show that's coming back in the fall. It was supposed to run thirteen weeks. Well, Sam and I took that show, and it did so well that the sponsor decided to keep it. So we ran a thirteen-week assignment into sixty-five weeks! Then on about the sixty-first or second week, we got the call to go to Jack Benny...That meant that in a few weeks I found myself on a train,...and I hadn't been on a train...since I came out at a very early age from Pennsylvania to the San Fernando Valley. I met Jack in New York--he [had been] in North Africa...doing a USO show for the Armed Forces, and I met Jack for the first time in

New York. We then wrote our opening show which was to be broadcast from New York...Preceding that, however, there was a press conference at the Sherry-Netherland Hotel with Jack having come back from his stint for the military, and somehow or other we came up with the idea for the interview that the press was conducting...and in order to do it, they needed someone to play a reporter. Well, I found before I knew it I was playing the part of a reporter, and this was for newsreels! So I went from this trip to New York for the first time to appearing in a newsreel, the next week appearing on the Benny show as myself as a writer--along with the other writers--and that's how fast things happened. It was just one beautiful progression of [events]...It lasted twenty-five years.

TO BE CONTINUED

Please send all tape orders, questions, comments, etc. to: Laura Lee, c/o International Jack Benny Fan Club Offices, 15430 Lost Valley Drive, Fort Wayne, Indiana 46845

Please friends, send no bombs.

Members make news!

He's loved those old radio shows since jr. high

By Martha Kaplan
Macon Telegraph and News

One of the most enthusiastic fans in Middle Georgia of 50-year-old radio shows is a 19-year-old Macon resident.

John Shores, a student at Macon Junior College, recalls his seventh-grade English teacher giving his class the assignment of writing a radio play. "We didn't do so well," Shores admitted.

Still, his mother checked out some tapes of old radio shows from Mercer University's library and brought them home to her son.

"Once I heard my first show — it was either 'Life With Luigi' or 'Amos and Andy' — I was hooked," Shores recalled.

Shores said when he became intrigued with old radio shows, he soon discovered that nobody in this area was selling such tapes. Then, a few years ago he was looking through a magazine and saw an ad from Ed Cole, a Florida dealer in old radio shows on tape.

Shores was off and running. He said he began writing to people all over the country who wanted to copy tapes and swap. Then, he began to get involved with trade publications.

Shores said he has written pieces on the history of radio for *The Illustrated Press* and *The Sounds of Yesterday* and is now busy preparing profiles of radio personalities. Not long ago, he had a long conversation with Jim Jordan who is his favorite radio personality and will be remembered by the public as Fibber of "Fibber McGee and Molly" fame.

Fibber's Molly (Mary Ann) died in 1961, but Jordan, now 90, lives in an apartment in Beverly Hills, answers his own phone and leads an active life.

"Not only are these old shows great entertainment," Shores said, "but they are a refreshing change. I think the material stands on its own."

Shores said he belongs to the International Jack Benny Fan Club. Its president is Laura Lee, a college student in Indiana. Lee has her own radio talk show which is devoted to old radio shows. The club has members in the U.S., Canada, Europe and Australia and include such fans as Ronald Reagan, Itzhak Perlman and Dennis Day.

"There are private dealers who sell shows to the public at lower prices than commercial outlets," Shores said.

Tapes from retailers normally run from $5 to $12 an hour, he said, whereas tapes from private dealers may sell for $2 an hour up.

Few of the popular radio shows ever made it to television, "Gunsmoke" being one of the few exceptions. "Have Gun Will Travel" has the distinction of being the only show that moved in the other direction, from television to radio.

Shores said he would like nothing better than to stimulate more interest in the area in old radio shows and is interested in talking with anyone interested in swapping tapes or starting a club. You can reach him at 4489 Tech Drive.

Sunday, March 1, 1987
Macon Telegraph – News

This article accompanied last Sept-Oct. (1987) Times cover.

READING TIME ● 4 MINUTES 5 SECONDS

BY IRVING WALLACE

11-29-41

WHEN Jack Benny saw Rochester's two-tone Buick station wagon, he was interested. When he saw Rochester's huge highly polished Lincoln Zephyr, he was more so. But when he finally laid eyes on his colored employee's new airplane, he promptly went to his writers and, as a gag, had them print and distribute throughout NBC and Paramount this headline:

"Extra! Extra! Jack Benny offers Rochester role of boss on his radio series. Benny bids for lucrative job of valet. 'I'm tired of working for glory,' says Benny. 'From now on I'm after the dough!'"

Which is a way of telling you that stocky cigar-puffing Eddie Anderson, alias Rochester, is in the chips. After years of struggle, he has pyramided

worked in an all-colored something called Struttin' Along. Next, he took to dancing with his brother Connie, and the two of them hit the Keith-Orpheum Circuit.

Then the talkies came. Rochester got small bits. He was Noah in The Green Pastures. He stole scenes in Jezebel. Mostly, in between times, he went hungry or picked up change hoofing in cafés. He blames his huge barbecue pit and his endless appetite on those lean years. "In my place, you'd eat too," he told me.

Four years ago, on an Easter Sunday, Jack Benny needed a Negro to play the brief part of a Pullman porter. Among the candidates was

$3,250 a Week For Laughs

The story behind an exciting rise to fame, fortune, and this week's Liberty cover

a remarkable comedy patter, a homemade talent at singing and dancing, and an adhesive lovable personality into an income of $2,500 a week from the movies and $750 a week from radio.

But Rochester has done even more. He has become Public Negro Good-Will Ambassador Number One, a credit to his race. His popularity knows no limits. His own people, dwelling in that Harlem of Los Angeles, Central Avenue, have elected him their official mayor. His boss, Jack Benny, without fanfare recently handed him a bonus of $10,000. And not long ago, on a personal-appearance tour, Rochester invaded the deep South, against the wishes of advisers —and the Charlotte, North Carolina, Observer spread his picture and his quotes across page one!

Rochester doesn't talk about money. Feels this might be bad policy for a Negro. His charities are tremendous —to Negroes *and* whites; to all institutions—but he won't let his publicists say a word about them (and he'll have my head for this line).

His minor ambition is to become a motion-picture director, but as his major ambition he wants President Roosevelt to establish a United States Army Aviation School for Negroes. He feels that a corps of great colored combat fighters—to be called "The Blackbirds"—would emerge. He has requested his Hollywood congressman, John Costello, to present the bill to the House. Today, with a plane of his own, he is not many solo hours away from his own pilot's license.

Now thirty-six years old, Rochester was raised in San Francisco, went to high school two years, and then, as a chorus boy and general handy man,

hungry Eddie Anderson. He won the audition, became a smash hit on the show, was brought back three different times, was dubbed "Rochester" by Benny simply because it sounded funny, and then was brought back for keeps. Today his scripts are written in good straight English, and he improvises Negro dialect into them. Incidentally, because he was born in the North, he had to learn a sound Southern Negro dialect.

His movie career progressed until today he is appearing with Bing Crosby and Mary Martin in Birth of the Blues and enacting his first semi-dramatic role.

However, neither Rochester's thirty suit-and-coat combinations, nor his yacht, nor his newly built fourteen-room, $35,000 colonial home off Central Avenue is as sharp as his incessant chatter. On the subject of Eddie Anderson, he's a three-ring circus. For instance—

On his physical appearance: "My face? Some one once said my face looks as though I slept in it. Another critic asked me if it was my original face or a retread. I wear my hair departed in the middle. Once I was even too lazy to walk in my sleep—so I hitchhiked!"

On his past: "Experience is something you get when you're looking for something else."

On himself and his job: "Just a lull in a big broadcast!"

Rochester always backs his horses. And always loses. A short time ago, at Del Mar, he tried out a two-year-old. It won. It paid $240 to $2 and—for the first time—Rochester wasn't on it! Besides horses, his tastes go to talks with pal Duke Ellington, milk for breakfast, classical music, watching motorcycle races, managing a down-and-out but talented prize-fighter, owning a night club, and joking with his wife and stepson.

Mrs. Anderson is an ex-court steno named Mamie who helped him in his climb, nicknamed him "Oozie-boozie," and stuck with him through thick and thin. His stepson and pride, twelve-year-old Billy, has taken over his swimming pool, his Little Theater in the basement, and his expensive miniature trains and tracks.

When I phoned Rochester, one of his four servants answered with, "This is the Anderson residence." Rochester grabbed the phone from her. He objects to formality. I told him I just wanted to check his height for this article. "My height?" he said. "Just write I'm so short that if I tried to pull up my socks I'd be blindfolded!"

Maybe. But also you know by now that he's an awfully big guy!

THE END

FAN CLUB

15430 LOST VALLEY DRIVE
FORT WAYNE, IN 46845

The Jack Benny Times

Volume VIII, Number 5   INTERNATIONAL DISTRIBUTION   September-October 1988

IMPORTANT DISCOVERY

THE FIRST* APPEARANCE OF THE "BATTLE CREEK FIDDLER" ON A BOX OF KELLOGG'S RICE KRISPIES.

*PLEASE NOTE THE COPYRIGHT DATE (1981).

PRESIDENT'S MESSAGE

Wow! Isn't that neat? Just thought you computer buffs out there would like to know that I am figuring out this thing so that the **Times** will be more interesting.

Anyhow, Jell-o again and all that stuff. You have probably already noticed on our cover that there has been another reported sighting of Jack Benny--this came from a member in California. He reports that he was just eating his breakfast, and BAM! There he was. If any of you have a sighting to report, please either drop me a note or call the "Si, Benny's Alive!" hot line at: (219) 637-2287.

The Television Academy Hall of Fame induction has been postponed until January 8th. Hope to be able to bring you an on-the-spot report, but still nothing is certain.

Did you vote on November 8th? (Those of you in the US, anyhow.) Down around Indianapolis, a couple of candidates had commercials on radio that were celebrity impersonations. One of them was Jack. Actually, it was the best one as the impersonator's natural voice sounded rather like Jack, you see. Anyhow, we will try to get a copy of it. Did any of you cable folks see the Town House Appliances commercial on Chicago channel 9? They even have a Maxwell!

A note of interest: Tom and Dick Smothers, two of our honorary members, are being featured on a channel of United Airlines. Why I Like United: they play wonderful music on their commercials (Gershwin's Rhapsody In Blue). It always gets my attention! Gershwin fans unite!!!

Well, let's get to it before my homework gets the best of me again. Now on with the show!

AND MORE WITH GEORGE BALZER

L: Could you give us a little breakdown of the cast...Mary, Rochester, Frank Nelson...just what they were like to work with...Was it easy writing the material for their character?
G: Well, in the first place, it was always easy to write for our people because Jack had so much respect for his writers...Anyone knew that if we put it on paper and it has gone through Jack, that nobody touches it. There was never any concern about the script; any members of the cast, they merely did what they were told. Not that we were always that "right," but that was the kind of situation. They had great faith in us...Sometimes we s

Copyright 1989, Laura Lee

would have a guest star booked, and...in conversation we might mention it to other writers on other shows. We'd say, "Next Sunday we're having So-n-so," and they'd say, "Oh, boy, he's a headache,"; and we'd say, "Well, he fit the part, so we'll have him on anyway." Well, this actor or actress would come on the Benny show, and they would be just as nice as could be. Now the reason for that was that they, too, knew that the Benny show would take care of them--that they would not be mistreated. They would be given good material, and they didn't worry about it. But when they appeared on other shows, they found out that they weren't getting quite that quality of material, or performance from the star, or whatever. So, we never really had any trouble with anybody. Jack had a philosophy which...proved to be so right...He's told this several times in interviews, and he said it to me personally. He said that he, Jack Benny, is number one because he's the star, and it's his show. Then next to him come his four writers. Then after the four writers come the shoe shine boy, the barber, the usher, the director, the producer; and you can put them in any order you want, but don't put anybody between me and my writers...What he was trying to say was that WE will put this show together, and we will do what WE think is right, and don't anybody interfere...It worked beautifully.

L: Were there many differences between the characters that the people portrayed and..."real life" character?...

G: No, the characters on the show were really different than the real-life people. I would say that everyone had their own off-stage character, but they came on and played these characters. Phil, you know, he looked the part with that dark, curly hair and real cocky attitude and so forth; so when he did that same thing on the show, he came off as that brash, young bandleader...God's gift to women. Dennis, of course, is completely different off-stage--he'd HAVE to be different! We had the BEST actors on our cast. Our supporting cast were really the top people in Hollywood. They were easy to get because they knew if they worked the Benny show, they would be getting called for many other shows, doing different things...That was a great goal for all the actors and actresses, to perform and appear on the Benny show.

L: ...What were they all like to "work with?" You said it's easy, but everyone has their own personality...

G: Well, let me start with Jack. I'm going to quote a thing that I did once. I was on the show as really just a young kid...but I was new on the show. Maybe within my first year or less, we had rehearsed a show, and we went into a conference room at NBC to rewrite and cut it down for air time. Jack came to a page in the script, and he said, "Fellas, I want a different joke here. I want something stronger, something funnier." We writers didn't say one word. He kept going, "What I need here is something that really pays off this whole business we've been doing." We don't say a word. He said, "What I want is just something...it just has to be better." After a pause, I leaned over and I said, "Jack, okay, we'll put something else in there." He says, "Oh! You agree with me, huh?" And I said, "No, but it's possible that the four of us could be wrong." Now you would think that right there, I would be through. But what happened was, he started to laugh, and he laughed and he laughed. He slid off his chair, down to the floor, and he sat there leaning against the wall laughing and screaming...He got up and said, "I wouldn't change that joke for a million dollars!" He didn't, we went on the air, it played beautifully; and we were all in the control room, and he looked up at us as if to say, "Oh, you cocky so-n-so!", and he went right on with the show...Now most comedians, I'm sure this is correct, after a discussion of that nature, would have purposely read the line badly so it wouldn't play, so he could say, "See? What did I tell you?" But not Jack. He was just great.

Mary could be tough when she wanted to be. By tough, I mean a little difficult. But I was fortunate. I was really very lucky in that for some reason or other, apparently Mary liked me. Don't ask me why--I don't know, but she was always nice to me...We didn't concern ourselves with any difficulty there because what we wrote, the writers and Jack, what we got on paper, that's what she had to do anyway.
L: Did she really have as much "microphone fright" as I've heard?
G: She was on the nervous side, yes, but not extensively. Mostly in television is where she got very nervous and eventually gave it up. But on radio she was fine. Of course, she used to do those crazy letters from her mother in Plainfield, New Jersey. As for anyone else...they were beautiful...Of course everybody says this, but we were a family. Well, we were **really** a family. We were back before shows really had working families. It was great.
L: One thing comes to mind when I think about Rochester. I read where there had been some news report that he had been lost at sea. Do you remember anything about that?
G: I remember everything about it. We were down in Palm Springs, and we had written a show, and we had a spot in it for Rochester...On the radio we heard a bulletin...this was...maybe on a Thursday. A bulletin was on the radio that Eddie Anderson, Rochester of the Jack Benny Program was lost at sea. We all were very concerned, not only about the fact that we had written a spot that we couldn't use, but that Roch was lost at sea! But somehow or other, with Roch you didn't worry too much until you got more

facts. So sure enough, he showed up. He was found and brought to shore, and he came on down to Palm Springs; and in the meantime, when we found out he was okay, that we were going to be able to have him on the show, we said,"Wait a minute. This thing has gotten national publicity." So we rewrote his appearance and tied it to the fact that he was lost at sea...It played very well because it was a real crazy, wild, typical Rochester spot. So it worked out very well for us. But Rochester was a kind of fellow who, I guess in his teasing, and I think that's what it was or at least I like to think that it was just teasing, he would kind of drive you crazy. Especially Jack. [Ed. note: I thought that was Dennis!] We travelled a lot, as you know, and whenever we went to the railroad station, in those days we travelled by train, somehow or other Roch was never there. But somehow or other as the train pulled out, he would swing aboard. Jack was always nervous and upset; he says, "Why does he always do this to me? He knows I worry about him not making the train." Well, one day we go down to Los Angeles Union Station, and we're all ready to go. We hear the "all aboard," we all get on, and a moment or two later the train starts to roll, and there's no Rochester. Jack says, "Well, it finally happened. It finally happened and I'm glad. Maybe this will teach him a lesson." Jack kept going on and on and on. He says, "Boy, I hope he learns a lesson." Now we're heading east, and about an hour later we're approaching San Bernardino where we're going to stop for maybe two minutes. And as the train pulls up to the stop, who do you thinks on the platform?...And he's got boxes and boxes of barbecued ribs!...All this barbecued food, and he steps on board the train. Later on that day, we're all on board the lounge car, and we're chewing on all this barbecue, and Jack was steaming. I said, "You know, Jack, it's awfully hard to be mad at a man when you're chewing on one of his spare ribs!" That's sort of typical Roch. Now I'll tell you another true story. When Roch passed on, that must be ten years now.

L: He passed away on my birthday, coincidentally...so I think it was 1978, February 28th I know for sure. I'll look it up. [Sorry, George, it was 1977. My mistake.]

G: Anyway, I couldn't make the funeral. I was either going to be out of town or something, but I had to be in the area of the funeral home two days before. So I stopped in for a few moments, went back and paid him a little visit for just the two of us. He didn't speak to me, and I didn't speak to him; he was laid out. Then I went up front...to a little flower shop that was in the same building, and I said that I want to order a sprig of flowers for the Eddie Anderson funeral. They said, "We'll be happy to take care of that. While you're waiting, would you like to select a card?" I said, "Yeah, sure,"

183

and without looking, I just sort of turned toward the card rack and pulled out a card; and I had half my name written on it when I noticed the card said "Get Well!" That's a true story! I said, "Look. Look what I did." So naturally I didn't use that card. However, if you stop to think about it, that was most appropriate. It was a way of saying, "Don't go." There was a hidden meaning there. I think if I had it to do over again, I would have just said, "I'm going to send this anyway to the family so they'll know what I mean." We really felt that way. When we lost Roch, I don't know, he was just such an important part of that show for many years.

L: Did you ever...have any racial problems with that?

G: No, and I'll tell you why. Because of the relationship that we created between the two of them, Jack and Roch, there was no racial problem, or at least if there was going to be any it would have to be reversed. We used to do lines such as: the phone would ring, Jack and Roch would be sitting in the living room...it would ring again, and Jack would say, "Rochester, answer the phone!", and Roch would say, "You're closer to it than I am!"...So he really took advantage of Jack, rather than Jack having a black working for him...Rochester first came on the show...as a Pullman porter. Originally, his name was Syracuse. That was just for one show. Then when he played so well and we decided to keep him on, they changed the name to Rochester and made him Jack's butler.

STILL TO BE CONTINUED!!

Please send all questions, comments, additions, corrections, ESPECIALLY ADDRESS CORRECTIONS, to:

Laura Lee, c/o International Jack Benny Fan Club Offices, 15430 Lost Valley Drive, Fort Wayne, Indiana 46845

Please friends, send no bombs.

P.S.   T'IS THE SEASON! (OH NO!)

Oh yes! Give a membership to the IJBFC this year for Christmas! It shows how much you care, and even more, it's FREE!!! Even Jack couldn't pass a bargain like that! A one-year subscription to the _Times_ is only $5.39. So give the gift that will make them say, "WELL!"

Benny Will Appear Weekly
Mary Will Step Out of Retirement To Help Launch Jack's 11th Season

By Bob Thomas

Hollywood — (AP) — There was much to-do when Gracie Allen retired from show business. Not generally known is the fact that her close friend, Mary Benny, has been virtually retired for almost a decade.

This was disclosed by Jack Benny as he prepared to kick off his eleventh and most strenuous season in TV. He'll face it without Mary, except for a brief appearance on his first show Sunday.

"I needed a scene in which someone would scold me - for going on TV every week," Jack explained. "Mary was the only one who could do it, because she is the only woman who has a close relationship with me. She agreed to do the short scene, but not before an audience, of course. She gets nervous even without an audience.

Worked at Home

"Actually, Mary never was crazy about performing. During our last days on radio, she did all her work at home, and the script girl read her lines with me before the audience. The people never minded, once I explained the situation to them."

While Mary has given up performing, she's still an important member of the Benny team, the comedian indicated.

"I always take decisions to her, because she has great insight," he said. "When I was thinking about going on TV every week, I asked her what she thought about it. I'd either do that, or stay on every other week and do a few specials.

"She advised me to go on regularly but to avoid the specials. 'You'll always be trying to top yourself with specials, Jack,' she said. 'You'll feel miserable if you don't.' She's absolutely right."

And so Benny is embarking on a weekly grind though he is 27 years beyond his legendary 39. He doesn't need the money. He doesn't need the fame. So why does he do it?

"I think it makes more sense in building an audience," he explained. "Before, no one knew exactly which week I was on; I didn't even know myself.

It was hard to maintain a rating, because people who liked my show might not like the alternate show, and vice versa.

"By doing a show every week, I can get into a regular routine. I don't have those dull periods when I'm anxious to get to work. The writers like it better, too; they know what their deadlines are and they prepare for them."

The schedule still leaves him time to play golf three or four times a week (though he groused about the loss of daylight saving) and to play fundraising concerts, as he will next month in Cleveland, Cincinnati and Indianapolis. It's a busy schedule at an age when a lot of folks are collecting social security.

"I think it's working that keeps me young," he observed. "If I had quit a couple of years ago, I'd be an old man by now. As it is, I just got the returns back from my annual checkup, and the doctor says I'm in fine shape."

BENNY IS BACK—Mary Livingstone will come out of retirement to join her husband for the season's premiere of the Jack Benny show on CBS-TV Sunday night. Jack is starting his eleventh season on television.

TV—Oct. 16

WOOD-TV Presents. 8.
Stagecoach West. 7.
Nat'l Auto Show. 3, 2, 13.
From the new Cobo Hall in Detroit, the 1961 model cars of U. S. manufacturers will be shown.

6:30—People Are Funny. 5, 10.
Spartan Football. 6.

7:00—Maverick. 8.
Bart and Beau win $6,000 at poker, but the money disappears in "Last Wire From Stop Gap."
Adventures in Paradise. 7.
Elsa Lanchester and Cecil Kellaway guest star.
Lassie. 3, 2, 6, 13.
Timmie gets a job at a circus.
(c) Shirley Temple. 5, 10.
"Madeline" starring Imogene Coca as governess of 12 girls.

7:30—Dennis the Menace. 3, 2.
Dennis won't split $1,650 with Mr. Wilson.
Navy Log. 13.
Biggie Munn. 6.

8:00—Islanders. 8.
A mysterious blonde is rescued by fliers Wade and Malloy, only to involve them in smuggling and murder.
National Velvet. 5, 7, 10.
Ed Sullivan. 3, 2. 6, 13.
Guests: Johnny Mathis, Mort Sahl, Peggy Lee, Dorothy Kirsten, Dave Brubeck. Premiere of Ed's new monthly series, "See America With Ed Sullivan."

8:30—Tab Hunter. 5, 7, 10.

9:00—(c) Art Linkletter. 8, 5, 7, 10.
Linkletter hosts "Love Is Funny," starring Chuck Connors, Zsa Zsa Gabor, Alan Young, Betty Garrett, Jimmie Rodgers.
Progress Theater. 3, 2, 13.
Anne Baxter and Ronald Reagan star in "Goodbye, My Love." A successful novelist's life is endangered by one drink.

9:30—Jack Benny. 3, 2, 6, 13.
Season premiere. Mary Livingstone comes out of retirement to guest on the first show of Jack's 11th TV season. Mike Wallace also will appear.

10:00—Loretta Young.

Jack Benny begins his eleventh season in television with a weekly, half-hour show. Mary Livingstone will join him in the season's premiere at 9:30 p. m. on channels 3, 2, 6, 13.

Monday
Johnny Midnight. 8, 5.

11:00—News. 3, 8, 6, 13.
Movie. 10.
"Sitting Pretty" (1948) with Clifton Webb, Maureen O'Hara. A genius becomes a babysitter.
Movie. 2.
"Smoky" (1946) with Anne Baxter, Burl Ives, Fred MacMurray. Story of a man and his horse.
Movie. 5.
"Rage in Heaven" (1940) with Ingrid Bergman, Robert Montgomery. Story about a paranoic.

11:15—Sports. 8.

FAN CLUB

15430 LOST VALLEY DRIVE
FORT WAYNE, IN 46845

The Jack Benny Times

Volume VIII, Number 6   INTERNATIONAL DISTRIBUTION   November-December 1988

BENNY'S ALIVE!!

PRESIDENT'S MESSAGE

Jell-o again and Merry Christmas, Happy Hanukkah, and what have you. Normally, this issue would be sent out at the end of December (come to think of it, it might be anyhow); but we will do it now just to get some of the enclosed information out in time for the holidays.

By the way, if any of you out there are interested in Laurel and Hardy or just old movies in general, I am in the middle of a book by Randy Skretvedt, a member of the club. It is entitled "Laurel and Hardy: the Magic Behind the Movies"--tons of illustrations, fine reading. A book definitely worth considering for the holidays for any movie buff. Will review it more fully when I have completed it.

Realized the other day that I was missing some of my mail; thought of a couple letters that I had not answered when I did my correspondence. It seems that someone cleaned out the library and 86ed some items. If you wrote a letter to me prior to the last three weeks and have not received a response, please let me know. So sorry.

Now for some good news.

CHRISTMAS MIRACLES

Remember last year we had a Christmas catalog selling "39 and holding" and Jack Benny Junior High School items (plus Dennis Day Christmas tapes)? Well, hope that everyone finally received their orders (life is never easy). If not, let me know. Anyhow, now that all is said and done with that (I hope), you, the members of the IJBFC, helped to raise $80.00 for the ALS foundation. (Applause!) A check for this amount will be presented to Patrick Day, Dennis Day's son, in Dennis' honor to find a cure for Lou Gehrig's disease. Deepest gratitude to everyone.

Doris Martin, a member in Illinois, was diagnosed some time ago with having cancer in many areas of her body. About a month ago, her doctor told her that somehow the cancer is almost gone. She informs me that her prognosis is good, and both she and her family are in high spirits. Who says miracles don't happen any more?!

Also, in the last few **Times** issues, we have been reporting information on the Television Academy Hall of Fame induction of Jack (and George and Gracie, etc.). Well, slam the door and ring the chimes...we will be bringing you an on-the-spot report of the proceedings. Just

Copyright 1989, Laura Lee

recently received the invitation (THANK YOU THANK YOU THANK YOU!!!), and will be flying to LA for the shooting at the Twentieth Century Fox Studios on January 8th.

Now on with the show!

EVEN MORE WITH

* GEORGE BALZER *

L: How about [the performing habits of] some of the supporting players like Mel Blanc or the telephone operators?
G: The telephone operators were...the only two characters I know who could step out of a swimming pool smelling of perspiration!
L: Now that's about the characters, not the ladies!
G: That's the characters! The characters were beautifully played by Bea Benadaret and Sara Berner. They were the original telephone operators, and did a marvelous job for us. Of course, they both played many parts on many different shows. In those days of radio, good actors or actresses would play maybe five or six shows a week, because they merely...changed their voice. In radio, actors could play two or three parts in the same show.
L: Mel Blanc.
G: That's right. Mel Blanc would do that for us many, many times. So they were really fine people to work with. No problems. We didn't have cast problems.
L: That's different from most other radio shows [about which] I've heard.
G: Well, it is because there's no one at the helm who is really respected. I contend that one trouble with television today, has been for a long while in comedy...is that from the time the writers finish the script and really believe that this is good, this is the way we want to do it; you turn it in, and from there on it goes downhill. People start picking at it, change it--they think they're fixing it but they're hurting it in most cases. Eventually what goes on the air is entirely different from what the writers had in mind. This is what they get stuck with.
L: Did you ever write for any of Jack's movies?
G: Not really. Of course, I came on after the "[Buck] Benny Rides Again" show, but "Horn Blows at Midnight" I think I had...a couple of lines in that. The only way we would work on Jack's movies would be...if he would bring a scene home from the studio that maybe he wanted strengthened...we might put in a line or two.
L: Jack...was successful on stage and radio and television, and really never made it "big" in the movies.

He did many of them, but why do you think he never really fit into the movies?

G: "To Be or Not to Be" was his best picture. His movies made pretty good money...Yet, I kind of know what you're saying--he was not a big success in pictures, but he was a success. As to why that would be, I don't know. Jack's greatest performance again was radio. That's where he was at his best. I see a lot of the old television shows now on cable, and I will say that most of them hold up just as well today as when they were first done. Yet I see that...at times, [Jack] is very evidently concerned from line to line that he say the right line. He shows his being a little uncomfortable. But...the ratings were always good, and the shows were well-received. You can't ask for more than that.

L: Did you ever have a favorite show?

G: Yes. The classiest show we ever did, I think, was the first Colman show. Jack went over...uninvited, but thinking he was invited, wearing his top hat, tie, gloves, etc., and spent the evening at the Colmans', has dinner and everything, and never knows he was not invited. That, to me, was a classy show because it was done with classy people. Are you familiar with the "I Can't Stand Jack Benny" contest?...[L: Oh sure!] Did I ever tell you how that came about? Usually when we go off the air on Sunday night, we never knew what we were going to do the next Sunday in radio. But somehow by Tuesday, we'd get an idea. We'd check it with Jack, and he'd say, "Yeah, that sounds like it could be something. Write it. See what you can do with it." So we would write Wednesday and Thursday; and then we'd go to Jack's home in Beverly Hills, and then on Friday we'd meet with him and spend a couple of hours cleaning it up, putting it together and so forth; and then send it down to NBC for mimeo; and on Saturday we'd rehearse; Sunday rehearse and do the show; and here we are again in the same fix. We don't know what we are going to do next week. But we always know that somehow by Tuesday afternoon, we'll think of something. Well, this one week, Tuesday afternoon came and we didn't think of anything. Wednesday morning we went over to Jack's house and said, "Nothing's happening. Maybe if we all sit here together for a while, something will come up." Well, we have no show for Sunday, and it's now getting about noon on Wednesday. I think it was Sam, my partner, said to Jack, "Why don't we have a contest where we ask our listeners to write lyrics for a song. Then they'll send them in, and then we'll have Mahlon Merrick, our musical director, put a melody to them; and then, we'll just have that kind of a contest." Jack says, "No, I don't want to go through that." So we're thinking a little bit more, and I said, "Jack, I have an idea. You know, we hear so much on the radio--"I like so-n-so toothpaste" in twenty-five words or less, and then you win a prize; or you like so-n-so potato chips in twenty-five words or less. Why don't we do this: we'll ask people to write in and say, "I can't stand Jack Benny" in twenty-five words or less, and give them a prize!" There's absolute silence in the room. Silence. The other three writers look at me. I don't know what to do. And Jack is looking at me. And he gets up out of his chair, and he walks across the room, puts his hand on my shoulder, and he says, "That's it. That's what we're gonna do." We said, "Jack, you can't..." He said, "That's what we're gonna do. And not in twenty-five words or less. We're gonna give them fifty words or less." And we did it. We were looking for one show. We ran that for eleven weeks. I think it was the first Colman show when we opened with the cast: Mary, Phil, Don, Dennis and so forth, they're reading the mail that came in. The joke mail, which we made up for the air. Then Jack says, "Well, I have to go over to the Colmans'. I've been invited for dinner..." Then that's when he first went to the Colmans'. Now that was, to me, the classiest show. When we started the contest, we had to put on eight women to handle the mail. It really came in. And Jack paid a price, too. He paid ten thousand dollars: five thousand to the winner in liberty bonds, and split up the other five [between] two other winners...[The winning entry] really said what everybody felt.

[Ed. note: This was the winning entry:

       I can't stand Jack Benny because
       He fills the air with boasts and brags,
       And obsolete, obnoxious gags,
       His cowardice alone, indeed
       Is matched by his obnoxious greed,
       And all the things that he portrays
       Show up my own obnoxious ways.

Contributed by Carrol P. Craig, Sr. of Pacific Palisades.]

G: I thought that was just great. We did not write that. That was sent in, and was the winning entrant. It worked out beautifully. And then...even a couple of years later when we were playing in San Francisco, doing a stage show up there--we did a broadcast also--and I remember two or three mailbags of letters came in in our premise. Jack says, "Oh, yeah. That must be from the 'I Can't Stand Jack Benny' contest I did two years ago." We always got a lot out of our material. It was fun to write that way, and Jack was very aware of not throwing away good material.

TO BE CONTINUED!

The next issue will probably concern itself with the induction, so stay tuned for more of George Balzer in March (or so)!

Laura Lee, International Jack Benny Fan Club Offices, 15430 Lost Valley Drive, Fort Wayne, Indiana 46845.

Have a safe and happy holiday, passez un joyeux noel, and all best wishes for a prosperous new year. Would like to leave you with Jack's speech of 12-30-45:

"Ladies and gentlemen, while history will point to 1945 as the year of victory, 1946 will be the start of a new era. An era in which people the world over must live together in peace and mutual respect. We won a lot more than just battles in this war. We won a realization that all men everywhere want to live out their lives in peace and freedom. While there are many different points of view of how this peace should be secured, the important thing is that all mankind wants it, and it will be accomplished. There's no place for hate, greed, suspicion and prejudice in a world that has the atomic bomb. The old era is dead, and 1946 is the beginning of the new one. The era of Wendell Wilkie's 'one world.' Happy new year, everybody."

The Ten Turning Points In Jack Benny's Life

Now that Jack Benny has reached the ripe old age of 39, he is apt to fall into a reminiscent mood more often than he did, say, ten years ago. In fact, "The Life of Jack Benny" was brought forcibly to his mind just this past week when a representative from the Simon and Schuster Publishing company approached him with the suggestion—well, it wasn't really a suggestion, it was a firm offer—that his life would make biographical fodder.

"My first thought was that I was too young to be biographed," said Benny. "At 39, how much has a man lived? Then, as a sort of a tentative thing, I thought back over my life and tried to select the points that were most important—at least to me."

And these are the points he thought of—as it turned out, ten of them.

No. 1—he was born. "The next nine wouldn't have happened if this didn't come first." He was born Benny Kubelsky on Feb. 14, 1894, in a Chicago hospital, but has always claimed Waukegan, Ill. as his home, because that is where he lived the major part of his youth.

No. 2—his father, Meyer Kubelsky, bought him a half-size fiddle when he was six-and-a-half years old. "This gave me my first taste of the show world, a taste which whetted my appetite, and which still hasn't been satisfied." Jack's subsequent teachers thought he'd make a fine violinist if only he'd practice. However he practiced just enough to be good, never great. But his years of sawing away at the fiddle weren't wasted. He started in show business by playing parlor concerts for friends and finally got a job when he was fifteen playing in the orchestra pit of Waukegan's sole legitimate theatre.

Navy Man

No. 3—World War I and Jack enlisted in the Navy at the Great Lakes Naval Station near his home. Prior to his enlistment, he had entered vaudeville, always as the violin part of a piano team. And he just played the violin, no jokes. But in the Navy, he was cast in the "Great Lakes Revue," playing "Izzy There, the Admiral's Disorderly." The director of the show, Dave Wolff, liked the way Jack read his first line and kept building the part. Jack discovered he had good delivery and timing. He also found he liked getting laughs. From then on he was a comedian first, a violinist second, then third, then fourth, then the worst violinist in the world.

No. 4—He met and married Mary Livingstone. They met first in Vancouver when Mary was twelve. He wasn't too impressed. They met later in Los Angeles. She was no longer twelve, and he was impressed. Their courtship was interrupted by the fact that he had to leave on tour. When he was in Chicago, he heard that she'd become engaged to another fellow. "I wasn't ready to get married, but I didn't want Mary to marry anyone else. So I asked her sister, Babe, who was also appearing in an act in Chicago, to persuade Mary to come and visit her. She did. Three days after her arrival, we were married, on Friday, January 14, 1937. It was the smartest thing I've ever done. I'm a lucky man."

No. 5—In 1929, after having signed a lucrative contract with Metro-Goldwyn-Mayer studios, he asked to have it cancelled. "This was a tough decision. It was the beginning of the depression. But the waits between pictures were too long. I felt my career was dying. I wanted to get back to Broadway. I talked it over with Mary. She wanted to do whatever would make me happy. So we did it. That was a real turning point."

No. 6—Ed Sullivan, who had a radio show in New York, asked Jack to make a guest appearance on it for free. This was in 1932. Jack's first words were: "This is Jack Benny. Now there will be a slight pause while everybody says, 'Who cares?'" A lot of people cared and the next day an advertising agency offered him $1,500 a week to go on the air in a show selling ginger ale. He accepted and has been in radio ever since.

No. 7—In 1934, Mary and Jack adopted a daughter, Joan, when she was six weeks old. "We always wanted children, but for some reason or other we never got around to it, so we adopted Joannie. We should have adopted more children; we were just negligent."

Few Changes

No. 8—On January 1, 1949, Jack's radio show began broadcasting on the CBS Radio network, where it has been heard every Sunday evening at 7 p.m. (EST) since. His show has consistently been in the No. 1 rating spot for many, many years. His cast has changed little in the twenty-three years he's been on the air. Announcer Don Wilson has been with him for twenty-one of those years. Rochester seventeen, Dennis Day, fifteen. And of course, Mary, who joined him on the show shortly after it started in 1932. His writers, Sam Perrin, George Balzer, Milt Josefsberg and John Tackaberry, have been with him for twelve years.

No. 9—In November, 1950, he made his coast-to-coast television debut on CBS with a line that compares favorably with the first he uttered on radio. When he stepped before the cameras he said: "I'd give a million dollars to know what I look like."

No. 10—this happened just a few weeks ago when his daughter Joan, who had married Seth Baker in March, 1954 in one of the most publicized weddings of the year, informed him that he was going to be a grandfather. "Which will make me one of the youngest grandfathers in show business."

A GREAT TEAM

JACK BENNY, "boy violinist," and his partner-in-comedy and in real life, Mary Livingstone. They were married on January 14, 1927.

FAN CLUB

15430 LOST VALLEY DRIVE
FORT WAYNE, IN 46845

The Jack Benny Times

Volume IX, Number 1   INTERNATIONAL DISTRIBUTION   January-February 198

"SPUDS" BENNY...

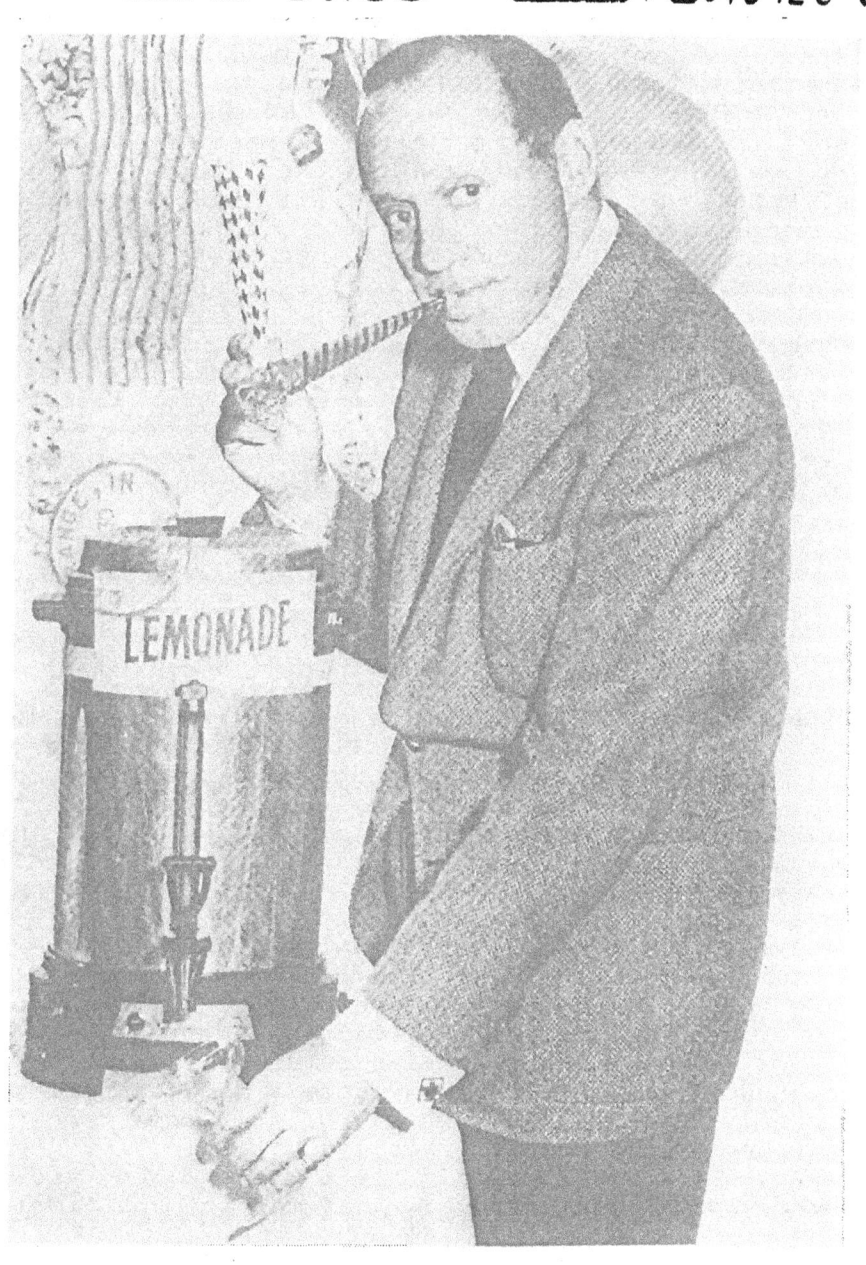

the <u>really</u> original party animal!

PRESIDENT'S MESSAGE

Jell-o again! As you probably have already noted, enclosed is the announcement for the release of the new Jack Benny log. Sorry for all the delays...hope the finished product is worth the wait.

Also, to my dismay, in lieu of numerous rising costs, we are being forced to raise the subscription fee from $5.39 to $6.39. My apologies. In lieu of this, is there anything that you would like to see in upcoming <u>Times</u>? How may the newsletters be improved? Hope no one has been offended by the "Jack Benny is alive" articles; we lost a member last year over the "Big Clip Club." I want this newsletter to reflect the things that you, the members, want to see and read. LET ME KNOW!!!

More apologies for the delays in responding to all my mail. The fact is early last December my mother had a stroke, and so I have taken over her work load. Hope the future months will bring a speedy recovery. Now some better news: yours truly is the newest employee of WEZV-WEZR radio of Ft. Wayne! An internship now, but hope it will continue over the summer. Now on with the show!

<u>CINDERELLA GOES TO THE BALL</u>

Must say "thank-you's" first. Thanks most of all to the party who arranged for my invitation...I will never be able to fully repay you. Los Angeles exceeded my greatest expectations; after nine years of trying to get there, you made it possible!!! A million thanks also are sent to Bill and Nancy Loomis who so generously allowed me to stay with them. Thanks to Morgan for the use of her room, to all females concerned for help with my makeup (had never worn it before), and thank you to Klaus for transportation.

Met two people individually while in LA: Sam Perrin and Chris Costello. Mr. Perrin and I had a great talk at his home for about an hour or so on all sorts of subjects; you can be certain that you will be reading it in upcoming <u>Times</u>! **Thanks again** for your time. Chris Costello (if you hadn't guessed) is the youngest daughter of the one and only Lou Costello. Have you seen that commercial for Bran News? There's a great story behind it. Recently a fan club for Abbott and Costello was started, and they are recruiting members. I know that many of you (including

_____   If this box is checked, $6.39 is due for
            another year of <u>The Jack Benny Times</u>.

Copyright 1989, Laura Lee

me) are also fans of the great comedy team, so let's get together and really get the club off to a big start! For information write to: **The Abbott and Costello Fan Club**, P.O. Box 2084, Toluca Lake Station, North Hollywood, CA 91602. Tell 'em Jack sent you!

Debated on how to present this report on the induction of Jack into the Television Academy Hall of Fame, and finally decided just to give you a play-by-play of the proceedings, and try to "take you there." I hope the following will communicate my own sensation of living a perfect dream, of experiencing an evening embodying an absolute joie de vivre.

Initially, an invitation was sent requesting a confirmation; then I received the two tickets--beautiful things...black engraving on silver. Neither cameras nor recording equipment were allowed; well, it was on television. I had gone through my closet immediately after getting the invitation, and had decided on a rather demure black dress with small rhinestone buttons. To put some sparkle in the outfit, I donned a necklace, bracelet, earrings and ring that really catch the light. Nancy Loomis accompanied me to the soiree. She had on a black and silver sequined top, black slacks and a diamond pendant. You can pick us out easily if you know where to look; to the far right of the stage, watch for the great-looking redhead who resembles Ann Margaret (that's Nancy), and the odd-looking one in the glasses with the bun in her hair (that's me).

So Nancy and I pull up to the gates of the 20th Century Fox studios, where a guard is posted to check the tickets. We both hold ours up to be seen; he smiles and says, "Go right ahead!" We are somebody!!! Proceeding onward, the first sight beyond the gates is the old set of <u>Hello Dolly</u> (so I am told). It is a lovely replica of an 1890's main street: boarding houses, bridle and saddle shops, and the like in very narrow buildings with about five or six floors. (Have I described that well enough?)

We follow the line of cars around the bend to the entrance. Naturally there is valet parking, and a gent with dark hair and a moustache escorts me out of my side of the car. There is the proverbial red carpet, all rolled out. Hey, we are somebody! Scattered all over the area are...is it "tiki torches?" You see, it had been rather cold--even snowed the day before, but no accumulation. We walk down the carpet a ways, and on the left are tables labeled with letters (i.e. A-D). Assuming that we are to "claim" our tickets here, I approach a blonde girl in a black dress at the L-N (or so) table. I give her my last name, she shuffles through some envelopes and replies, "Laura?" At this moment, one wishes to shout, "YEAH! THAT'S ME!" She hands me the tickets, and Nancy and I proceed to the cocktail area. I take the tickets out of the envelope, and see our table number: 7. How lucky!

A large tent is set up further down and to the left. The place is really packed. Unfortunately I am seldom able to recognize celebrities out of context, so Nancy kept a lookout. We eventually get near the bar for a drink, and a gentleman and his wife step up next to us. I really am not paying that much attention to them, but Nancy gently nudges me and cocks her head towards them. I look...hey...that's Vincent Price! Don't remember what they ordered...sorry. Nancy has white wine and I has a diet coke. I am able to hold my liquor well, but I don't want to be the least bit "impaired" this evening.

More people keep coming, so we go around to the far end of the tent where there is less congestion. There is a large model under glass of buildings which is near us; I think I remember someone saying that they were going to tear down this area and rebuild, so perhaps that is the proposed project (never stopped long enough to find out). On beyond there are searchlights scanning the skies...just like in the "fabled Hollywood." Decided to try to mingle through the crowd to "see some stars." Nancy decides to stay on the sidelines. I walk two steps and recognize someone—I'm so proud. Return to announce that I have successfully noticed and recognized Telly Savalas. "How could you miss him?" asks Nancy. I go further into the crowd and see Marla Gibbs. Other people look familiar, but I just cannot place the faces. Well, at least I recognized two people.

It is nearing time to go into the studio, and people are starting to file toward the entrance: a large archway outlined in chase lights. (The set is not visible from the outside.) Nancy points out Arlene Dahl to me. I think I see Lucille Ball...maybe, maybe not. We go in and turn to the left.

There it is...the set...as beautiful as it had looked in clips from the previous year. Michelangelo couldn't have made it any more spectacular. Generally, the arrangement is done in concentric semicircles:

(X is where we were seated.) I had been informed via a phone call on the 5th that we were sitting at Joan Benny's table. Joan Benny's table!!! Gee, we must be somebody!!! Joan is seated facing the stage, on her left is her son, on her right a female friend (sorry, it was too noisy to catch the name very well). I am seated on Joan's right, three seats down, and Nancy is on my right. (Got that?) The table centerpieces are "bushes" of yellow flowers; resemble daffodils, but not quite--narcissus perhaps? On each table is two plates of hors d'oeuvres: crackers with truly artful arrangements of shrimp, avocado and the like. Almost too pretty to eat!

Another couple sits down to my left--a young gent (maybe twenty years) and an attractive oriental girl, the girl being next to me. Digression: this really drove home the fact that fame is relative. In Morgan's room (where I slept), the back of the door was adorned with photos of male "teen idols"--no one I really knew. Nancy later informed me that the young gent two seats down on my left was named River Phoenix, and his photo was on the back of Morgan's door. Really? Big deal. Who is River Phoenix?

People are coming in gradually. I spot a couple walking towards us and immediately recognize the woman. I nudge Nancy and quietly mention them. They seem to be coming to the table...are they sitting here? Yeah! With an elegant smile she extended her hand and said, "How do you do? I'm Edie Adams." We all shook hands, and she sat on Nancy's right. OK now, going counterclockwise: Joan's son, Joan, Joan's female friend, River Phoenix, his date, me, Nancy, Edie Adams, Edie Adams' date, and an empty chair.

I decided to try to find Irving Fein, since we had been in touch about the program. Yours truly is so blind that I can't find the George Burns table. A waiter directs me. I made my way over, and we chatted briefly. He introduces me to his wife, Marion, who says that she also reads the <u>Jack Benny Times</u>. Wow! He also motions to a couple on his left and introduces them as Mr. and Mrs. Hal Goldman. Wow! The recent issues transcribing the George Balzer interview are mentioned. WOW! You mean <u>really</u> important people know what is in our newsletter? Anyhow, they point out other people standing around the table--a veritable who's who of show business. Bob Hope is talking to George Burns. Carol Channing is George Burns' date. Steve Allen and Jayne Meadows are coming over to say hello. Gregory Peck is around somewhere. Well, they are now asking us to take our seats. I am just about ready to "head back" to the table and am thanking everyone for their time, and I happen to notice someone just off to my right. I say, "(Gasp) Isn't that Fred deCordova?" My observation is

confirmed. We both are going to sit down, so in a burst of chutzpah, I walk up behind him and tap his shoulder. He turns around, and I introduce myself as we shake hands. "How do you do? I'm Laura Lee....International.."
"Yes, Jack Benny Fan Club!", he says. WOW! Maybe I am somebody! The show is about to start, so I gotta get back to the table. Gee! I've really met THE people!

One other funny note prior to "air time": how many of you remember my little Russian banjoist Boris? Well, if you saw them in 1987 on the Tonight Show, perhaps you will recall that Johnny Carson made a comment about Boris' resemblance to Red Buttons. Therefore, whenever people in America saw Boris, they would say "There's Red Buttons." Well, here comes Red Buttons himself across the hall, and I say, "Look! There's Boris!"

I must say that the awards have true "class"--really a beautiful piece of art work! I notice during the show that (speaking of) Johnny Carson is just a little ways off from us. Boy, his wife is a stunning woman--wish I could look half that good. I also notice a few people who later appeared on stage, i.e. Art Buchwald, Alex Haley, etc. Yeah, I can't recognize many celebrities, but I did notice Alex Haley. Don't ask me why. Was far enough to the side to be able to see things going on backstage--interesting! Also, I am only speaking from the audience perspective, but Tommy Tune is as tall as he looks on television.

Since I assume most of you saw the broadcast, I will not go into any great detail about that. However while watching the tribute to Jack, there was a consensus of sincere admiration; almost as if every person in the room had known him as a personal friend...a great sense of warmth. It truly supported the feeling that through his comedy, you perceived that Jack was someone close to you. One knew his weaknesses, accepted them, and even saw humor in them. Perhaps it is simply this: we feel we can know him so well, because **he**...is **us**.

After the show, the entire front of the stage is swarmed by media people, CNN, Entertainment Tonight, and the like. I just decided to stay put at the table. However, in another burst of chutzpah, I went over to Johnny Carson and introduced myself. I have heard people say that he has a way of putting you at ease. Well, I must say that he was about seventeen feet tall, but for that moment I did feel completely comfortable. I returned to the table and made a prediction (I guess "Carnac" rubbed off on me). Digression: First person outside of family says, "Who did you meet?" Well, one of the greatest name recognitions is probably with Carson, so I say, "I met Johnny Carson." My prediction was completely fulfilled as they say, "WOW! What's he really like?"

Dinner consisted of Cornish game hen, steamed asparagus, and half an avocado filled with shrimp salad. I found out that I love avocados--good stuff! The orchestra is playing Gershwin medleys. It doesn't get any better that this!!! Somehow, one of the flowers is knocked out of the arrangement. I start the bread basket around the table, and promptly drop a roll on the floor. As the old Beatles' song goes, let it be. For those who do not already know, I am a chocolate mousse addict. Everywhere we went in Los Angeles, I had to try the chocolate mousse. Here comes desert. It's chocolate mousse! Rah! A little different though. The mousse has a fruit sorbet in the middle. A half sphere of this luscious concoction is then covered with a hard, chocolate shell and topped with fruit to match the sorbet. Yum! Anyone not want theirs?

The place is clearing out...the party is drawing to a close. We decide to go, too. I suppose we all have to wake up sooner or later. Before we leave, on a whim I pick up the roll from the floor and the flower that was previously jostled from the arrangement. (The roll we are shellacking, and the flower is pressed in an 1860's family Bible.) The valets are bringing the cars around, so we stand and wait under one of the heaters. For whatever odd reason, I look up. On the tallest building in close proximity, they are projecting enormous photographs of past honorees. I keep an eye on it for a while, hoping to see Jack. Finally I start watching the people getting into their cars. A stretch limousine pulls over to the side, and David Brinkley and his wife stand about a foot in front of me waiting for it. Then, almost as a reflex, I looked up. There was Jack, thirty-nine feet high, grinning over all of us. I could hardly contain myself-- "Nancy! Look! Look!" Momentarily he gave way to a photo of another honoree, and I laughed at myself for being nearly as excited about seeing his picture as I might be about seeing him personally.

Well, here is the car. Two valets escort us to our seats and close the doors. Slowly we pull away, going back down the 1890's Main Street. Unwilling to go without looking back, I turn around to once again see Jack, bigger than life. No one could have scripted it better--as we rounded the last turn to go through the gates, I could only see that tallest building...and Jack...smiling.

FAN CLUB

15430 LOST VALLEY DRIVE
FORT WAYNE, IN 46845

The Jack Benny Times

Volume IX, Number 2 INTERNATIONAL DISTRIBUTION March-April 198

PRESIDENT'S MESSAGE

Jell-o again! Well, since we last talked I had my upper wisdom teeth taken out; my first (and last) date...Guess which one was more unpleasant (with a date they do not give you anesthetic)...have worked from being a radio station intern to being their primary on-air part-time person; had another newspaper article written about me; went to Grand Rapids to see the Leningrad Dixieland Jazz Band; started a campaign to have the band play here in Fort Wayne; been made editor-in-chief of another international newsletter; been accepted into the graduate program for my MBA; and invited to bring the whole fan club down to Frankfurt, Indiana to see the Maxwell. Hope to get down there some weekend this summer--you will hear it in the <u>Times</u> when I do!

<u>39 Forever</u> is a smashing success!!! Infinite thanks to Jay Hickerson...with his help, the first printing has completely sold out. Will be getting more soon. Also supplements are **in the works**; they will be available for a SASE. Announcements of release will appear in the <u>Times</u>.

Also thanks for all the nice comments about the Jan-Feb issue of the newsletter. I had hoped that the article on the Television Academy Hall of Fame soiree would be able to "take you there," and I guess it reached its goal.

The cover photo signifies all the mail that has piled up in the last few months. I have a portable typewriter which I take to work with me to answer letters while I am not on the air. Will try to get back to all of you soon!

Oh...I graduated from college, too. Now on with the show!

GUESS WHO'S COMING TO DINNER

L: The bloopers, like "chiss sweeze" and "grass reek" were sometimes good material for many weeks.
G: Now that was something where it just happened accidentally. "Chiss sweeze sandwich"..."Wait a minute! What did you say?"...and everybody was screaming. Then we did the thing about "grass reek" where (Mary) was supposed to say "grease rack." Then we were in Palm Springs (where Mary read a newspaper story about a skunk going across someone's yard, ending up with), "And boy, did that grass reek!" You see?

Copyright 1989, Laura Lee (Please note all Times issues are now protected by copyright.

This also brings in running gags. We had the Governor of California on as a guest at one time, Goody Knight, and it was on radio. He could not make it, and he was late for the broadcast...just a minute or two, and we knew he would be. So the broadcast was already underway, he came onstage, we hand him the script. He was not familiar, of course, with what happens in the script, but he was just going to do his part. In doing his part, he had a line...I forget what it was...and he stopped. Right on the air, he says, "Jack, I don't understand that at all!" Jack says, "You will! You will!" So he kept going, and then there was a line that "fit" what he had just said, and Jack says, "You see, Governor? You see how it all ties in?"

We did the running gags most every show, but not always. You cannot plan a running gag; it has to develop. There's no way you can say, "Let's do a joke on page 3, and then we'll do it again on page 7, then on 14 and again on 19." It just has to happen...and we usually made it happen.

L: Just to sidestep a bit...we had been talking about Jack, the man outside the show. I have heard so much about Jack's car trips across the country; it's rather hard to believe that he could just get in his car and drive to Chicago or wherever. Is it really true?

G: Yes, it's true, but I hesitate in that Benny would ride along--he usually had someone to go with him. I don't think he did that a large number of times, but he did do it a few times. One incident that happened on a trip like that; he was running out of gas in his Cadillac, and he stopped in a small town with very small gas stations. He's got this brand new Cadillac, and he says to the fellow, "Fill it up." (The attendant) says, "Okay," and he started walking to the back of the car...then he walked to the front....He couldn't find where to put the gas! Then Jack got out, and _he_ didn't know where to put the gas in! At that time, the gas cap was under a tail light--you'd push a button and lift that whole tail light up, and inside there was the gas cap. You would never know that unless you had been instructed. Jack, of course, was not mechanical at all, and had no idea...but eventually they found it.

But Jack was kind of a loner--he never had a large entourage as most comedians did. There were always five or six people that were always with them...but not Jack. He'd come to the studio...just the two of them...he and his violin. Between rehearsals, he'd go in the dressing room and...practice. Just to fill up the time. He enjoyed playing the violin. We used to say on the air when a picture came out many years ago..."Lust for Life" with Kirk Douglas--about Van Gogh...about playing his violin, Jack regarded himself as really an artist. He called himself "the Van Gogh of the violin." The reason he did that was because he was giving a concert one night in Dallas, Texas; and as he was playing his solo, a woman in the third row stood up and said, "My God, he's lost his ear!" He took this as a big compliment. Same thing as the first time he went to the Colmans. He's getting ready to leave; and their friend, Jack Wellington, says, "Good night Mr. Benny, and with my luck, we'll probably meet again!" (Jack) says, "Yes!"

L: Jack said about his violin playing, "You always hurt the one you love!"

G: ...Actually Jack was not a bad violinist. He wasn't a good violinist, but he wasn't bad. There's a difference there. He was good enough that when he played with the symphony orchestras, they covered him very well and he looked good playing it. He got by. He was a big attraction on the concert stage, actually, because the purpose of his being there was to raise money for the symphony orchestras. So he loved to play the violin, and he practiced as much as he could. He got a big kick out of it.

L: He asked Isaac Stern to fill in for him one time when he couldn't make a violin date, didn't he?

G: Yes. We also did a couple of television shows with Isaac Stern.

L: While you were working on Jack's show, did you do any work outside of that?

G: No, not really. The only outside thing we did was one summer during those first few years when everything was happening so fast, my partner and I had a chance to do a Broadway musical. We used the summer to do that, and it ran for about 18 months on Broadway. Other than that, we stuck pretty much to Jack.

L: Jack plugged that musical on his show?

G: Yes. I think it was 1945, and we plugged it when we went to New York to do a couple of radio shows live. "Are You With It?" was the title.

L: Jumping ahead to today, cliche question, but what do you think about today's comedians and comedy...how it has evolved since you were writing for Jack?...

G: Of course, Cosby is a very polished, professional performer who knows his craft; and this is after many years of being in it. He certainly deserves admiration. Most of the people, however, don't have that ability. It's awfully hard to say. They do so much stuff nowadays that I must say I can't judge it because I don't understand it. I really don't know what they're doing. If I know what they're doing, I usually say, "Gee...if they had only done it the other way, it's a bigger laugh." But the sitcoms today have become just very talky...It seems to me most of the time a lot of people running around who are not too sure of what they're doing. That's my impression. I could be wrong.

L: Do you think Jack's show would work today?

G: Oh, no question about it. It's kind of an excuse...when they say, "Well, things have changed." Well, comedy hasn't changed. What was funny years ago is still funny today. Your subject matter changes, but the mechanics of comedy have not changed. The mechanics of comedy--all those little things that make comedy play--are not really know by a lot of people who are involved in playing and producing comedy. I think the "old time" comedians and the older writers came up from a school...where you had to be familiar with those mechanics. Why a punch line should only have so many words in it. The minute you put in the extra word, you kill it. You hurt the timing. To make sure in the buildup conversation of one, two or three lines that there's enough information in those lines so that the fourth line pays off. The kinds of words to use, and the rhythm of the sentences to make it all play. I think they don't know about these things.

My opinion is that if Jack were just starting today, he would get laughs just as big as ever.

****
Our **sincerest thanks** once again to George Balzer for all his time and assistance.
****

If you have any questions, comments, corrections or additions, please send them to:

Laura Lee, c/o International Jack Benny Fan Club Offices, 15430 Lost Valley Drive, Fort Wayne, Indiana 46845

Please friends, send no bombs.

NEWSWEEK, DECEMBER 24, 1945

Please Kick Benny

"I can't stand Jack Benny because m[y] uncle likes him and I can't stand m[y] uncle."

"I can't stand Jack Benny because [of] those who know Jack Benny best it's Fre[d] Allen two to one."

These are samples of the 300,000-od[d] letters, wires, and records that have d[e]luged the Los Angeles postoffice sinc[e] Dec. 2. The reason: the latest contest [in] what is rapidly becoming, again, a co[n]test-mad nation. The rules are simple an[d] inviting as plugged on Benny's Sunda[y] night show (NBC, 7-7:30 p.m., EST[).] In 50 words or less—the usual 25-wo[rd] limit was discarded as too restricting[—]complete the sentence: "I can't stand Ja[ck] Benny because........." The prizes to[tal] $10,000 in Victory Bonds, with the funniest entry squeezing bonds worth $2,500 out of Benny—or more accurately, out of his sponsor, the American Tobacco Co.

The contest was born in the buzzing brains of Benny's gag writers, on the hunt for giggles. But even they were surprised when Benny took such wholesale self-derision seriously and screamed: "This is sensational, let's do it." Proof of Benny's perspicacity is the heaviest contest mail in the history of Los Angeles, the hurried plans of other sponsors for a return to the Why-I-Like days, and a round robin of plugs for Benny from a multitude of other entertainers.

The youngest contestant so far is aged 4, the oldest 103. But only a handful of letter writers have been seriously nasty and vitriolic.

Out of Pocket: The contest, which runs through Dec. 24, has three carefully qualified judges: Goodman Ace, for his knowledge of humor, Peter Lorre, for his mastery in handling weird jokes, and Fred Allen, for obvious reasons. Judge Allen confided to NEWSWEEK: I am the greatest living authority on Jack Benny. I have seen him reach for his pocketbook. No other living American can make that statement. I have known Jack Benny, man and boy, for 30 years. He was born a man and matured into a boy."

Asked what he would say, could he enter, Allen cracked: "I can't stand Jack Benny because with his legs that look like two nasturtium stems he can hardly stand himself, and if Mr. Benny can't stand himself, why should I try?"

As for Benny, he is glowing under the abuse. The only jar to his happiness: It is costing him about $4 a day, to make up due postage.

(Gene Trindl)

Jack Benny & Co.

In 30 years on radio and television, they've never missed a dividend, thanks to a stock of blue-chip jokes

Jack Benny, the 69-year-old comedian who looks about 50 but still says he's 39, has been a fixture of radio and/or TV for 30 years. During that time he has collected more medals, both real and imagined, than a Nicaraguan general.

Early in his career, his bouts with the late Fred Allen drastically altered the course of radio comedy. ("Benny," said Allen, "couldn't ad-lib a belch after a Hungarian dinner.") And by the 1940s, he had sold so much Jell-O that they switched him to Grape Nut Flakes. In 1948 he all but started a broadcasting war by defecting (for a reported $2,500,000) from one network to another. In TV, he has managed to hold his own impressively. And yet times have been changing rapidly. How has Benny changed?

Recently Benny sat with his four writers, whose combined time of servitude totals 68 years. They were discussing the script which they would be taping later that week. The guest star was to be Rod (*Twilight Zone*) Serling, and the idea of the show was that Benny, burdened in the script with writers who could barely write their names, was to hire Serling to give his writing staff some "class."

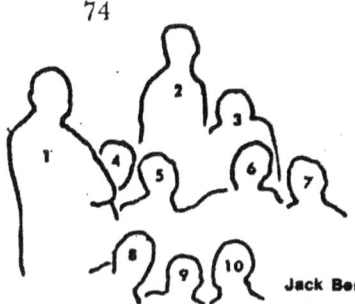

Jack Benny, Dennis Day, Eddie (Rochester) Anderson and Don Wilson above are respectively 1, 2, 3, and 8. The writers are Hal Goldman (4), Sam Perrin (5), George Balzer (6) and Al Gordon (9). Frederick De Cordova (10) is producer-director, and No. 7 in Irving Fein, executive producer and president of J&M Productions.

The jokes that week, as every week, were vintage Benny. In the beginning Jack is discovered washing his own windows—he is too cheap to hire anybody to do it for him. The Cheap Jokes and the Ego Jokes drop like heavy dew up to and through the moment of Serling's entrance. Serling is to come into Benny's office and explain why he is late: Benny's window-washing bucket has fallen off the ledge and hit him on the head.

Benny stops the read-through. "Fellows," he says soberly, "after my line, 'Gee, that's a shame, Rod,' how about if I say, 'Uh, you didn't bring it back up with you, did you?' Then Rod says, 'What did you say?' and I say, 'Oh, nothing.'" After the laughter had subsided, Cheap Joke #9999 is duly incorporated into the script.

Benny has been telling the Cheap Joke without cessation or apology since he first started in vaudeville during the 1920s. Explain its singular attraction and you explain Jack. Thriftiness is a universally human trait with which almost everyone can identify, and writer George Balzer (20 years with Benny) has said many times, "Everybody has an uncle who's cheap—just like Jack."

George Burns, Benny's oldest show-business friend and official Boswell, says, "With Jack it's not so much the Cheap Joke as the Cheap Man. He's always been in character." Burns, like Benny a great comedy technician, tends to see Jack as a man whose technique—particularly his masterful use of the Benny look—is so polished as to constitute an end in itself. "He is secure on the stage," says Burns. "He never sweats. The tempo is easy. If he tells a pointless joke and fails to get a response, he'll stop and do the look and the hand gesture. And if he holds it long enough, he'll *get* the laugh. He's such an institution they'll laugh because they're afraid there really is a point."

Benny has a simple explanation of his own comedy. "I emphasize character," he says. "The best humor I can possibly get is out of a stingy one. You can go as wild as you want. The audience has a point of reference: Everybody knows somebody who's real tight."

Jack's concern is only what he does *with* a joke. He likes to boast about his ability as an editor and about his eagle eye for contrived straight lines or for jokes—often very funny ones—which are inconsistent with the character he has spent 40 years creating. He is proud, too, of his sense for keeping his comedy techniques fresh.

He believes, for example, that one Cheap Joke prop that stood up for 20 years—the ancient Maxwell automobile—now is dated. But another familiar device, the bank vault where the Stingy One keeps his money, is still valid. "At some time I would have gotten rid of the Maxwell," he says, putting himself in the shoes of the fictitious tightwad he has created. "If I had a car, it would be a used car, but not a Maxwell. I wouldn't want to appear *that* cheap in public. On the other hand, a bank vault is a private affair.

"Oh, I've made other changes, too. Once I'd take out a loud-mouthed, homely-looking broad; today I take out a halfway decent one. You have to do that." He pauses. "The stingy character you can't help. If a man is stingy, he's stingy all his life."

Benny's writers point out that, except for Don Wilson, the members of the old stock company—Rochester, Dennis Day, Mary Livingstone, the French violin teacher, Mr. Kitzel, the parrot, the telephone operators, etc.—appear less frequently or not at all. This is attributable partly to the fact that television is less flexible than radio, which could build unlimited sets and situations in the imagination, and partly to the fact that the format calls for guest stars, around whom a protracted sketch must be built.

Jack the man is by and large totally different from Jack the comedian. He is truly generous and well organized, paying his real writers excellent salaries. If his comedy is "the comedy of frustration," as he says, then he is frustrated in at least one respect: He still seems to yearn to be the greatest violinist in the world. He owns a Stradivarius (an excellent one, says Isaac Stern) and practices two to three hours a day.

Next to most other comedians Benny sometimes seems all too colorless and workaday, a point about which he is sensitive. He prides himself on the fact that he is well liked, and urges would-be profilers to "go see my enemies—if you can find any."

Indeed, they are hard to come by. However, there are those who take a slightly less charitable view of the Benny comedy. "Benny can wring laughter out of a stone," says one highly placed comedy writer privately. "But he has to wring. I think all comedy is basically hostile. But Benny's is the comedy of petulance. For instance, when he begins to query his guest star Carol Burnett about her ex-boss, we know immediately what the joke is going to be. He wants Carol to knock Garry Moore and she won't do it. Benny is not only the most hostile comic going, but the one who most relentlessly satirizes the smallness of his fellow man."

That may explain something. But not everything. Philosophically, Benny is perhaps best left unexplained. Suffice it to say that at 69 he is still the most conscientious craftsman in the business. There is something rather touching about his devotion to just one joke—like a man playing a violin sonata on just one string.

But on that one string, ah! he is brilliant!

FAN CLUB

15430 LOST VALLEY DRIVE
FORT WAYNE, IN 46845

The Jack Benny Times

Volume IX, Number 3   INTERNATIONAL DISTRIBUTION   May-June 19[

IN MEMORIAM:

Mel Blanc
1908-1989

PRESIDENT'S MESSAGE

Jell-o again! No, your subscriptions have not been discontinued; I am just upholding the tradition of abominably late newsletters. Have an idea...what say we make the March-April issue the May-June issue, the May-June transferred to the July-August issue, etc.? No...I think that you would lose out in that deal. I think I made all my excuses in the last issue, so let us get on to more important things.

Of course, I am certain that everyone has heard by now about Mel Blanc's passing. If you will permit me a few cliches to demonstrate the mainstays he created, just fill in the blank (or Blanc); that train finally left on track five _____. The Maxwell will not start again (Oh fine. They just started playing "I Can't Get Started" on the radio). Carmichael spit out the gas man. The cimeron rolls have been delivered. The Tijuana Strings have finished playing. Oh say, can you si?...Now wait a minute! We have always said that no one is gone until they are forgotten. Not only is Mel still with us on tapes of the Jack Benny shows, but almost any time of the day you can turn on the television and see Bugs Bunny, Elmer Fudd, Yosemite Sam, Pepe Le Pew, and a million other characters which he created. Mr. Blanc is going to be around for a long, long time. In tribute to this immeasurable talent (what an understatement!), this issue is dedicated to Mel Blanc.

The Jack Benny tape library is off to a fine start. Some of you have expressed uncertainty as to the workings of the library, so I have included below an "outline" of our policies and procedures. Hope this helps. Also, several of you have queried me as to the trading of shows. Well, having discussed the financial end of this proposal with my father, we have agreed upon an order of blank tapes which will be used for these purposes. Ergo, anyone who is interested in trading tapes with the Jack Benny library is urged to send me a list of your shows along with your "want list." If you do not already have a copy of the library list, they are available for $1 plus a SASE (send to address at the end of the newsletter, as always). One other note on this topic...all new acquisitions will be listed in the *Times*.

On the topic of blank tapes, please note the JB classified section. (This includes you, Bill!) Anyone who is interested in purchasing 62-minute tapes (ultra-dynamic, voice grade) and/or Black Norelco boxes, but would be unable to make a minimum order is requested to notify me as soon as possible. On the last price list I have, tapes are 29 cents apiece, and boxes are 8 cents apiece. This offer is just to help "small consumers" out there to take advantage of these prices, since we are going to make an order anyhow. (Now why do I have to put something in the classifieds too?)

And finally, I noted this bio in the paper recently. Jack's mother? Was it in the show where Jack reminisces about the musicales in Waukegan? Or was it in one of the movies? Or am I just forgetting something obvious?

Other deaths

NORMA VARDEN, 90, a character actress whose lengthy stage, TV and film career included such roles as comedian Jack Benny's mother and the housekeeper in "The Sound of Music," died Thursday in Santa Barbara, Calif.

By the way, if you are within a fair radius of Windsor, Ontario, you might try tuning in AM 800 CKLW. I have known about the station for years, but never knew the frequency, Kenneth. (Remember that one?) Nice music.

Now on with the show!

LIBRARY PROCEDURES

Orders will be taken thusly: enclose a list of the items you wish, along with an adequate number of tapes for your order. For five or less hours, there will be a charge of $1.00 per hour to cover postage and service fees. For more than five hours, the charge will be reduced to 50 cents for each additional hour. These charges are to be paid with the initial order; the maximum order is ten hours.

BOOK REVIEW

Was fortunate enough to receive a copy of George Burns' new book _Gracie: A Love Story_ for my birthday. I placed it by my bed for reading a few pages each night before I retired. To be perfectly honest, I happily lost many hours of sleep over that book! It is similar in style to his _Living it Up_ and _Third Time Around_ (both of which should be procured at all costs...call your local used book shop). It is readily evident why it was on the best-seller lists for so long--even hitting number one. Sure, it has stories about Jack. Certainly, _Gracie_ is a fabulous tribute to an incomparable comedienne. As if that were not enough, the book has the engaging quality of enveloping the reader in every aspect of the people and the environment. You will feel as though you had known Gracie personally...and be richer for it.

SURE, BUT CAN HE PLAY LOVE IN BLOOM?

Recently was very fortunate to have a few moments with Itzhak Perlman after a concert at the Embassy Theatre in Fort Wayne.

I: We had a luncheon date...and he says, "Come to my office!"...I go in, and he was practicing. He was really practicing! He really adored to play the violin, and he knew he wasn't very good...He said people always thought he was kidding, but he (said), "They just don't realize that THAT'S IT!!!"
L: So many people ask me..."He supposedly was...terrific."
I: No, he was just a great fan. He had a very loose bow arm--that was very nice. But that was all!
L: What do you think the psychology is behind people (paying) however much to see you play Saint-Saens or Vivaldi, any yet would pay just as much to Jack play the same piece?
I: Well, that's entertainment. Ahem!...In his field, he certainly was an artist....Sometimes you have a crutch today, where people that want to be funny just utter four-letter words and they shock you. The thing is, Jack never did. He always relied on his persona and his history, and the fact that people knew he was "stingy." He also said, "The fact that I have all this (reputation) is costing me more money, because I'm always trying to prove (that I'm not cheap)."
L: Did you ever play in concert with him?
I: No, but he came to some of my concerts. He was real enthusiastic.
L: One last thing...what were the circumstances of your first meeting him?
I: I think he may have come to a concert...He was such a fan of music. I just remember that every time I would come to L.A., he would be there.

My sincerest thanks to Mr. Perlman for his time!

JACK BENNY CLASSIFIED

WANTED: Cassette tapes of 1930's "Popeye" radio broadcasts. Will trade for wants from extensive collection of pre-bop jazz and swing. Steve Smith, 1945 Coit Avenue NE, Grand Rapids, Michigan 49505

WANTED: People interested in trading shows with the JB tape library. Laura Lee, (address at end of newsletter).

AS PROMISED: People interested in ordering tapes (see description in "President's Message"). Please note quantity desired. For more information, contact (guess who): Laura Lee.

WANTED: Your favorite stories about Jack, or scenes from shows. If desired, just note show and scene, and I will transcribe. Laura Lee.

THE TALE PIECE

By these tidings may all ye know that "The Tale Piece" is the formalized name for a section containing your favorite Jack Benny "tales" and scenes. Just for the inquiring minds, the "tailpiece" is part of a violin.

This one was sent in by Don Taylor of Chula Vista, CA:

Jack Benny was invited by President Truman to an afternoon affair at the White House in honor of a group of reporters and photographers. Jack knew he would be called upon to entertain, as he always was, so he brought along his violin as a prop, and he also hoped that he could get Harry Truman to join him in a duet of The Missouri Waltz.

As he approached the gate, the guard, who not only recognized Jack, but had his name listed among those invited, stopped him as a mere formality and asked, "Your name, please?"

"Jack Benny."

The guard pointed at Jack's violin case and asked, "And what do you have in there?"

Jack, figuring he should live up to his reputation as a comic, answered, "I have a machine gun in there."

"Thank heavens!" replied the guard. "I thought it was your violin!"

****

Please send all questions, comments, additions, corrections, and orders to:

Laura Lee, c/o International Jack Benny Fan Club Offices, 15430 Lost Valley Drive, Fort Wayne, Indiana 46845

Please friends, send no bombs.

Mel Blanc, Who Provided Voices For 3,000 Cartoons, Is Dead at 81

By PETER B. FLINT

Mel Blanc, the versatile, multi-voiced actor who breathed life into such cartoon characters as Bugs Bunny, Woody Woodpecker, Daffy Duck, Porky Pig, Tweety Pie, Sylvester and the Road Runner, died of heart disease and emphysema yesterday at Cedars-Sinai Medical Center in Los Angeles. He was 81 years old.

He had been admitted to the hospital on May 19.

In a career spanning six decades, Mr. Blanc helped develop nearly 400 characters and provided a rich mix of voices for some 3,000 animated cartoons. In the 1940's and 50's he supplied the voices for 90 percent of the Warner Brothers cartoon menagerie, and in the 70's he was a co-producer of "The Bugs Bunny Show," an ABC-TV Saturday morning series that featured Looney Tunes characters in new adventures written for television.

In the 1960's he also contributed to "The Flintstones," the first animated situation comedy created for television and the first cartoon broadcast in prime time. For that series he supplied the voices for both Barney Rubble, the dull-witted neighbor of Fred and

---

He did dialogue for the 1988 film 'Who Framed Roger Rabbit.'

Wilma Flintstone, and Dino, the Flintstones' pet dinosaur.

Mr. Blanc was still active as he approached 80, when he made new recordings of five of his classic characters for the innovative 1988 live-animation film "Who Framed Roger Rabbit," rejuvenating Bugs, Daffy, Porky, Tweety Pie and Sylvester the cat.

Played Three Instruments

Melvin Jerome Blanc was born on May 30, 1908, in San Francisco, to Frederick and Eva Katz Blanc, managers of a women's clothing business. He attended elementary and high schools in Portland, Ore., and studied music, becoming proficient on the bass, violin and sousaphone.

He married Estelle Rosenbaum in 1933 and, soon after, they won contracts to appear on a daily radio program. The sponsors could not afford to hire additional actors, so Mr. Blanc used his voice to create a repertory company.

The couple then went to Los Angeles, where Mr. Blanc joined Leon Schles-inger Productions, an innovative cartoon workshop that eventually developed Warner Brothers' Looney Tunes and Merrie Melodies.

Mr. Blanc's first major character was Porky Pig, the shy stammerer. The second was Happy Rabbit, which he saved from oblivion by providing a new name, Bugs, from the nickname of the character's illustrator, Ben Hardaway. Mr. Blanc then developed a distinctively brash voice for the character and came up with Bugs's catchy cue: "What's up, doc?"

Events Changed Bugs's Character

Bugs's creators were very careful in shaping his personality. Events and other characters tormented him, bringing about a change in his naturally timid rabbit nature and pushing him to take the offensive. He became mischievous, but never mean.

In an interview Mr. Blanc explained Bugs Bunny's charm this way: "He's a little stinker. That's why people love him. He does what most people would like to do but don't have the guts to do."

The Blanc repertory company grew to include Tweety Pie, the devious canary known for the song "I Tawt I Taw a Puddy Tat"; the canary's enemy, Sylvester, whose favorite oath was "Sssssufferin' ssssssuccotash!"; the scheming Daffy Duck; the speedy "beep-beeping" desert bird Road Runner; the amorous French skunk Pepé le Pew; the shifty-eyed Wile E. Coyote, and the hot-tempered Yosemite Sam.

Mr. Blanc also created a dizzying range of sound effects. In the Jack Benny radio show he was Carmichael, the irascible polar bear who guarded the comedian's underground vault. He was also Mr. Benny's outspoken parrot; his violin teacher, Monsieur Le Blanc; his Mexican gardener, Sy, and even his troublesome Maxwell car.

Other roles created by Mr. Blanc were the wistful postman on "The George Burns and Gracie Allen Show" and a range of characters on programs starring Abbott and Costello, Dagwood and Blondie, and Judy Canova and Al Pierce.

Produced Commercials

In the 1960's Mr. Blanc formed his own company to produce and market commercials and fillers for radio and television. These included an unconventional announcement for the American Cancer Society in which a man was tortured to death by being forced to smoke one cigarette after another.

In 1976, the State of California hired Mr. Blanc to enlist his cartoon associates in producing 10 radio announcements to warn residents how to prepare for a major earthquake, how to survive one and what to do afterward.

In one announcement Bugs asks

Associated Press, 1988
Mel Blanc with one of his most famous characters, Bugs Bunny.

"What do I do when the shaking stops?" Daffy replies, "Stay away from damaged structures and power lines and remember to stay calm."

Mr. Blanc maintained a lifelong interest in music, and composed a handful of songs. Two of them, "I Tawt I Taw a Puddy Tat" and "The Woody Woodpecker Song," each sold more than two million records.

Mr. Blanc and his wife lived for many years in Pacific Palisades, Calif., where Mr. Blanc was the honorary mayor.

He had an insatiable curiosity about all kinds of sounds. "When I was a kid," he said, "I used to look at animals and wonder, how would that kitten sound if it could talk. I'd tighten up my throat and make a very small voice, not realizing I was rehearsing."

In 1985, he described his creative efforts thus: "What we tried to do was amuse ourselves. We didn't make pictures for children. We didn't make pictures for adults. We made them for ourselves."

Mr. Blanc is survived by his wife and their son, Noël.

Mel Blanc Dies; Gave Voice to Cartoon World

By PAUL FELDMAN, Times Staff Writer

Mel Blanc, the voice of Porky Pig, Bugs Bunny, Barney Rubble, Daffy Duck and countless other animated vertebrates, died Monday afternoon at Cedars-Sinai Medical Center.

He was 81 and had been hospitalized since May 19 suffering from heart disease and related medical problems, said hospital spokesman Ron Wise.

With Blanc when he died at 2:30 p.m. were his wife Estelle and son Noel, who now does most of his father's voices.

Although his lines were primarily written by others, Blanc's performances, like those of the Three Stooges and Marx Brothers, gave life and technicolor to a spirit of wise-aleckness in an era of gray flannel suits and proper manners.

"For the majority of us, the sassiness of our childhood, mustered alone in bed or nursed in sullen silence at the dinner table, had a secret champion in the voice of Mel Blanc," wrote Times comedy columnist Lawrence Christon in 1984.

Blanc, commenting on the personality of Bugs, put it in his own words: "He's just a stinker. In other words, he's more or less of a suppressed desire of what man would like to do that don't have guts enough to do."

Melvin Jerome Blanc was born May 30, 1908, in San Francisco, where his parents managed a ladies' ready-to-wear apparel business.

Even as a youngster, he displayed his one-of-a-kind vocal gift, regaling his classmates and teachers with the piercing laugh would later develop into Woody Woodpecker's signature call.

"[In] high school, I used to lay down the hall and hear the echo coming, you know.... So that's the Woody Woodpecker laugh," once told an interviewer.

Blanc, whose family moved to Portland, Ore., shortly after birth, turned immediately to show business following his graduation from high school in 1927. But the first five years, he made a living with musical instruments rather than the magic of his vocal cords. An accomplished bassist, violinist and sousaphone player, Blanc played in the NBC Radio Orchestra and conducted the orchestra at the Orpheum Theater in Portland.

In 1933, he married Estelle Rosenbaum, and soon after the couple began hosting a daily one-hour radio show in Portland called "Cobwebs and Nuts." Since management would not spring for additional actors, Blanc invented an entire repertory company.

"They wouldn't allow me to use anybody else because they were too damn cheap," he once said. "... It taught me these many, many voices. This went on for five years. Finally my wife said to me, 'You want to continue with show or do you want to have a nervous breakdown?'"

Opting for sanity, Blanc, accompanied by his wife, moved to Los Angeles, where he toiled as a character actor on radio shows while repeatedly seeking an audition with Leon Schlesinger Productions, the cartoon company that produced the original Looney Tunes and Merrie Melodies for Warner Bros.

Oral Test Passed

At Schlesinger, Blanc was rebuffed several times by the same production supervisor. But the man finally died. So after more than a year of knocking on the door as persistently as Wile E. Coyote chasing the Road Runner, Blanc was offered an oral test by the supervisor's successor.

The audition was rather unorthodox—at least for anyone other than a cartoon voice.

"One of the [directors] said, 'Can you do a drunken bull?' So I had to think for a moment and I said, Yeah,' . . . I'd shound, hic, like I was a little loaded, hic, and looking for the, hic, sour mash."

Blanc did better than the Coyote ever did. He got the job, and the rest, as they say, was history.

Blanc's first major memorable role was that of Porky Pig, which he was offered in 1937 after studio officials decided that the porcine personality, who was originally introduced in 1935, needed a face-lift.

"Leon called me in and asked me if I could do a pig—a fine thing to ask a Jewish kid," Blanc recalled. 'The guy they were using actually had a stutter and used up yards of film. But I could stutter and ad lib in rhythm."

Bugs Bunny followed a year later. "They originally wanted to call Bugs Bunny the Happy Hare. But the writer was called Bugs Hardaway and had a snappy way about him. He'd say things like, 'Hey, what's cookin'?' I said, 'Let's use it. It's modern.' That became 'What's up, Doc?' Bugs was a tough little stinker; that's why I came up with a Brooklyn accent. I always worked on creating a vocal quality to match the characters."

Blanc, indeed, was proud of his voices, proclaiming to interviewers: "I created every voice that I do except Elmer Fudd].

"I will not imitate. I think imitation is stealing from another person."

In the case of Porky, Blanc claimed to have visited a pig farm and "wallowed around" for two weeks in order to "be real authentic."

90% of Warner's Stable

In time, Blanc provided the voice for more than 90% of Warner's table of cartoon characters. For most of them, he helped develop the distinctive personas in tandem with such giants in the field as animator-directors Tex Avery, Chuck Jones and Robert McKimson.

"I create the personality when they tell me what the story is and so on," he once explained. "Sylvester was sloppy. Tweety was a baby with a baby's voice. Daffy was egotistical."

Known as "The Man of 1,000 Voices," Blanc was virtually never seen on the silver screen during the golden era of Merrie Melodies cartoons. Yet the myriad permutations of his acrobatic vocal cords have remained instantly recognizable by children of all ages around the globe for more than 50 years.

Among the many lines he repeatedly uttered that arguably rival those of Shakespeare in terms of familiarity, if not intellectual depth: "Eh . . . what's up, Doc?" through the lips of the wiseacre hare, Bugs Bunny; "I tawt I taw a putty tat," from the tart-tongued canary Tweety, and "SSSSSsssuffering SSSSSuccotash," courtesy of Sylvester the sloppy cat.

Not to mention Woody Woodpecker's signature laugh ("Hee, hee, heh, hah, ho. Hee, hee, heh, hah, ho"); both the laconic train conductor ("Anaheim, Azusa and Cuc-a-monga") and sputtering Maxwell auto of Jack Benny radio and TV show fame, and, of course, the stutter-strewn meanderings of Porky the wistful pig.

Over time, Blanc's reknowned "voice characterizations" became nearly as much a part of his own life as breathing.

In his later years, Blanc would often recount the scene as he lay in a coma at UCLA Medical Center following a nearly fatal 1961 car collision.

Bugs Bunny Invoked

"They say that while I was unconscious, the doctor would come into my room each day and ask me how I was and, nothing. I wouldn't answer him. So one day he comes into my room, he gets an idea, and he says, 'Hey, Bugs Bunny! How are you?' And they say I answered back in Bugs' voice. "Ehh, just fine, Doc. How are you?"

The doctor then said, "'And Porky Pig! How are you feeling?' and I said, 'J-j-j-just fine, th-th-th-thanks.'

"So you see, I actually live these characters."

For days following the head-on Sunset Boulevard collision, Blanc hovered near death.

But like his dynamic cartoon characters—who so often slammed into walls and shrugged their shoulders or were blasted by dynamite and proceeded to calmly wipe the gunpowder off their noggins—Blanc, after 21 days, finally awoke, picked himself up and went back to work.

Before signing an exclusive cartoon contract with Warners, Blanc also worked free lance for Walter Lantz, for whom he developed the laugh of Woody Woodpecker, and for Walt Disney. Unfortunately, his 16 days of work on Disney's Pinocchio wound up on the cutting room floor, except for a single hiccup by a cat named "Giddy."

It was one of the few cases in which Blanc was not successful. Blanc, in fact, eventually became the first voice specialist to earn over-the-title credits on cartoons.

Blanc later credited those credits with untapping a steady stream of radio work on such shows as Burns and Allen, Fibber McGee and Molly and Jack Benny.

On the Benny show, Blanc began with a growl—a bear growl. The bear was named Carmichael, and he guarded Benny's vault.

"Well, I did the bear growl for six months, and that's all I did was just the bear growl. Finally I said to him, 'You know, Mr. Benny, I can also talk.'"

Benny quickly submitted, tabbing Blanc to do the train station announcer, a parrot who called Benny a cheapskate, a harried retail salesman, Benny's exasperated violin teacher Prof. LeBlanc, and Cy from Tijuana, who answered most queries, "Si."

When Benny went to TV, Blanc made the transition too, doing on-camera stints in his character roles. Blanc also had bit parts in several movies and starred in his own forgettable comedy CBS Radio network show in 1946, in which he played the owner of a fix-it shop.

In 1960, Blanc turned to made-for-TV cartoons, providing voices for a Saturday morning Bugs Bunny show and for two of the characters on "The Flintstones"—Barney Rubble and the pet dinosaur, Dino. For a time following his 1961 accident, Blanc taped his part at home with a microphone suspended over his bed.

In the following years, further TV cartoon roles included Secret Squirrel, Mr. Cosmo G. Spacely on "The Jetsons," Hardy Har Har on "Lippy the Lion" and Droop-along on the "Magilla Gorilla Show."

Over time, though, the quality of cartoons deteriorated as animation costs rose and writing values changed, Blanc reflected.

"They're not as funny as they used to be, and they seem like they're just slapped together now," Blanc said in 1975. ". . . They're playing too much just to the children, not enough to the adults . . . [and] they're just not as animated as they should be."

By that time, Blanc had diversified, forming his own production company, along with his son Noel.

Since the early 1960s, the firm has produced commercials for such products as Kool Aid, Raid and Chrysler cars and for nonprofit agencies including the American Cancer Society.

In 1988, Blanc performed a bit part as Daffy Duck in the wildly successful film feature, "Who Framed Roger Rabbit?"

Blanc also kept busy during later years with his favorite ho collecting antique watches. His luminous collection, insured $150,000 as far back as 1 contained items dating to 1510.

Over the years, Blanc receiv slew of awards from civic organ tions, many of which he wa member. Among the plaudits w United Jewish Welfare Fund M of the Year and the Show Busi Shrine Club's first Life Achie ment Award.

One of Blanc's favored chari was the Shrine Hospital Childre Burn Center where the family a contributions in his name.

In 1984, Blanc was also hono by the Smithsonian Instituti During an informal ceremony Washington, he revealed, "In r life, I sound most like Sylveste without the spray." Blanc a disclosed what he considered so of his more demanding challer es—Bugs Bunny imitating El Presley and a Japanese nat imitating Bugs Bunny.

"You know, my wife talks to a lot about retiring," he once t an interviewer. "I say to her, 'Wi the hell for?' I never want to st When I kick off, well, I kick off."

Or, as Porky said over the many years:

"Thaaaaaat's all folks!"

15430 LOST VALLEY DRIVE
FORT WAYNE, IN 46845

THE JACK BENNY TIMES

Volume IX, Number 4 INTERNATIONAL DISTRIBUTION July-August 198[?]

And all this time I thought he said, "Please KICK Benny for me!!!"

PRESIDENT'S MESSAGE

Jell-o again! Say...just look at that cover. What a lovely masthead! Big, big thanks to Bobb Lynes for sending that. For those of you who are waiting for my response, patience is a virtue. Guess you have all accepted the fact that time is tight; I used to get all kinds of letters asking if I had discontinued subscriptions. This is probably the first bi-monthly newsletter to come out quarterly. Just figure that I'm living on Uranus.

Due to a new printing and mailing arrangement, names of persons whose subscription fees 39) are due will be listed in the PM. The following people are up for renewal ($6.39): Doug Brown, Wayne Ennis, Larry Gassman, Ina Goldsten, David Howell, Steven Kucsma, Misty Dawn Lane, Patricia Link, Kelly Malone, Lora Palmer, Daniel Pelletier, Joel Rasmussen, Greg Seltzer, Christopher Snowden, and Charles Wright. Please send all monies to the address at the end of the newsletter.

Folks, please note the "Coming Attractions" and "Do You Know?" columns. Perhaps you can help with these endeavors. Now on with the show!

NEW MEMBERS

****CHARLES E. WRIGHT****INA GOLDSTEN****LARRY GASSMAN****PEGGY RIFFLE****EMILY RIFFLE****JOSEPH RUSSELL****ALICE L. RUSSELL****CHRISTOPHER SNOWDEN****DOUG BROWN****DAVID A. HOWELL****PATRICIA A. LINK****STEVEN KUCSMA****SEDALIA PEARSON****GREG SELTZER****WAYNE L. ENNIS****BERNIE KELKER****MISTY DAWN LANE****JAMES V. ROGERS****ELINORE ROGERS****TODDY MYERS****FRANKLIN LOPSHIRE****GEORGE COURTESIS****MARK J. CUCCIA****STEVEN LEWIS****RICK CROUCHER****WILLIAM GRAFF****KEVIN B. SHAFER****STEVE BRENT****GLENN V. LAXTON****ALFRED BRUTON, III****STEVE LAKE****CAROLINE LAKE*****PATRICK DAY*****MARION FEIN*****HAL GOLDMAN

DO YOU KNOW?!?!

Alan Grossman sent me a letter a couple weeks ago regarding something he had acquired called a "VoicOgraph."

Copyright 1989, Laura Lee

Enclosed a couple xeroxes, and it is shaped like a 10" 78rpm record. I do not see a hole in the middle, so perhaps it is played some other way. There are outstanding montages on both sides; one having Jack wearing a dark coat and polka dot tie, Don, Andy Devine, an NBC mike, the word "Jell-o," and what looks like Phil. The other is a large shot of Jack in a somewhat checked coat, overlayed with Mary and Kenny Baker. This side is inscribed "Best Wishes from Jack Benny" across Jack's shoulder. The sleeve (or container of some sort) says "Jell-o presents Jack Benny via VoicOgraph." Alan estimates it to date from between 1936 and 1938. I agree, and would venture a more specific guess at late 1936 or early 1937. You see, late '36 was when many of the "Buck Benny" skits with Andy Devine were airing, and Phil joined the show in October of '36. If you know anything about this, please let us know.

Also, does anyone know whatever happened to the Jack Benny stamp campaign? Is it still going on, or has everyone lost interest? Every once in a while I will get a letter from someone who is interested in its progress; I have not heard anything about the campaign lately. I know that people have to be deceased a certain amount of time before they are allowed to be on a stamp (not sure how long), but them how can they even consider an "Elvis" stamp? Wait a minute...was it our July cover from last year that killed it?!?!?!

TAPE TRADING LIST

Ellen Barker, P.O. Box 1402, Reseda, California 91335

Jack Bloom, 8618 Stansbury Avenue, Van Nuys, CA 91402

Hal Bogart, 2029 Aldersgate Drive, Lyndhurst, Ohio 44124

Yosef Braude, 25 Longhorn Road, Providence, RI 02906

Rob Cohen, 6635 Helm Ave., Reynoldsburg, Ohio 43068

The Everills, 1558 Knox Dr., New Haven, Indiana 46774

Andrew Haskell, 160 West 39th Ave., Vancouver, British Columbia V5Y 2P2, Canada

Howard and Mary Joyce, 1050 Locksley SW, Grand Rapids, Michigan 49509

Laura Lee, 15430 Lost Valley Dr., Fort Wayne, IN 46845

John Malone, Rural Route #2, Wee-Ma-Tuk, Cuba, IL 61427

Bill Oliver, 516 Third Street NE, Massillon, Ohio 44646

Lewis and Sedalia Pearson, 240 Ridge Drive, Marion, Iowa 52302

Michael Pointon, 11 Kings Court, Kings Road, London SW19 8QP, England

Keith Scott, 4 Bellbird Crescent, Forestville 2087, N.S.W. Australia

Joyce Shooks, P.O. Box 307, Sparta, Michigan 49345

Steve and Kim Smith, 1945 Coit NW, Grand Rapids, MI 49505

Steve Szejna, 3334 South 15th Street, Milwaukee, WI 53215

James E. Treacy, Jr., 5395 Petersburg Rd, Dundee, MI 48131

Is that everyone?

COMING ATTRACTIONS

In the next issue we will begin transcription of the conversation with Sam Perrin in Los Angeles. Know from your letters that you kids like these interviews (thanks for all the kind words), and this promises to be another great one. Hope you enjoy it. Thanks also, of course, to Sam Perrin for his time. Just an aside: Nancy was asking if I wanted to go to Universal City or Knott's Berry Farm that day, but I just wanted to go see Sam Perrin. And I bet I had an even better time. Rather reminiscent of 1981 when we were going to Marriot's Great America, located just north of Chicago. I saw highway signs saying "Waukegan," so I begged to go there instead. Hmmm...I suppose most people would just call this a warped sense of values! However, I always had a great time.

Now, like we said before, we can use your help. This summer I went to see one of the Maxwells. Am planning on devoting an entire issue to the Maxwell, but data is very hard to find. If you have **ANY** data whatsoever on the Maxwell, the company, or anything associated with it, please let me know. (This is the main reason this issue is late...was trying to get enough background to write it).

Also, many thanks to Bill Graff for alerting me to the fact that one of Jack's houses is on a tentative demolition list. Did a little checking, and it is not the Roxbury Drive home. However, if anyone has any info about the house or the demolition plans, please contact me. Thanks so much.

OTHER CLUBS

Would like to take this opportunity to let you know about a couple other clubs which have been extremely helpful to us lately. As some of you know, Al Jolson is my favorite singer. The Al Jolson Society has been around for about 40 years; in fact, Jolie himself was an honorary member (perhaps even hon. Prez, if memory serves). For those of you who are also fans of the divine Mr. J, you must pursue this club. For more information, write to: Mike Modero, 476 Colonial Road, Roselle Park, New Jersey 07204. (And note number 2 of clipping!)

Headline Gallery (!)
Headlines you didn't see in this week's News-Sentinel*
1. "Startling New Evidence Of Life After Death!" (National Enquirer)
2. "We Were Captured By A Tribe Of Al Jolson Look-alikes!" (Weekly World News) ← and there were so mamm of them
3. "Snowbound Motorist Eats His Own Clothes!" (News)
4. "People Look Forward To Getting Old!" (Enquirer)
5. "Exclusive Interview With A Space Alien!" (News)

Source: News-Sentinel research

Also, some of you may be interested in the Antique Comb Collectors' Club. Saw the collection of their Secretary, and it is truly fascinating--even items dating back to B.C. (before Cantor, comedy, combs, etc.). For more information write to: Mrs. Betty Miller, Box 316, Homer, Arkansas 99603.

****

As ever, if you have any questions, comments, corrections, or additions, please send them to:

Laura Lee, c/o International Jack Benny Fan Club Offices, 15430 Lost Valley Drive, Fort Wayne, Indiana 46845

Please friends, send no bombs.

BLOOM COUNTY

Jack Benny's $400 Yaks

By CLEVELAND AMORY

Saturday Evening Post November 6, 1948

The businessman of comedy doesn't look funny, doesn't act funny, isn't quick with a quip. But he runs radio's biggest humor factory, and your laughter is worth $2000 a minute to him. Here's how he operates.

AT a broadcast some time ago Jack Benny became distressed just a few moments before he was to go on the air. Quickly he signaled for his writers, all four of whom invariably watch the show from the control room of the studio, and in marching order they trooped to his side.

"Boys," said Benny, looking critically at the end of his script, "I want to get something in here on the tag that says the part of the violin teacher was played by Mel Blanc."

One of the writers took the script. "The part of the violin teacher," he wrote quickly, "was played by Mel Blanc."

Much relieved, Benny thanked him and took back his script. Again the four writers trooped off. The one who had written the line, however, paused.

"Jack," he said quietly, "two of us could have done that."

At this, Benny collapsed. "That's wonderful!" he screamed, apoplectically clapping his hands and pounding the table. Then, using his favorite method of discussing a joke he likes, he yelled to everyone within hearing, "Did you get the way he threw the line away? Did you get that 'two'? Gee, that's wonderful!"

It is indeed wonderful. If Benny—who has so little confidence in his extemporaneous humor that he regularly employs his writers for his after-dinner speeches—had merely stayed in radio as long as he has, it would be no mean achievement. But he has done much more than this. On October third, after a personal appearance tour this summer in which he broke the existing box-office record at London's Palladium, his Benny Show, as it is known in the trade, opened its seventeenth season for NBC, which is the all-time radio record for any program's consecutive appearance on one network. Starting in 1932, it of course far antedates such new wrinkles as the Hooper system, but ever since 1937, when it first passed the Eddie Cantor Show, its over-all rating average is above that of any other show on the air, and in the course of its sixteen years it has lulled even radio's severest critics into deciding that it must be funny. "I have been listening to Benny so long," says John Crosby, radio editor of the New York Herald Tribune, "my critical sense is paralyzed."

Measured in cold cash, the Benny Show is the country's biggest single laugh industry. In this industry, the sponsor's "nut," as it is called, or the capital investment of the American Tobacco Company in the Benny factory, is the tidy sum of $55,000 per week. Benny's last-admitted salary, for 1947, was $27,500 a week, but out of this he had to pay for his own "package," or raw material. Currently, the two major slices of this are $7500 per week for the services of his five principals—Mary Livingstone, Rochester, Phil Harris, Dennis Day and Don Wilson—and $5500 per week for the services of his four writers.

Up to this year it would have been possible to figure Benny's own salary by directly subtracting these expenses, as well as the expenses of his other players and office staff. Now this can no longer be done, for under the present arrangement the show is packaged by an organization known as Amusement Enterprises, Inc., which pays all salaries except Benny's. The latter comes direct from American Tobacco and remains a secret. That his total personal earnings are close to $15,000 a week, however, leaked out inadvertently some months ago, when Benny, who works with his writers an average of three days a week on his script, became concerned with the fact that a friend of his had just lost $10,000 in one evening in a Palm Springs gambling house.

"You know," said Benny thoughtfully, "if I lost ten thousand in one evening, I'd feel like slitting my throat the next morning."

"Yeah, Jack," replied his friend, promptly getting the full impact of the philosophy, "just think—two whole days' work."

At the retail end of his factory, for thirty-nine weeks a year Benny delivers twenty-seven minutes and forty seconds of entertainment to between 25,000,000 and 30,000,000 people—two minutes and twenty seconds being taken up by individual station identification and by opening and closing commercials over which he has no control. Benny's time is further tailored by a middle commercial, which he does control and by a *(Continued on Page 81)*

Dennis Day song. Actual dialogue, with sound effects, usually runs about sixteen and a half minutes, and the "spread" of the show—the time consumed by transitions and by studio, and presumably home, laughter—averages about seven minutes, usually including some thirty-five individual "boffs," as they are called, or "yaks."

In the final analysis, Benny, who is not personally funny, but a likable, earnest, rather childlike man, ends up with something in the neighborhood of $2000 per air-time laugh minute, or $400 per yak, for being funny when it counts.

With the possible exception of Edgar Bergen, who is of course openly schizophrenic, the contrast between the personal Benny and the professional Benny has no parallel in the funny business. Such comedians as George Burns, Groucho Marx, Danny Kaye, Red Skelton and Milton Berle are out-and-out clowns, on and off the air. Bob Hope, Jimmy Durante and Eddie Cantor have their serious moments, but even when relaxing are invariably loaded with gags, for use with or without mike. Even dour Fred Allen and dead-pan Henry Morgan, who actually write some of their own scripts, and thus may be pardoned for occasional gloom, are basically funny guys.

Jack Benny is something else. In what has been called Hollywood's square-cut-emerald set, the society in which he moves, he is well liked, but not regarded either as witty or as a particularly sparkling dinner partner. In his $250,000 Beverly Hills home, which is complete with eight servants, a swimming pool, ankle-deep rugs and a living-room portrait of Mrs. Benny—the second ever painted by Claudette Colbert—Benny breakfasts rather shyly each morning in the pantry with his butler, and if he has a dinner party he would infinitely prefer to hear someone else tell a story than to tell one himself. Mrs. Benny, who is the Mary Livingstone of the show, and to whom the fifty-four-year-old comedian has been married twenty-one years—they have one adopted daughter—describes her husband with some difficulty. "Jack doesn't joke around the house," she says, "and he certainly doesn't look funny. I always think of him as—well, an attorney or something."

Nonetheless, the professional Benny has won the respect of all his rivals. Fred Allen, his public enemy and by no means as close a private friend as publicized, is, of course, rarely serious about Benny. "There are two kinds of jokes," he is fond of saying, "funny jokes and Jack Benny jokes." When pinned down, however, Allen freely declares that practically every comedy show on the air today owes its basic structure to Benny's idea of humor. Furthermore, Allen admits that some of his most publicized wisecracks have been those which became famous because they were based on Benny's well-developed professional character. When Benny was nominated to open a March of Dimes campaign, Allen thought little of the choice. "The dime hasn't been minted," he commented briefly, "that could march past Jack Benny."

Benny, who has plenty of confidence in his professional humor, earnestly joins in the general acclaim. "I have good programs," he says, "because I can't stand lousy ones. I don't like anything second rate. I might have been a fairly good violinist, maybe even the second-best violinist. But who cares about the second-best violinist? This way it's fine. I'm the world's worst violinist."

This philosophy is not particularly humorous, but there is a sort of naïve charm to it. Actually Benny sees nothing extraordinary about being a business comedian, and about not looking funny. His favorite humorist was the late Stephen Leacock, whom he never met, but to whose work he was introduced by Groucho Marx. Although he declares he reads little—"I fall asleep when I read"—he read everything the Canadian humorist wrote. "And remember," he says, "I've seen pictures of Leacock, and he was a very dignified-looking guy. Why, do you know he was a professor of economics?"

Ever since Benny became the acknowledged dean of radio salesmen, because of his five-year work with Jell-O for General Foods, he has enjoyed many privileges not shared by other air men. Chief among these is the honor of being the only man in radio to control his own time. As long as he wants it and has a sponsor satisfactory to NBC, his Sunday spot from seven to seven-thirty, Eastern Time, belongs to him—a time, incidentally, which is not so highly regarded as a later spot, since Benny has to start the Sunday-evening parade and has virtually no carry-over audience from previous programs.

Through the years Benny has managed to pass along some of his benefits to his co-workers. Disproving Samuel Goldwyn's Hollywood remark that a happy company makes a bad picture, the people under Benny are extremely content. Present-day radiomen use the phrase "working the Benny Show" in the same way old-time vaudevillians tossed the magic line "playing the Palace." Of Benny's stars, two of them, Phil Harris and Dennis Day, now have their own shows, Mary Livingstone and Rochester have been offered theirs, Don Wilson is perhaps radio's best-known announcer—though he now works no other show—and even the relatively new Sportsmen Quartet recently went big time and incorporated themselves. Six past producers of the Benny Show have become advertising-agency vice-presidents, and even bit players like Frank Nelson, Mel Blanc and Artie Auerbach make handsome livings from Benny work alone. Auerbach, the program's most recently developed character—the "peakle in de meedle" Mr. Kitzel—figured out that he was paid five dollars per spoken word for the year 1947 on the Benny Show.

The first step of each individual Benny Show takes place on Sunday evening in Benny's dressing room just off Studio C of NBC's Hollywood headquarters at Sunset and Vine. Here, directly following the broadcast of the preceding show, Benny and his four writers, Sam Perrin, George Balzer, Milt Josefsberg and John Tackaberry, meet to discuss the basic idea of the following week's show. While the writers declare that the chances are three out of four this basic idea will be Benny's, they are equally agreed that Benny could not possibly prepare his own script from scratch. Once the idea is decided, the next question is which two writers—they work in teams, two on the opening, or "cast," spot and two on the closing, or "drama," spot—will do which half of the program. When this is also decided, the writers have two full days off and Benny four, though he often communicates with them by phone when they are doing their teamwork on Wednesday and Thursday. On Friday the four writers and Benny again gather to put the script together, and as each section is okayed, Producer Hilliard Marks is informed by telephone of the characters wanted for bit parts. Marks telephones these, and after the Saturday rehearsal, which follows individual rehearsals of the orchestra, the Sportsmen and Dennis Day, the writers and Benny once again retire, this time for rewrite and cutting. On Sunday there are two rehearsals, one at one o'clock and the final, or mike, rehearsal at two.

In some of the other factory systems, radio writers have been known to work amid piles of old scripts, reference books and joke encyclopedias. Benny writers do not. Also, as befitting men who, during the weeks the show is on the air, draw individual weekly salaries that are approximately the size of that of the President of the United States, they consider themselves above even listening to other programs. For writers, they are extraordinarily extroverted, actually preferring collaboration to individual work, and they are also remarkably sure of themselves. In the summer of 1945, when Benny was off the air, the team of Perrin and Balzer wrote the musical Are You With It? in thirty-six days, and equal proficiency can be expected from the team of Josefsberg and Tackaberry. Ranging in age from thirty-one to forty-five, they have been doing their weekly stint for Benny for five years, and are apparently used to the idea of writing without waiting for the spirit to move them. On this subject, Perrin, senior of the group, speaks for all. "We move the spirit," he says briefly.

To the outsider, the most remarkable feature of a Friday script session with Benny and his writers is the immense amount of pleasure all concerned seem to get out of it. Benny, who has been known to arrive at a session in tails, white tie and top hat in a rather self-conscious effort to get the humor started, invariably howls with laughter when he sees the script, and his writers promptly join in the mirth, although they have written the gags. Even in places where Benny suggests a change—he does this rather timidly—they spout new routines so rapidly that it is not unusual for all four writers to contribute to the same routine at once. For example, one writer will give the "feed line," as it is called; the second will "punch it"; the third will "kick it around"; and the fourth will "pull the snapper." Illustrated by a past script, this would mean that one writer gave the feed line by having Benny compare himself with Robert Taylor, then add, "Why, we even have the same girl, Barbara Stanwyck." As they appeared in the final script, the punch, kicker and snapper were as follows:

HARRIS: Only *he* goes out with her.

BENNY: Is that so? I could get a date with Barbara Stanwyck, too, couldn't I, Mary?

MARY: You couldn't get a date with Barbara Frietchie.

When two or three of these punches or snappers are offered at the same time, it is up to Script Girl Jeanette Eymann, an attractive twenty-eight-year-old ex-schoolteacher from Pontiac, Illinois, to watch for Benny's okay as to which line goes in. Miss Eymann, who frankly admits she has the most enviable secretarial job in Hollywood, rarely contributes to the general hedlam of the script sessions, but has been known to come up with a gag now and then. Along with the writers, who are by no means backward about writing themselves into the script for short lines, whistles, and so on, she herself often speaks a bit part on the air and has a good time doing so.

All this enthusiasm carries over from the Friday session into the Saturday and Sunday rehearsals and right into the broadcast itself. At the Saturday rehearsal Phil Harris wisecracks, Rochester clowns, Don Wilson guffaws, and though Benny corrects readings freely—he is an acknowledged craftsman at inflection and timing—the volume of laughter of the cast is the barometer by which the script is revised during the afternoon rewrite.

Benny declares he is extremely dependent on a favorable studio audience, and to make sure he gets one he never allows his orchestra to hear the lines until the show is on the air. Keyed-in laughter by Frank Remley, a guitar player who begins his roaring with Benny's warmup routine—though Benny often uses the same one for months at a time—the orchestra in turn keys the laughter of everyone else. Remley, who is Benny's closest personal friend and travels with him on vacation trips, thinks Benny is wonderful. "Even when he tells a joke like that one about the traffic being so bad he had to come by way of Santa Barbara, there's something about the way he mugs it that makes me laugh. I think he's the funniest man alive."

This may be doubted, but there is no question that Benny can be a very able master of ceremonies. His writers may work on his banquet speeches, but Benny's satirical way of putting these talks over has won high praise. Having had to emcee several dinners at which Bing Crosby has received awards and yet has not been present to receive them, Benny has become slightly weary of the position. He first greets his audience with an elaborate tribute to Crosby, then declares, "If Bing doesn't come to these things, you know what people say—they say, 'Isn't he modest and sweet and cute?' If Bing does come, they say, 'Isn't that wonderful! Bing never goes to things like this, but he came here today. Good old Bing!'"

Here Benny pauses, still smiling. Then he puts on his famed frustrated look and concludes, "Now I ask you, do people ever say, 'Good old Benny! Benny goes to everything'?"

His treatment for Al Jolson is equally effective. More than once he has noted Jolson in his studio or banquet audience and has had the singer take a bow. Following this, he sentimentally recounts how he will never forget how, at a benefit a year ago, Jolson sang Irving Berlin's ballad, When I Leave the World Behind. Benny declares that he was terribly touched by Jolson's rendition of leaving the sunshine to the flowers, the springtime to the trees, the nighttime to the dreamers, the moon above to those in love, and so on.

Again comes the pause, and the look. Then, "There's Jolson, good old Al, a man worth at least twelve million dollars. And what's he going to leave us when he dies? Moonbeams!"

Benny is well aware that the effectiveness of these stories comes to a large extent from the fact they are based on truth. Crosby is known to be so secure in Hollywood that he can, and does, do what he pleases in the matter of attending dinners, and Jolson is by no means averse to accumulating money. In the same way Benny feels that a large part of the success of his show is due to the fact that people believe his radio character—that he wears a toupee, which he does not; that he is stingy, which he is not, and so on. Last year, for example, a Cleveland lawyer wrote him that he should be ashamed of his parsimony toward Rochester, and hinted at legal steps on the valet's behalf. Benny wrote that it was hardly a case for the courts. Rochester, who has never been anybody's valet, has a block-large estate and three servants of his own, drives an expensive car and a big station wagon, and when not working—which he does two days a week for some $700 per air-time minute—spends his leisure hours either yachting or supervising his well-stocked racing stable.

The lawyer's case is extreme, but character believability is vital to the Benny Show formula, now so imitated that it has become almost as standard radio fare as the back-and-forth joke routines which were in vogue when it started. Proud as he is of developing what he calls situation humor, Benny is even more proud of his show's reputation for good taste. "A lot of really strict people listen," he declares, "and remember, it's Sunday—that makes a difference." As an example of the Benny Show idea of taste, he recalls a broadcast last winter where he was getting ready to attend a Hollywood party and mentioned that Lauren Bacall would be with Humphrey Bogart, and Barbara Stanwyck with Robert Taylor. When he got to Lana Turner, he said, "And Lana will be with—Rochester, get me the evening paper."

Benny claims that if Miss Turner had been married at the time, as she is now, or if there had been any innuendo in the line beyond the joke that Miss Turner was fickle, the Benny Show would not have used it. A few years ago he did a program where, with Dennis Day, he went into Eddie Cantor's house, and in the living room noted pictures of every celebrity except himself. The snapper of the routine came when Day found Benny's picture in Cantor's bathroom, but, as Benny points out, Day had been established as entering the bathroom specifically to put a toothbrush there. NBC's Continuity Acceptance Department, which checks all scripts, objected to the routine, feeling that other comedy shows, which often take their cue from what the Benny Show is allowed to do, would promptly start working on more objectionable bathroom gags. Nonetheless, Benny stuck to his guns and, because of the toothbrush, won his case.

Benny also claims that his show has a higher standard than some others in the matter of advertising plugs. Constantly propositioned by manufacturers, stores and hotels—who would like to trade their product or service for a free mention on the air—the Benny writers maintain they use trade names only when they make the script funnier, and not because of the remunerative value involved. On one occasion at least, however, the Benny Show was brought up short in this matter. This was the case of a New York hotel which was mentioned in the script the week before the troupe descended on it. Confident that everything would be taken care of, the advance guard of the Benny party approached the manager of the hotel. "Well," they asked, smiling, "what do you do for actors?"

The manager smiled back. "We applaud them," he said, then added quietly, "at our regular rates."

Although he is charitably inclined toward other comedians—he declares that Danny Kaye "fractures" him and that George Burns can make him laugh at anything—Benny is not averse to pointing out that in the long history of the Benny Show it has established many firsts for which it has never been given credit. On the subject of Henry Morgan, for example, he likes to make clear that the Benny Show was satirizing commercials as far back as 1932, its first year on the air.

In one of its programs in June of that year the show included the reading of a wire purporting to be from the Canada Dry Ginger Ale representative in North Africa. As Benny read the wire, the representative, having found eight tourists who had been thirty days on the Sahara Desert without a drink, reported: "I came to their rescue, gave each of them a glass of Canada Dry, and not one of them said he did not like it!"

Also in that year the Benny Show did its Grind Hotel program, which was the forerunner of all drama satires on the air, and was so successful that people still mention it in fan letters. A typical routine from the first broadcast came when Benny, as the Baron, called on the dancer who burlesqued the part originally played by Garbo:

(Sound: *Heavy knock at door*)
Ethel: Who is it?
Benny: It's me—the Baron.
Ethel: Baron who?
Benny: Baron *von two three* . . .
Ethel: Four-five-six.
Benny: Seven-eight-nine.
Ethel: Come in, Baron.

As repeated a week later, the routine was revised as follows:

(Sound: *Heavy knock at door*)
Ethel: Who is it?
Benny: It's the Baron.
Ethel: Which Baron?
Benny: From Wilkes *Barron*, Pennsylvania.
Ethel: Ah! Come in, Baron.

In spite of such emphasis on puns, with Mary's letters from Plainfield and other features which have lasted to the present day, the Benny Show was beginning to develop. Working with only one writer, Harry Conn, Benny was still being introduced on the order of "our effervescent comedian"—after which he would say, "Effervescent for me, we would have a nice program"—but he was gradually breaking away from the routines of his vaudeville days, which invariably included stories about his girl's father who was so mean that . . . ; her sister was so fat that . . . ; her brother was so dumb that . . . ; and so on.

The two Benny writers who worked for him from 1936 to 1943, Ed Beloin and Bill Morrow, believe that Benny hit on his formula more by accident than by anything else. "He saw that he wasn't a fellow who could stand up and joke all over the lot," says Morrow, now producer of the Bing Crosby Show. "He had to have an attitude."

In any case, by 1937, when the Benny Show first topped the ratings, it was already established as a humorous program with a formula based not on surprise or reversal—ordinarily considered the essence of comedy—but on exactly the opposite. The Benny Show never surprises. Actually falling somewhere between comedy and soap opera, it began giving its fans a weekly saga of frustration, which not only maintained an intimate, family-joke appeal from week to week but also a high level of consistency for longer periods. When its fans clamor for more of the same on the Benny Show, the chances are they get it. It is easy to find programs of its early days which are still popular with its present writers.

For last February twenty-second the entire drama spot of the program, or approximately six pages of the twenty-page script, was an almost word-for-word repeat of the program for May 1, 1938. Where, ten years ago, Benny was building his house in Beverly Hills, this year, in virtually the same lines, he built his house in Palm Springs. Lately the Christmas-shopping program has become a Benny Show perennial. For Christmas, 1946, Rochester was picking out a necktie:

Salesman: Of course, it might be a little too plain for your boss. Is he a young man?
Rochester: No.
Salesman: Is he middle-aged?
Rochester: No.
Salesman: Is he elderly?
Rochester: *Wrap it up!*

For Christmas, 1947, Rochester wanted cuff links:

Salesman: I see. What type of man is your boss?
Rochester: Well, he's medium tall, medium weight and rather conservative.
Salesman: By conservative, do you mean he's penurious?
Rochester: Well . . .
Salesman: Parsimonious?
Rochester: Well . . .
Salesman: Frugal?
Rochester: Well . . .
Salesman: Thrifty?
Rochester: You're headed in the right direction, but there's a *long, long trail awinding!*

Obviously this can be repeated as often as desired, and Benny fans will love it. Only once did the Benny Show go into a real slump. This occurred in 1945, and Benny promptly came up with his celebrated "I can't-stand-Jack-Benny-because" contest. Since he is Jewish, Benny asked his cordon of twelve contest secretaries to hold out all definitely anti-Semitic letters. Out of 270,000 received, he had only three. Also in 1945, Benny conceived the idea of putting the Ronald Colmans—established as his next-door neighbors, though they actually live eight blocks away—on the show as guest stars.

"Frankly," says Colman, "when I read that first script I thought it was pretty corny, but when we started rehearsing it and everyone got laughing, I got into the spirit of the thing." So, apparently, did the audience, and in keeping with the Benny Show tradition, the Colmans have been on the program ten times since. Benny himself rates their first appearance, on December 9, 1945, as the best single program he has ever had, and claims that the cocktail scene, where the fashionable Colmans are trying to make the best of the fact that the upstart Benny got the invitation intended for their old friend Jack Wellington, was a situation so real that the script girl in the control room actually had tears in her eyes:

Colman: Well, the cocktails are ready. A toast! Benita, your health! [*Sound: Tinkle of glasses.*]
Colman: Wellington, happy days. [*Sound: Tinkle of glasses.*]
Colman: Benny, good luck. [*Sound: Glass breaking.*]
Benny: Whoops! Too hard! . . . I'm sorry, I didn't mean to break the glass.
Mrs. Colman: (*sadly*) Oh, and that set was a hundred and fifty years old.
Benny: Well, I'm glad I didn't break any of your new stuff.

Another Colman situation was responsible for the biggest single laugh in Benny Show history. This occurred on April 27, 1947, when Mrs. Colman, after having said she was hungry and been given an apple, was questioned by her husband. "Benita," he asked, "have you ever seen Phil Harris' musicians?"

"Please, Ronnie," replied Mrs. Colman, "I'm eating."

George Foster, NBC engineer for seventeen years, timed the laugh which greeted Mrs. Colman's remark at forty seconds and metered it as a plus-ten, the longest and highest in his experience, and the only laugh he has ever had to hold down in order not to overload his equipment. Benny names it his best "picture joke" and points out that it took twelve years of outlandish gags about the personal shortcomings of Phil Harris' men to get such a reaction. As a single program build-up, his most successful picture joke was the Benny Show satire of Gaslight, with Ingrid Bergman. The high point of this drama, first broadcast in 1945, but in line to be repeated soon, was the scene where Benny, playing Boyer's role as the tormentor of his wife, is finally caught by the detective and bound to a chair:

Bergman: (*emotionally*) There you are, Charles, tied to a chair like the criminal that you are. For years you have *tormented* me, *embarrassed* me, *degraded* my life, *ruined* my health, *tried to drive me mad* . . . DIDN'T YOU, CHARLES? . . . DIDN'T YOU? . . . *Charles, why don't you answer me?*
Benny: Because I'm tied up and can't turn the page!

Whether the Benny Show will ever go on television, and thus enable the home audience to share even more closely in its picture jokes, remains in doubt. In his only previous experience in a pictorial medium, Benny has not been, to put it gently, successful. Out of fifteen movies he has made, he has had only one, his latest, which was outstanding—and this was so only because the picture, The Horn Blows at Midnight, was so universally condemned that he has been able to capitalize on it as a running gag ever since.

Benny's frustrated-voiced "H'm's," which often take the place of a snapper line, are, of course, well known. But what Benny feels was his most satisfactory achievement in the realm of nothing occurred in what is known in Benny Show history as the "But" show of February 23, 1947. After having declared that he was sick and tired of being kicked around by his cast, Benny fired the Sportsmen Quartet and then pretended, at the conclusion of the program, to be called to the phone by Vincent Riggio, president of the American Tobacco Company:

Benny: Oh, oh, my sponsor. . . . HELLO, VINCE. . . . VINCENT? . . . OH, MR. RIGGIO, WHAT CAN I DO FOR YOU, MR. RIGGIO? . . . YOU'VE BEEN LISTENING TO THE SHOW? . . . WASN'T IT GREAT? . . . OH. . . . I SHOULDN'T HAVE WHAT? . . . BUT I HAD TO FIRE THEM; THAT QUARTET WAS THE WORST. . . . YOU DON'T THINK SO? . . . WELL, EVERYBODY'S ENTITLED TO HIS OWN OPINION. THAT'S WHY THEY PUT RUBBER MATS AROUND CUSPIDORS. (*silly laugh*) . . . WHAT? . . . I GUESS YOU'RE RIGHT; IT DIDN'T GET A LAUGH HERE EITHER. BUT ABOUT THAT QUARTET, MR. RIGGIO, I FELT THAT . . . I KNOW BUT . . . BUT, MR. RIGGIO . . . I KNOW, BUT . . . YES, BUT . . . . YOU MIGHT BE RIGHT, BUT . . . BUT . . . BUT . . . BUT . . . I KNOW, BUT . . . BUT . . . BUT . . . BUT . . . . BUT . . . . BUT, BUT . . . BUT . . .

The psychology of this laugh, Benny feels, was that his audience was amused not only by what they imagined Mr. Riggio was saying, but also at Benny's own gall in allowing so much "dead air," or at least air dead of anything but studio laughter. As Benny read the script, the space between the two most separated "but's" was timed at fourteen and a half seconds.

"I don't know how I did it," Benny concludes earnestly. "We've repeated sequences like it since, but never one with that much space. If you don't believe fourteen and a half seconds is a long time, take out your watch, read the script and time it for yourself."

THE END

FAN CLUB

15430 LOST VALLEY DRIVE
FORT WAYNE, IN 46845

THE JACK BENNY TIMES

Volume IX, Number 5   INTERNATIONAL DISTRIBUTION   September-October 19

JACK: Look at this! The Jack Benny Times says they found me in Battle Creek at a Stop-and-Go!

ROCH: Yeah! And I thought you were playing at a 7-Eleven!

PRESIDENT'S MESSAGE

Jell-o again...what a semester. The June-August *Times* was ready last October, but then this one was due. So here are both of them, even though now the N-D issue should be arriving. Patience, patience...and my apologies.

$6.39 is due from:

        THE RUSSELLS

Thanks.

Sorry I couldn't come up with a better caption for the cover photo. Well, come on you comedians out there--what do **you** think it should say? Send in some good ones and we will put them in the next *Times*.

Also have switched from doing the newsletter on Q&A to Word Perfect. Do not know if you can tell the difference...if you have any suggestions, let me know.

Once again thank you for your patience. Now on with the show!!!

LIBRARY ACQUISITIONS

And amendments, etc. Several shows have been misdated, outdated, debated...they are as follows:

PREVIOUSLY DATED	ACTUAL DATE
1- 4-42	12-28-41
4-18-43	3-26-44
5- 7-44	1-16-44
2-24-52	2-26-50
10-12-52	10- 5-52
2- 1-53	9-28-52

Additionally, the last third or so of the 4-12-53 show is gone...vamoosed. How a part of a radio show gets up and walks away I'll never know; perhaps the Evil Mad Magnet has been at work.

The following new shows have also been obtained:

    3-28-37*   2-27-38   4-17-38   4-24-38
    5- 1-38

3-28-37 does not have the most clear sound, but it is reputedly Rochester's first performance. Finally, the following Dennis_Day_Shows have been contributed:

    4-18-46   11-14-46   12-25-46   1- 1-47
    3- 5-47   9- 3-47   12-17-47   6-23-48
    3-26-49   4-16-49   5-27-49   6-25-49

Many thanks to all contributors. All future acquisitions will be printed in the Times.

DO YOU KNOW?

Below is something I clipped out of Parade magazine; silly me, I did not write a date on it. However, it notes that Jack Douglas wrote for Jack. Hit all three books on Jack, and cannot find anywhere that he worked with him. Does anyone know if this is true; and if so, when they were associated. By the way, is it just me or does his wife look a little like an oriental Marlo Thomas?

Q. I would like some background information on Jack Douglas, the comedian and writer who used to appear on "The Merv Griffin Show" and wrote the book "Shut Up and Eat Your Snowshoes." —Barbara H. Anderson, Linthicum, Md.

A. Jack Douglas, humorist and writer who worked for many of the leading comics in show business—Bob Hope, Red Skelton, Jack Paar, Woody Allen, Jack Benny and others—died on Jan. 31 in Los Angeles at age 80. At one time early in his career, Douglas was a chorus boy in Warner Bros. musicals but left dancing to develop into a successful comedy-writer and performer. Among the 12 books he wrote, some of the best were "My Brother Was an Only Child," "A Funny Thing Happened on My Way to the Grave," "The Adventures of Huckleberry Hashimoto," "What Do You Hear From Walden Pond?" and "Shut Up and Eat Your Snowshoes." Douglas is survived by his singer-wife, Reiko, who used to appear on various TV programs with him, and two sons: Timothy, a musician-writer; and Bobby, a TV production assistant.

Humorist Jack Douglas at age 70, with wife Reiko

FAVORITE SCENES

PHIL: I've decided to reorganize my band.

JACK: Why?

PHIL: I want to move the piano player from the left side of the band to the right side.

JACK: Why?

PHIL: 'Cause that's the side the piano's on!

IT'S SAM PERRIN TIME!

Know how much you kids like interviews, so here comes another. When I was in Los Angeles last year, I had the great fortune of being able to share some time with Mr. Perrin and talk over his career, Jack, and current work. The tape starts just after I made an apology for referring to Jack on a first-name basis. "Don't worry about it," he said and related the following anecdote:

S: Irving Fein was the President of Jack's company.

L: J and M Productions.

S: Yes...and Jack was in Irving's office talking about something. Jack went out, and Irving said to his secretary, "Oh, I just thought about something. Tell him to come back." She ran out and said, "OH JACK! Mr. Fein wants to see you!"

L: ...You listen to the show and they're almost friends. Oh, that's Jack and Mary and Rochester, etc...Chris [Costello] asked me this last night...how much family did Rochester have?

S: Well, his first wife...her name was Mae. I don't believe I ever met his second wife.

L: Did he have any children?

S: Not that I know of.

L: ...Were you involved in any of the specials?

S: I didn't do all of his specials after '65 [the year the television show was discontinued]; I may have done two, possibly three.....Jack brought me out here in 1936, for The Big Broadcast of 1937.

L: Did he have intentions of putting you on the staff for the radio show?

S: Oh, when we first met in 1932, yes. His original writer, who I think was sensational, [was] Harry Conn. I was writing a vaudeville act.

230

L: Anybody we'd know?

S: Not necessarily. There was a fellow named Al Burns, no relation to George Burns, but [Jack, George and Al] were very close...I wrote an act for Al Burns, and vaudeville started to slip. So the booking office bought the act. I didn't have a dime, and Al promised to send me my percent commission. He never sent it. So he went around the whole circuit--what was left--and when he came back, he tried to get the circuit again. The booking agent said, "I can't now. But if you get another act I'll be able to." So Al called me, told me the circumstances, and said, "Would you write me another act?" I said, "No," because he hadn't paid me for the first act. At that time, I was married to an Irish girl, and she said, "You can't write an act for someone that doesn't pay you." Her name was Peggy. Everybody loved Peggy.

L: Was she in show business at all?

S: Never...Mary loved Peggy. If Peggy said anything, it was like if I said something...If we were doing a picture, and I said, "Jack, I think...", he'd say, "Hold the camera!" The same thing with Mary and Peggy. As a matter of fact...we were in London, and I had tickets to fly home. Mary said, "Sam, Jack and I want to go to the south of France, and we'd like you and Peggy to stay [with us]. Phil needs a ticket to fly home, so would you give your ticket to him [and come with us]?" They didn't want to go back to the states; they wanted to go on vacation, because Jack had played the Palladium and was "working." So I told Peggy, and she said, "That would be nice." So we went with them to the South of France.

As ever, **TO BE CONTINUED!**

Please send all questions, comments, additions, corrections, etc. to:

Laura Lee, c/o International Jack Benny Fan Club Offices, 15430 Lost Valley Drive, Fort Wayne, Indiana 46845

Please friends, send no bombs.

Newsweek
12-24-45

(See also
July-August 1989
cover!)

Please Kick Benny

"*I can't stand Jack Benny because my uncle likes him and I can't stand my uncle.*"

"*I can't stand Jack Benny because with those who know Jack Benny best it's Fred Allen two to one.*"

These are samples of the 300,000-odd letters, wires, and records that have deluged the Los Angeles postoffice since Dec. 2. The reason: the latest contest in what is rapidly becoming, again, a contest-mad nation. The rules are simple and inviting as plugged on Benny's Sunday-night show (NBC, 7-7:30 p.m., EST). In 50 words or less—the usual 25-word limit was discarded as too restricting—complete the sentence: "I can't stand Jack Benny because . . ." The prizes total

$10,000 in Victory Bonds, with the funniest entry squeezing bonds worth $2,500 out of Benny—or more accurately, out of his sponsor, the American Tobacco Co.

The contest was born in the buzzing brains of Benny's gag writers, on the hunt for giggles. But even they were surprised when Benny took such wholesale self-derision seriously and screamed: "This is sensational, let's do it." Proof of Benny's perspicacity is the heaviest contest mail in the history of Los Angeles, the hurried plans of other sponsors for a return to the Why-I-Like days, and a round robin of plugs for Benny from a multitude of other entertainers.

The youngest contestant so far is aged 4, the oldest 103. But only a handful of letter writers have been seriously nasty and vitriolic.

Out of Pocket: The contest, which runs through Dec. 24, has three carefully qualified judges: Goodman Ace, for his knowledge of humor, Peter Lorre, for his mastery in handling weird jokes, and Fred Allen, for obvious reasons. Judge Allen confided to NEWSWEEK: I am the greatest living authority on Jack Benny. I have seen him reach for his pocketbook. No other living American can make that statement. I have known Jack Benny, man and boy, for 30 years. He was born a man and matured into a boy."

Asked what he would say, could he enter, Allen cracked: "I can't stand Jack Benny because with his legs that look like two nasturtium stems he can hardly stand himself, and if Mr. Benny can't stand himself, why should I try?"

As for Benny, he is glowing under the abuse. The only jar to his happiness: It is costing him about $4 a day, to make up due postage.

SKETCH 3959
Issued March 1, 1956

JACK BENNY
Comedian

Born February 14, 1894

[EDITORS: The following is a substitute for Sketch 3437 issued April 15, 1948.]

(By The Associated Press)

Jack Benny made a fortune out of being the butt of his own jokes. He rarely kidded anyone else—he was kept too busy as a target for gags that others bounced off him. Perhaps that was one reason he made so few enemies—maybe none at all—during his many years in show business.

For it was hard to get mad at the perennial fall-guy, the fellow who had trouble finding girl friends, the timid man who tried to be a hero. He typified the timorous, ineffectual little guy.

The easy-going, deadpan Benny was one of the first comedians to play straight for the other people in the cast. He took the falls and let the others heckle him.

Joke topics familiar through the years included his supposedly thinning hair, his pretended stinginess, his perennial age of 39, his make-believe feud with comic Fred Allen and his sputtering museum-piece automobile.

The fiddle, on which he sawed sour practice phrases and the tune, "Love in Bloom," was a standard accessory in his bag of tricks.

Superb Sense of Timing

But laughmaking to this funnyman was a serious business Behind every program was a lo of careful preparation. Then hi superb, almost uncanny, sens of timing often provided th spark that gave the final hilarious touch.

He might be talking on th telephone to his boss about "raise" and let the audience on how badly he was doing b just a series of perfectly space "buts."

The audience could plainl understand from this sputterir that Benny not only wasn't ge ting the raise but instead w getting an embarrassing dres ing down for something.

It was said he could get mo laughs out of a simple "hmmr than some comics got from so jokes. "But don't forget," sa Benny, "that a lot went befc that 'hmmm' to make it sou funny at the time." 232

He built up a reputation his radio and television p grams for stinginess with su... jokes as these:

"Why in the world did you give Jack Benny only one glove?" one clerk asked another, and got the reply, "that's all he needs, he never takes his right hand out of his change pocket."

Rochester: "The boss really got a bargain on this second hand airplane luggage. It's genuine airplane luggage, too. It used to belong to Orville Wright."

'Money or Life' Dilemma

Then there was the time a holdup man poked a pistol against him and gave the ultimatum: "Your money or your life." There was complete silence from Benny while the audience's interest built up. Just as the interest reached its peak, Benny hit the jackpot for laughs with his laconic reply—"I'm thinking it over."

Actually this amiable miser of the air was the most generous of men. He was a notorious overtipper, a perpetual gift giver and charity contributor. But he preferred to keep his benefactions secret.

Eddie Cantor told of the time he invited Benny to his home for dinner. During the course of the meal, Cantor, an active worker for the cause, discussed a Bonds for Israel campaign.

"I could see Jack was interested," Cantor recalled, "but he floored me when he wrote out a check for $25,000."

Cantor added: "The only reference I ever heard him make about it was once when he told a mutual friend: 'Don't ever eat at Cantor's house. He serves the most expensive meals in town.'"

His toupee was just a myth too, for he possessed a good head of hair.

Expert Violin Player

Another Benny myth was his lack of violin skill. At the turn of the century his native Waukegan, Ill., knew him as a child prodigy with the violin. His father had hopes that he would become a virtuoso.

While still in grammar school Benny was good enough with the violin to play in the local vaudeville house. Later on the vaudeville stage himself his specialty was playing "The Bee," the piece that was to figure in the feud between him and Fred Allen.

Actually it was "The Bee" that started the whole thing. Once a child on an Allen program played the selection in a skit that was a takeoff on amateur programs. Allen commented it had been Benny's old vaudeville specialty and wisecracked to the child performer:

"Only 8 and you already can play 'The Bee.' Why, Jack Benny ought to be ashamed of himself."

Through the years the violin remained Benny's great love, next to his wife and daughter. Successful as he was as a comic, he occasionally wondered about what might have happened had he practiced more on the violin as a child.

Born Benjamin Kubelsky

The cigar-smoking radio and TV star, movie actor and sauve master of ceremonies was known as the Waukegan Wit because he was reared in Waukegan, Ill. He was born Benjamin Kubelsky on St. Valentine's Day, 1894, in a hospital in nearby Chicago.

His father, Meyer Kubelsky, was a Polish immigrant who had peddled wares with a pack on his back in and around Chicago. In Waukegan, where he had married Emma Sachs, the elder Kubelsky operated a furniture store.

Benny Kubelsky was a boy in knickerbockers when his father gave him a $50 violin.

He gave a few performances in the Barrison Theater when he was 8, later was a ticket taker and usher there and still later a regular violinist—the only musician who didn't shave. With Farmer's Orchestra he played for social events around the town.

At 17 Jack went into vaudeville as a violinist with a pianist partner. He called himself Ben Benny or Ben. K. Benny. Years later he changed his stage name to Jack Benny to prevent confusion with another wise-cracking violin player, Ben Bernie.

Became Comic in Navy

He joined the Navy in World War I and went as a "gob" to the Great Lakes Naval Training Station, Chicago. When a call was issued for talent for a Naval Relief Society show to be called the Great Lakes Revue, he reported for a tryout.

While resting from his violin playing Jack tossed off spontaneous quips for the entertainment of his fellow sailors. The show's writers worked his quips into the script, and Benny's career as a comedian was launched.

"Up until then," he said later, "for six and a half years I'd never opened my mouth on the stage. I'd been a violinist. People think my violin's a gag. I go along with the gag."

After the war, Jack returned to vaudeville as a single, doing a monologue and fiddling. He played the Palace Theater in New York, goal of all vaudevillians, and joined a musical, "Great Temptations."

When the show was in Los Angeles in 1926 he was introduced to Sadye Marks, who was working as a department store clerk. They were married the next year. Some years later they adopted a daughter, Joan.

Her Wedding Lavish

The daughter's marriage in 1954 to Seth Baker, a New York stock broker, was one of the most lavish weddings in Hollywood history. Benny estimated the cost at more than $25,000. He contrasted it with his own wedding.

"We did it in Waukegan at the home of a friend," he recalled. "There were six or seven people there, and the cost was nil. We didn't have time to have a reception. We were married in the afternoon and I had to grab the train to Chicago, where I was appearing in a show that night."

Some time after Benny went on the radio, the script called for a girl to play the role of a fictional fan named Mary Livingstone. After several New York radio actresses had auditioned, Mrs. Benny tried the lines. She stayed on—as Mary Livingstone.

Jack's first radio appearance was on March 29, 1932, as the guest of newspaper columnist Ed Sullivan, who then had an air program. At the time Benny was on Broadway in Earl Carroll's Vanities.

The first words he spoke over the air were "Hello, folks. This is Jack Benny. There will be a slight pause for everyone to say 'Who cares?'"

Soon Got Regular Spot

Shortly afterward, he was appearing at a Miami Beach night club when a telegram asked him to audition for a sponsored program. He flew back to New York and started on the air in the summer of 1932. That was the beginning of his long run on the National Broadcasting Company network for a succession of sponsors.

NBC in 1941 gave Benny a lifetime option on the Sunday half hour between 7 and 7:30 p.m., Eastern time, so long as he had a sponsor approved by the network. Benny owned the show.

At the beginning of 1949, Benny switched to the same hour over the Columbia Broadcasting System network. CBS disclosed that the total money involved in the transaction was $2,260,000. Benny's personal share amounted to $1,356,000, of which he was required to pay approximately $1,030,000 in personal income taxes.

The price paid by CBS for the show represented the purchase of Amusement Enterprises, Inc., of which Benny owned 60 per cent of the stock.

In the fall of 1950 the droll comedian made his debut on television.

His Success Recipe

How did he manage to remain among the top entertainers on the air for so long?

The secret, he said, "is giving the audience credit for having intelligence."

"We play up to them, not down to them," he explained. "I think all you have to do is keep your humor adult. You can do that and even the kids get it today. I don't think anybody on the air is too intelligent for the audience. But it's deadly to be patronizing."

It irked him when "somebody who is getting $8,000 a week" would say at the end of the show, "Thanks for letting me into your living room."

"I don't thank the audience for letting me into their living room. A lot of them watch me because they have to—there's nothing else on in their city. And how do I know their set is even in the living room? It may be in the bedroom, or the den, or the basement.

"The audience doesn't like to be thanked. They just want to sit back and have fun—and feel free to give you the devil if they don't think the show was good."

Entertained Service Men

In World War II Benny made five worldwide trips to entertain troops. He had just recovered from pneumonia in 1943 when he headed a USO troupe that visited Africa, Egypt, the Persian Gulf and Sicily. Their plane, "Five Jerks to Cairo," was said to have been the first flown to entertain on conquered Italian soil.

The next year he toured Pacific outposts. On July 4, 1945, shortly after Germany's defeat, he and others played for 20,000 troops in Adolf Hitler's former Sportspalast.

During the subsequent Korean war he traveled between 25,000 and 30,000 miles with an entertainment troupe. They played before troops and wounded veterans in Hawaii, Japan, Okinawa and throughout Korea. Part of the time during that six week trip he slept in a dirt floor tent close to the front lines.

Benny commented that his soldier audiences were highly appreciative. They howled at all references to his pretended stinginess, such as "That Tokyo is a fast town; I was there just a few days ago and 50 yen went just like that." As for his violin playing, "You'd think I was Heifetz."

He and Fred Allen had known each other from their vaudeville days. Over the years they exchanged a thousand quips in their make-believe feud. Both mined paydirt from their pretended dislike for each other.

Age a Constant 39

Benny began basking in the 30's when he reached the age of 50. On his half century birthday his script writers had Mary Livingstone ask how old he was. For no particular reason, they put down 36 as Jack's answer. Listeners thought that was pretty funny—Jack Benny only 36.

A year later he observed his 37th birthday on the air. He was 37 for two years, 38 for three and 39 from 1950 on.

Waukegan had a Jack Benny Day in April, 1937, with brass bands, marching high school cadets and special newspaper editions. The citizenry jammed the high school auditorium to greet the one-time Benny Kubelsky.

The high school principal made a welcoming speech, then brought up Jack's scholastic record. Jack couldn't resist gag. He slid off his chair and crawled offstage on his hands and knees.

Jack's first movie preceded his start in radio. It was a musical in color called "Hollywood Revue." Later he appeared in "Transatlantic Merry Go-Round," "Broadway Melody," "The Big Broadcast of 1936," "The Big Broadcast of 1937," "College Holiday," "Artists and Models Abroad," "Man About Town," and "Buck Benny Rides Again."

With Fred Allen he made "Love Thy Neighbor," then came "Charley's Aunt," "The Meanest Man in the World," "To Be or Not to Be," "George Washington Slept Here," and "The Horn Blows at Midnight."
— GENE HANDSAKER —
Los Angeles
—wtc—

JACK BENNY
(1954)

Newsweek, March 4, 1946

RADIO

Bennyphobia (CIO)

Jack Benny, who recently spent $10,000 in prizes to find out why people "can't stand" him (Newsweek, Dec. 24, 1945), had an unsolicited answer last week. The CIO, some of whose members are on strike against the American Tobacco Co. for higher wages, sent a gag-minded picket line to NBC's Hollywood studios while Benny was on the air (Sunday, 7-7:30 p.m., EST). One of their placards read: "I can't stand Jack Benny because he is sponsored by Lucky Strike." Benny, meantime, happily out of range, was broadcasting from Palm Springs, 100 miles to the southeast.

HA HA!

  **FAN CLUB**

15430 LOST VALLEY DRIVE
FORT WAYNE, IN 46845

The Jack Benny Times

Volume IX, Number 6   INTERNATIONAL DISTRIBUTION   November-December 19

PRESIDENT'S MESSAGE

MERRY CHRISTMAS!
HAPPY HANUKKAH!

Belated, of course. Anyhow thank you so much for the lovely cards--greatly appreciated. Hope you all had a happy holiday, and I wish you the best for the coming year, decade, millennium, etc.

You probably have already heard that George Burns has a new book out entitled All My Best Friends. Am in the process of reading it, and will give a more full review of it later; however, it looks like a must-read for Benny fans.

Now on with the show!

$6.39 DUE

JACK ABIZAID ** DAVID ANDERSON ** HAL BOGART ** BOB BURNS ** JOHN BURNS ** FRANK DALY ** GARY DUNN ** PHIL EVANS ** THE EVERILLS ** THE FILLENWARTHS ** J. ED GALLOWAY ** DONALD J. MARIS ** DORIS MARTIN ** DONALD PALMER ** THE RAPPOLTS ** SCOTT SEVERSON ** THE SMITHS (Steve, this means you!) ** THE TAYLORS ** THE TINTORRIS ** LARRY VALLEY

A HAPPENING IN WAUKEGAN

Oops. Found this in the "Upcoming Times" file, but must have passed over (passed up, passed out) it several times. Well, as we like to say, (ahem, ahem) "Better late than never!" The following is an excerpt from a letter by Lynn Schornick, Superintendent of Cultural Arts in Waukegan. It describes the proceedings of the "1989 Benny Birthday Bash!" at the Jack Benny Center for the Arts.

"On Saturday, February 11, approximately 75 people joined together to celebrate the 39th birthday of the namesake of the Jack Benny Center for the Arts in Waukegan, Illinois. The evening began with hors d'oeuvres and a cash bar with guests mingling through the halls of the Center, enjoying the art works on display from the Lake County Art League.

"At 8:00 P.M. the show began, featuring comedian Bob McEvilla (our favorite Jack Benny impersonator), and his friend Bob Rumba. They slipped skillfully in and out of skits which have been longtime favorites of Benny fans, including the 'See-Saw' [Si-So, I assume?] sketch with Bob's young son lending a hand. "Jack" was presented with a gift from his former violin teacher. It was, of course, a gun! Bob and Bob, with the help of the Benny Center's theatre director Ken Smouse, recreated the trip to the vault to get $2.50.

"Spirits were high and the laughs were constant as the third annual Benny Birthday Bash! went through its paces. A special Jack Benny Award was given to Mayor Robert Sabonjian of Waukegan for his support of the arts and dedicated service to the community of Waukegan. This will be an annual award. Mayor "Bob" is ending his tenure as Mayor of Waukegan this year. He was mayor when the Jack Benny Center for the Arts was founded in 1964.

"We at the Waukegan Park District's Jack Benny Center for the Arts hope we will have the pleasure of seeing many of the Jack Benny Fan Club members at the next Bash!"

THE TEN BEST

Recently talked with a member who informed me that he was largely unacquainted with the Jack Benny radio shows. Like me, he had enjoyed Jack through television first, and was now starting to discover his prior years on radio. Requested that I choose ten shows which would give a well-rounded picture of those programs.

What an enjoyable task! Think about it...23 years of shows, narrowed down to ten. Naturally had to amend the original list according to the shows in the library, but thought I would share my original ten with you. If you would like, feel free to send me your list of ten; can publish them occasionally in a separate column, similar to "Favorite Scenes." These are listed in chronological order.

1-10-37: First show after Fred Allen's comment on the "Bee" by Stuart Canin. The style of this show is rather representative of the early years. It also contains the first buds of the Benny-Allen feud; plus a sketch of the famed "Buck Benny Rides Again," naturally preceding the movie of the same name.

1-7-45: Debut of the vault, "Hey, Bud," and "Anaheim, Azusa, and Cuc...amonga" skits.

12-9-45: Dinner at the Colmans'. This was the first appearance of the Colmans on the show; George Balzer has also commented that this was the "classiest" radio show they ever did.

3-28-48: Your money or your life. Need I say more?

4-25-48: Guest Dorothy Kirsten. Jack always claimed that this show elicited the longest laugh ever received on the program.

3-13-49: Loses $4.75 at Santa Anita. Along with being a good show, has some historical (hysterical?) significance. The following day many people bet 4-7-5 in the California numbers game. The winner was a combination of those three digits, and it was the biggest losing day for the state.

4-9-50: Gives $1.00 to a panhandler. Have had lots of members tell me that this is their favorite show. Yup, it's good...(crash)!

4-12-53: Jack showers with peeled potato. Has one of the cimeron roll bits (crumbs?). The last half concerns itself with Jack inheriting a sum of money from a long-lost relative; love that last line!

2-14-54: Jack turns 40 (or 39). Lots of good stuff in this one...you just have to listen to it.

ALSO...any of the Christmas Shopping shows. Take your pick.

BACK ISSUES

Like to put this in every once in a while just FYI. Back issues are available for 50 cents apiece. Including this issue, there are 34 issues available. Also, (and I am sure this will instill real confidence in you) I believe that all orders up to this moment have been filled. However, if somehow yours has slipped through the cracks, let me know.

Going to cut this short so you can have all of the article without abbreviation or reduction. Please send all questions, comments, additions and corrections to:

Laura Lee, c/o International Jack Benny Fan Club Offices, 15430 Lost Valley Drive, Fort Wayne, Indiana 46845

Please friends, send no bombs.

RADIO

It's Benny Two to One

Not even among comedians is there much argument. Right now Jack Benny is the funniest man on radio. Back in 1945, after Benny had been on the air for thirteen rib-tickling years, his program abruptly skidded. The comedy became dusty and labored. Listeners demoted him from his customary post among radio's top four or five shows to twelfth place. The smart alecks whispered that he was finished. But not Benny. The next fall he clamped more tightly on his ever-present cigar and paced the floor more nervously—and the show recaptured some of its old verve.

This week, after exactly fifteen years in radio, Jack Benny is back in full stride, as he has been all season. Against the toughest competition of his career, the Jack Benny Show (NBC, Sunday, 7-7:30 p.m., EST) has copped the top spot on the bimonthly Hooperatings twice in six months, and week in, week out gives the Bob Hopes and the Fibber McGees a hard, fast run for the win money.

Unlike some of his competition, notably Hope, Benny pulls his radio way almost unaided by outside activities. Of the fifteen movies he has made, he has had two real hits. During the war he successfully toured battle zones, but his personal appearances for home-front civilians have been few. Nevertheless, Benny's potential draw as a performer on the stage of urban movie houses is such that this May the radio star and a small troupe move into the Roxy in New York for a minimum gross take of $40,000 a week. It is the highest salary ever paid for a theater date.

For all this Variety in its annual showmanship issue two weeks ago was moved to give Benny a special award. The cryptic and critical trade paper said: "The story of Benny is the story . . . of a comedian who, thanks to his own particular savvy, has grown up with the changing techniques in radio. Variety salutes him because the program represents the acme in smooth cooperation between scripters, production crew, and cast."

It's Hard to Be Funny: At 53, Benny, off mike, looks and acts like a successful businessman. He is exactly that: a success at the very serious business of comedy. Unlike the Fred Allens of the trade, Benny has little natural, spontaneous wit. What gags he ad-libs on the air are those anyone would soak up after 37 years of hanging around professional funny men. In a private gathering of show people Benny is no showoff. He would much rather and usually does sit and listen to others strut their stuff. For them he is a wonderful audience. Even a minor gag can provoke a Benny belly laugh. It is the appreciation of what makes a line laughable that keys his radio program. Benny is the industry leader in the business of manufacturing radio comedy. Like the Henry Fords and the Alfred Sloans, he can't manufacture his product alone. Hence he has surrounded himself with a production team that clicks like castanets.

Benny gives all the credit for his stature to this outfit. "Where would I be today," he asks, "without my writers, without Rochester, Dennis Day, Mary Livingstone, Phil Harris, and Don Wilson?" That he himself hand-picked both the writers and the cast is something Benny never admits. He dismisses lightly the fact that he directs his own rehearsals, down to the last, fine reading of a line. Nor will he ever say part of his success stems from his own sense of timing and showmanship.

This belittling is not new. It was evident in the first words that Benny ever spoke on the air. He said: "Hello, Folks. This is Jack Benny. There will now be a slight pause for everyone to say 'Who cares?'" That was March 29, 1932. Benny was appearing on Broadway that year in Earl Carroll's Vanities. He was a successful graduate of vaudeville and had already hit Hollywood for a couple of movies. Ed Sullivan, the columnist, who then had his own radio program, had invited Benny to try this new medium. Four weeks later, on a Monday, May 2, Benny opened his own show for Canada Dry Ginger Ale over the old NBC-Blue network. He has never been without a program or a sponsor since then.

The Perfect Fall Guy: Benny's first crack in radio may have been characterized by modesty. But it was never to be so again. The Jack Benny of radio is a cheap, tightfisted blowhard who gets knocked down by everyone and comes right back for more. The balding Benny character of the air let his vanity force him into buying a toupee. The character insists Benny is a violinist—though he has never gotten through more than a few

Benny album: With Mrs. Benny (1933) . . . as "Charley's Aunt" (1941) . . .

. . . on a wartime South Pacific battle zone tour with Carole Landis . . .

squeaky, sour bars of "Love in Bloom." This is the Benny that is a mirror for a million human foibles—the perfect fall guy. Yet all of this is completely manufactured. The radio and stage Jack Benny is the opposite of the private Jack Benny. And it is a difference which Benny has to fight hard to maintain.

When he was still a kid in knickerbockers in Waukegan, Ill., Benny was given a violin by his father. He learned to play it so quickly that he got a job in the pit orchestra of a local theater before he was in long pants. At 17, calling himself by his real name, Benjamin Kubelsky,* he went into vaudeville with his violin tucked under his chin. At home Benny still plays his violin, not too badly,

*While he was still a smalltime vaudeville violinist Benjamin Kubelsky changed his name to Ben K. Benny. During a stint in the Navy of the first world war he worked up a monologue routine to go with his violin. Shortly after the war, however, the confusion between the up-and-coming Ben K. Benny and another musician with a sense of humor named Ben Bernie became too great. Thus Benjamin Kubelsky became Jack Benny once and for all.

for his own amusement—and as proof to the skeptics that he can.

Though his hair is gray and thinning, Benny is a long way from being bald. To prove this to the public, Benny rarely wears a hat and never a toupee except on movie lots. But Benny's worst fears are that people will take him for a genuine skinflint. He estimates conservatively that it costs him an extra $5,000 a year in lavish tipping and the like to disprove the nonexistent failing.

That Benny feels he must disprove his stinginess is, of course, perfect proof of the success of his radio character. That character was born on Benny's first regular program in 1932. For four and a half years Benny worked out the type with his gagwriter, Harry Conn. How much credit for the idea goes to Conn and how much to Benny is and probably will remain a moot question. In 1936 Benny and Conn split. Three years later Conn sued Benny for $65,500, charging that the comedian was still using Conn characters,

quips, and sequences. The matter was settled out of court, and the Benny of the air has continued to grow—and to serve as the basis for the situations around which the show is built.

Happy Family: Looking back over old Benny scripts is like thumbing through a family album. The family group is all there. Don Wilson, the announcer, fills the same foil role once held by an earlier Alois Havrilla. Dennis Day, the timorous tenor, is the successor to a line of timorous tenors which included Frank Parker, James Melton, and Kenny Baker. Phil Harris, his bourbon, his consummate ego, and his orchestra, joined Benny in 1936, following Frank Black and Don Bestor. Eddie Anderson, who plays Rochester, was hired for a one shot in 1937 to play a Pullman porter. But the public liked him so much that Benny hastily put him to regular work as his valet.

Last but certainly not least in the Benny corral is Mary Livingstone. Unlike the rest of the cast, Miss Livingstone was not a professional. Benny met her in 1926 when a vaudeville tour took him to Los Angeles. She was then a 17-year-old clerk in the May Co. department store. Her name was Sadye Marks—shortly thereafter changed to Mrs. Benny. Five years later on his program Jack needed someone to read a short poem supposedly written by an addled fan named Mary Livingstone. Sadye Marks Benny stepped into the bit role—and stayed on as Mary Livingstone to become almost as famous as her husband. On the air, however, she is just the girl who gets in what is left of Benny's hair.

So thoroughly are these characters established on Benny's show that this year two of them got their own programs, playing elaborations of their Benny roles. Dennis Day, whose talents never get a complete workout on the Sunday program, sings and acts on Wednesday night in what is one of the year's most promising situation-comedy shows, A Day in the Life of Dennis Day. Phil Harris, joining forces with his wife, Alice Faye, follows Benny on Sunday with what is supposed to represent a day in the life of the Harris family. Unlike Day's, Harris's show is perhaps the year's outstanding flop. Away from the smart, glib typewriters of the Benny writers, the Harris radio character fizzles into a boring loudmouth with very few vestiges of humor.

Behind the Gags: In fifteen years on the air Benny has had only seven writers. When Conn left, he took on Bill Morrow and Ed Beloin, who worked for him until 1943 and were then succeeded by his present staff, John Tackaberry, Milt Josefsberg, Sam Perrin, and George Balzer.

Benny probably prizes his writers more than any other part of his organization. They are under exclusive contract to him and are among the highest paid in radio, with combined salaries totaling about $5,000 a week. When Benny's program

...with George E. Stone and Tom Dugan in "The Medicine Man" (1930)...

Acme, Culver

...and at a recent rehearsal-conference with his writers and crew

blueprint of a perfect cocktail

You'll enjoy a Manhattan when you use G&D Sweet Vermouth ...For G&D has all three: quality, flavor, color. And for a perfect Martini use G&D Dry Vermouth.

Write for new, free recipe booklet "So You're Going To Give A Cocktail Party". It shows you how to make Cocktails the professional way. Address a postcard to G&D, 19 Park Row, N.Y. 7.

HAS ALL THREE quality, flavor, color

GAMBARELLI & DAVITTO
Division of Italian Swiss Colony

---

slipped in 1945, instead of hiring new writers, he held onto his four and trained them even harder in the Benny ways. Now, he gives them full credit for pulling the show out of the doldrums.

His writers' work begins right after each Sunday's broadcast. With Benny, they sit down and work out the situation for the following week. Some of the ideas come from the writers, but more of them are Benny's. By Thursday the writers have put together the script, which goes to Benny for astute editing. On Saturday there is a cast reading and Sunday morning is spent in loose rehearsal. Benny doesn't like a final dress rehearsal, saying it spoils the program's spontaneity. Occasionally, this theory backfires, resulting in fluffs and all too obvious ad-libs.

The most serious criticism of the Benny program has been that his show seldom changes. The comedian violently disputes this idea. True, the basic part of each week's humor arises out of the well-established characters and their well-known reactions to given sets of circumstances. But the circumstances, Benny points out, always have an element of surprise. Over the years Benny has resorted to such diversified gimmicks as a polar bear, a talkative parrot, a feud with Fred Allen, a museum relic of an automobile, and the gravel voice of Andy Devine, whom Benny once paid $500 just to say "Hi ya, Buck."

The Lifetime Guarantee: Out of the fact that the Bennys live next door to the Ronald Colmans in fashionable Beverly Hills, Calif., Benny got one of his funniest situations: the socially correct and veddy British Colmans entertaining the social climbing, inelegant Benny. Last year the comedian brought the names of three small Southern California towns into the show. Now the mere mention of Anaheim, Azusa, and Cucamonga brings a laugh. Jack started a national nuisance when he got involved with a character named Kitzel who sold him a hot dog with "peekel een the meedle and the mustard on top."

This year's major contribution to the nation's giggles is Benny's quartet. He hired them first for laughs and secondly to help hurdle that necessary evil, the middle commercial. The quartet, professionally known as the Sportsmen but around the Benny show as "Mmmmmm," take the middle plug for Lucky Strike cigarettes and sing or chant it in ridiculous and clever verse. The commercial is written by Benny himself, with the help of Mahlon Merrick, the show's musical director.

For comedy reasons, Benny accepts the quartet only as a major nuisance and recently "fired" them to get a laugh-provoking situation. Last week the situation had been built up to a temporary substitute—and extraordinary—quartet consisting of Dennis Day, Dick Haymes, Andy Russell, and Bing Crosby. In the million-dollar clambake that followed baritone Bing stumbled on a high note and nearly broke up the show by ad-libbing loudly "Who the hell picked this key, Dennis Day?"

Only a Crosby could get away with profanity on a Benny show. Throughout his radio career, Benny has avoided any off-color, muddy humor. His care to keep his show clean is even greater than his reliability in coming up with comedy 35 Sundays a year.

For as long as Benny cares to stay in radio, listeners can be sure they may tune him in on the 7 p.m., EST spot Sundays. In 1941, when it looked as if Benny might move to another network, NBC made the unprecedented move of giving him a lifetime option on what is one of radio's most valuable half hours. So long as he has a sponsor satisfactory to NBC, Benny can use that half-hour as he sees fit. Two weeks ago he was assured of NBC's satisfaction for three more years when the American Tobacco Co., Benny's fifth and current sponsor, renewed his contract through 1950. The terms: $25,000 a week for the packaged program, which Benny owns, plus $250,000 a year to advertise and publicize the show. Benny will earn it.

Associated Press
Beethoven, Bach, and bats for MacPhail

Play Bach

Larry MacPhail president of the New York Yankees, has never been at a loss to promote his club. Last week he turned up with a stunt that reeked with culture. Starting April 14 the Yankees will sponsor 55 minutes of symphonic music a day, seven days a week, over WQXR, New York's most highbrowed radio station. The pauses between the Bach and the Beethoven on the program (Symphonic Matinee, 4:05-5 p.m., EST) will be filled with the latest inning scores of Yankee games and institutional messages about baseball in general and the New York American League team in particular. MacPhail explains his newest exploit by saying: "There are many baseball players who enjoy good music. What we hope to do is to induce more music lovers to enjoy good baseball."

ALL I REALLY NEED TO KNOW I LEARNED IN KINDERGARTEN

Most of what I really need to know about how to live and what to do and how to be I learned in kindergarten. Wisdom was not at the top of the graduate school mountain, but there in the sandpile at Sunday school. These are the things I learned:

Share everything.
Play fair.
Don't hit people.
Put things back where you found them.
Clean up your own mess.
Don't take things that aren't yours.
Say you're sorry when you hurt somebody.
Wash your hands before you eat.
Flush.
Warm cookies and cold milk are good for you.
Live a balanced life—learn some and think some and draw and paint and sing and dance and play and work every day some.
Take a nap every afternoon.
When you go out into the world, watch out for traffic, hold hands and stick together.
Be aware of wonder.

ISBN 0-394-57102-9

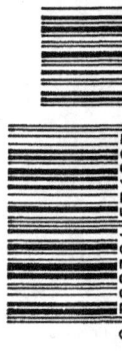

Jack Benny FAN CLUB

15430 LOST VALLEY DRIVE
FORT WAYNE, IN 46825

www.ingramcontent.com/pod-product-compliance
Lightning Source LLC
Chambersburg PA
CBHW080359170426
43193CB00016B/2764